Communication Technologies for the Elderly:
Vision, Hearing, and Speech

Communication Technologies for the Elderly:
Vision, Hearing, and Speech

Edited By

Rosemary Lubinski, Ed.D.

D. Jeffery Higginbotham, Ph.D.

Department of Communicative Disorders and Sciences
University at Buffalo

Singular Publishing Group, Inc.
San Diego · London

Singular Publishing Group, Inc.
401 West A Street, Suite 325
San Diego, California 92101-7904

Singular Publishing Ltd.
19 Compton Terrace
London N1 2UN, U.K.

e-mail: singpub@mail.cerfnet.com
web site: http://www.singpub.com

© 1997 by Singular Publishing Group, Inc.

Typeset in 10/12 Palatino by SoCal Graphics
Printed in United States of America by McNaughton and Gunn

Library of Congress Cataloging-in-Publication Data

Communication technologies for the elderly : vision, hearing, and
  speech / edited by Rosemary Lubinski, D. Jeffery Higginbotham.
      p.   cm.
  Includes bibliographical references and index.
  ISBN 1-56593-634-5
    1. Communicative disorders in old age—Patients—Rehabilitation.
  2. Communication devices for the disabled.   I. Lubinski, Rosemary.
  II. Higginbotham, D. Jeffery.
    [DNLM: 1. Communication Aids for Disabled—in old age. 2. Sensory
  Aids—in old age.   WL 340.2 C7345 1997]
  RC429.C6533   1997
  618.97'685503—dc21
  DNLM/DLC
  for Library of Congress   96-46039
                                               CIP

Contents

Foreword

When Pablo Casals reached 95, a young reporter threw him the following question. "Mr. Casals, you are 95 and the greatest cellist that ever lived. Why do you still practice six hours a day?" Mr. Casals answered,"Because I think I'm making progress."

My 89-year-old mother quilts tenaciously 3 hours daily, because it is fun, but more importantly to maintain the skill of quilting 10 stitches to the inch and progress toward a desired goal of quilting 12 stitches to the inch.

Both of these examples demonstrate the desire on the part of older persons, not necessarily to continue to function as they have for many years, but to change, improve their ability and skills, or as Mr. Casals said,"make progress."

We all desire to make progress, and this is something I was struck with in reading the chapters in this text. Our understanding of the aging process is continually improving, and the wealth of information contained in these chapters is a real demonstration of the progress being made, especially as it relates to the communication behavior of older persons.

Lubinski, in her chapter, gives us eight reasons why communication is vital to older persons and clearly points out how communication skills change as we advance in years. Although the changes are subtle, she points out they are interrelated and complicated by physical, sensory, psychological, and sensory functioning. Steinfeld calls our attention to the ways in which the environment can affect the communication behavior of us all, but particularly older people. As he points out, the process of environmental design can be a powerful arena for facilitating communication among older people and those of us who interact with them.

The effect of sensory deficits on the behavior of older persons, especially communication, is well discussed in the chapters by Schumer and Orr (vision) and Strouse et al. and Weinstein (hearing). The up side to the fact that both vision loss and hearing impairment are frequent problems of older persons is the fact that present day technology provides for life-enhancing devices that allow for increasing independence.

There are wonderful new technologies available to older persons in their quest to remain a part of their respective mainstream cultures. But Higginbotham and Scally point out very aptly that communication specialists have a responsibility to extend beyond the provision of technology to enable older persons with impairments and disabilities to resume being competent communicators within their social worlds. They go on to make a valuable point that, "We are obliged to learn how elderly individuals communicate within their social contexts and to determine strategies that will promote success with their technologies in their daily living situations."

Yorkston and Garrett, in their two chapters, bring us to look broadly at intervention strategies for older persons with communication impairments. They point out that communication abilities change and assistive technology needs change as well. Consequently, it is important to follow through with these changes and provide appropriately for meeting the needs of the individual. One of their statements with which I could not agree more, and which I hope will be emblazoned on the brains of each person reading their chapter, is the notion that, "Many traditional approaches to treatment (*of communication disorders*) focus on remediating the individual's communication *deficits*, rather than simultaneously acknowledging the elder's preserved *competencies*."

The reader will find suggestions in chapters by Newton and Mann for applying assistive technology for purposes of increasing safety and ensuring more independence. But as Broehl points out so realistically, "Successful implementation of assistive technology is directly related to the availability of funding." She offers some good strategies for addressing this problem. After all, improving of quality of life and care of elderly persons is greatly dependent on the accessibility of the technology that is on the market.

One of my disappointments with this book is that none of the authors is an "older person." Perhaps that is why the editors asked me to write the foreword, to have at least one senior citizen listed among the contributors. I would like to have read a chapter written from the perspective of an older person to provide an elder's insight on this topic. For as Bessie Delany (101) says in her book, *Having Our Say, The Delany Sisters' First 100 Years*, "When you get real old, honey, you lay it all on the table. There's an old saying: Only little children and old folks tell the truth." Perhaps that perspective would add an additional element of "truth" to what you will read in this book.

When Dee and I moved to Chapel Hill, North Carolina, 10 years ago, we found a pleasant rural community in which to purchase our home. Little did we realize at the time that we would be living in a village where 90% of the people are retired. We found these retired persons had moved to our village from many places throughout the United States. Many of them were formerly CEOs of large corporations, professional people making a lifestyle change; the majority of them had held major positions in public life. I was and continue to be impressed with the way my neighbors and the village citizenry evolve into this new stage of life called "older" and "senior." Their lives are full of activities, many of which involve skill acquisition and skill improvement. Above all, I have been impressed with an attitude that life is good and exciting for them in this period of "growing older." Hugh Downs, the famous TV personality, has said in his regard, "A happy person is not a person in a certain set of circumstances, but rather a person with a certain set of attitudes." Attitudes are forever coloring our perceptions of who we are and what we can do. Likewise attitudes color the way we see others and what our expectations of them are and can be. What attitudes do we have about older persons and aging? I am sure that reading the chapters in this book is bound to change some attitudes. If it doesn't, then we had better reread the book.

Grandma Moses, as we know, did not become well known until she was elderly. Her attitude was that, "Life is what we make it, always has been, always will be." If we can live by that quote, growing older, which we are all doing, can be good.

The story is told by a grandmother about her 5-year-old granddaughter who was intently drawing on a piece of paper. When asked what she was drawing, she answered that she was drawing God. "But no one knows what God looks like," the grandmother said. "They will when I finish this picture!" she answered. Like the little girl, the respective authors of this text have drawn a "picture" of the role of communication and behaviors related to the well being of older adults. You will know what communication "looks like" during the process of aging when you finish reading the book.

David E. Yoder, Ph.D.
Professor and Chair
Department of Medical Allied Health Professions
University of North Carolina at Chapel Hill

BIBLIOGRAPHY

Canfield, J., & Hansen, M. V. (1993). *Chicken soup for the soul.* Deerfield Beach, FL: Health Communication.

Canfield, J., & Hansen, M. V. (1995). *A 2nd helping of chicken soup for the soul.* Deerfield Beach, FL: Health Communication.

Delany, S., & Delany, A. E. (1993). *Having our say, the Delany sisters' first 100 years.* New York: Kodansha America.

Preface

"He didn't wear his dentures. What makes you think he'd wear a hearing aid?"
" I've given up reading. Not much worth reading. "
"Who cares if I talk. What I say doesn't make a difference."

These comments reflect a demoralizing and persisting attitude toward the communication needs of elders. At a time of life when being able to communicate effectively is clearly linked with independence and quality of life, such discouraging remarks pose barriers between elders and the benefits of interaction. Communication is not an ancillary need for elders but an essential skill.

What many elders and their families or caregivers do not realize is that one's communicative ability is vulnerable to the process of aging and secondary pathologies. Vision and hearing changes can occur so subtly and insidiously that their effects are like a thickening veil shrouding out sensory information. The effects of pathologies such such as stroke, progressive neurological diseases, and dementia on communication are observable and devastating. Regardless of the etiology, the effect of reduced receptive and/or expressive communication skills is that the elder will have fewer meaningful and successful communication experiences.

This book is about enhancing the communication opportunities of elders through the use of communication technologies. Advances in technologies for enhancing vision, hearing, and expression make it possible for many elders and their families or caregivers to interact more effectively. Such technologies may help elders remain safely in their homes, express themselves to care providers and others, and benefit from the stimulation inherent in communication. The technologies described in this text range from simple "usual" devices such as magnifying glasses to more sophisticated computers that speak for the elder at the push of a button. The technologies also range from personal devices such as hearing aids to environmental assistive listening devices and architectural design.

This book is also about the physical and social contexts of elders. A basic premise underlying the philosophy of each of the chapters is that for technology to be accepted and effective, the physical and social environments must be responsive to the communication needs of elders. Fitting an elder with a state-of-the-art hearing aid will be futile if the elder uses it in a noisy environment. Similarly, providing simple environmental aids that help an elder with low vision live independently will be wasted if caregivers anticipate every need. No assistive device will be needed or useful if there is a scarcity of meaningful activities that generate conversations or a lack of desired communication partners.

Finally, the text is about the larger societal issues that frame how elders, families, and caregivers will perceive and access technologies that enhance vision, hearing, and speech. Will technologies have the opportunity to meet the needs of the burgeoning number of elders? At a time of cost cutting, technologies for elders may be viewed as beneficial but too costly, desirable but not essential, and effective but complicated. These sentiments must be neutralized by the commitment of communication professionals to provide reasonably priced technologies that are appropriate, essential, and easy to use. These professionals must also provide research to document the effectiveness of communication technologies to elders and caregivers.

This text is designed to help communication and other professionals understand the process of aging and the scope of technologies available to enhance the vision, hearing, and speech of elders. The book begins with two introductory chapters that provide a broad conceptual framework of aging, communication, and technologies. The text proceeds with two chapters that describe the changes in vision with aging and assistive devices for elders with vision impairments. This is followed by a chapter that details the hearing problems of elders and two chapters that focus on individual and environmental hearing technologies. The next two chapters discuss the nature of expressive communication impairments of elders with aphasia, dementia, and dysarthria and the technologies appropriate to meet their communication needs. The final chapters of the book elaborate on special issues related to elders and communication. One chapter focuses specifically on the telephone, and two chapters discuss architectural and safety issues. The final chapter taps into the vital issue of why funding may or may not be available for communication technologies for elders.

It is not so long ago that the only technology available for the elder who was hearing impaired was a conspicuous ear trumpet; the elder who had cataracts removed wore coke-bottle eye glasses; and the person with aphasia had a magic slate to communicate. Although the technologies of today may look as antiquated in just a few short years, it is hoped that they will benefit their users in the same way—with effective communication, enhanced self-esteem, and greater quality of life for elders and their communication partners.

Rosemary Lubinski
Jeffery Higginbotham

Contributors

Fred H. Bess, Ph.D.
Professor and Director
Bill Wilkerson Center
Vanderbilt University, Division of
Hearing and Speech Sciences
Nashville, Tennessee

Margot E. Broehle, P.C.
Broehl and Waldron, Attorneys at Law
Wooster, Ohio

Albert R. DeChicchis, Ph.D.
Department of Communication
Sciences and Disorders
University of Georgia
Athens, Georgia

Katherine L. Garrett, Ph.D.
Clinical Assistant Professor
Department of Communication
Sciences and Disorders
University of Pittsburgh
Pittsburgh, Pennsylvania

D. Jeffery Higginbotham, Ph.D.
Associate Professor
Department of Communication
Disorders and Sciences
University at Buffalo
Amherst, New York

Rosemary Lubinski, Ed.D.
Associate Professor
Department of Communication
Disorders and Sciences

University at Buffalo
Amherst, New York

William C. Mann, O.T.R., Ph.D.
Professor and Director, Rehabilitation
Engineering Research Center on Aging
University at Buffalo
Buffalo, New York

Mariana Newton, Ph.D.
Director of Graduate Study in
Communication Disorders
University of North Carolina at
Greensboro
Greensboro, North Carolina

Alberta L. Orr, M.S.W.
National Program Associate in Aging
American Foundation for the Blind
Department of Programs and Policy
Research
New York, New York

M. Kathleen Pichora-Fuller, Ph.D.
Assistant Professor
University of British Columbia
School of Audiology and Speech
Sciences
Vancouver, British Columbia, Canada

Christine Scally, M.A.
Speech-Language Pathologist
Clark County School District
Las Vegas, Nevada

Robert A. Schumer, M.D., Ph.D.
Assistant Clinical Professor
Mount Sinai School of Medicine
Manhattan Eye, Ear and Throat
Hospital
New York, New York

Edward Steinfeld, Arch. D.
Professor
Department of Architecture
University of Buffalo
Buffalo, New York

Anne L. Strouse, Ph.D.
Audiology and Speech Pathology
Service
VA Medical Center
Mountain Home, Tennessee

Barbara E. Weinstein, Ph.D.
Associate Professor of of Audiology
Lehman College, City University of
New York
Hunter Mt. Sinai Geriatric Education
Center
Graduate School, City University of
New York

Kathryn M. Yorkston, Ph.D.
Professor
Department of Rehabilitation
Medicine RJ-30
University of Washington
Seattle, Washington

Dedication
To our parents

1

Perspectives on Aging and Communication

Rosemary Lubinski, Ed.D.

INTRODUCTION

As the 21st century approaches, North Americans must contend with four inextricably related phenomena: the rising number and percentage of elders, numerous advances in technology, the escalation of health care costs, and a smaller group of young to care for the old. North Americans face the challenge of how to meet the health care needs of a rapidly growing aging population in a cost effective manner but also with care that promotes quality of life and not just length of life. Advances in a wide variety of technologies complicate the problem in that they hold the potential to increase length and quality of life but frequently add to the health care financial crisis (Berk, 1993). Successful aging in a time of financial restraint may be achieved through judicious development of technologies that support the independent functional ability of elders to accomplish activities of daily living. Some technologies may actually contribute to prevention of disabilities, reduce overall health care costs, increase quality of life and independence for elders, and lessen the burden for younger generations.

The first test that technologies for the elderly must meet is that they must be based on a careful understanding of the complicated and individual process of aging that crosses physical, sensory, cognitive, emotional, and social domains. The simplified cause and effect model of identifying an impairment and assuming that functional limitations are solely and directly related to that impairment does not hold true with elders. For example, hearing loss associated with aging has a general set of symptoms but affects elders differently depending on a variety of factors such as physical and cognitive status, the nature of everyday communicative experiences, available support systems, motivation, and willingness to use technologies to facilitate hearing. Because of the number and complexity of such factors, two elders with similar hearing loss profiles may require different technological approaches to meet their hearing accessibility needs.

The purposes of this chapter are to provide a broad conceptual framework for understanding aging and communication and to lay a foundation for the use of communication technologies by elders taking into account their physical and social environments. The underlying premise of this chapter is that the ability to communicate effectively is an essential component to the wellness, adjustment, and functional competency of individuals during their elder years. The chapter begins with a demographic profile of elders and the value of communciation to them. It is followed by a brief discussion of how communication changes with aging and ends with a discussion of service delivery implications for communication, medical, and other rehabilitation specialists.

DEMOGRAPHY OF AGING

From the newstand to the research article, evidence is presented daily about the increasing number of elders in our population. In 1950, those aged 65 and older constituted about 12 milllion persons, less than 10% of our total population. By 1991, these numbers had multiplied to 31.7 million individuals comprising over 12.6% of the total population (Centers for Disease Control and Prevention, 1995). These numbers will continue to rise precipitiously in the next century as the "baby boom" cohort born between 1945 and 1962 moves into old age. It is predicted that by the year 2020 there will be 52 million individuals over age 65 (16.9% of the population) and close to 70 million elders by the year 2040 (21.7% of the population) (Brock, Guralnick, & Brody, 1990). The discrepancy in age expectancy for men and women yields a greater number of elderly women than men across old age although this is most obvious among the very old. Age expectancy is about 71 years for Caucasian men and about 78 years for Caucasian women. Male and female minorities generally have lower age expectancies (Brock et al., 1990).

The fastest growing group of elders comprises individuals aged 85 years and older. It is expected that this group of "very old'" will nearly triple in the years between 2000 and 2040 and will compose nearly one-half of the total population aged 65 and over (Brock, et al., 1990; McGinnis, 1988). These elders tend, as a group, to have a greater number of serious impairments that result in functional limitations requiring more frequent and intense health care and part- or full-time assistance in either the community or long-term care settings. The growth rate of the very old is important because the increasing number of elders is not being matched by an equal rise in the number of younger individuals who can provide financial, physical, and social support during old age. This increase in the dependency ratio will have major political implications for allocation of health care and social resources in the coming years. Although it is well recognized that health care costs associated with aging will multiply in the next 25–40 years, it is less clear who will assume the financial responsibility for these mammoth increases. The increase in the dependency ratio also translates into practical issues for elders, their families, and their communities, who must meet the needs of elders on a daily basis.

The vast majority of elders reside in the general community with only about 5% of elders living at any one time in long-term care settings such as nursing homes (United States Senate Special Committee on Aging, 1986). It should be noted, however, that 44% of elders will spend *some* time in *some* type of long-term care setting (Scanlon, 1988). Six in 10 elders live in metropolitan areas. Males are more likely to live in their own or another family member's home than are females across all racial groups. Very old women are among the most isolated and impoverished, generally outliving their spouses and experiencing low economic status. The current cohort of elders is not highly educated; 60% of them have completed eighth grade or only some high school education. The vast majority of elders (80%) consider themselves retired and live on incomes that vary from one-third to two-thirds less than their preretirement wages. Poverty is more prevalent among elderly women, minorities, and those living in a nonfamily context (Biggar, 1985).

Chronic health conditions are highly prevalent and tend to be multiply occurring among those aged 65 years and older. Most of the common chronic conditions (arthritis, hypertension, heart disease, orthopedic impairment, cataracts, hearing loss) are not immediately life-threatening but do contribute to functional limitations. These chronic conditions tend to have a more serious impact on those over age 75 years. Of particular interest in this book are impairments that result in sensory, cognitive, or expressive/receptive communication difficulties. Although these impairments may be considered more "invisible," the isolation, depression, and reduction in quality of life caused by them may be devastating.

The prevalence of hearing and vision impairment increases with age and is most dramatic among those aged 85 years and older. The prevalence of self-reported hearing loss (partial loss to complete deafness) for those in the community is estimated to be about 26% for those aged 65–74 years, 36% for those aged 75–84 years and 50% for those aged 85 years and older (National Center for Health Statistics, 1987). The prevalence of hearing loss surges upward for those residing in long-term care settings. In three recent studies the prevalence of measurable hearing impairment for institutionalized elders was found to hover between 70 and 80%, with the level of hearing loss increasing dramatically with advancing age (Garahan, Waller, Houghton, Tisdale, & Runge, 1992; Schow & Nerbonne, 1980; Voeks, Gallagher, Langer, & Drinka, 1990). Hearing loss is also highly common among those with dementia, and the severity of their loss tends to be greater than that of an age-matched group of older persons without cognitive impairment (Uhlmann, Rees, Psaty, & Duckert, 1989; Weinstein & Amsel, 1986). (See Chapter 5 for more details on prevalence and characteristics of hearing loss among elders.)

Impaired vision affects about 10% of those aged 65–74 years, 16% of those aged 75–84 years, and 27% of those aged 85 years and above (Brock, Guralnik, & Brody, 1990). The most common causes of vision difficulties are cataracts, glaucoma, macular degeneration, and diseases of the retina, resulting in some degree of impairment from low vision to blindness. The prevalence of coexisting hearing and vision loss among elders is not well documented, but is likely to be more prevalent among the very old. (Chapter 3 describes the nature of vision loss.)

It is difficult to determine the percentage of elders with expressive/receptive communication problems who reside in the community. Best estimates are that expressive/receptive communication problems exist among 10% of community-based elders and between 52 and 63% of nursing home residents (Mueller & Peters, 1981; Sorin-Peters, Tse, & Kapelus, 1989). Smith-Worrall, Hickson, and Dodd (1990) estimated that as many as 90% of those in residential care may have one or more communication disorders. These problems can be attributed to hearing loss, dementia, stroke-related aphasia and apraxia, head trauma, cancer of the larynx, and progressive neurological disorders such as Parkinson's disease. In addition to the previous communication problems, the high percentage of those in nursing homes with communication problems is likely due to dementia, usually Alzheimer's disease. At least 63% of nursing home residents of all ages have some degree of memory impairment (Hing, 1987). Finally, the communication problems of elders in both the community and long term-care settings are immeasurably complicated by a plethora of other problems, including vision impairment, depression, overall physical frailty, and social isolation.

AGING

Aging can be defined from a number of perspectives: what happens at a biological level throughout the body's systems; the manifestation of these changes in physical, mental, emotional, and social functioning; and finally, in how aging individuals and their societies perceive and adapt to the changes. Aging is not something that happens mysteriously on one's 65th birthday; rather it is revealed as a holistic, subtle, individual, progressive, and lengthy process of change and adaptation. What is happening in the quiet of the body has cumulative effects on persons, communities, and nations.

Although each of life's stages from infancy through adulthood can be viewed as change and adaptation, the process of aging involves adapting to progressive and cumulative changes in structure and function with a reduced resource base. Health and physical skills may decline or be impaired, as may cognitive and emotional competencies. Social support systems may also be transfomed, particularly with the loss of a spouse, relocation from familiar surroundings, or increased dependency on adult children or formal caregivers. For some elders, financial income may be limited, thus reducing access to potential resources.

The process of aging is holistic in that it involves shifts or declines to at least some extent in all physical, sensory, psychological, and emotional systems. The number, co-existence, progression, and effects of these changes will differ among individuals and even within an individual. In addition to the normal changes associated with aging, the individual may have to cope with an overlay of other problems such as depression and health problems secondary to aging including stroke and heart attack. The impact of the changes will be affected by the individual's perception of the modifications and the environment's ability to cope with them.

At its best, aging is subtle in that many changes emerge gradually, providing time for the individual and environment to accommodate naturally or with planned assistance. These changes may be so gradual and the accommodations so instinctive, that individuals and their social partners do not realize for some time the real effects of the changes. This frequently happens in the case of hearing loss where elders and their social partners unconsciously modify their communicative interaction to meet the hearing ability of the elder. It is not until the elder communicates with a less familiar partner or in a less accommodating environment that the reality of the hearing loss is realized. At worst, the changes may be immediate and sharp, leaving little room for incremental accommodation. This can happen, for example, as a consequence of acute stroke.

Adaptation involves appraisal of one's goals and values, self- or other-initiated assistance or modification, and continuing reassessment of the degree of and satisfaction with the results of adaptation. Adaptation can be viewed as an example of systems theory involving elders, their immediate social network, and the larger social framework. As changes occur, elders and their families or caregivers must continually reassess priorities. During early retirement, the priorities may include how to contend with changed social roles and to use increased leisure time in a meaningful way; the development of new interests and relationships with family (particularly adult children and grandchildren); and adjustments in financial resources. In later years, assessment of priorities may also include adjustment to loss of spouse; relocation to a new environment; an increase in the number and severity of health, sensory, or psychological concerns; and increased need for some type and degree of assistance. In still later years, priorities may shift to simultaneously meeting health care needs while maintaining the individual's dignity, independence, and overall quality of life.

Successful adaptation during aging may be transient in that an elder may successfully adjust during one phase and be less successful during another. For example, an elderly man with moderate vision and hearing losses may adapt well in a supportive environment with a spouse, but upon the death of that spouse and relocation to an unfamiliar institutional living situation, he may be less successful even though the level of impairment remains the same. Further, successful adaptation cannot be measured easily. What may appear as successful for one individual may be more or less efficacious for another, depending on personal values and expectations. One person may experience isolation after relocating to a daughter's out of state home; whereas another person might consider the relocation to be a fair trade for frequent contact with and support from the daughter.

The process of aging, and thus of adaptation, is progressive and lengthy. People are living longer, many at least 20 years postretirement. The process has no clearly definable starting point for most individuals but eventually ends in death. The adaptive strategies that individuals bring to the aging process may well be rooted in the experiences of both childhood and adulthood. Some individuals come relatively well-prepared physically, mentally, emotionally, financially, and socially. For example, some individuals come with a supply of strategies that includes a combination of a lifetime of health care maintenance, knowledge of stress management techniques, a variety of interests that contribute to self-actualization, a strong and accessible support system, experiences with elders who have successfully aged, and financial security. Others have fewer or less robust personal and social resources as they move through the aging process.

Finally, the process of aging must be viewed from a broad instead of an individual perspective. The process of aging for each individual must be multiplied over 32 million times in the United States alone. We are no longer a society where elders are the exception or where a maiden daughter remains at home and cares for her aging parents until they die. Although individual families of elders are faced with unaccustomed pressures that tax them physically, emotionally, and financially, the larger society faces the cumulative, unprecedented, and complicated demands and effects of aging.

The most obvious societal concern is monetary. The basic question is not whether we want to provide quality care for our elders, but rather what is the minimal level of care our society is willing to financially support for their welfare? As people live longer, even those who have saved for retirement may find that their resources do not equal their increasing needs. At some point, care needs must be reprioritized to meet available finances and other resources, care must be withdrawn, or the larger society has to help fund these endeavors. Individuals, families, professionals, and other payors must make hard choices regarding care options for elders.

Also of concern is the question of whether society is structured to adapt to the increasing number of elders. At the family level, a variety of adjustments may need to be made, from occasional informal assistance with activities of daily living and financial aid, to cohabitation or direct, intensive daily care, to long-term institutionalization. These family adaptations have repercussions for the primary caregiver and his or her family. They eventually reverberate to larger work and social networks. The increase in the number of women working outside the home, smaller family size, increased mobility, and changing family structures all have an impact on the available resources for elders.

At a professional level, there is a need for specialists qualified to meet the variety and complexity of the aging population. This may be as simple as training customer service representatives to communicate more effectively with elders to specialized training and education for home health care assistants, medical and rehabilitation professionals, and others who serve the elderly. Not only must society be willing to financially underwrite services to the elderly, but working with and for elders must be valued within our culture. Although elder care does not have an aura of professional glamour now, in years to come the sheer number and high expectations of elder consumers will create demands for new and improved quality services as well as for practitioners who specialize in the problems of aging.

Finally, policy makers at all levels of society must grapple with how to provide for the needs of a burgeoning number of elders. Areas such as housing, safety, health care, and ethical matters are just a few of the important issues leaders must address. Leaders must meet the immediate needs of elderly individuals while considering larger societal values and priorities. Meeting the needs of the elderly will become the great balancing act of the 21st century at both family and societal levels.

AGING AND COMMUNICATION

What role does communication play in the aging process? At a time of life when so many abilities are changing, many of which are placing increased demands on individuals, their families, and society, the ability to understand and express oneself may seem like a trivial necessity. How can communication compete with health, physical functioning, the need for appropriate housing, and so forth? At a basic level, are we not meeting our obligation to elders if we address their daily living activities including eating, toileting, walking, and dressing? Given its pre-eminence over other abilities and functions, communication may be the single most important skill to maintain or improve to a functional level if we are to help elders adapt to the aging process as successfully as possible.

Lubinski (1995) proposed that communication is vital to the elderly for at least eight reasons: (a) to develop and maintain a sense of identity; (b) to transmit and receive information vital to self-care and care provided by others; (c) to relieve loneliness, depression, and anxiety; (d) to help others through listening, reflecting, and offering possible solutions; (e) to exert influence and power; (f) to reflect on the continuity of the past, present, and future; (g) to interact with sensory and interpersonal stimuli, thus stimulating thinking; and (h) to receive the benefits of the aesthetic environment and humor.

Maintaining elders' morale or sense of well-being is the concept common to each of these reasons why communication is important to elders. The ability to communicate empowers elders to participate in their own care, maintain social networks with individuals of choice in activities of choice, and preserve some degree of control and independence. Through communication, elders retain an active adult role in their environments. From a family members' perspective, an elder who can communicate effectively can maintain a productive role in decision-making and contribute to family life. Elders who can communicate effectively are also more able to participate in the public arena of politics and policy making. For many elders, communication is the key to their psychological independence even when physical dependence increases.

As with other abilities, communication skills change as individuals advance in years. These changes are often subtle, interrelated, and complicated by physical health, depression, and changes in cognitive functioning. Aging is responsible for structural and morphological changes of the speech mechanism and the peripheral and central auditory systems. In general, muscles related to speech production undergo some atrophy and become less elastic. Nonmuscular tissue also becomes stiffer, and there is a subsequent reduced range of motion. Neuron loss associated with normal aging results in a slowing of cognitive functioning and also of control over the peripheral speech mechanism. Such changes, unless complicated by sequelae of other disorders, may show few observable effects on speech production (Benjamin, 1988).

Language skills appear to be affected differentially by age. Some language skills remain intact well into old age, including vocabulary, automatic speech, sentence comprehension, grammatical judgment, repetition ability, and sentence completion. In contrast, changes become evident in comprehension of complex utterances, production of complex syntax, and active vocabulary or naming (Obler, Au, & Albert, 1995). As many listeners are well aware, some older speakers say more words but offer less information with less referential specificity. Elders are also likely to recall less information in both immediate and delayed conditions (Obler et al., 1995). How problematic these changes become depends on the overall physical and cognitive well-being of the individual as well as the communication context and expectations of both the elder and the communication partner. (For detailed information on changes in the speech and language abilities of elders, the reader is referred to recent reviews of this literature by Benjamin, 1988; Kahane & Beckford, 1991; Rochet, 1991; Rosenfeld & Nudelman, 1991; Ryan, 1995; Sonies, 1991; Weismer & Liss, 1991.)

Aging also affects the peripheral and central auditory systems. Structural changes in the outer ear such as the hardening and elongation of the pinna and the increase in hair and cerumen are likely to have minor but real effects on the transmission of sound to the middle ear. Age-related changes in the middle ear include the thinning of the ear drum, increased rigidity and ossification of the ossicular chair, atrophy of the tensor typani and the stapedius muscles, and less efficiency in eustacian tube function. Most evident and problematic are changes in the inner ear, particularly loss of hair cells within the cochlea, loss of nerve fibers along the auditory nerve, and changes in the central auditory system marked by loss of neurons in the superior temporal gyrus (Nerbonne, 1988). The potential co-existence of changes in the peripheral and central auditory systems creates a complicated hearing profile for elders. These peripheral and central changes result in a bilateral sensorineural hearing loss with greatest loss in the high frequencies, poor discrimination ability, difficulty processing in a background of noise, and a slowing in rate of auditory processing. (Again, for in-depth resources on changes in hearing with aging, the reader is referred to Chapter 5 as well as to the Committee on Hearing, Bioacoustics, and Biomechanics [CHABA], 1988; Grimes, 1995; and Nerbonne, 1988.)

To further confound these age-related changes across the speech and hearing systems, there is a potential effect of secondary problems such as stroke, progressive neurological disorders, dementia, cancer, and depression. General physical frailty and relatively simple dental problems may also be factors mitigating communication abilities. Expressive and receptive communication impairments are sequelae of each of these disorders and thus complicate differentiation of normal aging from pathological aging.

Stroke affects 400,000 individuals each year in the United States, the majority of whom are elders. The incidence of stroke increases about eight times between the ages of 60 and 80 (Funkenstein, 1988). About 80,000 of these individuals develop aphasia, difficulty in one or more expressive and/or receptive modalities (American Speech-Language-Hearing Association, 1994). The actual prevalence of aphasia among elders residing in the community and in institutional settings is difficult to determine because of differences in assessment methods across studies and the high frequency of comorbidity with other disorders such as dysarthria, apraxia, hearing loss, and dementia. O'Connell and O'Connell (1980) found that, although aphasia was the most common diagnosis of residents referred for speech-language pathology services in a nursing home, 38% of these referrals had multiple diagnoses. Worrall, Hickson, and Dodd (in press) screened residents of nursing homes and elder hostels in Australia and found that 43% and 31% of the residents, respectively, failed the *Frenchay Aphasia Screening Test*. They found that 70% of residents failed two or more communication screening measures, again suggesting multiple diagnoses.

The largest group of elders with communication problems is composed of those with dementia. Dementia is characterized by (a) a progressive decline in cognitive function and memory from previously attained intellectual levels, (b) change in ability to independently accomplish activities of daily living, and (c) impairment in at least three of five areas of mental activity including language, memory, visuospatial skills, emotion or personality, and abstraction, calculation, and judgment (Cummings & Benson, 1983; Molloy & Lubinski, 1995). The prevalence of dementia, particularly Alzheimer's disease, among community-based elders may be as high as 10.3% for those 65–74 years, 18.7% for those aged 75–84 years, and 47.2% for those over age 85 (Evans, Funkenstein, & Albert, 1989). Approximately two-thirds of nursing home residents have been categorized as demented (National Center for Health Statistics, 1991). Communication impairment is one of the inevitable and progressive changes associated with dementia.

Depression is a frequent partner of aging and the communication problems that accompany aging such as hearing loss, aphasia, apraxia, and dysarthria. It affects 13% of elders in the community (Gurland, 1976) and 17% of those in nursing homes (National Center for Health Statistics, 1991). According to the DSM-III-R (American Psychiatric Association, 1987), the diagnostic criteria for depression include a dysphoric mood or loss of interest or pleasure in all or most usual activities Symptoms include some constellation of appetite changes, sleeping disturbances, psychomotor retardation or agitation, decrease in sexual drive, fatigue, feelings of worthlessness, recurrent thoughts of death or suicide, and hallucinations or delusions. Depression may be considered a natural consequence of awareness of significant losses such as spouse, home, and communication ability (Tanner & Gerstenberger, 1988). It becomes pathological when it begins to severely affect daily functioning and interaction.

Depressed elders are less able to avail themselves of the benefits inherent in stimulating activities and conversations. Because of their pessimistic mood they often are not chosen as communication partners by friends or caregivers. Thus, depressed elders who also experience other communication problems such as aphasia or hearing loss are in double-jeopardy of losing needed communication opportunities.

Communication change during aging is further complicated by personal variables such as communication style, personal motivation to communicate, and the physical and social environment that creates a backdrop for communication. Less research has been directed toward these variables primarily because of their multivariate nature.

Despite the general preservation of basic linguistic communication skills for most elders in good health, their communication style has variously been described as loquacious, focusing on the past, and sincere. Shewan and Henderson (1988) found that elders took a longer period of time to transmit the same amount of information as younger speakers, thus giving them a decrease in communication efficiency (p. 154). The conversation of elders is also somewhat more ambiguous than that of younger speakers because of less topic shading and more incomplete ties that facilitate cohesion (Stover & Haynes, 1989). When investigating topics initiated by elders, Shadden (1988) found that the most common topics focused on aspects of past life, followed by health and family. Life review, reminiscing, and story-telling may serve a role in adjustment to the aging process for at least some elders (Huntley, 1995). Ryan, See, Meneer, and Trovato (in press) found that both older adults themselves and younger groups perceived elders to be more sincere in their communication style than younger speakers.

The communication of elders is also related to their physical and social environment. The physical environment entails natural phenomena, manmade objects, space utilization, and multidimentional sensory characteristics (visual, auditory, olfactory, tactile, and taste) (Lubinski, 1995). The physical environment creates the backdrop against which topics can be developed and conversations can happen. Elders need easy, independent, or aided access within their physical environments to activities and individuals that will stimulate communication. The physical environment can be structured to enhance access to communication activities and partners, or conversely, it can contain impedances that become barriers to communication fulfillment.

How individuals interact with each other creates the social environment. With aging, the social environment of elders shifts over time due to circumstances involving family relationships, loss of spouse, changes in the cohort of colleagues and friends, and possible relocation to unaccustomed environments. The specific effects of these changes on communication have received modest research attention. Two exemplary studies provide insight into the social communication environment of elders. Shadden (1988) interviewed elders in the community and in nursing homes, their adult children, and a variety of professionals involved in working with elders. She found that older persons had a restricted range of communication partners comprised primarily of age peers and family members. Lubinski, Morrison, and Rigrodsky (1981) also found that the social environment of nursing homes had a deleterious effect on communication opportunities of elderly residents. Residents perceived the social environment as one where there were few communication partners of choice, few topics, few reasons to talk, and numerous rules governing conversational interaction with other residents and staff. Other studies have focused on the communication style of caregivers toward elders particularly in long-term care settings (e.g., Caporeal, 1981; Caporeal, Lukaszewski, & Culbertson, 1983; Jones & Jones, 1985). These studies generally found that the communication partners of elders use "overaccommodating" speech, infantalizing communication, and interactions that support dependence and incompetence (Orange, Ryan, Meredith, & MacLean, 1995). Such studies on speech accommodation call into question many of our findings of communication changes associated with aging. It may be that some of the changes are reactions of elders to the communication styles of those around them. Furthermore, this corpus of studies indicates that the communication environments of elders in the community and institutional settings may be considered impaired in themselves.

A final component in the complex communication equation of elders is their motivation to communicate. Ryan et al. (in press) found that elders do not perceive their language performance as positively as do younger adults and that awareness of communication and memory problems may lead to anxiety and to changes in the elder individual's motivation to communicate. In contrast, the institutionalized elders in the study by Lubinski et al. (1981) indicated that they enjoyed talking but felt that their communication efforts had little meaning or contribution in that environment. It is likely that motivation is influenced by the individual's internal state as well as by the external physical and social environment. Motivation to participate in communicative interaction is maximized when communication opportunities are present and easily accessed, and when elderly individuals have functional communication skills or access to technologies that will compensate for communication impairments.

AGING, WELLNESS, AND COMMUNICATION

As priorities for elders become better defined, two related concepts emerge as having potential for increasing quantity and quality of life while being cost efficient. These synchronous concepts are prevention and wellness. Many individuals have long realized that a lifestyle of physical and psychological wellness is critical to preventing problems that manifest themselves as disabilities later in life. Wellness is defined as "a process of moving toward greater awareness of and satisfaction from engaging in activities that move the whole person toward fitness, positive nutrition, positive relationships, stress management, clear life purpose, consistent belief systems, commitment to selfcare and environmental sensitivity/comfort" (Clark, 1986, p. 12). Individuals who approach aging from a wellness model focus on the individual rather than the disorder, a positive approach to living, internal locus of control and responsibility, and maintaining quality rather than length of life (Armentrout, 1993).

Communication is a key factor in both prevention and wellness for elders. Elders who can communicate effectively are better able to receive information from reading and listening that can contribute to a healthy lifestyle. Knowledge becomes a powerful prevention strategy. Communication also allows elders to participate more fully in health prevention programs and consultations with health care providers. Elders who are capable of and comfortable with communicating their needs are more likely to have their needs appropriately addressed.

Being able to communicate effectively is a natural and essential component of a wellness model of health care and aging. One of the fundamental tenets of wellness is internal locus of control and responsibility. Individuals can better assume a self-governance and self-reliance approach to aging when they can accurately understand others and can clearly communicate their perceptions, needs, and values. Further, a positive approach to living becomes more realistic for elders who maintain meaningful social roles within their environment. The more opportunities elders have to communicate in a variety of productive roles, the more likely they will be attracted to and achieve a wellness approach to living. Elders who can communicate effectively are more likely to be perceived as socially competent within their environments. Such perceptions generate more opportunities for demonstrating competence and thus more need to maintain wellness. Finally, effective communication may be a key to coping successfullly with acute, chronic, and daily life stressors that range from diagnosis of stroke, to daily management of an elder with Alzheimer's disease, to frustrating conversations with a roommate who is severely hearing impaired. A cornerstone of stress management is the availability of interpersonal support or the availability of frequent meaningful conversations with partners of choice who exhibit warmth, empathy, and good listening skills. What is not achieved through traditional medical and pharmaceutical approaches may be realized through meaningful conversations and appropriate nonverbal communication with partners of choice.

IMPLICATIONS FOR SERVICE DELIVERY

Those of us in service delivery professions such as medicine, rehabilitation, and social services face numerous, simultaneous, and often subtle challenges in effectively meeting the communication needs of elders. Few beyond the professions directly involved in hearing, vision, and speech fully understand the complex nature of communication and are totally aware of the critical importance of effective communication in the daily life and well-being of elders. Effective communication is too often totally neglected or considered a secondary or even tertiary priority of care.

Our society is approaching a crossroads regarding how we manage the aging of our population. The present crisis in Social Security and Medicare that our leaders face today will pale in comparison to the numbers and problems that will begin to emerge in about 15 years as members of the Baby Boom generation become the Elder Boom. Our society will undertake an unprecedented juggling act of values, needs, and dollars. A national dialogue must begin regarding the nature of these values, the scope of realistic needs, and the national and personal financial investment required to equalize value and need. Somewhere in this national dialogue must be a discussion of the communication needs of elders and how to maximize these abilities.

As our national agenda concentrates on cost efficiency and cost reduction, it becomes the obligation of communication professionals to develop programs and technologies that provide observable, measurable, and functional outcomes at a reasonable cost. It is the job of professionals in fields such as speech-language pathology, audiology, and vision to clearly identify the real, everyday communication needs of elders and their caregivers in a variety of environments. This information must then be translated into practical, convenient, and realistic programs and technologies that these consumer groups will accept, purchase, and use. It is also the obligation of professionals to clearly articulate evidence that these programs and technologies make a difference in the lives of elders and their formal or informal caregivers. Government programs, private insurers, and individuals will pay for services that have a positive cost/benefit ratio, particularly when the benefits consist of receptive and expressive communication skills functional for daily life, increased independence, better utilization of wellness activities, reduced caregiver burden and stress, and enhanced quality of life for elder and caregiver. Communication professionals thus need to generate new models of care delivery and formulate outcome measures that are consistent with the functional needs of elders and caregivers.

Financial and programmatic challenges are not the only ones that professionals must consider in meeting the communication needs of elders. The general public, particularly elders themselves and their caregivers, must be better educated as to the practical value of enhancing the communcation effectiveness of elders. Just as public education has greatly enlightened consumers as to the harmful effects of cigarette smoking, public education can be used to motivate elders and their caregivers to seek quality programs and technologies that enhance elders' ability to communicate effectively. Such public education must unambiguously explain why communication is vital to all elders, the scope of programs and technologies available, and how to access these interventions. Caring for one's ability to communicate should be viewed as a key ingredient in promoting the physical and mental wellness of elders.

Such changes in the public arena will not take place without the full and sustained commitment of professionals in hearing, vision, and speech. Commitment begins with basic and continuing academic grounding in aging, knowledge of the scope and appropriateness of various interventions including communication technologies for elders, and appropriate practicum experiences. Professionals need to learn more about the effects of aging on both individuals and their physical and social environments. Professionals must better appreciate the influence of significant others on the carryover of therapeutic strategies into the everyday life of elders and on the acceptance or rejection of communication technologies. Professionals must go beyond the traditional focus on impairment and disability to the idea that elders and their environments may be communication handicapped. To this end, payors, particularly third party insurers, must include adequate reimbursement for service to elders and their caregivers. In addition to traditional assessment and fitting services, practitioners should be adequately reimbursed for elder and caregiver counseling, in-home follow-through, and environmental assessment and intervention.

Further, professionals need to be creative in marketing a range of low to high technologies to a public that is potentially fearful of, skeptical about, or uninformed regarding communication assistive devices for the elderly. Elders may perceive such devices as stigmatizing, too complex, too expensive, too troublesome, or inappropriate for their stage of life. Others have had poor experiences with devices or have "heard" founded or unfounded stories of malfunctioning, unsuitable devices that received little or no follow-up service. Caregivers may consider technologies as intrusive and burdensome to learn and maintain. Elders, caregivers, and even other professionals must be convinced of the unquestionable and functional value of assistive devices in enhancing interaction and in facilitating care.

Professional commitment also entails greater willingness on the part of service providers to view technologies as but one component of a full service delivery continuum. An unmistakable theme throughout this text is that the provision of technologies must be viewed as part of a *comprehensive* nine-step approach to communication care for elders (Table 1–1), including (a) education of the professional and lay public; (b) easy physical access to assessment and follow-up service; (c) functional, individual, environmental, and often interdisciplinary assessment; (d) provision of functional therapies and a range of low to high technologies; (e) instruction in how to use and adapt strategies and technologies in everyday environments; (f) enhancement of the physical and social environment to accept these strategies and technologies; (g) continued monitoring of the effectiveness of the these approaches; (h) reinforcement of the elder and significant others for using and adapting communication strategies and technologies; and (i) research devoted specifically to improving the communciation life of elders. Elders and caregivers who *perceive* that they will have easy access to functional services and long-term support in using communication strategies and assistive devices will more likely accept, appropriately adapt, and use them. They are also the best sources for new developments in assistive devices and strategies for enhancing communication. Finally, research efforts and monies must be devoted to better understanding the nature of communication changes with aging and the types of therapies and technologies that make a real difference in their everyday lives.

The interest in aging and communication is in its infancy stage. New communication technologies will emerge to meet the diverse needs of the elderly, and with this evolution in technology will come the need for continuing professional education and practice changes. Although not an answer in themselves, technologies for hearing, speech, and vision will

Table 1-1. Comprehensive nine step approach to communication care for elders.

1. Education of professionals and public regarding communication needs and services for elders
2. Easy physical access to assessment and follow-up services
3. Comprehensive, functional, and interdisciplinary assesment
4. Functional therapies and a range of low to high technologies
5. Instruction in strategies and technologies in everyday environments
6. Enhancement of physical and social environment
7. Continued monitoring of outcomes
8. Reinforcement of the elder and significant others for using communication strategies and technologies
9. Research devoted to improving the communication life of elders

be an exciting part of the equation that leads to communication effectiveness and enhanced quality of life for elders in the century to come.

SUMMARY

The postretirement years bring diverse challenges and fulfillments for elders. Being able to communicate effectively plays a fundamental role in the wellness of elders. Changes in hearing, vision, and speech associated with the normal process of aging or problems secondary to aging are highly prevalent among community-based and institutionalized seniors and influence how they will adjust to the aging process itself. Professionals must be committed to understanding the communication changes associated with aging and the specialized needs of elders and their social partners, and to providing age- and setting-appropriate communication strategies and technologies. Communication technologies are on the cusp of a revolution that will unfold as the number of elders proliferates in the next 20 years.

BIBLIOGRAPHY

American Psychiatric Association. (1987). *Diagnostic and statistical manual of mental disorders* (3rd ed.). Washington, DC: Author.

American Speech-Language-earing Association. (1994). *Communication facts.* Rockville, MD: Author.

Armentrout, G. (1993). A comparison of the medical model and the wellness model: The importance of knowing the difference. *Holistic Nurse Practitioner, 7,* 57–62.

Benjamin, B. (1988). Changes in speech production and linguistic behavior with aging. In B. Shadden (Ed.), *Communication behavior and aging* (pp.163–181). Baltimore, MD: Williams & Wilkins.

Berk, P. (1993). Restructuring American health care financing: First of all, do no harm. *Hepatology, 18,* 206–215.

Biggar, J. (1985). Demographic, socioeconomic, and program aspects. In G. Maguire (Ed.) *Care of the elderly: A health team approach* (pp. 3–16). Boston: Little, Brown.

Brock, D., Guralnik, J., & Brody, J. (1990). Demography and epidemiology of aging in the United States. In E. Schneider & J. Rose (Eds.), *Handbook of the biology of aging* (3rd ed., pp. 3–23). San Diego: Academic Press.

Caporael, L. (1981). The paralanguage of caregiving: Baby talk to the institutionalized aged. *Journal of Personality and Social Psychology, 40,* 876–884.

Caporael, L., Lukaszewski, M., & Culbertson, G. (1983). Secondary baby talk: Judgments by institutionalized elderly and their caregivers. *Journal of Personality and Social Psychology, 44,* 746–754.

Centers for Disease Control and Prevention. (1995). *Vital and health statistics trends in the health of older Americans: United States, 1994.* Washington, DC: U.S. Dept. of Health and Human Services.

Committee on Hearing, Bioacoustics, and Biomechanics (CHABA). (1988). Speech understanding and aging. *Journal of the Acoustical Society of America, 83,* 859–895.

Clark, C. (1986). *Wellness nursing: Concepts, theory, research and practice.* New York: Springer.

Cummings, J., & Benson, D. (1983). *Dementia: A clinical approach.* Boston: Butterworth.

Evans, D., Funkenstein, H., & Albert, M. (1989). Prevalence of Alzheimer's disease in a community population of older persons: Higher than previously reported. *Journal of the American Medical Association, 262,* 2551–2556.

Funkenstein, H. (1988). Cerebrovascular disorders. In M. Albert & M. Moss (Eds.), *Geriatric neuropsychology* (pp. 179–210). New York: Guilford Press.

Garahan, M., Waller, J., Houghton, M., Tisdale, W., & Runge, C. (1992). Hearing loss prevalence and management in nursing home residents. *Journal of the American Geriatrics Society, 40,* 130–134.

Grimes, A. (1995). Auditory changes. In R. Lubinski (Ed.), *Dementia and communication* (pp. 47–69). San Diego, CA: Singular Publishing Group.

Gurland, B. (1976). The comparative frequency of depression in various adult age groups. *Journal of Gerontology, 31,* 283–292.

Hing, E. (1987). Use of nursing homes by the elderly: Preliminary data from the 1985 National Nursing Home Survey. In *Advance data from vital and health statistics.* (Publ. 87–1250). Hyattsville, MD: Public Health Service.

Huntley, R. (1995). Promoting and preserving elders' communication skills. In R. Huntley & K. Helfer (Eds.), *Communication in later life* (pp. 225–242). Boston: Butterworth-Heinemann.

Jones, D., & Jones, G. (1985, Fall). Communication between nursing staff and institutionalized elderly. *Perspectives,* pp. 12–14.

Kahane, J., & Beckford, N. (1991). The aging larynx and voice. In D. Ripich (Ed.), *Handbook of geriatric communication disorders* (pp. 165–186). Austin, TX: Pro-Ed.

Lubinski, R. (1995). Environmental considerations for elderly patients. In R. Lubinski (Ed.), *Dementia and Communication* (pp. 256–278). San Diego, CA: Singular Publishing Group.

Lubinski, R., Morrison., E., & Rigrodsky, S. (1981). Perception of spoken communication by elderly chronically ill patients in an institutional setting. *Journal of Speech and Hearing Disorders, 46,* 405–412.

McGinnis, J. M. (1988). The Tithonus syndrome: Health and aging in America. In R. Chernoff & D. Lipschitz (Eds.), *Health promotion and disease prevention in the elderly* (pp. 1–15). New York: Raven Press.

Molloy, W., & Lubinski, R. (1995). Dementia: Impact and clinical perspectives. In R. Lubinski (Ed.), *Dementia and communication* (pp. 2–21). San Diego, CA: Singular Publishing Group.

Mueller, P., & Peters , T. (1981). Needs and services in geriatric speech-language pathology and audiology. *Journal of the American Speech and Hearing Association, 23,* 627–632.

National Center for Health Statistics. (1987). Aging in the eighties, functional limitations of individuals age 65 years and over. *Advance data from vital and health statistics* (No. 133, DHHS Publ. No. PHS 87-1250). Hyattsville, MD: Public Health Service.

National Center for Health Statistics. (1991). *Mental illness in nursing homes: United States, 1985.* (Series 13, No. 105). Washington, DC: Vital & Health Statistics.

Nerbonne, M. (1988). The effects of aging on auditory structures and functions. In B. Shadden (Ed.), *Communication behavior and aging* (pp. 137–162). Baltimore, MD: Williams & Wilkins.

Obler, L., Au, R., & Albert, M. (1995). Language and aging. In R. Huntley & K. Helfer (Eds.), *Communication in later life* (pp. 85–98). Boston: Butterworth-Heineman.

O'Connell, P., & O'Connell, E. (1980). Speech-language pathology services in a skilled nursing facility: A retrospective study. *Journal of Communciation Disorders, 13,* 93–103.

Orange, J. B., Ryan, E., Meredith, S., & MacLean, M. (1995). Application of the communication enhancement model for long-term care residents with Alzheimer's disease. *Topics in Language Disorders, 15,* 20–35.

Rochet, A. (1991). Aging and the respiratory system. In D. Ripich (Ed.), *Handbook of geriatric communication disorders* (pp. 145–164). Austin, TX: Pro-Ed.

Rosenfeld, D., & Nudelman, H. (1991). Fluency, dysfluency and aging. In D. Ripich (Ed.), *Handbook of geriatric communication disorders* (pp. 227–238). Austin, TX: Pro-Ed.

Ryan, E. (1995). Normal aging and language. In R. Lubinski (Ed.), *Dementia and communication* (pp. 84–97). San Diego, CA: Singular Publishing Group.

Ryan, E., See, S. Meneer, W., & Trovato, D. (in press). Age-based perceptions of language performance among younger and older adults. *Communication Research.*

Scanlon, W. (1988). A perspective on long-term care for the elderly. *Health care financing review, annual supplement.* Washington, DC: Social Security Administration.

Schow, R., & Nerbonne, M. (1980). Hearing levels among nursing home residents. *Journal of Speech and Hearing Disorders, 45,* 124–132.

Shadden, B. (1988). Communication and aging: An overview. In B. Shadden (Ed.), *Communication behavior and aging.* (pp. 1–11). Baltimore, MD: Williams & Wilkins.

Shewan, C., & Henderson,V. (1988). Analysis of spontaneous language in the older normal population. *Journal of Communication Disorders, 21,* 139–154.

Smith-Worrall, L., Hickson, L., & Dodd, B. (1990). Communication disorders and the elderly in residential care. In R. B. Lefroy (Ed.), *Proceedings of the 25th annual conference of the Australian Association of Gerontology, Canberra* (pp. 65–68). Parkville: Australia Association of Gerontology.

Sonies, B. (1991).The aging oropharyngeal system. In D. Ripich (Ed.), *Handbook of geriatric communication disorders* (pp. 187–204). Austin, TX: Pro-Ed.

Sorin-Peters, R., Tse, S., & Kapelus, G. (1989). *Journal of Speech Language Pathology, 13,* 63–70.

Stover, S., & Haynes, W. (1989). Topic manipulation and cohesive adequacy in conversations of normal adults between the ages of 30 and 90. *Clinical Linguistics and Phonetics, 3*, 137–149.

Tanner, D., & Gerstenberger, R. (1988). The grief response in neuropathologies of speech and language. *Aphasiology, 2*, 79–84.

Uhlmann, R., Rees, T., Psaty, B., & Duckert, L. (1989). Validity and reliability of auditory screening tests in demented and non-demented older adults. *Journal of General Internal Medicine, 4*, 90–96.

United States Senate Special Committee on Aging. (1986). *Developments in aging: 1985* (Vol. 3). Washington, DC: Government Printing Office.

Voeks, S., Gallagher, C., Langer, E., & Drinka, P. (1990). Hearing loss in the nursing home: An institutional issue. *Journal of the American Geriatrics Society , 38*, 141–145.

Weismer, G., & Liss, J. (1991). Speech motor control and aging. In D. Ripich (Ed.), *Handbook of geriatric communication disorders* (pp. 205–226). Austin, TX: Pro-Ed.

Weinstein, B., & Amsel, L. (1986). Hearing loss and senile dementia in the institutionalized elderly. *Clinical Gerontologist, 4*, 3–15.

Worrall, L., Hickson, L., & Dodd, B. (in press). Screening for communication impairment in nursing homes and hostels. *Australian Journal of Human Communication Disorders.*

2

Aging and Assistive Technology: A Critique

D. Jeffery Higginbotham, Ph.D.
Christine Scally, M.A.

INTRODUCTION

Over the last several decades, technological innovations have increasingly focused on augmenting or replacing parts of human beings rendered unusable through injury, illness, or prolonged use. These innovations include the technologies used to replace human tissue and organ systems such as artificial hearts, kidneys, skin, lenses, blood and blood vessels; replacements for missing limbs and damaged joints; neural prosthetics that transduce light and sound and directly stimulate the nervous system; as well as a bevy of external devices like vision and hearing aids and technologies used to augment or enhance one's memory and organizational abilities. With increased sophistication and miniaturization, computerized assistive communication technologies are now being developed to enhance or supplement higher order cognitive skills and social communication (e.g., memory aids and augmentative communication devices). In American society we have come to accept these innovations and to view them, at least from a distance, as beneficial to the individual and to society. The primary recipients of these assistive technologies are mature and elderly individuals who present a somewhat perplexing problem for the service provider. Although during their lifetimes the elderly have experienced the most significant technological changes in the history of the human race, as a group, they reportedly have substantial problems operating modern technologies.

23

As purveyors of these technologies, it is incumbent on professionals to develop a broad-based perspective as to what might influence their elder clients' successes or failures using hearing, vision, or expressive communication devices. All too often, failure to make appropriate use of a communication technology is attributed to an inability on the part of the elderly client when the real answer may reside elsewhere or constitute a more complex set of circumstances.

This chapter provides a backdrop and counterpoint to the other chapters in this text by scrutinizing some of our assumptions about technology and elderly individuals. It suggests a critical approach to analyzing the use of technology as an intervention strategy by focusing on clinical interaction and technology design factors as a means to provide appropriate, competent, and humanistic intervention.

OVERVIEW OF ASSISTIVE COMMUNICATION TECHNOLOGIES

The use of technologies as assessment and intervention tools for all people with disabilities is expanding rapidly. Technology by its nature continuously increases in quantity and sophistication. It would be short-sighted to devote much room to descriptions of particulars about current assistive technologies as they will soon be replaced by different and more sophisticated systems. Rather, to help expose the issues facing elderly persons today, it may be helpful to examine the current and future trends in assistive technology development with respect to assessment, service delivery, interface, and device intelligence.

Assessment

The future will bring about radical changes in the types of assistive communication technologies available to individuals who are elderly and disabled, but it will also bring about a revolution in the types of devices professionals employ for assessment. Yoder (1996, personal communication) foresees the day when speech and language screenings will be conducted by a computer at the neighborhood pharmacy—just like the technologies that monitor heart rate and blood pressure today! One can imagine sitting down at a machine, responding to a few questions, then waiting for a few seconds until the computer spits out the results, as well as some home-therapy hints! Even today there are assessment and therapy report programs used to automate a variety of assessment and intervention procedures.

Artificial intelligence-based diagnostic tools will facilitate clinical decision making by comparing the responses of the client to a world-wide database of individuals with similar communication problems. Additionally, the daily activities of a disabled and elderly individual at risk may be remotely monitored by computers which could then analyze various aspects of the individual's behavior and report back to a central office. Such documentation could be used to determine the individual's future course of therapy—or even whether therapy is justified. In the future, the clinician may not just be assisted by machines—it just might be one.

Service Delivery

Use of the Internet could have dramatic implications for intervention and service delivery to elderly clients using assistive communication technologies. The Internet and associated technologies will drastically transform today's expressive communication aids into knowledge tools, tailored to the specialized needs of the individual. For example, the increasing availability of low-cost cellular phone and Internet access technologies may allow elder augmented communicators to have "internet boxes" on their laptrays and desktops that will connect them to the world. Their vocabularies will be stored on the Internet and rapidly downloaded and used when needed. Connection to the Internet will allow the elderly client's communication software to be easily accessed for modification by the clinician or upgraded by the manufacturer. Rehabilitation curriculum developers will dispense and update their curricula over the Internet to individual clients. Software modules will take care of any modifications required to meet the needs of the individual who is disabled. The individual's responses to the programs will be remotely monitored and responded to by a computer located somewhere on the Internet.

The Internet will also offer elders with communication and mobility problems the ability to interact with other individuals in *virtual worlds*. Upon downloading a piece of software, an individual will be able to enter a graphic realm in which all people are represented by humanoid images called "avatars." The world itself consists of landscapes, sky, buildings and other structures. Avatars can walk, run, and fly over the this virtual world and interact with other avatars. Such applications provide new ways to access information, make commercial transactions, and interact with other people on the Internet.

For individuals with mobility restrictions, virtual worlds will provide new avenues for them to explore and interact socially without suffering the consequences of being stigmatized because of their disability. With the advancements in neural sensors and artificial intelligence, an individual with disabilities may be able to perform as competently as any other inhabitant of these cyber-communities. Older individuals will also inhabit these virtual worlds in the future. Like their younger disabled comrades, they can avoid being stigmatized in this virtual world through their graphical identity. That is, if their view of social interaction is to be found through the internet.

Interface

Interface refers to the information display presented by the technology and the integrated or peripheral equipment the individual uses to access and alter the information display. Currently, individuals access visual (text and graphic), tactile, and auditory displays using a variety of means including keyboards, pointing systems (e.g., joysticks, mice), touchscreens, and switches. Neural interfaces are currently being used in cochlear implants, in some experimental vision aids for the blind, and in redirecting impulses from severed spinal nerves. However, this work only marks the beginning of the application of these techniques to persons with disabilities. According to the research findings at a recent Rehabilitation Engineering Society of North America research symposium (RESNA, 1995), neural interface technologies will soon be able to reliably sense and interpret the electrical activity generated by the brain, skeletal nerves, and muscles. This will enable persons with disabilities to control a variety of communication, transportation, and environmental control devices. Research has already demonstrated the ability of computerized sensing systems to detect choices made by an individual (e.g. via EEG) within a fraction of a second. In the near future, individuals could be fitted with a series of subcutaneous electrodes placed under the scalp or worn in a headband or skin patch. This sensing system could translate simple changes in neural activity into actions used to control computer systems. For elders with memory problems, we may be able to provide consistent prompting and assistance through cochlear and optic nerve implants. Further into the future we are likely to find machines that, through direct cortical interface, will translate sound and light into thought and be able to translate our communicative thoughts and directives into machine-produced speech and action.

Intelligence

Intelligent applications are just starting to make their appearance in the augmentative communication arena. Word prediction systems employ grammatical and semantic information to provide efficient and appropriate word choices. Sophisticated hardware systems such as the Prentke Romich Unity program automatically switch back and forth between spelling and icon code mode, saving the user time and keystrokes. In the future, however, the impact of intelligent technologies appears to be much more dramatic. Ongoing research at the corporate and university level is focused on converting telegraphic, misspelled, and ungrammatical input into fully elaborated sentences. In the future, augmented communicators will be able to speak in full utterances, five to six times faster than current communication rates, without a required focus on syntactic concerns. With these new conversational aids, users will not have to concentrate on issues regarding interpersonal focus or verb tense, and the devices will be able to modulate communications with respect to emphasis, sarcasm, and urgency (Higginbotham & Wilkins, 1995; Todman, Alm, & Elder, 1994). For elders with disabilities, such technological improvements could significantly facilitate their participation in society—if they can learn to use the technology.

PROBLEMS WITH TECHNOLOGY

Although this look at the future of assistive technology may be exciting, it should also make us feel uncomfortable. We know that technology is not always benevolent nor are its effects on society entirely predictable. We only need to look back over the last century at the massive personal and social problems such as unemployment, pollution, starvation, and social unrest to see that technological innovation is implicitly related to these predicaments. It would also be naive to assume that new technological developments will have any less of an impact on our lives or on the lives of our clients who are elderly and disabled. How will these new technologies actually affect our clients and our professional pursuits?

So far, comparatively little attention has been given to the ethical and societal implications of assistive technology for persons who are elderly or disabled. Issues regarding depersonalization, stigmatization, and utility of new technologies are of paramount importance to these individuals in their attempts to be a part of mainstream culture. However, if we are to understand the problems engendered by the use of technology by older persons, it is critical that we understand the social-communicative context in which the dispensing and use of assistive communication technologies takes place.

The Portrayal of Age and Disability in Our Culture

For many years, research on individuals who are elderly has focused on how the elderly individual compares to young and middle-aged adults across a variety of physical, sensory, perceptual, cognitive, and language tests. Not surprisingly, the results of many of these studies indicate that the performance of elderly persons declines with age—a finding that in many ways supports our cultural suppositions about the aging process. For example, as we age, our performance on tests of digit-span memory, syntactic processing, and so forth significantly declines compared to younger adults. Professionals often use such findings to explain why elderly persons have difficulty using modern technologies.

Although the specifics of these studies are not necessarily refutable, there are good reasons to dispute the generality of these findings, as well as the commonly held view that an elder's skills necessarily decline because of the aging process. For example, many cognitive and language tests place significant demands on memory and processing abilities and are sensitive to small changes in cognitive and language performance in experimental and clinical contexts. Although these may be desirable methods for studying cognitive and linguistic behavior, the results obtained by such measures may not account for performance during everyday activities that take place in different physical and social contexts and may not tax specific abilities as much as in formal testing. It is not always clear how the cognitive/communicative declines demonstrated in older persons necessarily impact their daily lives, or whether some elder may develop strategies to mitigate the effects of performance decreases (Hummert, Nussbaum, & Wiemann, 1992; Morrow, Leirer, Altieri, & Tanke, 1992).

Norman (1988), for example, noted that all of us, young and old, make adaptations to compensate for various kinds of memorization problems that we face during our daily lives. Natural adaptations such as keeping lists, parking in the same part of the parking lot at a store, and using the same password for all our banking and checking accounts represent just a few of the common strategies that we all employ to compensate for our memory limitations. Long-term experience with these adaptations may lead to a decline in skill areas that are not practiced. The effect of practice on the cognitive skills of elderly persons is clearly demonstrated by the work of Smith, DeFrates-Densch, Schrader, and Crone (1994). They found that elderly adults who played bingo on a regular basis performed similarly to younger adults across a variety of cognitive tasks. They suggested that the social-environmental factors of bingo play a role in enhancing the adults' cognitive skills. This finding suggests that cognitive declines in persons who are elderly are due in part to a lack of sufficient practice and are not necessarily a "fact of old age."

Aging as a Social Construction

If declining skills are not a necessary result of getting older, the social construction of "old age" is in our society. There is a growing body of sociolinguistic literature showing that aging is a socially constructed phenomena in our society in which older persons are typically regarded and treated as being frail, sick, and/or incompetent (Caporeal, 1981; Coupland, Coupland, Giles, & Henwood, 1991; Hummert et al., 1992; Ryan, Hamilton, & See, 1994; Ryan, MacLean, & Orange, 1994; Taylor, 1992).

Hummert (1994) showed photographs of individuals ranging in age from 55 (young-old) to over 75 (old-old) to a group of undergraduate students and asked them to rate the pictures according to a set of positive and negative attributes associated with elderly persons (e.g., positive = "perfect grandparent, distinguished looking, conservative, mellow healthy, capable"; negative = "forgetful, rambling, ill-tempered, selfish, sedentary, victim of crime, neglected, sick"). On the basis of physiognomic cues alone, subjects associated the positive stereotypes with the young-old photographs and associated the negative ones with the old-old pictures. Such research reflects a pervasive, negative societal stereotype of the language, cognitive, and social abilities of the elderly (Ryan, Maclean, & Orange 1994). As noted by Hummert (1994), beliefs and attitudes of individuals lead to inappropriate intergenerational communication.

Sociolinguistic research on language use during intergenerational communication provides strong evidence for accommodation by both the young toward the elderly, and vice versa, perpetuating the previous stereotyped views. Researchers have shown that younger adults manifest their stereotypic views of the elderly by adapting their language in consort with these attitudes. These speech styles have been called *patronizing speech*, or *elderspeak*, and are characterized by slow rate, simple grammar, controlled articulation, increased vocal loudness, and so forth. The most patronizing form, *babytalk*, incorporates patronizing speech style plus high pitch and exaggerated intonation (Ryan, Hamilton, & See, 1994). Caporeal (1981) found that caregivers in a residential facility used this form of talk with elder residents regardless of their cognitive or communicative status. Researchers have argued that patronizing speech and babytalk evidence the speakers' negative attitudes toward their elder interlocutors. Over time patronizing speech erodes the self-esteem of the elders and promotes dependency.

Four types of language strategies have been proposed by Ryan, Giles, Bartolucci, and Henwood (1986) and Coupland and Coupland (1988) to account for the language accommodations found in young to old talk. *Overaccomodation due to physical and sensory handicaps* reflects the overcompensation made by younger individual's based on their presumption of the other individual's hearing loss or limited physical disabilities. Many of the speech characteristics associated with this strategy are used with adults speaking to young children. An overbearing, directive, and disciplinary speech style reflects a *dependency-related overcompensation*, and is used to make the older person more dependent on the younger individual. *Age-related divergence* highlights differences between the younger and the older individual and may be reflected in the content of the younger person's talk. Finally, *intergroup overaccomodation* reflects a common strategy used in young to elderly talk in which younger persons talk about the older person in terms of their negatively stereotypic views of elderly individuals as a group. That is, older individuals are linguistically depersonalized and not treated as individuals. Elderly individuals may also incorporate these strategies, as well as others, into their discourse. Adoption of these strategies reflects the elders' acceptance of age-related stereotypes, need for protection, and expression of group solidarity (Giles & Williams, 1984, Ryan, Hamilton, & See, 1994).

Elderspeak in the Human Service Domain

Clinicians must understand the ramifications of accommodating conversational and narrative discourse styles. When pejorative discourse styles are employed, they can place older persons, without respect to their individual circumstances, into a depersonalized, incompetent, and dependent position in our society. By virtue of being elderly, the individual can now be characterized as frail, dependent, and incompetent. Unfortunately, the professional establishment frequently promulgates these stereotypic attitudes and engages in patronizing talk (Hummert et al., 1992; Nagy, Beal, Kwan, & Baumover, 1994).

In a review of the literature, Ryan, Hamilton, and See (1994) indicated that elderspeak is a common discourse style of professionals working with elderly persons and functions to foster a climate of dependency and compliance by the elder residents. For example, they noted that many professional caregivers of elderly persons in institutions believe that their elderly clients prefer babytalk, even though most elder residents disapprove of being addressed in that manner. These attitudes and communication practices also appear to be prevalent among physicians who work with the elderly. Studies of doctor-patient interactions indicate that physicians often significantly control interaction during conversations by focusing on medical issues and conforming to their stereotypic beliefs about their patients' competencies. As a result, physicians frequently failed to investigate potentially significant medical issues evidenced in the discourse of their elderly patient.

Interactions Around Assistive Technology

When a clinician and an elderly client enter into an interaction regarding a technological solution, each brings to that interaction certain assumptions about technology—assumptions that are often contradictory. In addition, there are socially constructed assumptions regarding the roles played by each that affect interaction and therapeutic outcomes at a tacit level, but which may not be consciously recognized by the interactants. Problems inherent in this interaction, in addition to the abilities of the client or the features of the particular technology, may be responsible for the client's failure to appropriately use a piece of technology.

Elderly individuals may enter the clinical interaction with negative perceptions and attitudes regarding using technology to compensate for their disabilities. Gitlin (1995) reported that technology is the major problem faced by elderly people today. In her review of the literature on technology abandonment, Gitlin advanced three themes to account for the abandonment of assistive technology by elderly individuals: (a) ability related, (b) device related and (c) sociopsychological problems. With respect to ability related problems, poorness of fit between the individual and the technology is perhaps the most widely recognized problem, followed by the individual's lack of knowledge about the technology and inability to use a particular piece of technology in combination with another assistive technology (e.g., problems using trifocal lenses with a telescopic magnification system; Mann, 1995; Mann, Hurren, & Tomita, 1993, 1994). Improvement of the older individual's functional abilities frequently contributes to technology abandonment, but is less recognized. Wylde (1995a, 1995b) points out that elders have inadequate access to the technology market due to a lack of information about the kinds of assistive technologies available in the community and money to purchase the technologies. Because of an insufficient information base, elders are often at risk for purchasing superficially attractive products that do not meet their expectations or needs. Device related problems (i.e., loss, failure) are also frequently related to technology disuse and abandonment.

Older individuals may decide to not use a technology because it makes them feel embarrassed, diminishes their self-esteem, or makes them appear less competent. Elders may deny that they even need an assistive device, even if prescribed by a clinician, fearing that use of a device may signify a change in competence and incur negative social judgments. Also, many individuals find that the presence of assistive technologies calls attention to their disabilities, thereby encouraging, rather than abating, stigmatization.

As technology interventionists, clinicians enter clinical interactions with a somewhat more positive view of the role of technology in their clients' lives. They may view technology, in general, as being the best, most appropriate, or the only solution available for their clients. By virtue of being active professionals, clinicians are less likely to have personally experienced the particular problems faced by their elder clients. Combined with the fact that assistive technologies are *designed* to improve one's quality of life, these factors make it difficult for clinicians to recognize that the technologies they are about to recommend may also possess dehumanizing and isolating qualities.

Wylde (1995b) pointed out that problems with assistive technology are often due to failure of the professional and service-delivery system to provide individualized services to the elderly individual. Despite the wide array of existing technologies, individual clinicians may only be familiar with a subset upon which they base their clinical decisions (Higginbotham, 1993; Wylde, 1995b). Further, younger professionals generally do not experience the problems faced by their elder clients and may not understand how products fail to accommodate to their changing needs. It is easy to see how such mismatched attitudes and perceptions could occur in the clinical relationship and threaten the success of the outcome of the intervention.

Technology and Assessment

In the clinical domain, a client's competencies are often defined by his or her success or failure with a communication device and/or an assessment protocol (i.e., behavioral technology). If an individual succeeds in learning or performing well with a technology, we tend to view this accomplishment as a reflection of his or her communicative and intellectual abilities. Conversely, when an individual is unable to use a device, particularly after repeated attempts with several devices, his or her motivations and abilities may be doubted. Thus, success with technology often serves as a criterion by which we evaluate an individual's potential. What is inappropriate with this view is that this assessment of an individual's abilities is technology-dependent, based on the qualities and limitations inherent in the technology or technique and on the client's ability to adapt to the characteristics of the particular technology.

Assessments in the field of communication disorders often focus on, or are mediated by, some form of technology (e.g., hearing aid, augmentative communication device, audiometric evaluation, language test). Professionals invest considerable time and effort to master the technologies of their trade and invest much faith in the validity and reliability of the results rendered from these systems. However, it is important to realize that, although these technologies can provide insight into the nature and solution of an individual's problems, they also may pose barriers in terms of revealing the true nature of the client's competencies. Besides the daunting nature of an assessment situation, clients may not be able to use or effectively make sense of some aspect of the technology that may render them incompetent to use the device or participate in the assessment. These problems occur more frequently than we admit. Because of the high status accorded to technology in our culture, professionals are at risk for finding fault with the client rather than with the technology.

Dehumanization and Isolation Through Technology

Although assistive technologies are designed to improve the quality of an individual's life, they can also dehumanize and isolate the individual from society. For example, the human voice is a primary means of self-expression and interaction and is inextricably linked to one's self-image (Pettygrove, 1982). Although providing a means for more efficient information exchange, augmentative communication devices employing synthetic speech may also reinforce certain stigmatizing views of the communicator with disabilities due to the slow rate of communication, the less intelligible and robotic voice qualities of synthetic speech, the lack of natural gesture accompanying speech output, and the obtrusive presence of the "electronic box" with which the individual communicates.

Technological interventions can lead to social isolation by creating a barrier that separates individuals from desired social contact and interaction with their friends and community. Unfortunately, this side effect of technology intervention frequently goes unrecognized, and its consequences are devalued by the professional. For example, augmentative communication devices can alter normal social interaction processes, resulting in less desirable communication experiences. Compared to the less technologically evolved word and letter boards, computerized communication aids diminish the need for interactants to actively attend and cooperate in the message production process. Although the augmented communicator is now more independent, message production becomes a solitary enterprise. Social interaction can be postponed for minutes at a time while the message is being constructed.

As computerized technologies become increasingly able to remotely monitor the health and safety individuals who are elderly or disabled, face-to-face social contact with health care providers will be less frequent. Thus, the increasing technical sophistication of our cost-conscious health care market may contribute to further social isolation of older individuals, who, with advancing age, are losing their social communities.

Society is also at risk of isolating individuals who are elderly and disabled through the pace of technological innovation itself. With each new technological innovation, humans must learn to use it, possess the skills and motivation to make use of it, and be able to physically and perceptually access the controls and information displays. Vanderheiden (1983) noted that computers present the most significant current threat to social participation by persons who are disabled, because their design prevents many individuals with cognitive and physical differences from using them. For example, the colorful, interesting, and informative graphic characteristics of the World Wide Web, are not accessable by many individuals with disabilities because a certain degree of visual acuity and manual dexterity is required to control the computer. Also, as more information and services become available on the internet, individuals without the financial means or technological knowledge will increasingly lose access to important social resources.

Although the current generation of middle-aged adults may not experience the types of problems with computer technology faced by their elders today, they can expect to have the same types of problems with the new technologies of the twenty-first century. Will this generation of adults be ready to utilize the new artificial intelligence, virtual reality, or neural interface technologies on the horizon? Unfortunately, if there is anything to be learned from the technology-related problems faced by our elders, it is that we will likely face similar problems with yet unforeseen technological advances as we grow older.

MAKING TECHNOLOGY MORE USABLE AND HUMANE

Technology Use

Several factors have been associated with successful assistive technology use (Enders, 1995; Gitlin, 1994, 1995; Pirkle, 1995; Wylde, 1995b). With respect to the consumer, Gitlin (1994, 1995) pointed out that predisposition to technology use and early professional intervention promote device use, but that age and gender are unrelated to successful assistive technology use. Gitlin suggested that some of the most important indices predicting successful device use relate to elder persons' perceptions that the assistive technology is comfortable to use, tasks will be easier to perform, and the technology will provide increased safety and emotional security, and will facilitate independence and functionality. Gitlin (1995) noted that these personal factors may not be the ones valued by the professional community, which often places greater emphasis on functional gain issues than on less measurable personal goals (p. 45). Extended exposure to the device, frequent consultation, and the use of universal-type design devices can "enable the professional to portray device use as normal and to minimize the social stigma some older adults associate with these tools" (Gitlin, 1995, p. 44).

Characteristics of Successful Technology

Technology acceptance and successful use can be facilitated by good design. As consumers of technologies, we have all had problems operating common devices such as audio and video equipment, telephones, automobiles, and computers. How many of us can type without error, program our video recorder, operate our business phone for call forwarding or conference calls, or transfer voice mail from one source to another? Problems relating to the understanding and error-free use of technology are major concerns for engineers and manufacturers and are due, in part, to their misassumptions about the consumers' understanding and motivations regarding the device (Norman, 1988). The discrepancy between the designer's and the consumer's mental model of the product underlies many design problems facing the manufacturing industry today. Poorly designed features for a critical piece of technology may prevent individuals from engaging in important learning or social activities or prevent them from gaining needed independence.

One overall strategy for achieving good design is to build technologies with a universal design emphasis (Alm, 1993; Newell; 1992; Wylde, 1995b). That is, the technology would be developed for use by *anyone* interested in using it. Large button telephones are a good example of a universal design approach as large buttons are easier to locate, read, and push than are the smaller buttons on regular telephones. Such modifications provide increased access to technology across lifespan and ability levels.

For the elder person, good design considerations would include technologies that are easy to learn, flexible, and functional, but do not stigmatize the consumer by their presence. Wylde (1995a, 1995b) and Newell (1992) promoted the development of universal and transgenerational design in which the design of the device has wide application across ages and ability levels.

SUMMARY

In our quest to find the means to assist elderly and disabled individuals, it is critical that we carefully regard the role that technology plays in our determination of an individual's communication problems and potential solutions to those problems. As discussed in this chapter, present and future technologies hold both great promise for and potential threats to improving quality of life. Because technology is regarded by general society and professional culture as providing solutions to our problems, we run considerable risks in allowing technology to become the defining factor in assessment and intervention. Elderly individuals face many challenges due to societal discrimination and technological changes that have little to do with their inherent competence.

As professionals we need to understand how these factors relate to the elderly individual's clinical situation. The application of technology in assessment or as a communication aid should be carefully considered with respect to the elderly individual's background and social context. We perform our interviews, make our evaluations, and deliver our therapies through interaction and conversation. It is within these contexts that we also form our impressions of our clients and make decisions about their rehabilitation programs. We also convey our impressions about their competencies and our attitudes and beliefs about their social status and value as human beings in our society. If we engage in elderspeak or hold stereotypic attitudes about elders, we are at risk of perpetuating ageist beliefs and attitudes and of compelling elders to assume a dependent, disabled relationship with us, other professionals, caregivers, and their family members.

As communication therapists, our responsibilities extend beyond the provision of technology to enable our clients to resume being competent communicators within their social world. We are obliged to learn how elderly individuals communicate within their social contexts and to determine strategies that will promote success with their technologies in their daily living situations. This would include learning about the attitudes, beliefs, and practices of the client's social group concerning elderly persons and the use of communication technology and promoting the rights of elderly clients as communicators within these contexts.

REFERENCES

Adelman, R., Greene, M. Charon, R., & Friedman, E. (1992). The content of physician and elderly patient interaction in the medical primary care center. *Communication Rsearch, 19,* 370–380.

Alm, N. (1993). The development of augmentative and alternative communication systems to assist with social communication. *Technology and Disability, 2,* 1–18.

Caporeal, L. (1981). The paralanguage of caregiving: Baby talk to the institutionalized aged. *Journal of Personality and Social Psychology, 40,* 876–844.

Coupland, J., & Coupland, N. (1994). "Old age doesn't come alone": Discursive representations of health-in-aging in geriatric medicine. *International Journal of Aging and Human Development, 39,* 81–95.

Coupland, J., Coupland, N., Giles, H., & Henwood, K. (1991). Formulating age: Dimensions of age identity in elderly talk. *Discourse Processes, 3,* 101–132.

Coupland, N., & Coupland, J. (1988). Accommodating the elderly: Invoking and extending a theory. *Language in Society, 17,* 1–41.

Enders, A. (1995). The role of technology in the lives of older people. *Generations, 19,* 7–12.

Giles, H., & Williams, A. (1994). Patronizing the young: Forms and evaluations. *International Journal of Aging and Human Development, 39,* 33–53.

Gitlin, L. N. (1994, May). Technology and self-care: What can social science research contribute to an understanding of technology use and aging? Paper presented at Conference on Research Issues Related to Self-Care and Aging and the Administration on Aging, Washington, DC.

Gitlin, L. N. (1995). Why older people accept or reject assistive technology. *Generations, 19,* 41–46.

Greene, M., Adelman, R., Charon, R., & Hoffman, S. (1986). Ageism in the medial encounter: An exploratory study of th doctor-elderly patient relationship. *Language and Communication, 6,* 113–124.

Higginbotham, D. J. (1993). Assessing augmentative and alternative communication technology. *Technology and Disability, 2,* 42–56.

Higginbotham, D. J., & Wilkins, D. (1995). Frametalker: A system and method for utilizing communication frames in augmented communication technologies. Unpublished technical report. University of New York at Buffalo.

Hummert, M. L. (1994). Physiognomic cues to age and the activation of stereotypes of the elderly in interaction. *International Journal of Aging and Human Development, 39,* 5–19.

Hummert, M. L., Nussbaum, J. F., & Wiemann, J. M. (1992). Communication and the elderly: Cognition, language, and relationships. *Communication Research, 19,* 413–422.

Mandler, J. (1984, December). Six grave doubts about computers. *Whole Earth Review,* pp. 10–21.

Mann, W. (1995). NIDRR rehabiliation engineering research center on assistive technology for older persons. *Generations, 19,* 49–53.

Mann, W., Hurren, D., & Tomita, M. (1993). Comparison of assistive device use and needs of home-based seniors with different impairments. *American Journal of Occupational Therapy, 47,* 980–987.

Mann, W., Hurren, D., & Tomita, M. (1994). Assistive device needs of home-based elderly persons with hearing impairments. *Technology and Disability, 3,* 47–61.

Morrow, D., Leirer, V., Altieri, P., & Tanke, E. (1962). Elders' schema for taking medication: Implications for instruction design. *Journal of Gerontology Psychological Sciences, 46,* 378–385.

Nagy, M. C., Beal, S. C., Kwan, A. Y., & Baumhover, L. A. (1994). Are health care professionals ready for Alzheimer's disease: A comparison of U.S. and Hong Kong nurses. *International Journal of Aging and Human Development, 39,* 337–351.

Newell, A. F. (1992). Today's dream-tomorrow's reality. *Augmentative and Alternative Communication, 8,* 81–88.

Norman, D. (1988). *The psychology of everyday things,* New York: Basic Books.

Pettygrove, W. B. (1982). A Psychosocial perspective on the glossectomy experience. *Journal of Speech and Hearing Disorders, 50,* 107–109.

Pirkle, J. J. (1995). Transgenerational design: Prolonging the American dream. *Generations, 19,* 32–36.

Rehabilitation Engineering Society of North America. (1995, June). Developments toward a direct brain interface to control assistive technologies. Proceedings of the Rehabilitation Engineering Society of North America 1995 annual conference, Vancouver, BC, Canada.

Ryan, E. B. (1994). Intergenerational communication: Evaluations and analyses of talk exchanged between older adults and younger adults. *International Journal of Aging and Human Development, 39,* 1–3.

Ryan, E. B., Giles, H., Bartolucci, G., & Henwood, K. (1986). Psycholinguistic and social psychological components of communication by and with the elderly. *Language and Communication, 6,* 1–24.

Ryan, E. B., Hamilton, J. M., & See, S. K. (1994). Patronizing the old: How do younger and older adults respond to baby talk in the nursing home? *International Journal of Aging and Human Development, 39,* 21–32.

Ryan, E. B., Maclean, M., & Orange, J. B. (1994). Inappropriate accommodation in communication to elders: Inferences about nonverbal correlates. *International Journal of Aging and Human Development, 39,* 273–291.

Smith, M., DeFrates-Densch, N, Schrader, T., & Crone, F. (1994). Age and skill differences in adaptive competence. *International Journal of Aging and Human Development, 39,* 121–136

Taylor, B. C. (1992). Elderly identity in conversation: Producing frailty. *Communication Research, 19,* 493–515.

Todman, J., Alm, N., & Elder, L. (1994). Computer aided conversation: A prototype system for nonspeaking people with physical disabilities. *Applied Psycholinguistics, 15,* 45–73.

Vanderheiden, G. (1983, Summer). Non-conversational communication technology needs of individuals with handicaps. *Rehabilitation World,* pp. 8-12

Wylde, M. A. (1995a). If you could see it through my eyes: Perspectives on technology for older people. *Generations, 19,* 5–6.

Wylde, M. A. (1995b). How to size up the current and future markets: Technologies and the older adult. *Generations, 19,* 15–19.

3

Changes in Vision and Aging

Robert A. Schumer, M.D., Ph.D.

INTRODUCTION

This chapter presents an overview of an ophthalmologist's approach to disorders of the aging eye. This approach emphasizes recognition of diagnostic entities, techniques of functional assessment, principles of medical and surgical management, and a knowledge of epidemiology and demographics.

With aging comes change in the function of most physiological systems and, concomitantly, in performance. The apparatus of sight is not spared from this truism. Often the changes manifest as a decline in performance. Nevertheless, it is only seldom that the changes result in substantial, irreversible impairment. Furthermore, impairments that do occur often can be significantly corrected through a four-fold program of diagnosis, medical treatment, use of assistive devices, and behavioral adaptation. This chapter will concentrate on the first two of these components. The second two are discussed in Chapter 4.

BASIC DEFINITIONS

Changes in vision that occur with aging may be "normal," occurring as part of senescence in general, and not, as such, the result of disease. They may, alternatively, be pathological or disease-related. It is of key importance to distinguish between these two. Both require proper recognition by the eye-care professional, and both may benefit from various interventions. Both are also amenable to clinical and scientific study. Pathological changes, however, when properly diagnosed, may also benefit from treatment of an underlying condition. Therefore, a major aspect of approaching vision changes in the elderly must be to distinguish between changes that are normal and those that are not.

In approaching changes in visual function in general, it is useful to bear in mind several fundamental conceptual dimensions. First, changes may be due to either optical or neural factors. This distinction has implications not only for the nature of the defect and the impairments that are to be expected, but also for the likely severity and correctability of the change. Neural defects tend to be permanent, whereas optical ones may often be corrected. Changes in vision may also affect either central or peripheral vision. This important functional distinction has implications for the tasks that a change in vision may impact. Changes further may characteristically affect either one eye (monocular sight) or both eyes (binocular sight). Additionally, as already mentioned, changes may be those of normal aging, or senescent, or they may be abnormal for the patient's age, or pathological. Finally, functionality must be assessed. This is usually done using numerous standard vision tests that are available. Functionality is itself a complex, multidimensional concept, which depends not only on the sensory apparatus but on skill level, need, and training of a particular individual. A partial listing of major visual functions is given in Table 3–1. Examples of functional assessment include Snellen (letter) acuity, peripheral visual field testing (perimetry), color vision testing, pupillary reaction testing, eye movement testing, and electroretinography. Assessment of functionality is itself complex in that for each test there is a range of (usually quantitative) values that results may take, and each test must always be recognized as being imperfect in describing the visual status of an individual.

At a more concrete level, specific normal changes of senescence as well as specific common medical entities of the elderly can be identified. The proper approach to changes in vision in the elderly individual requires accurate recognition of these diagnostic categories. Often, detailed knowledge of anatomy, physiologic function, natural history of a particular condition or disease, and understanding of the range of treatment and management options is required.

The remainder of this chapter elaborates a general framework to aid in the understanding of vision changes in the elderly, provides introductory accounts of the most common and important specific changes in vision that accompany aging, and illustrates, using specific examples,

Table 3–1. Commonly measured visual functions.

Acuity

Peripheral vision

Accommodation (ability to focus)

Color discrimination

Light and dark adaptation

Glare sensitivity

Pattern detection

Pattern discrimination

Night vision

Motion detection

Stereopsis (depth perception)

Temporal resolution

Cross-modal sensory compensation

how the general framework for understanding vision changes can be applied. It is hoped that a useful basis for understanding and managing vision changes among the elderly can thereby be obtained.

THE VISION PATHWAYS

The reader should be aware of the major structures in the visual pathways, including those of the eyes as well as the central nervous system. Major structures of the eyeball—referred to by ophthalmologists as "the globe"—include the *cornea*, the *anterior chamber*, the *iris*, the *ciliary body*, the *lens*, the *retina*, and the *optic nerve*. The cornea is the clear window" over the front of the globe. Its transparency is achieved by the extraordinarily regular packing of the collagen of which it is composed. Its curvature, acting as a lens, provides some 75% of the refracting power of the eye, and its power is fixed in magnitude. The *anterior chamber* is the space immediately behind the cornea and in front of the colored iris. The anterior chamber is normally about 2.25 mm in depth, and is filled with a clear, watery fluid called aqueous humor. *Aqueous humor* is secreted by the *ciliary body*, which is a specialized structure at the posterior base of the iris. Aqueous humor is rich in nutrients and electrolytes, and bathes the structures of the inside of the front of the eye. It is continuously produced and continuously drains in and out of the eye through the *trabecular meshwork*, which contains tiny specialized channels and is located at the angle between the base of the iris and the inside corner of the cornea. Aqueous humor also is important because its volume accounts to a large degree for the regulation of pressure inside the globe. When its drainage is impaired, as may happen in numerous pathological states, pressure inside the globe may become elevated, leading to the common occular disease, glaucoma.

The iris is significant because it gives color to the eye, and also because the opening in its center is the *pupil* through which light enters into the posterior segment of the eye, where it is focused by the lens onto the retina. The *retina* contains numerous neural elements and is responsible for visual sensation, providing photoreception and many important early stages of neural image processing. The lens lies behind the iris and assists the cornea in focusing light rays. The lens is remarkable for its capacity to alter its refractive power substantially by changing its shape. This ability is largely lost with aging. Finally, the *optic nerve* is composed of axons of the ganglion cells of the retina, the last cell layer in the neural chain of cells within the retina. These axons exit the globe at its posterior pole and travel, as the optic nerve, to the visual centers of the brain.

Thus, optical images of the ambient environment are formed on the retina, the heterogeneous neural layer that lines the inside of the eye. Light rays enter the cornea, pass through the pupil—or central opening—of the iris, pass next through the lens, and then through a clear, fixed substance called the vitreous gel, pass then through most of the retina, and are focused (by the cornea and the lens) on the photoreceptors which are at the back of the retina. Photoreceptors transmit their detection of patterns of light, dark, and color to the ganglion cells via a complicated series of interneurons. Ganglion cells send their axons out of the eye in a bundle forming the optic nerve. The origin of the optic nerve is visible, using the ophthalmoscope or similar optical devices, at the back center of the retina and is referred to as the *optic disc*. This structure is very important in clinical evaluation; it is also the only part of the central nervous system that can be viewed noninvasively in the living human being.

Some 4–6 centimeters behind the globe, each eye's optic nerve divides, and about one-half of each nerve crosses at the optic chiasm to the contralateral hemisphere, the other part projecting ipsilaterally. Fibers then proceed to the interior of the brain, where they form synapses mainly with cells of the lateral geniculate nucleus, and also with other brain structures. From there, other nerve fibers originate, and then travel farther to the back of the brain, to the neocortex of the occipital lobe, where higher brain processing of visual images occurs and high-level visual perception is believed to begin.

NORMAL CHANGES OF AGING

Numerous changes in the visual structures and in visual function occur as a normal part of aging. These change result from the loss of cells, from the alteration of cells, and from the loss of function of cells.

Miosis

Miosis is the state in which the pupil, or entry hole through the iris, is small as compared to its normal size. Typically, and throughout life, miosis occurs as a moment-by-moment physiological response to light, and also occurs when the eye is focused on nearby objects. It may also occur either as a response to drugs (such as pilocarpine, used to treat glaucoma), as a result of neurological impairment (such as Horner's syndrome, which affects the sympathetic fibers of the autonomic nervous system that innervate the pupil), or as a result of inflammation of the eye. It also occurs as a normal consequence of aging.

A small pupil allows less light to reach the retina. Normally, pupil size ranges from diameters of about 8 mm in the dark to about 2 mm in bright sunlight. Therefore, the ratio of normal pupillary areas (proportional to the square of the pupil's radius), and thus the ratio of the amounts of light permitted into the eye by different pupil sizes, is about 16:1. If a pupil is abnormally small, or miotic, even though the eye is in dark illumination, about 1/16 the normal amount of light therefore enters the eye, and this will limit visual performance for both central and peripheral vision (Weale, 1992, p. 48). This optical limitation is a normal consequence of aging, although the elderly miotic pupil may be larger than 2 mm. Normal miosis with aging contributes to reduced visual performance. This may be partially compensated for by brighter lights; night vision is thus particularly adversely impacted by miosis.

Presbyopia

For images to be seen sharply, light rays that fall on the front corneal surface must be properly refracted by the eye to be brought into sharp focus on the retina. As mentioned, the cornea actually accomplishes the majority of the eye's focusing, but is fixed in power. The lens performs the remainder of the refraction, and has the virtue of being unconsciously changed in its shape so as to focus either far-away images or near ones, as needed, a process known as *accommodation*.

One of the changes that occurs with aging is a "hardening" of the lens, which causes loss of elasticity, loss of ability of the lens to change shape, and consequent loss of accommodative ability—mostly, the ability to focus at near. This condition is called *presbyopia* (Weale, 1992, p. 82). The common experience that, beginning in one's forties, one often needs to hold reading material increasingly farther away from the face is the result of this change. The eye simply cannot focus as near as formerly was possible. By the fifties, many people cannot read at all without "reading" glasses that externally provide the needed focusing power for the eye. Presbyopia is virtually universal; only the occasional individual, for unknown reasons, retains useful accommodative amplitude into the sixth or seventh decades.

Presbyopia is corrected by reading glasses or use of bifocals. It is purely optical in nature, usually affects both eyes symmetrically, and mostly affects central vision, as peripheral vision is inherently of too poor acuity to be much affected by the loss of focus caused by presbyopia. Of interest, people with pre-existing mild to moderate myopia— near-sightedness—will often be able to focus at near without any reading glasses, simply by removing their normal refractive correction for distance. This is a trick of nature, in a sense, as the removal of all correction in these lucky few is the optical equivalent to adding the normal reading correction to their myopic correction—a net optical result of zero refractive error for near points!

An elderly person with trouble seeing at close distances but without impairment at far distances may have inadequate correction for his or her presbyopia. This is perhaps the commonest visual problem of the elderly. Fortunately, once recognized, it is easily corrected.

Cataract

As mentioned in reference to presbyopia, the lens and cornea are responsible for focusing images onto the retina. Cataract occurs when there is an opacity or clouding of the lens. It is nearly universal among the elderly and, if significant, can lead to severe loss of optical clarity. When it occurs in isolation in an elderly individual, there is no accompanying neural loss. (Cataract occurring in a child, on the other hand, may lead to a permanent neural deficit, a condition called *amblyopia*, sometimes referred to as "lazy-eye"; this does not happen in the adult.)

Cataract is by definition a monocular condition, although often the two eyes may be comparably affected. It usually affects both central and peripheral vision, and may affect either near or distant vision more than the other, or may affect them equally.

Cataract is the most common cause of blindness worldwide (Foster, 1991). It accounts for vision loss in more than half of the 23 million persons worldwide with best-corrected Snellen acuity of 20/400 or worse (Kupfer, 1984), and 30 to 45 million persons worldwide have been estimated to be visually impaired from cataract (World Health Organization Programme Advisory Group, 1989). Within the United States it is estimated that about 40,000 persons are legally blind from senile cataract, representing 35% of existing visual impairment (National Society to Prevent Blindness, 1980).

The prevalence of adult cataract in the United States is known from the Framingham Eye Study (Kahn et al., 1977; Sperduto & Siegel, 1980) and the 1971–1972 National Health and Nutrition Examination Survey (Leske & Sperduto, 1983). In the Framingham study, for example, among the 2,631 participants, cataract was present in 42% of persons ages 52 to 64, in 73% among those 65–74, and in 91% among those 75 to 85. Percentages of total blindness in the U.S. due to cataract are smaller, but showed corresponding increases with age: 0.07% of those 52–64, 0.82% of those 65–74, and 2.03% of those 75 or older.

Cataract is correctable by a surgical procedure in which the cloudy lense is removed through a small opening in the front of the globe. In economically developed countries like the United States, a polymethacrylate (plexiglass), silicone, or acrylic replacement lens is usually implanted in the eye to restore a fixed focus without the use of thick spectacles, but in developing countries, the cost of these implants is often prohibitive. Cataract surgery is the single most commonly performed operation in the United States among persons over 60, with more than 1 million cataract operations being performed annually (U.S. Department of Health and Human Services, 1987).

Causes of cataract are not well understood, but risk factors have been identified, which include age (Schwab & Taylor, 1990), diabetes (Ederer, Hiller, & Taylor, 1981), numerous drugs (e.g., corticosteroids, phenothiazines, cancer chemotherapy agents, diuretics, major tranquilizers, and gout medications; Harding & van Heyningen, 1987; Leske & Sperduto, 1983), ultraviolet exposure (Bochow et al., 1989; Taylor et al., 1988), and gender (women are more frequently afflicted; Schwab & Taylor, 1990). Of note, the presence of diabetes and drug use independently increase with age so that numerous risk factors contribute to the dramatically high prevalence of senile cataract.

The kinds of vision disturbances that may arise from cataract include general absorbtion of all wavelengths of light (causing loss of brightness of the image), selective absorption of one wavelength of light (causing color shifts), scatter of light (causing lack of contrast, blur, glare, or all three), changes in refractive power of the eye (causing a shift in the corrective spectacles needed), or prismatic effects (causing double, triple, or even multiple images in the affected eye's view; Hemenger, 1984; Hess & Woo, 1978).

There are numerous kinds of cataract. They are distinguished for the most part by their clinical appearance. Nuclear sclerosis, cortical, posterior-subcapsular, oil-droplet, snowstorm, and sunflower cataract are some of the descriptive names that are used. The first three mentioned are the most common normal cataracts that occur with aging (Sperduto & Hiller, 1984). Most people have some detectable degree of cataract by the age of 40 or so, although often it may not be visually significant for many years thereafter.

Changes in Glasses

Often a need for change in corrective lenses (glasses) occurs in the elderly eye. This occurs for two main reasons. The first is presbyopia, or loss of ability to focus at near (accommodation), as discussed earlier. The second is a shift in the refractive index of the eye caused by biochemical alterations of the lens that accompany cataract. Typically, this change leads to a relative increase in near-sightedness, so as to bring the natural focal point of the eye closer to the patient and to partly (or sometimes completely) compensate the loss of ability to accommodate. In any case, refraction (selection of corrective lenses) can usually restore sharp vision, although rapidly changing refraction can be confusing to the patient, a burdensome expense (for examination and to purchase new glasses frequently), and occasionally disabling if only one eye changes so as to be intolerably different from the other, a condition that may make glasses unwearable and effectively lead to monocular blindness.

Posterior Vitreous Detachment

The typical symptom of posterior vitreous detachment (PVD) is the impression of "floaters," small black spots, a fine, lace-like mesh, or perhaps small, dark, curly lines that seem to "float" about in the field of view. These floaters are actually the shadows of small fragments of tissue hovering in the middle of the vitreous chamber of the eye. They arise from attachment points between the vitreous gel and the inside wall of the eye, mainly blood vessels, the optic nerve, and the perifoveal retina. With aging, the vitreous gel commonly liquefies and liquid vitreous may dissect into spaces between the remainder of the gel and these other inner-eye structures. In many instances, the gel is then pulled from its attachments, and as this happens, glial attachment tissue floats freely in the liquid vitreous. Although such fragments usually assume a stable position within the vitreous, they may float back and forth, and are perceived as floaters. If they are in the central zone of the vitreous chamber and move with the movement of the eye, they may interfere with vision, although usually only mildly.

PVD is a benign condition, and although floaters may cause concern in the patient, it is a common, normal senescent change. The incidence of PVD has been reported to be 53% in persons age 50 or more and 65% in those over age 65 (Linder, 1966). The incidence increases with aging because the underlying cause of PVD—vitreous humor liquefaction—increases with aging. More than half of the vitreous body has been found to be liquefied in 25% of those age 40 to 49 and in 62% of those age 80 to 89 (O'Malley, 1976).

The presence of floaters indicates that the vitreous gel has pulled loose from its retinal attachments. This event, which necessarily involves some degree of vitreous traction or tugging against the retina, usually ends in successful separation of the vitreous from the retina. However, detachment may be partial, and continued traction may result in formation of a hole in the retina. Such a hole may be stable or may lead to retinal detachment.

Therefore, the development of new floaters may be a warning of a new retinal hole or of an impending retinal detachment, although this development is relatively uncommon, and PVD usually follows a benign course. Onset of new floaters of a significant degree should generally lead a patient to obtain a thorough retinal examination to search for retinal holes (American Academy of Ophthalmology, Quality of Care Committee, Retinal Panel, 1994).

CHANGES IN LIDS AND SKIN

With aging, there is a general loss of muscle tone, breakdown of the tissue planes that hold subcutaneous fat layers in place, and a stretching and thinning of skin. All of these lead to increased sagging of upper and lower eyelids and adjacent areas. This usually has a cosmetic effect only (which may contribute to changes in the patient's self-image and perception by others), but sometimes may lead to genuine visual disability.

There are two main means by which this may happen. One is a sagging of the skin folds on the upper lid. The other is a weakening of the muscle that holds the upper lid in its normal, open position. This results in a droop of the upper lid, called *blepharoptosis* (or more simply, *ptosis*). Both may cause the lid to sag over the upper part of the visual field, causing loss of sight for superiorly placed objects. Occasionally, the condition is severe enough that the pupillary axis is actually partly occluded, which can lead to dimming and blurring of sight in general, including central vision. Correction is surgical, and requires either tightening or reinsertion of the upper eyelid muscles, excision of excess skin, removal of prolapsed fat, or some combination of the three. Results are usually satisfactory to the patient.

Normal Changes of Aging: Summary

Most older people have good vision. Comprehensive eye examinations for all adults can lead to early detection of most conditions, and the prevalence of disabling eye conditions is not really that great. The Framingham Eye Study (Leibowitz et al., 1980) found that visual acuity of 20/25 or better is seen in 98% of those between 75 and 85. Further, Sommer et al. (1991) studied the rate of bilateral blindness in an urban population, and reported the the prevalence of bilateral blindness (defined as Snellen acuity of 20/200 or worse in both eyes) was 64 persons out of 5,308 studied overall, or only 1.21%. Notably, 86 of the 128 blind eyes (67.2%) were persons over the age of 65. Although Sommer et al. (1991) concluded that health services are underutilized, and that at least some blindness in the United States could be prevented simply by increased access to care, the rate of blindness they found indicates that most persons, including the elderly, will have useful vision throughout their lives.

PATHOLOGICAL VISION LOSS IN THE ELDERLY

As summarized in Table 3–2, the causes of visual impairment in the elderly can be divided into those that are common and those that are uncommon. Prevalence estimates for these conditions are, however, just that: estimates. Accurate data are difficult to collect, and many problems cloud our knowledge. Important issues include absence of a federal registry for medical as well as specifically ocular conditions; widespread use of clinic-based (as opposed to population-based) data, which introduces bias from self-selection, leading to overestimation as well as other

Table 3–2. Causes of pathological vision loss in the elderly in the United States.

A. Common Causes
  Cataract
  Glaucoma
  Age-related macular degeneration
  Diabetic retinopathy

B. Less Common Causes
  Eyelid and skin changes
  Corneal degenerations
  Ischemic optic neuropathy
  Vascular occlusions
  Retinal detachment
  Tumors
  Posterior vitreous detachment

sources of errors; and errors and differences among specialists concerning diagnosis.

Cataract

Please refer to the previous section of this chapter on the normal changes of aging for a discussion of cataract.

Glaucoma

Glaucoma refers to a heterogeneous group of conditions which all display similar optic nerve degeneration resulting in characteristic abnormalities of, typically, peripheral vision. Most glaucoma patients have elevated intraocular pressure (IOP) as part of the spectrum of this disease, although this is now recognized as not being either a necessary or even a defining co-condition. Most commonly, the condition occurs in a familial pattern of poorly understood genetic pedigree (Lichter, 1994) and has no known inciting cause. In this case the disease is regarded as "primary open-angle glaucoma" (POAG). This is the commonest variant, and other, "secondary," types of glaucoma, which are less common, will not be discussed here.

The second most common cause of blindness in the United States, and the most common among African Americans, POAG is insidious because many are unaware they have the disease until late in its course.

It is estimated that 2 mllion Americans have glaucoma, with about half of them unaware of it. About 80,000 Americans are blind from POAG (Armaly, 1966; American Academy of Ophthalmology, Quality of Care Committee, Glaucoma Panel, 1996; Bankes, Perkins, Tsolakis, & Wright, 1968; Hollows & Graham, 1966; Leibowitz et al., 1980).

Among those over age 50, it is estimated that about 2% of Caucasians and 8–12% of African Americans in the United States have glaucoma (Tielsch et al., 1991). Glaucoma increases dramatically with age. In one study (Tielsch et al., 1991) there was a prevalence of 0.92% among Caucasians age 40–49, 0.41% among those age 50–59, 1.76% among those age 60–69, and 3.47% among those age 70–79. Glaucoma was much more prevalent among African Americans. For example, in the age range 60–69, there was a prevalence of 6.59% among African Americans and among African Americans age 79–79, 10.51%. Also, glaucoma tends to occur earlier in African Americans than in Caucasians. Among Caucasians, few under the age of 50 have the disease, but among African Americans, it may commonly be present before the age of 40 (Tielsch et al., 1991).

Glaucoma is a progressive degeneration of the optic nerve. It is diagnosed by (1) a typical optic nerve head appearance and (2) a typical pattern of vision loss in visual field (peripheral vision) testing. Risk factors for the development of glaucoma include (a) elevated IOP, (b) a family history of glaucoma, (c) myopia or near-sightedness, (d) increasing age, and (e) African American descent. Elevated IOP is the most common co-occurring ocular condition, but there are many people with elevated IOP who do not have glaucomatous vision loss. Conversely, many with typical glaucomatous loss have never had elevated IOP. Therefore, elevated IOP has, at present, an uncertain role in causing POAG (Schumer & Podos, 1994), although it is conventionally regarded as the immediate cause.

Glaucoma has a "silent" presentation, it usually is without symptoms until quite late in the disease. The reasons for this are fourfold. First, the loss of sensitivity to light is typically a relative loss, and is not absolute, so if one eye has suffered some loss, it may be subtle, and the other eye, if it has normal vision in the same region of the affected eye's field of view, may mask the loss. Second, glaucoma typically affects peripheral vision, sparing central vision. Patients often are unaware of any loss, even after it is readily demonstrable by appropriate testing. Third, considerable damage can occur to the optic nerve before any loss of sight has occurred. Nevertheless, in such situations, the loss is real, often progressive, and may be the basis for subsequent rapid deterioration. Finally, the disease is usually painless, and there are no symptoms, nor is there any discomfort, other than loss of sight, even when such loss is quite advanced.

The treatment of POAG, although simple in concept, is often difficult in practice. The only accepted goal of treatment is the lowering of intraocular pressure. Typically, this is achieved with medications (Schumer & Podos, 1993). If medications prove either inadequate or intolerable because of side effects such as allergy or systemic (medical) reactions such as gastrointestinal upset, dizziness, or fatique, then laser treatment or surgical creation of a drainage channel in the wall of the eye are further options.

There are many medications available for lowering IOP. Currently approved drugs fall into two main classes, those that lower the production of fluid (aqueous humor) by the ciliary body and those that increase the drainage of fluid by the trabecular network. Since elevated IOP in POAG is invariably due to a decreased outflow of fluid, the latter approach may be physiologically more sound. However, the chief drugs that can accomplish an increase in outflow are acetylcholine receptor activators (agonists), of which pilocarpine is the main example. These drugs cause severe pupillary constriction (miosis) and may thus aggravate cataract, which often co-exists in the elderly population likeliest to have POAG.

Several other classes of drugs are available; each has various side effects that may limit its usefulness, and each may or may not be effective in any individual patient. Many patients with POAG require more than one drug for adequate IOP lowering, and, especially in an elderly population, the proliferation of drugs with different dosing schedules and different side-effect profiles can lead to an overly complex and sometimes toxic regimen.

The overall prognosis for POAG is variable. Many patients can achieve an acceptable lowering of their pressure and thereby reduce the rate of progression of their vision loss so as to retain useful sight for the rest of their lives. A smaller but still disturbingly large number of patients seem to progress despite any and all efforts, no matter how successful, to lower their pressure. We do not understand the full pathophysiology of POAG, and elevated pressure is likely to be only one component of the mechanism of the disease. For example, as many as 15% of patients with glaucoma do not appear to have elevated IOP at all. Lowering pressure in these people is often inadequate in the long run (Shumer & Podos, 1994).

Visual function that is lost due to glaucoma results from neural loss and, as such, is permanent. Glaucoma is usually a bilateral condition, but may asymmetrically involve the two eyes. Loss of peripheral vision usually occurs first, often in the nasal hemifield (the left side of the right eye's field of view and the right side of the left eye's field of view), and it progresses to central vision last. When nasal peripheral vision is lost, the affected individual may have difficulties reading, driving, or walking. When central vision is lost, usually late in the course of the disease, patients lose the ability to read, recognize faces, write, or perform detailed, visually guided tasks such as sewing, typing, or cooking. Loss is often relative at first, and absolute later. Late in the course of disease, patients may have complete loss of peripheral vision, so that their field of view is limited to a small central zone, often only a few degrees in extent. Even this central zone is often blurry. Patients will typically be forced to use their small central zone of vision like a spotlight, ambulating slowly and searching with gross head movements for visually important targets like faces or obstacles.

Age-Related Macular Degeneration

Age-related macular degeneration (ARMD) describes a progressive spectrum of related conditions, ranging from small focal deposits beneath the retina, through hemorrhagic retinal detachments, to severe subretinal scarring. What is common to them is that each involves the macula, or central portion of the retina, upon which we depend for reading, acuity, and scrutiny. The various conditions form a progressive series, variable in its expression and rate of advancement, but generally afflicting the elderly and sometimes devastating in its consequences (Hampton & Nelson, 1992).

ARMD has been divided into six stages: (1) low risk nonexudative ARMD, (2) high risk nonexudative ARMD, (3) geographic atrophy, (4) pigment epithelial detachment, (5) choroidal neovascularization, and (6) subepithelial fibrosis (American Academy of Ophthalmology, Quality of Care Committee, Retinal Panel, 1994a). The first two stages are characterized by the appearance of *drusen*: yellowish spots that are small deposits lying underneath an inner layer of the retina, the *pigmented epithelium*. Patients with large collections of drusen, or many confluent drusen, are at high risk of progressing to later stages and must be closely monitored. There is no known treatment for the nonexudative forms of ARMD

In more advanced stages, there is loss of the pigment epithelium and of the overlying photoreceptors. Following this, choroidal (subretinal) neovascularization, or new vessel growth, may occur. Evaluation of the extent and degree of new vessel growth is often assisted by retinal angiography, or dye injection with rapid-sequence photography. New vessels, being abnormal, may leak clear serum or may bleed, resulting in, respectively, serous or hemorrhagic pigment epithelial detachments. In advanced cases, fibrosis, or scar formation, may occur under the macula, effectively destroying the central retina.

The only stage that is at present treatable is choroidal neovascularization, and treatment has been shown to be effective only before severe vision loss has occurred, and only for a small, select group of patients (Macular Photocoagulation Study Group, 1982, 1990, 1991, 1993; Moisseiev, Alhalel, Masuri, & Treister, 1995). Also, there is a high rate of recurrence even after successful treatment. Treatment consists of laser photocoagulation, or burning, of the abnormal blood vessels, which may cause those vessels to regress.

One of the best means of monitoring ARMD is by home self-examination. The patient regularly examines an Amsler grid, a pattern regularly spaced sharp horizontal and vertical lines. Any distortions seen on this grid ("metamorphopsia") may indicate progression of ARMD to an exudative stage.

New, investigational techniques that are being explored at present include new kinds of laser treatment, antioxidant vitamin therapy (Eye Disease Case-Control Study Group, 1993), submacular surgery (Wade, Flynn, Olsen, Blumenkranz, & Nicholson, 1990), retinal transplantation (Algvere, Berglin, Gouras, & Sheng, 1994), and genetic therapy (Bok, 1993). None are yet of proven value. Because treatment is not beneficial for most patients with ARMD, close monitoring in the early stages and referral for low vision services in the late stages is strongly recommended (American Academy of Ophthalmology, Quality of Care Committee, Retina Panel, 1994a).

The limitations experienced by those afflicted by advanced ARMD include loss of the visual abilities that are dependent on central, high-resolution tasks, and fine depth perception.

Diabetic Retinopathy

One of the most common compliations of diabetes mellitus, diabetic retinopathy, encompasses a range of related conditions all involving the blood supply of the retina.

Diabetic retinopathy is the leading cause of new cases of legal blindness among working-age Americans. It afflicts both those with insulin-dependent diabetes (Type I) as well as those with non-insulin-dependent diabetes (Type II). Patients with Type I diabetes have a higher incidence of proliferative retinopathy, but there are far more patients with Type II diabetes (American Academy of Ophthalmology, Quality of Life Committee, Retina Panel, 1993).

Long-term diabetes appears to lead to breakdown of vascular integrity throughout many bodily systems, including the vessels of the eye. Initially, there may be leakage from normal retinal vessels, which can cause fluid swelling within the retina. Often, this involves the macula, and is called macular edema. Leaking vessels can also produce small, focal hemorrhages, leakage of lipid deposits, or small capillary wall weakenings. This stage is called background diabetic retinopathy. Retinal capillaries may also close off, leading to oxygen deprivation of patches of retina and subsequent death of nerve cells. In more advanced cases, new vessel growth (neovascularization) occurs on the retina or on the optic nerve head. This is called proliferative retinopathy. These new vessels may cause tractional retinal detachment or may leak and cause hemorrhage into the vitreous chamber. Additionally, new vessel growth can sometimes be seen in the front of the eye, on the iris, causing adhesions that block the normal outflow of fluid from the eye and leading, secondarily, to neovascular glaucoma.

Regarding treatment, first and foremost, intensive medical control of hypoglycemia with insulin in Type I patients delays the onset and slows the progression of diabetic retinopathy (The Diabetes Control and Compilations Trial Research groups, 1993). Since many stages of diabetic retinopathy are treatable, frequent eye examinations are warranted, with the frequency of examination increasing with the severity of disease. Newly diagnosed patients should be seen by an ophthalmologist as soon as possible, since prior duration of the disease is often unknown and the extent of eye disease may be greater than suspected.

Early stages of diabetic retinopathy are merely observed; progression may warrant increases in the aggressiveness of medical therapy. If there is visually significant involvement of the eye, laser photogcoagulation can be effective. Laser photocoagulation of the retina induces new, abnormal retinal vessels to regress and can reduce macular degeneration. Also, surgical evacuation of the vitreous cavity plus repair of tractional retinal detachments have been proven valuable early in cases of vitreous hemorrhage with severe proliferative retinopathy.

Macular edema affects the macula, and therefore causes loss of central, high-acuity vision. Capillary dropout deprives focal patches of retina of their blood supply. Proliferative retinopathy usually affects the posterior half of the retina and may cause a tractional detachment affecting a quadrant or more of the visual field, or may cause a hemorrhage completely preventing some or all light from reaching part or all of the retina. Therefore, diabetic retinopathy is protean in its manifestations, and can cause either optical or neural, and either central or peripheral, loss.

Ocular Surface Degenerations

Numerous age-related changes of the cornea and conjunctiva may occur. Most are benign, but, especially if they affect the central part of the cornea, each may cause optical degradation of the visual image (Kenyon, Hersh, Starck, & Fogle, 1992). Corneal degenerations are a group of conditions that have no apparent hereditary or developmental pattern and are usually seen among elderly individuals, although they may also result from inflammatory disease.

The whitish ring that appears around the peripheral cornea among many elderly people is one such degeneration. Called *arcus senilis*, this degeneration is an accumulation of cholesterol esters, triglycerides, and phospholipids (Cogan & Kuwabara, 1959; Walton, 1973). Another common degeneration is the *pterygium*, which is a triangular, fleshy, overgrowth of the conjunctiva onto the cornea. This degeneration is, histologically, a fibrous, vascular alteration of normal conjunctival collagen. Pterygia may be accompanied by irritation, burning, and foreign body sensation. Ptergia are horizontally positioned between the upper and lower lids, on either the nasal or, less commonly, the temporal side of the cornea. Their development appears to be related to accumulated exposure to ultraviolet energy, and thus they are more common in the elderly (Townsend, 1988) and more common in more tropical and equatorial latitudes. They are benign, but if they grow centrally on the cornea, they may distort or block the visual image. They are often self-limited in their growth, but if they become troublesome they may be removed surgically.

Anterior Ischemic Optic Neuropathy

Stroke of the optic nerve head (anterior ischemic optic neuropathy, or AION) is a relatively common affliction of the elderly. The hallmark of this condition is painless, sudden, monocular loss of vision with accompanying swelling of the optic nerve head, readily observed ophthalmoscopically (Glaser, 1989). There may be some recovery, but generally the loss is permanent. The cause is not understood. There are two generally recognized forms: arteritic AION and nonarteritic AION. They differ in that the former appears to be a manifestation of a vascular inflammatory disease, and often is accompanied by symptoms such as malaise, weight loss, fever, tenderness in the region of the temporal arteries of the forehead, jaw pain following chewing, or muscle aches (myalgias) of the large trunk muscles. Also, the erythrocyte sedimentation rate (ESR) is usually elevated. This condition, with many or most of the previous features, is also called temporal or giant cell arteritis. The nonarteritic form of AION is idiopathic, meaning without known cause, although systemic hypertension, or elevated blood pressure, appears in about 50% of cases of nonarteritic AION.

The typical age for nonarteritic AION is 60–65 years, whereas for arteritic AION it is somewhat older, about 70–80 years of age. Both forms are by far most common among the elderly. For example, the prevalence of arteritic AION is about 33/100,000 between ages 60–69 and rises to 844/100,000 for those over age 80 (Hauser, Ferguson, Holley, & Kurland, 1971). Other differences are that second eye involvement occurs in about 40% of cases of nonarteritic AION and up to 70% of cases of arteritic AION, and the loss in the arteritic form tends to be more devastating.

Treatment of the arteritic form consists of high doses of systemic steroids. This does not reverse the loss that has already occurred, but decreases the likelihood that the second eye will become involved. The nonarteritic form has no known treatment, but, as mentioned, is fortunately less severe.

Loss of vision from either form of AION can be dramatic, sudden, and profound. The loss is neural, essentially consisting of a monocular stroke, or infarction, of the optic nerve. Recovery is rare. The loss is often "altitudinal," meaning it affects the lower or, less commonly, the upper half of the field of vision in one eye. Loss of the lower half may be more devastating than loss of the upper half of the field of vision, as loss of the lower half interferes with walking, seeing the street, and seeing the hands. Sadly, central vision is often lost as well. Management consists primarily of protecting the other eye.

Eyelid and Skin Changes with Aging

The skin of the eyelids and the underlying connective tissue structures, ligaments, and tendons all tend to relax, thin, and atrophy as a normal part of aging. However, in certain individuals, such changes may become especially pronounced and pathological in nature, and lead not only to a cosmetically undesirable appearance but to functionally significant impairments. Normal functioning of the eyelids is important in protecting the corneal surface from trauma and from drying, in pumping tears from the eye surface into the nasolacrimal ducts that drain into the nose, in cleaning the cornea of foreign matter, and in providing the lipid component of the tear film. Laxity of the eyelids may interfere with any or all of these functions.

Ectropion and *entropion* are the terms used to describe, respectively, the out-turning or in-turning of the lid margins. Among the elderly, the commonest cause of both ectropion and entropion is involutional (senile) skin, muscle, and connective tissue degeneration, although tumors, scar-forming diseases, inflammation, neurological disorders, or other causes may be involved (Doxanas, 1993). The lower lid is more commonly involved that the upper.

If uncorrected, lid laxity can lead to severe corneal disorders, which include vascularization or drying and subsequent infection of the cornea, loss of acuity from corneal surface irritation, and scraping of the cornea by in-turned eyelashes. Conservative steps, such as use of lubricant eye drops or bedtime lubricant ointment, or surgical procedures, such as tightening or shortening of underlying tissue planes or muscles, are available, as indicated.

Blepharoptosis, or lid droop, was mentioned earlier in the context of normal changes of the lid skin. There are also other, less common, pathological causes of lid droop that are seen in an elderly population. An important such cause is isolated palsy of the oculomotor (third) cranial nerve, which leads to loss of neural innervation of the muscle that holds the eyelid in its normal elevated position. This is commonly seen in the setting of diabetes, and may also be caused by an aneurysm, among other causes, all of which have increased incidence in the elderly population. Myasthenia gravis, a disease of the neurotransmitter system for acetylcholine, also can present with lid droop (Glaser, 1988).

Dry Eye Syndrome

Dry eye syndrome (*keratoconjunctivitis sicca*) occurs when there is deficiency of the tear film that bathes the corneal surface, which results in excessively rapid evaporation of the tear film and consequent loss of its normal functions. This generally results from deficiencies in the make-up of the tear film. Tears are secreted mainly by the lacrimal gland, which resides in the upper, outer corner of the eye, under the upper lid, and also by numerous other small glands that line the eyelid margins and lie within the conjunctiva. With aging, all of these glands lose their effectiveness as a result of loss of cells and decreased productivity of the cells that remain.

The functions of the normal tear film are numerous (Lemp & Chacko, 1991). Tears smooth out irregularities in the corneal surface and thus act as the anterior-most refractive surface of the eye. Tears also aid in regulating the state of hydration of the cornea. Moreover, atmospheric oxygen dissolved within the tears provides the corneal surface with its primary source of oxygen. The tears further act as a lubricant for the blinking upper eyelid in its movement over the ocular surface. Tears additionally contain substances with antibacterial properties. And, finally, the movement of tears over the ocular surface serves to rinse the surface of the eye, removing exfoliated cells, debris, and foreign bodies. As can be surmised, the tear film is essential to the health of the cornea, and its decline in quality with aging may result in numerous corneal disorders.

The normal tear film has three layers: an outer lipid layer; a central, aqueous, or watery, layer, which comprises about 90% of the tear film by volume; and an inner mucin layer. In dry eye syndrome, there may be loss of any of the three layers. The symptoms typically worsen throughout the day as evaporation from the tear film proceeds.

Symptoms of dry eye syndrome include a foreign body sensation with "gritty" feeling, itching, burning, redness, and excessive tearing. The latter seems paradoxical, but is in fact a reflex attempt by the eye to address the aforementioned deficiencies in the tear film by producing more tears, which, in an unfortunate vicious cycle, are not any less deficient in quality. This cycle leads to excessive tear formation and the common complaint of constant wetness in the eye, or even the uncontrolled production of tears streaming down the cheek.

Dry eye syndrome is common and usually not very serious. An excess (deficient) tear film, if present, can however cause blurring of vision through optical distortion of the corneal front surface, while inadequate protection of the cornea can lead to a downward spiral of drying of the cornea, tissue breakdown, accumulation of cellular and foreign debris, and, finally, infection of a disturbed corneal surface. In more extreme cases of dry eye syndrome, in which the lacrimal apparatus is not merely deficient but is frankly underproductive, there may be little or no tears secreted at all and the hazards of drying may become severe problems requiring very frequent application of artificial tears (physiologically balanced synthetic wetting drops or ointments). Treatment of milder caes is usually managed by occasional instillation of a tear subtitute.

SIGNS AND SYMPTOMS OF POTENTIAL EYE PROBLEMS

Although this chapter cannot hope to educate the reader about techniques for diagnosing eye disorders, or about the very many other conditions besides those discussed that may be seen, anyone working with the aged will profit by being familiar with certain signs, symptoms, and conditions that may indicate the presence of either normal or pathological changes in vision (Table 3–3). If such signs and symptoms are present, referral to an eye care specialist should be considered, and this should be carried out with urgency if the changes noted are sudden or severe.

Table 3–3. Signs and symptoms of potential eye problems.

Decreased vision

New floaters

Flashes of light

Curtain or veil blocking vision

Loss of depth perception

Haloes

Pain

Redness of eye or lids

Discharge

Bulging of eye

Double vision

Diabetes

Family history of eye disease

Interventions

Although a chapter such as this cannot provide guidelines for rehabilitation of the visually impaired individual, which requires considerable individualized assessment (American Academy of Ophthalmology, Quality of Care Committee, Refractive Errors Panel, 1994; Faye & Stuen, 1992), several concepts from this area are worth mentioning, if only to give examples of the simple techniques that sometimes can be very helpful in improving sight and visual performance. Several applications of the concepts in the text are given by way of illustration.

One of the simplest things that can be done is to provide enhanced illumination. This often results in greater contrast and improved ease of reading text, seeing shapes and surfaces, and ambulating. For eample, a 60-watt bulb in a gooseneck lamp positioned 1 foot from a page of text provides far more illumination than does the light from a 150-watt bulb positioned 12 feet from the page. The impact of many of the visual conditions mentioned in this chapter, which result from optical loss of retinal illumination, can be eased by use of this one simple technique.

On the other hand, sometimes too much light reflected off the page can cause light scattering within the eye (if the ocular media are partly optically opaque, such as occurs in cataract), and this may cause glare, which actually reduces contrast. This is especially troublesome with glossy pages such as are found in magazines. In this case, lower illumination may paradoxically increase contrast. Another approach in this instance would be to use a pale amber acetate sheet over the reading material, which increases contrast by absorbing "blue" (short) wavelengths of light, which scatter far more than do "red" (long) wavelengths.

In conditions in which there is loss of effective contrast on the retina (which may arise from either optical or neural causes), techniques to enhance the contrast of reading material may be useful. Text that has crisp, dark letters on a flat white background will achieve this. Photocopies of newsprint will often have higher contrast than the original newsprint, which often has grey letters on a yellowish background.

Reading material should be held perpendicular to the line of sight, so as to maintain the entire page in the focal plane of the eye. A page of newsprint, for example, laid out on a table may cause text at the top or bottom of the page to exceed the focal range of the eye, especially with an elderly eye having little or (after cataract surgery with intraocular lens implant) no accommodative amplitude.

Another strategy is to place a black sheet of cardboard under the line of text being read. Acting as a ruler, this aids the eye in following a line across the page and also eliminates unnecessary glare arising from the page below the line of text being read. Larger print publications, or devices to enlarge the print, such as simple magnifiers, reading machines with lens systems, or closed circuit television systems, can also be very useful.

In Chapter 4, Orr further details of the kinds of assistive devices and inventions that can be helpful in aiding visually impaired individuals to achieve better functionality in all areas of life. It should be stressed that assistive devices and rehabilitative techniques can provide greatly improved visual function for many persons, even those with substantial vision loss. Underutilization of services and devices by professionals and patients alike remains one of the largest barriers to improved performance.

VISION LOSS AND HEARING LOSS

As described elsewhere in this text (Chapters 5, 6, and 7), age-related hearing loss, or presbycusis, is also a common experience of the elderly, and, hence, hearing loss often co-occurs with age-related vision loss. Functional problems that may arise for those with loss of both hearing and vision go beyond what either alone may cause. For example, those with limited hearing rely more heavily on speechreading as an aid in speech perception. Limited central acuity, from any of the causes mentioned, will therefore exacerbate a preexisting problem in the hearing and perception of speech. In fact, a common complaint of the elderly is that their hearing is suddenly worsening, when in fact it may be that their sight, which until then sustained their hearing through visual augmentation, has begun to decline. A careful history will often suggest such a mistaken self-diagnosis. As another example, for those with limited sight, the ability to walk out of doors can be increased by use of environmental sounds as cues to location and to potential hazards. Similarly, the ability to communicate with passersby may enhance mobility in the seeing-impaired; additional loss of hearing can be a devastating additional deficit.

Another aspect of combined hearing and sight loss is the psychological fear that this may engender in the individual who grows to fear complete loss of both of these modalities, and who would thus be cut off entirely from the world of sight and sound. It is therefore worth reassuring such an individual that the two systems, hearing and seeing, are essentially independent of one another, and that decline in one system in no way entails or causes decline in the other.

PSYCHOSOCIAL ASPECTS OF VISION LOSS

I have already alluded to the fear of severe sensory isolation in the patient with combined sight and hearing loss. The patient facing declining sight may also, as a consequence, suffer from acute depression or anxiety. There are numerous other psychosocial aspects to vision loss. Burack-Weiss (1992) outlined some of these. She noted that late life is a time of many losses: loss of health, of independence, of significant others, and of favored activities. Vision loss interacts with many of these and adds further strain to an already growing list of burdens. Ways in which vision loss, along with other losses, may impact on an elderly person's psychosocial profile include the precipitation of social withdrawal and isolation, the promotion of communication misunderstandings and even paranoid ideation, development of a feeling of being part of a pitied or stigmatized population ("the blind"), and loss of privacy, as others take on new roles in caring for one's personal matters. Additionally, loss of vision may contribute to an increased sense of vulnerability, dependence on others, and fear of further loss.

Vision loss in the elderly often interacts with other late-life changes to produce a more complex disability than the loss of sight would seem to explain. Therefore, full rehabilitation or comprehensive medical care may require referral to psychiatric or counseling specialists or to appropriate social services.

SUMMARY

As individuals age, many can expect to incur changes to their vision either as a consequence of the aging process itself or as secondary pathologies. Common vision problems associated with normal aging include presbyopia, miosis, cataract, posterior vitreous detachment, and changes in the lid and skin of the eyes. In addition, pathological causes of vision loss among the elderly include glaucoma, age-related macular degeneration, diabetic retinopathy, and several other less common disorders. Elders experiencing signs and symptoms of potential eye problems such as decreased vision, double vision, and pain should consult their ophthalmologist or other eye care specialist for assessment and intervention. Co-existing hearing loss should also be addressed to maximize sensory and social functioning. Elders' quality of life will be enhanced when their vision needs are identified and remediated.

RESOURCES

Organizations

American Academy of Ophthalmology
655 Beach Street
Box 7424
San Francisco, CA 94120
(415) 561-8500

American Foundation for the Blind
15 West 16th Street
New York, NY 10011
(212) 620-2000/(800) 232-5463

American Optometric Association
243 North Lindbergh Boulevard
St. Louis, MO 63141
(314) 992-4100

Association for Macular Diseases
210 East 64th Street
New York, NY 10021
(212) 605-3719

Fight for Sight, Inc.
160 East 56th Street
New York, NY 10022
(212) 751-1118

Foundation for Glaucoma Research
490 Post Street
San Francisco, CA 94102
(415) 986-3162/(800) 245-3005

Helen Keller National Center for Deaf-Blind Youths and Adults
South Central Regional Office
4455 LBJ Freeway, LBJ#3, Suite 317
Dallas, TX 75244
(214) 490-5998

Jewish Guild for the Blind
15 West 65th Street
New York, NY 10023
(212) 769-6200

Lighthouse National Center for Vision and Aging
111 East 59th Street
New York, NY 10022
(212) 821-9200

National Association for the Visually Handicapped
22 West 21st Street
New York, NY 10010
(212) 889-3141
and
3201 Balboa Street
San Francisco, CA 94102
(415) 221-3201

National Eye Care Project
See American Academy of Ophthalmology
(800) 222-EYES

National Eye Institute
National Institutes of Health
Building 31, Room 6A 32
Bethesda, MD 20892
(301) 496-5248

National Library Services for the Blind and Physically Handicapped
The Library of Congress
1291 Taylor Street
Washington, DC 20542
(202) 287-5100

National Society to Prevent Blindness
500 East Remington Road
Schaumberg, IL 60173
(312) 843-2020/(800) 221-3004

Research to Prevent Blindness
645 Madison Avenue
New York, NY 10022
(212) 752-4333

Textbooks and Monographs

Albert, D. M., & Jakobiec, F. A. (Eds.). (1994). *Principles and practice of ophthal-mology*. Philadelphia: W. B. Saunders.
Faye, E. E. (Ed.). (1984). *Clinical low vision* (2nd ed.). Boston: Little, Brown.
Faye, E. E., & Stuen, C. S. (Eds.). (1992). *The aging eye and low vision: A study guide for physicians*. New York: The Lighthouse, Inc.
Podos, S. M., & Yanoff, M. (Eds.). (1992). *Textbook of ophthalmology*. New York: Gower Medical Publishing.
Sekuler, R., Kline, D., & Dismukes, K. (Eds.). (1982). *Aging and human visual function*. New York: Alan R. Liss.
Tasman, W., & Jaeger, E. A. (Eds.). (1995). *Duane's ophthalmology*. Hagerstown, MD: J. B. Lippincott.
Weale, R. A. (1992). *The senescence of human vision*. Oxford: Oxford University Press.

Journals

Ophthalmology
American Journal of Ophthalmology
Archives of Ophthalmology
Investigative Ophthalmology and Visual Sciences
Clinical Visual Sciences
Vision Research

REFERENCES

Algvere, P. V., Berglin, L., Gouras, P., & Sheng, Y. (1994). Transplantation of fetal reginal pigment epithelium in age-related macular degeneration with subfoveal neovascularization. *Graefe's Archive of Clinical and Experimental Ophthalmology, 232,* 707–716.

American Academy of Ophthalmology, Quality of Care Committee, Glaucoma Panel. (1996). *Preferred practice pattern. Primary open-angle glaucoma.* San Francico: Author.

American Academy of Ophthalmology, Quality of Care Committee, Retinal Panel. (1993). *Preferred practice pattern. Diabetic retinopathy.* San Francisco: Author.

American Academy of Ophthalmology, Quality of Care Committee, Refractive Errors Panel. (1994). *Preferred practice pattern. Rehabilitation: The management of adult patients with low vision.* San Francisco: Author.

American Academy of Ophthalmology, Quality of Care Committee, Retina Panel. (1994a). *Preferred practice pattern. Age-related macular degeneration.* San Francisco: Author.

American Academy of Ophthalmology, Quality of Care Committee, Retina Panel. (1994b). *Preferred practice pattern. Precursors of rhegmatogenous retinal detachment in adults.* San Francisco: Author.

Armaly, M. F. (1966). On the distribution of applanation pressure and arcuate scotoma. In G. Patterson, S. J. H. Miller, & G. D. Paterson (Eds.), *Drug mechanisms in glaucoma* (pp. 167–189). Boston: Little, Brown.

Bankes, J. L., Perkins, E. S., Tsolakis, S., & Wright, J. E. (1968). Bedford glaucoma survey. *British Medical Journal, 1,* 791–796.

Bochow, T. W., West, S. K., Azar, A., Munoz, B., Sommer, A., & Taylor, H. R. (1989). Ultraviolet light exposure and risk of posterior subcapsular cataracts. *Archives of Ophthalmology, 107,* 369–372.

Bok, D. (1993). Retinal transplantation and gene therapy: Present realities and future possibilities. *Investigative Ophthalmology and Visual Science, 34,* 473–476.

Burack-Weiss, A. (1992). Psychosocial aspects of aging and vision loss. In E. E. Faye & C. S. Stuen (Eds.), *The aging eye and low vision: A study for physicians* (pp. 29–34). New York: The Lighthouse, Inc.

Cogan, D. G., & Kuwabara, T. (1959). Arcus senilis: Its pathology and histochemistry. *Archives of Ophthalmology, 61,* 553–560.

The Diabetes Control and Complications Trial Research Group. (1993). The effect of intensive treatment of diabetes on the development and progression of long-term complications in insulin-dependent diabetes mellitus. *New England Journal of Medicine, 329,* 977–986.

Doxanas, M. T. (1993). Eyelid abnormalities: Ectropion, entropion, trichiasis. In W. Tasman & E. A. Jaeger (Eds.), *Duane's opthalmology* (Vol. 6, chap. 118). Hagerstown, MD: J. B. Lippincott.

Edener, F., Hiller, R., & Taylor, H. R. (1981). Senile lens changes and diabetes in two population studies. *American Journal of Ophthalmology, 91,* 381–395.

68 ≡ COMMUNICATION TECHNOLOGIES FOR THE ELDERLY

Eye Disease Case-Control Study Group. (1993). Antioxidant status and neo-vascular age-related macular degeneration. *Archives of Ophthalmology, 111,* 104–109.

Faye, E. E., & Stuen, C. S. (Eds.). (1992). *The aging eye and low vision: A study guide for physicians.* New York: The Lighthouse, Inc.

Foster, A. (1991). Patterns of blindness. In W. Tasman & E. A. Jaeger (Eds.), *Duane's ophthalmology* (Vol. 5, chap. 53). Hagerstown, MD: J. B. Lippincott.

Glaser, J. S. (1988). Infranuclear disorders of eye movements. In W. Tasman & E. A. Jaeger (Eds.), *Duane's ophthalmology* (Vol. 2, chap. 12). Hagerstown, MD: J. B. Lippincott.

Glaser, J. S. (1989). Topical diagnosis: Prechiasmal visual pathways. In W. Tasman & E. A. Jaeger (Eds.), *Duane's ophthalmology* (Vol. 2, chap. 5). Hagerstown, MD: J. B. Lippincott.

Hampton, G. R., & Nielsen, P. T. (Eds.). (1992). *Age-related macular degeneration: Principles and practice.* New York: Raven.

Harding, J. J., & van Heyningen, R. (1987). Epidemiology and risk factors for cataract. *Eye, 1,* 537–541.

Hauser, W. A., Ferguson, R. H., Holley, K. E., & Kurland, L. T. (1971). Temporal arteritis in Rochester, Minnesota, 1951–1967. *Mayo Clinic Proceedings, 46,* 597–602.

Hemenger, R. P. (1984). Intraocular light scatter in normal vision loss with age. *Applied Optics, 23,* 1972–1974.

Hess, R., & Woo, C. (1978). Vision through cataracts. *Investigative Ophthalmology and Visual Sciences, 17,* 428–435.

Hollows, F. C., & Graham, P. A. (1966). Intraocular pressure, glaucoma, and glaucoma suspects in a defined population. *British Journal of Ophthalmology, 50,* 570–586.

Kahn, H. A., Leibowitz, H. M., Ganley, J. P., Kini, M. M., Colton, T., Nickerson, R. S., & Dawber, T. (1977). The Framingham Eye Study. I. Outline and major prevalence findings. *American Journal of Epidemiology, 106,* 17–32.

Kenyon, K. R., Hersh, P. S., Starck, T., & Fogle, J. A. (1992). Corneal dysgeneses, dystrophies, and degenerations. In W. Tasman & E. A. Jaeger (Eds.), *Duane's ophthalmology* (Vol. 4, chap. 16). Hagerstown, MD: J. B. Lippincott.

Kupfer, C. (1984). Bowman lecture: The conquest of cataract: A global challenge. *Transactions of the Ophthalmological Societies of the United Kingdom, 104,* 1–35.

Leibowitz, H. M., Krueger, D. E., Maunder, L. R., Milton, R. C., Kini, M. M., Kahn, H. A., Nickerson, R. J., Pool, J., Colton, T. L., Ganley, J. P., Loewenstein, J. I., & Dawber, T. R. (1980). The Framingham eye study monograph: An oph-thalmological and epidemiological study of cataract, glaucoma, diabetic retinopathy, macular degeneration, and visual acuity in a general population of 2631 adults, 1973–1975. *Survey Ophthalmology, 24*(Suppl.), 335–610.

Lemp, M. A., & Chacko, B. (1991). Diagnosis and treatment of tear deficiencies. In W. Tasman & E. A. Jaeger (Eds.), *Duane's ophthalmology* (Vol. 4, chap. 14). Hagerstown, MD: J. B. Lippincott.

Leske, M. C., & Sperduto, R. D. (1983). The epidemiology of senile cataracts: A review. *American Journal of Epidemiology, 118,* 152–165.

Lichter, P. (1994). Genetic clues to glaucoma's secrets. The L. Edward Jackson Memorial Lecture. Part 2. *American Journal of Ophthalmology, 117,* 706–727.

Linder, B. (1966). Acute posterior vitreous detachment and its retinal complications. *Acta Ophthalmologica, 87*(Suppl.), 1–108.

Macular Photocoagulation Study Group. (1982). Argon laser photocoagulation for senile macular degeneration: Results of a clinical randomized trial. *Archives of Ophthalmology, 100,* 912–918.

Macular Photocoagulation Study Group. (1990). Krypton laser photocoagulation for neovascular lesions of age-related macular degeneration: Results of a randomized clinical trial. *Archives of Ophthalmology, 108,* 816–824.

Macular Photocoagulation Group. (1991). Laser photocoagulation of subfoveal neovascular lesions in age-related macular degeneration: Results of a randomized clinical trial. *Archives of Ophthalmology, 102,* 1220–1231.

Macular Photocoagulation Study Group. (1993). Laser photocoagulation of subfoveal neovascular lesions in age-related macular degeneration: Updated findings from two clinical trials. *Archives of Ophthalmology, 111,* 1200–1209.

Moisseiev, J., Alhalel, A., Masuri, R., & Treister, G. (1995). The impact of the Macular Photocoagulation Study results on the treatment of exudative age-related macular degeneration. *Archives of Ophthalmology, 113,* 185–189.

National Society to Prevent Blindness. (1980). *Vision problems in the U.S.: A statistical analysis prepared by the operational research department.* New York: Author.

O'Malley, P. (1976). The pattern of vitreous syneresis: A study of 800 autopsy eyes. In A. R. Irvine & P. O. O'Malley (Eds.), *Advances in vitreous surgery* (pp. 17–33). Springfield, IL: Charles C. Thomas.

Schwab, L., & Taylor, H. R. (1990). Cataract and delivery of surgical services in developing nations. In W. Tasman & E. A. Jaeger (Eds.), *Duane's ophthalmology* (Vol. 5, chap. 57). Hagerstown, MD: J. B. Lippincott.

Schumer, R. A., & Podos, S. M. (1993). Medical treatment of newly diagnosed open-angle glaucoma. *Journal of Glaucoma, 2,* 211–222.

Schumer, R. A., & Podos, S. M. (1994). The nerve of glaucoma! *Archives of Ophthalmology, 112,* 37–44

Sommer, A., Tielsch, J. M., Katz, J., Quigley, H. A., Gottsch, J. D., Javitt, J. C., Martone, J. F., Royall, R. M., Witt, K. A., & Ezrine, S. (991). Racial differences in the cause-specific prevalence of blindness in east Baltimore. *New England Journal of Medicine, 325,* 1412–1417.

Sperduto, R. D., & Hiller, R. (1984). The prevalence of nuclear, cortical, and posterior subcapsule lens opacities in a general population sample. *Ophthalmology, 91,* 815–818.

Sperduto, R. D., & Seigel, D. (1980). Senile lens and senile macular changes in a population-based sample. *American Journal of Ophthalmology, 90,* 86–91.

Taylor, H. R., West, S. K., Rosenthal, F. S., Munoz, B., Newland, H. S., Abbey, H., & Emmett, E. A. (1988). Effect of ultraviolet radiation on cataract formation. *New England Journal of Medicine, 319,* 1429–1433.

Tielsch, J. M., Sommer, A., Katz, J., Royall, R. M., Quigley, H. A., & Javitt, J. C. (1991). Racial variations in the prevalence of open angle glaucoma. The

Baltimore Eye Survey. *Journal of the American Medical Association, 266,* 369–374.

Townsend, W. M. (1988). Pterygium. In H. E. Kaufman, B. A. Baron, M. B. McDonald, & S. R. Waltman (Eds.), *The cornea* (pp. 461–483). New York: Churchill Livingstone.

U.S. Department of Health and Human Services. (1987). *The National Advisory Eye Council: Vision research: A national plan 1983–1987: 1987 Evaluation and update.* (NIH Publication No. 87–2755). Washington, DC: Government Printing Office.

Wade, E. C., Flynn, H. W., Olsen, K. R., Blumenkranz, E. C., & Nicholson, D. H. (1990). Subretinal hemorrhage management by pars plana vitrectomy and internal drainage. *Archives of Ophthalmology, 108,* 973–978.

Walton, K. W. (1973). Studies on the pathogenesis of corneal arcus formation. I. The human corneal arcus and its relation to atherosclerosis as studied by immunofluorescence. *Journal of Pathology, 111,* 263–274.

Weale, R. A. (1992). *The senescence of human vision.* Oxford: Oxford University Press.

World Health Organization Programme Advisory Group. (1989). *Report of the Eighth Meeting of the WHO Programme Advisory Group on the Preventionof Blindness.* (WHO Publication No. 89.17). Geneva, Switzerland: Author.

4

Assistive Technologies for Older Persons Who Are Visually Impaired

Alberta L. Orr, M.S.W.

INTRODUCTION

Age-related vision loss touches the lives of approximately half of middle-aged and older adults through either their own personal experience or that of a family member, friend, or co-worker. It is among the most frequently reported impairments affecting the elderly population. Relative to the chronic health problems and disabilities encountered by older persons today, visual impairment has received limited attention despite to its prevalence. Most people are not aware of the vision-related rehabilitation services and adaptive devices available to ameliorate the impact of vision loss on the older person, and yet vision loss is potentially one of the most disabling conditions associated with aging.

Even in the 1990s, limited awareness of and access to services contributes to excess disability among older persons and unnecessary dependence on others for routine daily tasks. When this occurs, the impact of vision loss extends beyond the individual to the already overburdened social service and health care systems and to individual family caregivers.

Vision-related rehabilitation services and adaptive technology can enable an older person with deteriorating vision to continue to carry out life-sustaining and valued activities with increasing independence. Therefore, public and professional education about vision issues, needs, and services available for elders is as important as providing the services directly to them. Lack of information is the greatest barrier to accessing what is available. Service providers in the aging network and health arena can play a critical role in informing consumers about these services and how to access them.

The goal of this chapter is to provide professionals, family members, and elders themselves with current information regarding vision assistive devices and programs. Specifically, this chapter describes the demographics of aging and vision loss, the vision-related service delivery system, the range of high- and low-technological devices available, and the issues in delivering available and affordable vision services to this growing population.

DEMOGRAPHICS OF AGING AND VISION LOSS

It is impossible to overlook the fact that American society is increasingly becoming an aging society and part of the phenomenon of "global aging." As the elderly population increases, we can expect to witness a significantly higher incidence of age-related vision loss. Here are some illuminating data (Orr,1995):

- There are 32.8 million people over age 65 in this country, 12.7% of the population.
- Vision loss is among the most frequently reported disabilities affecting the elderly.
- An estimated 4.1 million Americans age 55 and over are blind or severely visually impaired and have a vision loss severe enough to interfere with their ability to carry out routine daily tasks independently (Nelson & Dimitrova, 1993).
- One in eight people age 55 and over is severely visually impaired.
- One in four people age 85 and over—the fastest growing age group—is severely visually impaired.
- Sixty-six percent of visually impaired older people have at least one other chronic condition, such as heart disease, arthritis, hypertension, or hearing impairment.
- Sixty-six percent of older people who are visually impaired live in their own home.
- A minimum of 500,000 older visually impaired persons now live in nursing homes (Kirchner, 1989).

- There will be 70.2 million Americans over age 65 by the year 2030, 20% of the population.
- The current older visually impaired population will double by 2030 when the last cohort of the baby boom generation reaches its senior years.
- Even sooner—by the year 2010—there will be 1.6 million severely visually impaired people age 85 and over.

The population of older persons who are visually impaired generally comprises those for whom vision loss is new. They are individuals who have lived 60, 70, 80, or more years as sighted persons, and the onset of vision loss occurs at a life stage associated with other critical losses of loved ones, productive roles, health, and well being. Visual impairment is common among people age 55 and over because of four major age-related eye diseases associated with the aging process: (a) macular degeneration, (b) cataracts, (c) glaucoma, and (d) diabetic retinopathy. Macular degeneration is overwhelmingly the leading cause of vision loss among older adults, but most individuals with this eye condition do not become totally blind. Chapter 3 details these and other vision problems of elders.

In a 1995 survey designed to gather current data and to raise public awareness, The Lighthouse, Inc., and Louis Harris and Associates, Inc. , found the prevalence of vision loss to be even higher than the data presented previously (The Lighthouse, Inc., 1995). Data on blindness and severe visual impairment have typically been collected beginning at ages 55 to 65, primarily because of eligibility for services and benefits at these age milestones. (Age 55 is used for eligibility for the federally funded independent living services program for older persons who are blind or visually impaired.) This 1995 survey included individuals age 45 and older and found that one in six American adults (13.5 million people) age 45 and older report moderate or severe visual impairment. This proportion jumps to one in four among those age 75 and over.

Although vision loss cuts across all social and economic strata, it is more prevalent among those with limited social and economic resources. Of particular note is the fact that older people who are African American, Hispanic, and American Indian are at a greater risk of vision loss because of the higher incidence of diabetes and the diabetic retinopathy associated with it in these groups. African Americans also experience glaucoma at a higher than average rate. This has significant implications for service planning and delivery in the areas of outreach services to identify these harder to reach populations and in overcoming language and cultural barriers to service.

Blindness and visual impairment have traditionally been classified as a low-incidence disability. Among older persons the opposite is true, and this is an important mind-set to change. Approximately 80% of all individuals in the United States who are blind or visually impaired are age 55 or over. It is conceivable, however, that advances in medical intervention in many areas, including ophthalmology, in the coming decades may have an impact on these numbers.

It would seem obvious that both the current and projected demographics should play a powerful role in shaping public policy now and in the future. It has taken the vision field several decades of population growth to begin to influence public policy concerning the need for increased funds for expansion of vision-related programs and services. Such services must be made increasingly available, accessible, affordable, and covered by health insurance. Much remains to be done, particularly in the area of third party reimbursement, and the current political and economic climate makes the task just that much more arduous.

VISUAL IMPAIRMENTS AND VISION-RELATED SERVICES

Definition of Vision Terms

Standardized definitions of terms used to describe varying degrees of vision loss are important to help everyone understand eligibility for vision-related services, for individuals and their family members to understand the "labels" assigned to the individual with a vision problem, and for documenting the number of older persons with a specific degree of vision loss and/or level of vision function. For example, how "visual impairment" is defined in each research study is critical to the data gathering procedure.

Many terms have been used over the last several decades to describe those who have some vision loss but still have some degree of remaining vision. The term **visual impairment** is defined as a decreased visual ability that impacts on daily activities. Visual impairment occurs along a continuum, ranging from total blindness at one extreme to partial vision at the other.

Legal blindness is defined as a visual acuity of 20/200 or a visual field of no greater than 20 degrees in the better eye with the best possible correction. A designation of legal blindness is used by governmental agencies to determine eligibility for vision-related rehabilitation services and disability benefits. However, many older persons who experience significant functional vision problems that are severe enough to interfere with their ability to carry out routine daily tasks are not legally blind. **Severe visual impairment** has been defined as having difficulty reading newspaper print.

Because most older persons with vision loss are not totally blind, the term **low vision** is typically used to describe a lower degree of functional vision, or a visual acuity of 20/70 or less in the better eye with the best possible correction. Vision is a complex sense made up of the ability to see contrasts and sharpness of detail and to evaluate the location of objects in the environment. In healthy aging eyes, changes in vision can be corrected by glasses or contact lenses. If an individual is told by an eye care professional that his or her vision cannot be fully corrected by ordinary prescription lenses, medical treatment, or surgery, and still has some usable vision, this is referred to as low vision. This term is commonly used in the eye care and rehabilitation fields. The individual with low vision still has some good usable vision and can make the best use of it by learning adaptive techniques to carry out daily tasks and by using assistive technology.

Low vision can result from the four leading eye conditions previously mentioned or from a stroke. The individual with low vision may experience one or more of three types of vision problems:

- *overall blurred vision,* which can be caused by cataracts, scars on the cornea, or diabetic retinopathy;
- *loss of central or center vision*, frequently caused by macular degeneration; and,
- *loss of peripheral or side vision*, most commonly caused by glaucoma or stroke.

It is important to understand the kinds of functional issues related to vision loss, such as its impact on mobility, near vision, ability to read print, communicate with others, drive, work, manage money, and household and personal management. Further, the psychosocial aspects of aging and vision loss are key to understanding how individuals react to vision loss, begin to "adjust" to vision loss, seek and accept services, interact with others, and perform basic tasks (Burick-Weiss, 1991; Orr, 1991). Lifelong coping skills, responses to change, loss, and stress, and the availability of a support network help to determine how each older person deals with vision loss. Other factors include determination to function as independently as possible, isolation, level of frustration, level of dependence, loss of privacy, and the need to continue productive activity, recreational activities, and social functioning. The process of adjusting to vision changes can be better managed when elders, families, and professionals realize what vision-related services are available and how techniques and devices can facilitate independence.

Vision-Related Rehabilitation Services

Because this book focuses on communication technologies that positively affect the independent functioning of older persons who are visually impaired, discussion of adaptive devices will highlight information access and communication issues within the broader context of vision-related rehabilitation services.

The most important message for all professionals to communicate to older persons and their family members is that help is available. Specialized vision rehabilitation can restore function after vision loss, just as physical therapy restores function after a person loses the use of a limb. Vision-related rehabilitation services include some combination of:

- low vision examination and devices
- individual counseling to help in the adjustment to vision loss
- support groups that provide opportunities to discuss similar problems and coping strategies
- training in adaptive techniques and the use of adaptive devices.

Learning to use such interventions will facilitate:

- home and personal management skills (such as meal preparation, personal care techniques, managing money, labeling medications)
- communication skills (including the use of readers, tape recorders, braille, large print, computers with screen magnification or speech output, writing guides, telephones, and timepieces)
- orientation and mobility (independent movement and travel skills), learning to orient oneself in familiar and unfamiliar environments, asking for assistance from others when appropriate, and moving about using a long white cane or other devices.

These vision-related rehabilitation services are provided by specially trained rehabilitation professionals, such as vision rehabilitation teachers, orientation and mobility specialists, rehabilitation technology specialists, and low vision specialists. They are available to varying degrees across the country. Every state has a state rehabilitation agency and that agency administers the Independent Living Services for Older Individuals Who Are Blind Program, Title VII Chapter 2 of the Rehabilitation Act. Many communities also have private agencies serving people who are blind or visually impaired. Some agencies have fees for services; others do not. Title VII Chapter 2 funding is the most important, because it is the only federal funding targeted to serve older blind and visually impaired persons. A select list of resources on agencies that provide assistance to those with vision problems is provided at the end of this chapter.

Low Vision Services

The first step toward good eye care for the older person is to see an ophthalmologist, a medical doctor with specialization in vision. An ophthalmologist diagnoses and treats eye diseases, in some cases prescribing medications or surgery to improve or prevent the worsening of vision-related conditions. An optometrist diagnoses eye conditions and can prescribe corrective lenses. If the vision loss cannot be completely corrected and interferes with everyday living, then it is time to consider vision-related rehabilitation services to help maintain or restore independent living skills. There are both ophthalmologists and optometrists with special training in low vision.

An older person with vision loss but with remaining usable vision should be referred by his or her eye care professional to a low vision specialist for a special type of eye examination called a low vision evaluation. A low vision specialist can determine the extent of remaining vision and prescribe optical devices that help make the best use of this remaining vision. Most low vision specialists will want a referral from the patient's eye care physician.

Low vision services are the first essential component of full scale vision-related rehabilitation services. Unlike the standard acuity measures conducted during an eye examination where the visually impaired person is able to see only a very limited portion of the eye chart, the low vision examination maximizes the patient's success. Through discovery of what the low vision individual can see, under what optimum circumstances, and with what special optical device(s), patients complete the examination feeling that there is something that can help them make better use of the vision they still have. Older persons experiencing difficulty carrying out routine tasks should have a low vision evaluation. If an eye care physician does not make this recommendation, all older persons should ask for a referral.

Fangmeier (1995) emphasized the most critical point about low vision optical devices. He cautioned that one must know what optical devices can and cannot do. They do not restore lost sight or normalize vision. Optical devices do help in three basic ways: by magnifying, filtering, or increasing the usable field of vision. Examples of devices most commonly used by older persons include:

- hand-held or stand magnifiers for reading print or performing other near tasks;
- high-intensity lamps for reading and other close-up tasks such as writing or sewing;
- pocket-sized telescopes for distance vision, such as reading a street sign or identifying the number of an approaching bus; and
- closed-circuit televisions for reading that magnify and project printed materials onto a television screen.

Several factors are essential for the successful use of any low vision device by older persons. These include: (a) training in the correct use of each device, (b) practice using the device in the environment in which it is needed, and (c) follow-up visit(s) as needed to ensure that the device is being used correctly. The follow-up component of low-vision rehabilitation is an extremely critical element if older consumers are to make maximum use of their prescribed low vision devices, such as hand-held magnifiers, telescopes, and high intensity lighting. Agencies must give priority to the follow-up phase of instruction so that fewer devices are left in drawers because "they just don't work."

Although low-vision services are becoming increasingly available throughout the country, some states have only one organization with a low vision center or clinic, and the scope of the services offered in these programs varies widely. Elders who live outside major metropolitan areas may be less aware of available services. Further, low-income and minority elders may have limited access to low-vision services and eye care. Limited insurance coverage prevents many elders from obtaining low vision services and optical devices.

Independent Living Services for Older Individuals Who are Blind: Title VII, Chapter 2 of the Rehabilitation Act

In 1978, reauthorization of the Rehabilitation Act of 1973 put the rehabilitation needs of older people on the public policy agenda in the form of Title VII, Chapter 2 (initially enacted as Title VII, Part C), Independent Living Services for Older Individuals Who Are Blind. However, rehabilitation services for this population did not become a priority until 1986 when the first funds were allocated and 25 grants of approximatedly $200,000 were made to state rehabilitation agencies. In 1994, 8.9 million dollars were funded, and it was not until 1995 that all states received Chapter 2 funds for the first time, a major and long-awaited coup.

In 1995, draconian cuts proposed by both the House and Senate threatened the Chapter 2 program. Considerable advocacy efforts, including those of the National Coalition on Aging and Vision and its Chapter 2 Task Force convened by the American Foundation for the Blind, succeeded in preserving the program and in maintaining level funding at 8.9 million dollars. This was a major triumph in light of the current threats to human service funds in Congress. The core services outlined under Chapter 2 include orientation and mobility training, communication skills, communication aids, activities of daily living, low vision services, family and peer counseling, and community integration including outreach and information and referral.

The annual analysis of the program's achievements (Herndon, 1993; Stephens, 1994) describes the range of services being provided through Chapter 2 and the number of individuals receiving each type of service in each state. Each year, only a fraction of the newly visually impaired older population seeks and receives vision-related rehabilitation services. Frequently, 5 to 7 years pass from the onset of deteriorating vision before older people seek services.

Stephens (1995) reported that, although 14,968 older persons were served in 1994, an average of 468 per state, less than 1% of those eligible for these services is being reached. This is in keeping with one of the major findings of the Lighthouse survey (Lighthouse, Inc., 1995) which revealed underutilization of vision-related resources, including rehabilitation services, adaptive devices, and optical devices.

Components of a Comprehensive Rehabilitation Program

An agency's comprehensive service delivery model begins with a comprehensive intake process that assesses overall needs specific to vision loss and those more generally related to the aging process. Comprehensive services include:

- independent living skills training, including instruction in adaptive techniques to accomplish routine tasks, as well as instruction in the use of adaptive devices;
- communication skills training, including braille instruction as desired; orientation and mobility training;
- low-vision services;

- support groups; family caregiver support groups;
- individual and family clinical or counseling services;
- vocational rehabilitation and job placement;
- recreation and socialization programs; and
- opportunities for community integration.

Innovations in service delivery strategies and programs help to round out a comprehensive program. Some examples include:

- models that create opportunities for productivity through mentorship and leadership roles or volunteerism;
- empowerment and advocacy skills training programs;
- a family rehabilitation model;
- collaborative models with the aging network, the medical arena, or other related fields and disciplines;
- innovative outreach strategies to the community; and
- strategies for improving access to community-wide resources and services for older consumers.

These core and innovative components constitute a comprehensive model of service to older persons that views and serves the older person holistically. Self-help or mutual aid support groups are the fastest growing and most highly valued support service for older people who are visually impaired. These groups play a critical role in helping older people deal successfully with vision loss as they work their way through an adjustment process. They provide newly visually impaired individuals the opportunity to share their experiences, frustrations, and adaptations with others in similar circumstances. Support groups can be an effective vehicle for discussion of the psychosocial factors associated with using assistive devices. Support groups for caregivers also provide family members with a safe and healthy forum in which to address their fears, frustrations, loss, and anxieties with others undergoing similar experiences and concerns.

Providing opportunities for productive activity and contributing roles must be an essential part of vision-related rehabilitation services. Increasingly, agencies are training older persons who are blind or visually impaired and have recently completed vision rehabilitation to serve as peer counselors. Such programs provide these individuals with opportunities to develop skills in mentoring and leadership. Empowerment and Advocacy Skills Training Programs are a critical part of service models both in the 1990s and into the 21st century.

Service Delivery Methods

Agencies provide individual or group services on site at an agency or in elders' homes. A home-based model is particularly important to serve older consumers who would otherwise not go to an agency for services because of geographic distance, transportation difficulties, limiting physical conditions, or chronic health problems. The home-based model has other functional advantages such as helping elders learn adapted skills and the use of assistive equipment in their primary environment. Thus, the service provider can tailor instruction to the individual's style and pace of learning. The major disadvantage of the home-based model is that the older individual does not have the opportunity to meet other older people who are experiencing some of the same challenges and frustrations associated with adjustment to vision loss.

The family rehabilitation model is an important model for the 1990s and the 21st century. In this model, a family member who frequently serves as a caregiver assumes an active role in the vision rehabilitation process. This caregiver also includes significant others in independent living, orientation, and mobility instruction. Such involvement benefits both the family member and the newly visually impaired person. Family members learn the adaptive skills and the use of adaptive devices along with the elder. They come to understand that their relative can learn practical techniques that promote safety and confidence. Their involvement supports the elder and reinforces the skills taught by service providers. In a recent study, the anxiety level of family members about the older person's safety was greatly reduced by knowing that their elderly relative had been taught adaptive techniques and the use of adaptive devices (Crews & Frey, 1993).

TECHNOLOGIES FOR INDEPENDENT LIVING AND COMMUNICATION

This is an exciting time in the area of adaptive devices for people with vision problems. For many years, adaptive devices related to blindness or visual impairment have been a small, specialized market, keeping availability limited and unit prices high. As the population ages and increasing numbers of older persons have vision, hearing, and physical difficulties, more adaptive devices will become available on the open market . Large face and large print watches are an excellent example. Universal design has made a major difference in an individual's willingness to use new technology.

One study of the use of and need for assistive devices among non-institutionalized older visually impaired persons found this group to have a high rate of device utilization (Mann, Hurren, Karuzza, & Bentley, 1993). The interviewees also expressed the need for additional devices and made suggestions for the development of new devices. Some of these devices are already on the market. The array of devices used by two older persons in the following examples is representative of many older persons with low vision.

1. A 73-year-old man uses tactile markings on stove, oven, and furnace controls, a talking alarm clock, a talking book machine, a timer with raised marks, a Wonder Knife, pins attached to specific areas on garments to code for color, a Visual-Tech Print Enlargement System, and a white cane.
2. An 81-year-old woman uses a kitchen timer and a dial phone with raised enlarged numbers, an electronic hot water measure, oven controls with color and tactile markings, large print labels on medication bottles, a talking clock, a hand-held magnifying glass with a built-in light, a wristwatch with a large face, and a white collapsible cane.

Most older people who are visually impaired learn to use adaptive devices while receiving vision-related rehabilitation services. Rehabilitation teachers and rehabilitation technology specialists provide this instruction, the latter specializing in high technology devices. Rehabilitation teaching combines the best principles of andragogy (the principles of adult learning), adaptive rehabilitation skills, and counseling to facilitate learning new skills. The goals of rehabilitation teaching are to enable clients to carry out their daily activities, to manage their lives more efficiently within their environment and to reach their potential for maximum independence, self-esteem, and productivity.

Rehabilitation teaching uses an individualized, problem-solving approach. If clients are fully aware of their options, they can explore adaptive techniques and devices that may be useful at a later time if their vision or needs change. Rehabilitation teachers also use counseling skills to help newly visually impaired persons and their families learn to adjust to severe visual impairment. They also assess the older person's environment and make suggestions for modifications such as improved lighting and the use of color contrasts to make the living space easier to manage.

Cost is minimized when existing appliances are adapted. One example might be removing the face of a bedside clock so that the individual could tell time tactually. The introduction of adaptive devices typically begins with low technology devices. High technology devices are introduced as needs and interests dictate.

An important consideration in the rehabilitative approach to elderly persons is the importance of what may seem to be small gains in function. Such small gains can make all the difference between being able to live in one's own home or requiring care in a long-term care institution (Williams, 1984). This is particularly relevant to the introduction of adaptive devices. Rehabilitation teachers serving older persons also recognize that skills training merges with the philosophy of geriatric rehabilitation. Most rehabilitation teachers would probably agree with Williams' (1984) observation that:

> Rehabilitation is an approach, a philosophy, and a point of view as much as a set of techniques. The aim of rehabilitation, to restore an individual to his or her former functional and environmental status, or, alternatively, to maintain or maximize function, in order to help them continue to live as full a life as possible. (1984, p. xiii)

Consider the example of Mrs. Grey, who experienced deteriorating vision. When Mrs. Grey's vision began declining 3 years ago, she ignored the initial changes: diminished ability to see at night, which gradually limited her driving to daylight hours; blurring of print letters, which prevented her from reading with her usual ease; uncertainty in reading and writing handwritten correspondence, which decreased the number of letters she wrote to friends and family members; difficulty in reading the telephone book, which caused her to dial incorrect numbers; and stumbling in unfamiliar environments, which discouraged her from going outdoors alone.

By the time Mrs. Grey and her family recognized the extent of her visual impairment and saw an ophthalmologist, she was fearful that she would not be able to care for herself or her home or continue the activities she enjoyed. When she met with a rehabilitation teacher, she identified several skill areas in which her limited vision caused a problem such as writing legibly or on a straight line, reading regular print size, pouring liquids without overflowing, identifying clothing, and dialing the telephone. She also needed help in reestablishing her self-confidence. Mrs. Grey and her rehabilitation teacher developed learning objectives and goals that focused on the general areas of self-care, home management, and communication. These included learning such skills as use of a tape recorder for personal correspondence and a four-track Library of Congress cassette playback machine for reading. Other skills included sighted guide techniques for ease and safety when walking with other people; a reliable tactile method for dialing the telephone; use of writing guides for writing a check, addressing an envelope, or writing a letter; and methods for identifying clothing and pouring liquids.

ACCESS TO INFORMATION AND COMMUNICATION THROUGH THE USE OF ADAPTIVE DEVICES

Like hearing loss, the loss of vision greatly affects standard methods of acquiring information and communicating with others. Reading a newspaper or a book, writing a letter or a check, jotting down a phone number, or telling time become increasingly difficult. Through adaptive methods and the use of assistive devices, the older person can continue to have access to numerous information sources and communication opportunities. Of equal importance is the need for family members and others to recognize how they might make various forms of communication accessible to the elder with vision difficulty.

Print Alternatives: Adaptive Technologies for Writing and Reading

Written communication methods include braille, large print handwriting, typing, portable electronic braille note takers such as the Braille n' Speak, and computers with screen magnification and synthetic speech. Any of these media can be adapted by visually impaired persons to fulfill their daily activities, including writing checks, messages, letters, or shopping lists. For some elders, it may help them enter or remain in the workforce.

Large Print

Large print is a catch-all term that encompasses a wide variety of print-material forms. Large print is not a technically definable term, but for many older persons a print size of 16 point or 18 point is effective.

Commercially produced large print materials are increasingly easier to find. Public libraries have large-print books, and many commercial printing houses publish large-print books. Most large-print material is published in 18-point type. This size type can be read by many visually impaired persons without using low vision aids or other adaptations.

The successful use of large print depends on several factors in addition to the size of the print. These include:

- the spacing of the letters and the lines,
- the contrast between the print and the background,
- the availability of good lighting,
- the angle at which the book or other material is being read, n the use of low vision aids, such as magnifiers or closed-circuit televisions,
- the need and motivation of the person who is doing the reading.

Further, the effective use of large print requires individualized training. Again, the case of Mrs. Grey can serve as an example. From a complete low vision evaluation, it was found that Mrs. Grey could read some large print when using a magnifier. Because she had been a fast and efficient reader, she found that using the magnifier and large print slowed down her reading rate and frustrated her. Therefore, with the assistance of the rehabilitation teacher, Mrs. Grey learned to use the four-track cassette playback machine for recreational reading and worked with her magnifier and large print for short tasks. She uses large-print recipes and large-print playing cards and labels foods and medicines in large print for ease of identification. Her pharmacy now prints medicine bottle labels in large print for her.

Braille

Many older people with age-related vision loss do not learn braille. However, it can be a useful communication skill for some and an important independent living skill for many. Braille is the most widely known form of written communication for people who are blind. It is used for English and foreign languages; mathematics, computer, and scientific notations; and music. It can be written by hand with a slate and stylus, by the Perkins Brailler (a manual braille writer), or by a computer connected to a braille printer. The braille "cell" consists of six embossed dots. The configurations of the dots represent a letter, a word, a portion of a word, a number, a punctuation mark, a composition sign, or a symbol specific to the subject (such as music). Grade 1 braille consists of the alphabet, numbers, punctuation marks, and limited composition signs that are specific to braille. Grade 2 braille is more complex than Grade 1 braille and includes many contractions (single symbols for commonly used combinations of letters such as "ing" or whole words). Most reading materials are produced in Grade 2 braille, although less than 20% of legally blind people use Grade 2 braille.

Because Grade 1 braille is relatively easy to learn, it should be introduced during rehabilitation to older visually impaired people who are exploring alternatives to reading and writing print particularly as an independent living tool. Grade 1 braille is especially useful for labeling, marking items, noting telephone numbers and addresses, and keeping brief notes. Braille labels can also be used for marking stove dials, clocks, timers, washers, dryers, and other appliances. Family members can visually learn to read and write Grade 1 braille. Jumbo braille can also be useful for some older adults. Jumbo braille dots are larger and spaced farther apart than are standard braille dots so they are easier to feel.

Braille technology may also be useful to those older persons who are already using technology or who are comfortable learning to use new devices. Electronic braille notetakers such as the Braille 'n Speak are often used instead of the slate and stylus or a braille typewriter. The braille notetakers are small, portable devices with braille keyboards for entering information. They use a speech synthesizer or braille display for output. Braille printers can be hooked up to computers to produce hard braille copy. Refreshable braille display technology consists of a long strip of movable pins that provide braille respresentation of a line of text on the computer screen. As the user cursors up and down the screen, the refreshable braille device continuously updates its 80 character information display.

Handwriting and Typing

Many older people with useful residual vision also have the lifelong habit of handwriting. Simple adaptations such as a felt-tip marker or pen and a handwriting guide can make writing possible. A number of writing guides are commercially available. The guides have designated writing spaces that enable the person to write on a straight line. These include a guide on a clipboard that has a movable right-hand margin and uses standard paper, bold-line paper with heavy black lines that are spaced farther apart than in conventional notebook paper, and tactile handwriting guides for writing signatures, checks, and addressing envelopes. These guides are helpful to clients with all degrees of vision loss including those who are totally blind.

Typing can also be an efficient way to communicate. It is used primarily for personal correspondence, addressing envelopes, filling out checks, and preparing lists and messages for other persons. Its limitations arise from the fact that visually impaired persons cannot read what they have typed unless large-print elements are used that are available only for some typewriters. Nevertheless, many older people enjoy the challenge of learning this skill, knowing that what they have typed can be easily read by others.

Computer Technology

Now that computers are so widely utilized, older persons who lose vision and have been using computers in the workplace or at home can continue to do so by installing a large print software package for on-screen magnification and by using a scalable font to print in the font size of choice—usually 16 or 18 point or more. Scalable fonts make it easier for others to produce materials in a large-print accessible format for the visually impaired reader.

Synthetic speech programs can also be loaded into a computer's memory. A synthetic speech system is composed of two parts: the synthesizer that does the speaking and the screen access program that tells the synthesizer what to say. Synthesizers used with personal computers convert written text to synthesized speech. It takes time and training to understand some synthetic speech which can be difficult for anyone with a hearing impairment; however, recent improvements in these technologies have made the speech more intelligible. Current computer technologies with outputs in braille, large print, and voice continue to increase the accessibility of print for blind and visually impaired persons. These technologies also make it possible for blind and visually impaired persons to access the information superhighway and to "surf the Internet."

Closed-Circuit Television

Over the years considerable research has been conducted on methods of making print accessible to blind people. New vision enhancement systems or closed-circuit televisions (CCTVs) based on video and computer technology offer help to the older person who is experiencing vision loss. A CCTV consists of a stand-mounted or hand-held video camera with a zoom lens that projects a magnified image onto a video monitor or a television screen. Reading material is placed under the camera and moved across and down the page. The reader adjusts the size of the magnification. The magnification capabilities of CCTVs allow many individuals with low vision to see the printed word. Along with the magnification, the reader can also adjust the light/dark contrast of the image on the screen.

An increasing variety of models of closed captioned televisions (CCTVs) are on the market, and prices are decreasing. Portable hand-held cameras are designed to magnify almost anything within reach, including labels on medications or on packages of food in the supermarket. The average cost of a hand-held camera is approximately $2,000, although some models are as low as $1,300. Lower cost CCTVs that plug into a TV are in the $500–$1,000 price range. New model CCTVs are attractive and easy to use and provide "ease and independence without stigma," which Harper (1995) described as the critical element in successful usage. One model called the Aladdin Personal Reader received the American Society on Aging's Platinum Award in 1995.

Optical Character Recognition (OCR) Technology

The optical character reader is frequently referred to as a scanner. It offers blind and visually impaired people the ability to scan printed material and to save the text to a computer that speaks it back using synthetic speech. The three processes of OCR technology consist of scanning, software conversion of the scanned image into characters and words, and producing the text as recognizable synthetic speech. The information is stored in an electronic form, either on a personal computer or in the memory of the OCR. Prices range from $2,000–$3,000.

Technology for Reading by Listening

Listening devices include tape recorders and Talking Book four-track cassette players. Tape recorders are remarkably versatile devices, but for older people they sometimes seem like high technology. Therefore, a rehabilitation teacher may need to help visually impaired persons select the machine that will be most useful and train them in its use.

Many visually impaired persons use a standard two-track cassette recorder for personal correspondence and everyday use. More advanced cassette recorders have four tracks, indexing capabilities, variable speed adjustments, compressed speech capabilities, and memory. Compressed speech is produced at a speed faster than normal speech. With aural training, visually impaired persons can learn to understand compressed speech and therefore read recorded material at a faster rate. This is frequently a preferred option for the individuals who were once rapid and avid visual readers.

The tape recorder serves many purposes for blind and visually impaired persons. For example, it can serve as a family message center, store gourmet recipes, and record a business meeting. With instruction, older visually impaired people can learn to use a tape recorder to fulfill many daily needs.

The National Library Service (NLS) of the Library of Congress provides a free state-of-the-art four-track cassette playback machine with rechargeable batteries. This machine enables blind, visually impaired, physically handicapped, and print-handicapped persons to hear books, magazines, and other reading materials that are available on loan through the National Library Service. Applications for and further information about the National Library Service are obtainable through state and local associations for the blind, public libraries, and state and regional libraries for the blind and physically handicapped.

The NLS provides additional aids to make its machines accessible to physically handicapped persons. For example, a remote control to turn the machine on and off is available, as are headphones with individually adjusted amplifiers and pillow speakers for persons who cannot use the headphones. (See the Resource section at the end of this chapter.)

Radio Reading Services

Many communities have a Radio Reading Service so that visually impaired individuals can listen to materials read over the air. This is done via a special radio receiver that is provided free of charge. There is a wide array of materials such as the daily newspaper, magazine articles, gardening tips, and recipes. This service is extremely popular among older persons. In general, both radio and television provide the older visually impaired person with access to current information.

High-Tech Reading Machines

The Kurzweil Reading Machine uses a computerized voice output to read printed materials. These machines are housed in many libraries for use by the public. The training for the Kurzweil machine is short; machines are costly and limited in availability. The Reading Edge, the current version of the Kurzweil Personal Reader, is a compact version and is designed for purchase by individuals for home or office use.

Time Device Technology

Clocks and watches in large print and with speech output are now readily available in the mainstream market, although many are also available from vision-related resources. Large print and braille kitchen timers are also available through distributors of independent living aids and devices. See the Resource section at the end of this chapter.

Receptivity to Assistive Technologies

Many older people, and younger people as well, once introduced to a new piece of adaptive equipment, undergo an internal, personal struggle that involves accepting or rejecting the new device. On the plus side, adaptive devices enable older persons to continue to perform routine tasks in a new and adapted way. They also promote self-reliance and self-confidence. On the minus side, deciding to use the device means accepting the fact that "I am blind" and that "I can no longer do without it."

In many instances, when older persons decide to use high or low technology assistive devices such use eliminates or drastically reduces reliance on another person to provide assistance with the task. For older persons who have become socially isolated, giving up the one-to-one contact for a piece of equipment may be a serious threat to psychological security. This factor is important for service providers and family members to consider when introducing new adaptive devices to an older person. Time may also be an important factor in helping persons adjust to using adaptive devices (Orr & Piqueras, 1991).

How elders perceive their public image and acceptance when using an adaptive device will influence their eventual use of the devices. Using a device in public is quite different from using it at home. Even using the device at home in the presence of family members requires a level of self-acceptance that is frequently difficult to reach. Rejection of a device can be anticipated when older persons are concerned about its appearance and their awkwardness in using it (Gitlin, 1995). Many older people become accustomed to using a device during the rehabilitation process, but afterward continued independent use may be troublesome.

Psychosocial factors greatly influence elders' adjustment to vision loss as well as their receptivity to new vision technologies and methods. Important psychosocial factors include established patterns of coping with change and/or loss and the availability of a support network of other older visually impaired persons.

Far too often, adaptive devices end up in a drawer out of frustration, resistance, or denial. This can be the case with what may seem the simplest devices, such as hand-held magnifiers. Magnifiers must be positioned at just the right distance from the page and one's eyes to focus the printed material. If an older person has been given more than one magnifier, and each works differently, proper use can be confusing and frustrating, especially when the elder feels resistant, anxious, and/or depressed. Sufficient training and follow-up are critical to ensure that the elder is completely comfortable using the device.

Trends in Vision-Related Assistive Technologies

As the baby boomers age, growing numbers of people will have a greater level of experience, interest, and confidence in trying new devices. As the demand for devices increases, and unit prices come down, greater numbers of older persons will have access to life-enhancing technologies for vision loss.

One of the greatest challenges in access to technology in the last 2 years has been the difficulty in accessing Microsoft Windows by individuals using screen magnification or speech output. Manufacturers of assistive technology have experienced problems in developing programs that can describe auditorially the visual environment of Windows. Advocacy efforts reached the Federal Communications Commission and Microsoft has recognized and addressed the concerns of people with vision problems.

These adaptive technologies along with many of the other assistive technologies discussed here have been and will continue to be evaluated by the National Technology Center at the American Foundation for the Blind (AFB). Product evaluations are published in each issue of the *Journal of Visual Impairment and Blindness News Services*, published six times a year by AFB Press. These product evaluation reports can also be obtained directly from the American Foundation for the Blind.

Although the development of these technologies is extremely exciting, many of the high-technology devices are far removed from the daily lives of older people. Some older persons are not interested in or do not perceive a need for the devices. For others, costs are prohibitive, and rehabilitation professionals are often hesitant to mention the devices for fear of offering their clients false hopes. Each individual's needs and interests play a critical role in determining what assistive devices will enable him or her to live as fully and asindependently as possible.

THE NEED FOR COLLABORATION BETWEEN THE AGING AND VISION NETWORKS

Leaders in the field of aging and vision loss also call for increased collaborative efforts between agencies serving visually impaired persons and agencies serving older persons at the community and state levels. Cooperative activities and networks are an essential element in the provision of comprehensive services to older visually impaired persons. Agencies receiving funds under Title VII, Chapter 2 are establishing cooperative relationships with their counterparts in the field of aging.

They are focusing on collaborative planning and service delivery to improve and expand services and to create greater access to services. The vision-related rehabilitation field also needs the joint advocacy efforts of the aging network to increase funds, expand services, and create innovative models of service delivery that will allow it to best serve the growing population of older persons experiencing vision loss.

Collaborative planning and service delivery are essential to ensure that older persons have both the general and specialized services they need associated with aging and disability (Orr, 1992). Service providers in the aging and vision fields should get to know their counterparts in both public and private agencies. This will facilitate effective and appropriate referrals. Much can be accomplished through collaboration, crossdisciplinary partnerships, and networking between the aging and vision rehabilitation fields. Serving older persons who are blind and visually impaired is a combination of good practice, public and professional education, legislative advocacy, and research efforts to bring about the level and quality of services and resources needed to ensure maximum independence.

SUMMARY

As the older population grows, agencies in the aging network, both in home- and community-based long-term services and in residential care settings will see more older people with vision loss. Professionals in the aging and vision rehabilitation fields need to understand and meet the needs of this expanding population. By working together, the aging and vision fields can plan and implement comprehensive services for elders experiencing vision loss.

Older persons who are visually impaired may also benefit from services available through the aging network, including home-delivered meals, door-to-door transportation services, escort services, telephone reassurance, housekeeping and chore services, entitlements counseling, financial management assistance, legal services, housing assistance, adult day care, and respite services. An agency serving visually impaired persons that provides holistic services must work cooperatively with agencies serving the elderly to help clients obtain these services.

The essential message to communicate to older people who are losing their vision is that "you don't lose your knowledge and skills when you develop a vision problem, but you may need to learn new techniques and to use new devices to carry out everyday activities." Older persons' needs will depend on their particular vision problems and the tasks they want to accomplish. Vision loss need not be the end of reading, watching television, cooking dinner, or managing finances. Social isolation and depression need not be naturally associated with deteriorating vision. Services are available. More people, including physicians and allied health professionals, service providers in the aging network, and older persons and their family members, need to know what services exist and how to access these services. Elders with some remaining vision will benefit from such minor adaptations as larger and darker print, increased lighting, glare reduction, and adaptive devices. Each of these, independently or in combination, can enhance productivity and quality of life.

Here is a summary of suggestions for frequent concerns. These tips are efficient, easily incorporated, cost-effective, and can make a difference in the lives of older persons experiencing vision loss.

For difficulty reading or identifying items:

- Try brighter light that is more evenly distributed. This may mean using more than one source of light in a room and adjusting blinds and draperies to make the best use of natural light.
- Avoid glare from windows or mirrors. Blinds can be adjusted to let natural light into a room, while keeping streams of bright glaring light out of the room. Nonglare floors also reduce glare.
- Be organized. This will help in locating and identifying important items easily. Explain to family members the importance of keeping items in the same place, including items in a kitchen, bathroom, and linen closets or the placement of furniture in a room.
- Label all medicine containers so that they can be identified independently, either in large print or by a tactile indicator.
- Ask a local librarian about large-print books and Talking Books on tape.

For concerns about moving around the home or other familiar environments:

- Replace worn carpeting, and remove area rugs. Move electrical cords away from walkways. Use nonskid, no-gloss products to clean and polish floors.
- Use contrasting colors to make doors and stairs easier to see.
- Move furniture out of the main traffic areas in your home and keep desk chairs and table chairs pushed in.
- Keep cabinet, closet, and room doors fully opened or fully closed—not half open.

- Make sure that lighting in hallways and stairwells is bright and even.
- Use railings when climbing stairs.
- Make it easy to locate electrical outlets and light switches, oven dials, hot pads, and doorknobs by using color contrasts.

For traveling safely outside of the home:

- Wear comfortable and supportive shoes.
- Plan your route before you go. Identify landmarks that are easy for you to detect and use them as reference points.
- Cross streets only at crosswalks. If you are uncertain about when it is safe to cross, do not hesitate to ask for help.
- When walking with another person, it may be helpful to hold onto his or her arm slightly above the elbow and walk about a half step behind. This will allow the person to guide you comfortably.
- Wear sun shields to reduce glare from sunlight.

RESOURCES

Books and Videos on Aging and Visual Impairment from AFB Press

American Foundation for the Blind
11 Penn Plaza, Suite 300
New York, NY 10001
212-502-763

Books

PRESCRIPTIONS FOR INDEPENDENCE: Working with Older People Who Are Visually Impaired (1993) by Nora Griffin-Shirley, Ph.D., and Gerda Groff
Prescriptions for Independence is a hands-on book with practical suggestions for improving the life and promoting the independence of older persons with visual impairments. Easy-to-read, it gives concrete examples and suggestions in non-technical terms.

OUT OF THE CORNER OF MY EYE: Living with Vision Loss in Later Life (1991) by Nicolette Pernot Ringgold
A personal account of sudden vision loss and subsequent adjustment that is full of practical advice and cheerful encouragement, told by

an 87-year-old retired college teacher who has maintained her independence and zest for life. Subjects covered include initial reactions as well as ongoing accommodations to loss of vision and ways to continue one's activities both indoors and out. An extensive resource section listing more than 40 sources of information and services completes this essential guide.

VISION AND AGING: Crossroads for Service Delivery (1992) edited by Alberta L. Orr

An overview textbook of the service delivery systems in the aging and vision rehabilitation fields that covers the essential issues concerning vision loss among older persons in this country, the growth of visual impairment among the increasing number of elderly people in the United States, and the policy and service questions that will demand national attention throughout this and the coming decade. Fifteen chapters authored by experts cover such diverse topics as the physiological, psychological, and social aspects of aging and visual impairment; low vision, rehabilitation, and orientation and mobility services; home- and community-based long term care, collaborative planning, self-help and advocacy; and current and future trends relating to aging and vision loss.

MAKING LIFE MORE LIVABLE (1983) by Irving R. Dickman

Shows how simple adaptations in the home and environment can make a big difference in the lives of blind and visually impaired older persons. The suggestions offered are numerous and specific, ranging from how to mark food cans for greater visibility to how to get out of the shower safely.

VISUALLY IMPAIRED SENIORS AS SENIOR COMPANIONS: A Reference Guide for Program Development (1992) by Alberta L. Orr

Older visually impaired persons can become active participants in their community, volunteer, and reenter the work force. This useful guide, a joint project of the American Foundation for the Blind and ACTION, assists service providers and others who work with blind and visually impaired older people to train, place, and match them with other older visually impaired clients so they can help each other. It describes the Senior Companion Program that is intended to help broaden opportunities for older persons with disabilities.

VISUAL IMPAIRMENT: An Overview (1990) by Ian L. Bailey, O. D., and Amanda Hall, Ph.D.

An up-to-date, overall look at the common forms of vision loss and their impact on the individual. Includes drawings that explain the parts of the eye and how it functions, as well as photographs that simulate how people with vision loss see.

CREATIVE RECREATION FOR BLIND AND VISUALLY IMPAIRED ADULTS (1988) by Irene Ludwig, Lynne Luxton, Ed.D., and Marie Attmore

Shows how sports, hobbies, and leisure-time pursuits can be adapted to the needs and abilities of visually impaired persons. Among the activities are running and jogging, bicycling, bowling, skiing, swimming, canoeing, hiking, performing in community theater, visiting museums, learning languages, doing crafts and needlework, cooking, and gardening.

Directory

AFB DIRECTORY OF SERVICES FOR BLIND AND VISUALLY IMPAIRED PERSONS IN THE UNITED STATES AND CANADA, 24th Edition

The must-have reference guide to programs and services for millions of blind and visually impaired Americans and Canadians. An invaluable resource containing almost 3,000 local, state, regional, and national services for blind and visually impaired persons of all ages and their families throughout the United Sates and Canada.

Videos

AGING AND VISION: Declarations of Independence

A very personal look at five older people who have successfully coped with visual impairment and continue to lead active, satisfying lives. Their stories are not only inspirational, but also provide practical, down-to-earth suggestions for adapting to vision loss later in life.

BLINDNESS: A Family Matter

A frank exploration of the effects of an individual's visual impairment on other members of the family and how those family members can play a positive role in the rehabilitation process. It features interviews with three families whose "success stories" provide advice and encouragement, as well as interviews with newly blinded adults currently involved in a rehabilitation program.

Pamphlets

AGING AND VISION: Making the Most of Impaired Vision (1985; Revised 1987)

This pamphlet, produced in association with the American Association of Retired Persons, reviews the four major causes of vision loss and tells senior adults how to enhance vision by improving lighting, decorating with contrasting colors, using devices for independent living, and learning how to move around in the safest fashion possible.

RESOURCE PACKETS (Available from the American Foundation for the Blind)

Building Bridges: A Resource Packet for Serving Older Visually Impaired Persons
  This resource packet is designed for service providers in the aging network.

"We Help Those Who Don't See Well, Live Like Those Who Do"
  This is an information packet designed for older consumers and their family members.

Catalog Houses That Sell Products for People Who Are Blind or Visually Impaired

The companies listed here sell products for blind and visually impaired people such as computer- and noncomputer-related access products (including electronic and optical magnification products) and household, personal care, recreational, medical and electronic items.

American Printing House for the Blind
P.O. Box 6085
Dept. 0086
Louisville, KY 40206-0085
502-895-2405
Specializes in instructional aids, tools, and supplies.

Ann Morris Enterprises
890 Fams Court
East Meadow, NY 11554
516-292-9232

Carolyn's
P.O. Box 14577
Bradenton, FL 34280
800-648-2266
813-761-8306 (fax)

Easier Ways
1101 North Calvert St.
Suite 405
Baltimore, MD 21202
410-659-0232

Independent Living Aids
27 East Mall
Plainview, NY 11803
516-752-8080
516-752-3135 (fax)

Maxiaids
42 Executive Blvd.
Farmingdale, NY 11735
800-522-6294; 516-752-0521
516-752-0689 (fax)

National Association for the Visually Handicapped
22 West 21st St.
New York, NY 10010
212-889-3141; 415-221-3201 (CA)
212-727-2931 (fax)
Specializes in non-computer-related products for persons with low vision.

The Lighthouse, Inc.
111 East 59th Street
New York, NY 10022
212-821-9200

Sense-Sations
Associated Services for the Blind
919 Walnut St.
Philadelphia, PA 19107
215-627-0600, ext 202

TFI Engineering
529 Main St.
Boston, MA 02129
800-331-8255; 617-242-7007
617-242-2007 (fax)

Vis/Aids
102-09 Jamaica Avenue
Richmond Hill, NY 11418
718-847-4734
718-441-2550 (fax)

Organizations Associated with
Vision Impairment and Blindness

American Academy of Ophthalmology
1822 Fillmore Street
PO Box 7424
San Francisco, CA 94120

American Bible Society
1865 Broadway
New York, NY 10023
212-581-7400

American Council of the Blind
1155 15th St. N.W., Suite 7209
Washington, DC 20005
202-467-5081

American Foundation for the Blind
11 Penn Plaza, Suite 300
New York, NY 10001
212-620-2000

**Association for Education and Rehabilitation of the
Blind and Visually Impaired**
206 North Washington Street
Alexandria, VA 22314
703-548-1884

Association for Macular Diseases
210 East 64th Street
New York, NY 10021
212-605-3719

Bible Alliance, Inc.
PO Box 1549
Bradenton, FL 3
813-748-3031

Canadian National Institute for the Blind Library for the Blind
1929 Bayview Avenue
Toronto, Ontario Canada M4G 3E8
416-480-7520

Council of Citizens with Low Vision
Riley Tower 2 Suite 2300
600 N. Alabama Street
Indianapolis, IN 46204
800-733-2258

Helen Keller National Center
111 Middle Neck Road
Sands Point, NY 11050
516-944-8900

Lions Clubs International
300 22nd Street
Oak Brook, IL 6-570
312-571-5466

National Association for the Visually Handicapped
22 West 21st Street
New York, NY 10010
212-889-3141

National Eye Care Project
PO Box 9688
San Francisco, CA 94101
800-222-EYES

National Federation of the Blind
1800 Johnson Street
Baltimore, MD 21230
301-659-9314

National Library Services for the Blind and Physically Handicapped
Library of Congress
1291 Taylor Street, NW
Washington, DC 20542
202-707-5100

New York Times Large Type Weekly
229 W. 43rd Street
New York, NY 10036

Reader's Digest Large-Print Edition
PO Box 241
Mt. Morris, IL 61054
815-734-6963

BIBLIOGRAPHY

Burick-Weiss, A. (1991). In our own words: Elders' reactions to vision loss. *Journal of Gerontological Social Work, 17*, 15–24.

Crews, J. E., & Frey, W. D. (1993). Older people who are blind and the family members who care for them. *Journal of Visual Impairment and Blindness, 87*, 6–11.

Fangmeier, R. (1995). Optical devices: A vital link. *Maximizing Human Potential, 3*, 5–6.

Gitlin, L. (1995). Why older people accept or reject assistive technology. *Generations, 19*, 41–46.

Harper, D. (1995). Ease and independence without stigma: Three new products that work. *Generations, 19*, 58–60.

Herndon, G. (1993). *Analysis of Title VII, Part C, Independent Living for Older Americans with Visual Impairments, fiscal year 1991–92*. Mississippi State University, Rehabilitation Research and Training Center on Blindness and Low Vision.

Kirchner, C. (1989). *Prevalence estimates of blindness and visual impairment in the United States: Late 1980's*. Unpublished manuscript, American Foundation for the Blind.

Mann, W. C., Hurren, D., Karuzza, J., & Bentley, D. W. (1993). Needs of home-based older visually Impaired persons for assistive devices. *Journal of Visual Impairment and Blindness, 87*, 106–110.

Nelson, K. A., & Dimitrova, E. (1993). Severe visual impairment in the United States and in each state, 1990. Statistical Brief #36. *Journal of Visual Impairment and Blindness, 87*, 80–85.

Orr, A. L. (1991). The psychosocial aspects of aging and vision loss. *Journal of Gerontological Social Work, 17*, 1–14.

Orr, A. L. (1992). *Vision and aging: Crossroads for service delivery*. New York: American Foundation for the Blind.

Orr, A. L. (1995). Innovative models of services delivery for older persons who are blind and visually impaired. In Orr, A. L., Lidoff, L., & Scott, J. (Eds.), *Building bridges: A resource packet for serving older visually impaired persons*. New York: American Foundation for the Blind.

Orr, A. L., & Piqueras, L. S. (1991). Aging, visual impairment, and technology. *Technology and Disability, 1*, 47–54.

Stephens, B. (1995). *Independent living services for older individuals who are blind, annual report for FY 1994*. Mississippi State University, Rehabilitation Research and Training Center in Blindness and Low Vision.

Stephens, B. (1994). *Analysis of Title VII, Chapter 2, Independent Living for Older Americans with Visual Impairments, Fiscal Year 1992–1993*. Mississippi State: Mississippi State University, Rehabilitation Research and Training Center on Blindness and Low Vision.

The Lighthouse, Inc. (1995). *The Lighthouse National Survey on Vision Loss: The experience, attitudes and knowledge of middle-aged and older Americans.* New York: Author.

Williams, T. F. (1984). *Rehabilitation in the aging.* New York: Raven.

5

Changes in Hearing with Aging

Anne L. Strouse, Ph.D.
Albert R. DeChicchis, Ph.D.
Fred H. Bess, Ph.D.

INTRODUCTION

Hearing loss ranks as one of the three most prevalent chronic conditions affecting the elderly (Feller, 1981). Although estimates vary depending on the criteria used to define hearing loss, most studies reveal that 25 to 40% of persons older than 65 years are hearing impaired (Bergman, 1971; Davis, 1983; Feller, 1981; Herbst, 1983; Moss & Parson, 1986). The prevalence increases with each succeeding decade, reaching 70 to 80% for individuals who are in their seventh and eighth decades of life (Moss & Parson, 1986). The prevalence of hearing impairment among institutionalized elderly has been reported to be as high as 80 to 85% (Hull, 1980).

The hearing impairment associated with age, *presbycusis*, is characterized as a symmetrical, mild-to-moderate, bilateral sensorineural loss primarily at high frequencies. A common accompaniment of presbycusis is difficulty in the ability to perceive speech. This difficulty in speech understanding is exacerbated when the listening task is made more difficult by the presence of noise or competing sounds (Working Group on Speech Understanding and Aging, 1988).

Although hearing loss is so prevalent, its potential effects on the elderly individual are often overlooked. Hearing impairment in the elderly has been associated with the psychological features of depressive symptoms, confusion, inattentiveness, increased tension, and negativism (Bess, Lichtenstein, Logan, Burger, & Nelson, 1989; Harless & McConnell, 1982; Herbst, 1983; Herbst & Humphrey, 1980; Mulrow et al., 1990; Weinstein & Amsell, 1986). Hearing impairment has also been associated with the functional problems of poor general health, reduced mobility (e.g., reduction in activities and excursions outside the home), and reduced interpersonal communications (Bess et al., 1989; Herbst, 1983).

This chapter focuses on audiological changes associated with aging and reviews the pathological changes throughout the auditory system associated with aging, audiological findings commonly seen in elderly listeners, and the functional impact of age-related hearing loss.

Pathophysiology

Presbycusis has no clear-cut etiology; however, several variables in addition to the aging process are thought to be involved. During the life span of an individual, the auditory system can encounter insult from a variety of exogenous and endogenous sources including noise exposure, genotype, vascular disease, systemic disease, faulty diet, neoplastic problems, inflammations, concussive damage, ototoxic drugs, heavy metals, solvents, industrial reagents, pollutants, hyperlipidemia, and tobacco (Hawkins & Johnsson, 1985). Of these, noise is perhaps the most common factor that causes damage, complicating the study of presbycusis. Thus, when we talk about hearing impairment and aging, the process of aging should be viewed as encompassing the effects of exogenous and endogenous factors. Indeed, any attempt to completely separate such factors from the etiology of presbycusis would be counterproductive.

Physiological Effects of Aging on the Ear

Pathophysiological changes associated with aging have been reported at nearly every level of the auditory system. This discussion of presbycusis begins with a review of anatomical and physiological correlates of aging, progressing from the outer and middle ear to the central auditory system.

OUTER AND MIDDLE EAR   A number of age-related changes have been observed within the structures of the outer and middle ear. The outer ear consists of two primary components, the pinna and the ear canal.

The pinna is the most visible portion of the ear, extending laterally from the side of the head. The ear canal is the long, narrow canal leading to the eardrum. Maurer and Rupp (1979) summarized changes that may occur within these structures as a result of aging. These include hardened and frequently longstanding wax deposits, hair growth in and around the external auditory canal, and a prolapsed external auditory canal. There may also be changes in the physical properties of the skin, including loss of tissue elasticity of the pinna and external auditory canal, and enlargement of the pinna, which might affect acoustical properties of the ear (Tsai, Fong-Shyong, & Tsa-Jung, 1958). Although these changes do not greatly affect hearing in most elderly people, it is conceivable that they could alter the characteristics of sound transmission to the eardrum or change the nature of sound shadows necessary for accurate spatial localization. Thus, the contributions of outer ear structural changes to age-related hearing problems may sometimes be significant (Maurer & Rupp, 1979).

The middle ear consists of a small air-filled cavity lined with a mucous membrane. It forms the link between the outer and inner ear. This link is accomplished mechanically via three tiny bones, the ossicles. Numerous investigators have documented age-related changes in middle ear structures. These include stiffening and/or thinning of the tympanic membrane (eardrum), degeneration of middle ear musculature, calcification of ligaments, and ossification of middle ear bones (Belal, 1975; Goodhill, 1969; Gussen, 1969; Rosenwasser, 1964). Such age-related changes are reportedly common in the aging ear and thus raise questions about possible effects on sound transmission. Histologic and audiometric studies, however, do not support a significant conductive hearing loss associated with age-related changes in middle ear structures.

INNER EAR   The inner ear is a complex structure that resides deep within a very dense portion of the skull known as the petrous portion of the temporal bone. The cochlea, which contains the sensory organ for hearing, is housed within the inner ear. To determine the effects of aging on inner ear structures, the classic work of Schuknecht (1955, 1964, 1974) is recognized. In this seminal research, histological evidence, case history, and audiological examination were combined to delineate four specific types of presbycusis, which distinguish between pathology of various cochlear structures including the organ of corti, spiral ganglion cells and their processes, the stria vascularis, and other structures related to cochlear mechanics.

In *sensory* presbycusis, the primary changes are in the organ of corti, involving degeneration of hair cells and supporting cells at the base of the cochlea and subsequent cochlear fiber degeneration. Sensory presbycusis is known to produce an abrupt, high frequency sensorineural hearing loss, with speech recognition remaining relatively well preserved. *Neural* presbycusis is characterized by a loss of ganglion cells or their peripheral processes, resulting in problems of transmission information coding. This type of presbycusis also causes high frequency hearing loss, but discrimination scores are poorer than would be expected from the audiometric information. Although Schuknecht (1974) urged that more histopathological evidence for central auditory nervous system degeneration would be useful, he presented no direct evidence for such involvement. Nevertheless, he did state that individuals with neural presbycusis tend to have diffuse central nervous system degeneration including motor control problems, memory loss, and intellectual deterioration.

A third type of presbycusis coined by Schuknecht is *strial* or *metabolic* presbycusis. As the name implies, strial presbycusis results from degeneration of the stria vascularis, causing disruption of the nutrient supply necessary for maintaining cellular function and resulting in changes in metabolic, chemical, and/or bioelectric properties throughout the cochlea. Strial presbycusis is known to produce a flat audiometric configuration usually accompanied by very good speech recognition. The final category identified by Schuknecht is *mechanical* presbycusis, also known as *cochlear conductive* presbycusis. Mechanical presbycusis represents a hypothetical type of presbycusis resulting from mass/stiffness changes in the basilar membrane and/or spiral ligament atrophy. Presumably, these changes could alter the motion mechanics of the cochlea, hence the alternative term "cochlear conductive." Mechanical presbycusis produces a straight line audiometric configuration with descending bone conduction scores; speech recognition is generally good.

Aside from Schuknecht's four categories, at least three additional forms of presbycusic pathophysiology have been reported in the literature. For example, Nadol (1979) made reference to the loss of outer hair cell afferent synapses, although light microscopy showed presence of outer hair cells and normal myelinated fibers. Thus, a normal light microscopy examination of the cochlea does not guarantee the presence of functional hair cell fiber synapses. Synaptic damage has also been implicated as a potential factor in noise-induced hearing loss (Saunders, Dean, & Schneider, 1985).

Hawkins and Johnsson (1985) noted two additional types of peripheral presbycusis, *hyperostotic* and *vascular*. Hyperostotic presbycusis represents an abnormal growth of bony tissue within the internal auditory canal. It has been suggested that this new growth could then compress the eighth nerve and internal auditory artery, causing subsequent dysfunction/degeneration of the eighth nerve fibers and inner ear tissue (Hawkins & Johnsson, 1985; Krympotic-Nemanic, 1971; Makishima, 1978). Johnsson and Hawkins (1972) also discussed the possibility of devascularization involving capillaries and arterioles of the inner ear, particularly in the regions of the spiral lamina and the lateral wall of the cochlea. Similar observations have been noted by Fisch, Dobozi, and Greig (1972). Because devascularization could naturally lead to cochlear ischemia, it is likely that the stria vascularis with its aerobic metabolism and high metabolic rates would be influenced most by oxygen and glucose insufficiency. Damage to the stria vascularis would reduce the endolymphatic potential and thus interfere with the modulation process of ionic currents through hair cell membranes during the transduction process.

Figure 5–1 illustrates the various types of presbycusis and their associated sites of pathologic change. It is important to note that individuals with presbycusis may not show any of these degenerative changes in a pure form, but rather in a mixture of the various types.

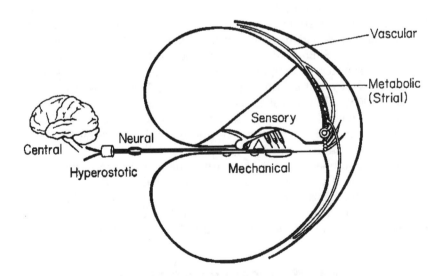

Figure 5–1. Cross section of the human cochlea to illustrate the types of presbycusis and the accompanying sites of pathologic change. (Adapted with permission from *Pathology of the Ear* by H. F. Schuknecht, 1974, Cambridge, MA: Harvard University Press, 1974.)

AUDITORY NERVE The auditory nerve provides the link between the cochlea of the inner ear and the central auditory system. Little information is available on age changes in auditory nerve physiology. Rasmussen (1940) identified an average of 32,500 fibers in the auditory nerve of subjects aged 2 to 26 years and 30,300 fibers in subjects aged 44 to 60 years, representing a 7% decrease in the number of auditory nerve fibers over this age range. Spoendlin and Schrott (1989, 1990) also counted nerve fibers in the auditory nerve, reporting a decrease in fibers of elderly patients with sensorineural hearing loss. The contribution of such changes to age-related hearing problems, however, remains unknown.

CENTRAL AUDITORY PATHWAYS Once action potentials have been generated in the auditory nerve, the electrical activity progresses up toward the cortex. This network of nerve fibers is frequently referred to as the auditory central nervous system (auditory CNS). The nerve fibers that carry information in the form of action potentials up the auditory CNS toward the cortex form part of the ascending pathways. Nerve impulses can also be sent toward the periphery from the cortex or brainstem centers. The fibers carrying such information compose the descending pathways. Degenerative changes associated with aging have been observed throughout the brainstem and cortical areas of the ascending auditory pathway, involving a reduction in the number of functional neurons of the cochlear nuclei, superior olivary complex, lateral lemniscus, inferior colliculi, and medial geniculate complex (Hansen & Reske-Nielsen, 1965; Kirikae, Sato, & Shitara, 1964; Schuknecht, 1964). Cortical atrophy has been demonstrated in temporal lobe and corpus callosum areas where the majority of auditory fibers project (Brody, 1955; Hansen & Reske-Nielsen, 1965). Although it is likely that damage to neural structures should influence auditory function, actual age-based correlations between function and structure are not available (Working Group on Speech Understanding and Aging, 1988).

This section has reviewed structural changes throughout the auditory system that occur with age. The functional significance of these changes on the hearing problems of elderly listeners, as we have seen, is not always conclusive. The following section describes typical findings seen in elderly listeners on the audiological test battery.

AUDIOLOGICAL CHARACTERISTICS ASSOCIATED WITH AGING

As previously noted, the aging auditory system typically exhibits a loss in threshold sensitivity and a breakdown in the ability to understand comfortably loud speech. The audiological manifestations often reflect the pathological changes occurring within the auditory system. Because one or more types of presbycusis are often present, it is difficult to determine the site of lesion from audiometric data. Nonetheless, age-related findings are common in nearly all areas of audiologic assessment.

Acoustic Immittance Measures

Acoustic immittance is a sensitive and objective diagnostic tool used to identify the presence of fluid behind the tympanic membrane, to evaluate Eustachian tube and facial nerve dysfunction, to predict audiometric findings, and to assist in the diagnosis of different auditory disorders. The immittance battery administered to evaluate the middle ear system in older adults generally includes tympanometry, static admittance, and determination of acoustic reflex thresholds. In order to accurately interpret immittance test results, the audiologist must recognize the manner in which age affects the various test parameters.

TYMPANOMETRY AND STATIC ACOUSTIC IMMITTANCE Tympanometry is the measurement of the mobility of middle ear structures when air pressure is varied within the external ear canal. Results from tympanometry are generally plotted on a graph, with air pressure along the x axis and immittance, or compliance, along the y axis. There is limited information available on tympanometric measurement in the elderly population. The presence of excessive negative pressure has been reported among older persons and is thought to be due to poor Eustachian tube function in this population (Gordon-Salant, 1991; Nerbonne, Schow, & Gosset, 1976).

Static acoustic immittance measures the ease of the flow of sound through the middle ear. It is generally recognized that static acoustic immittance decreases as a function of age. For example, Jerger, Jerger, and Mauldin (1972) examined impedance data on 700 individuals spanning eight age decades. They found a slight tendency for older groups to demonstrate decreased static compliance and reported a greater variance in compliance values among elderly groups. Despite concurring data, reported values are typically within the range considered to be normal for young adults, and thus age-related norms are probably not warranted (Gordon-Salant, 1991; Nerbonne, Bliss, & Schow, 1978).

ACOUSTIC REFLEX The acoustic reflex threshold is defined as the lowest possible intensity needed to elicit a middle ear muscle contraction. The effect of age on the acoustic reflex is minimal. Reflexes are usually present at expected hearing levels but may be abnormal in terms of elevation or absence due to the presence of peripheral hearing loss. Age is, however, known to influence acoustic reflex amplitude. Hall (1982) reported the maximum reflex amplitude decreased by about 56% over the age range of 20 to 80 years. The amplitude changes are typically greater for uncrossed reflexes and are thought to reflect age changes in the innervation of the stapedius muscle (Hall, 1979) or degeneration of the middle ear musculature.

Pure Tone Threshold Measures

We have seen that presbycusis is associated with a variety of audiometric configurations, ranging from a flat response across frequencies to various degrees of high frequency sensorineural hearing loss. The hearing loss most typically measured among individuals 60 years of age or older primarily affects the high frequency signals above 1000 Hz. The sensitivity changes that are known to occur as a function of age are shown in Figure 5–2. The progression is somewhat more rapid for men than for women, which may not be due to differences in age, but rather reflect a more frequent participation of men in noisy recreational activities. The data in Figure 5–2 suggest that aging results in a sloping high frequency loss, becoming progressively more severe with

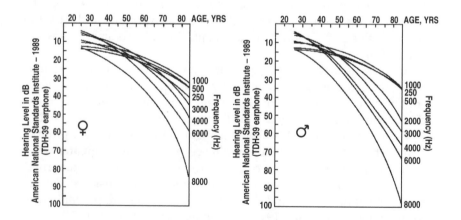

Figure 5–2. Hearing loss progression as a function of age in women *(left)* and men *(right)*. (Adapted with permission from "The presbycusis component in occupational hearing loss" by C. P. Lebo and R. C. Reddell, 1972, *Laryngoscope, 82,* 1399–1409, 1972.)

advancing age. Although it is important to recognize that other forms of audiometric configuration might be observed, the sloping high frequency audiogram representing Schuknecht's *sensory* category is the most common type of presbycusis realized.

Speech Recognition Measures

The speech reception threshold (SRT) is a measurement included in the basic hearing evaluation which represents the intensity at which an individual can identify simple speech materials approximately 50% of the time. Changes in SRT are observed with increasing age, and correspond with observed changes in pure tone measures. An example of the decrease in SRT with increasing age is shown in Figure 5–3.

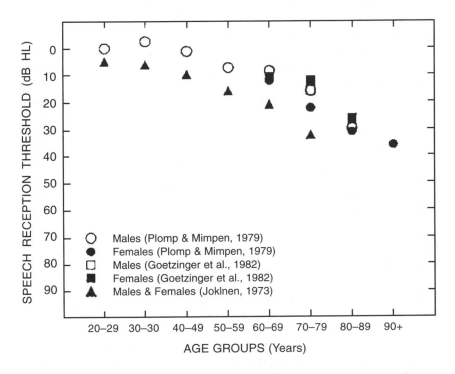

Figure 5–3. Speech recognition thresholds (SRT) as a function of age. Data taken from several studies. (Reprinted with permission from "Basic Hearing Evaluation" by S. Gordon-Salant in H. G. Mueller and V. C. Geoffrey (Eds.), *Communication Disorders in Aging*, 1987, pp. 301–333, Washington, DC: Gallaudet University Press.)

Although the SRT provides an index of the degree of hearing loss for speech, it does not offer any information regarding a person's ability to understand conversational speech, and thus the assessment of suprathreshold speech recognition is an important component of the hearing evaluation. It is well recognized that older persons experience difficulty understanding speech, especially when presented in a background of noise. In general, difficulty in speech understanding increases with age, especially with individuals more than 60 years of age. A review of the research provides three alternate hypotheses as explanations for the age-related decline in speech understanding among elderly listeners. Some investigators have attributed degradation in speech understanding to a *peripheral problem* associated with presbycusis that can be primarily described by pure tone thresholds. Others have suggested that such degradation is due to the elderly person's inability to perform speech audiometric tasks due to senescent changes in *cognition*. Still others believe that auditory processing disorders result from changes in the *central auditory nervous system* (CANS), which create an auditory deficit in speech perception that is both independent of cognitive decline and separable from the effects of peripheral hearing loss. The following discussion briefly examines these hypotheses.

In its simplest form, the peripheral hypothesis maintains that most of the individual variability in speech understanding performance can be explained by individual variations in hearing loss as measured by the pure tone audiogram. Because high frequency sensitivity is known to decline systematically with age, and because high frequency sensitivity impacts many speech audiometric measures, it can be argued that the systematic decline in speech audiometric scores with age results from age-related decline in high frequency hearing sensitivity. Several recent studies have directly examined this question (Helfer & Wilber, 1990; Humes & Christopherson, 1991; van Rooij & Plomp, 1990, 1991; van Rooij, Plomp, & Orbelek, 1989).

Humes, Christopherson, and Cokely (1992) examined each of these investigations, revealing that the percentage of systematic variance in speech recognition scores that could be accounted for by peripheral hearing loss of elderly listeners ranged from 70% to 95%. Jerger, Jerger, and Pirozzolo (1991) reached a similar conclusion in a recent study of 200 elderly people. In this study, results also showed that degree of hearing loss had a significant effect on speech recognition in the elderly, overall accounting for nearly 75% of the variance in speech recognition scores. Based on these studies it seems reasonable to conclude that speech recognition in elderly subjects may be largely explained by the progressive high frequency hearing loss associated with aging. However, several studies have demonstrated that even elderly subjects with essentially normal peripheral hearing exhibit poorer speech recognition ability in noise than do younger subjects.

Dubno, Dirks, and Morgan (1984) demonstrated that elderly subjects with normal and mild hearing losses experience considerable difficulty in speech understanding under varying signal-to-babble (S/B) ratios. The patients with mild hearing loss performed much poorer than did aged listeners with normal hearing. Figure 5–4 illustrates the S/B ratios required for 50% recognition in the four groups evaluated. It is seen that the more favorable S/B ratios are needed for subjects as the speech material increases in difficulty. Furthermore, more favorable S/B ratios are needed for the older subjects, even those with normal pure tone sensitivity. These data support the presumption that performance in noise deteriorates with age with or without increases in threshold sensitivity. Similar findings were reported by Jerger (1992). Subjects aged 50 to 90 were evaluated. Pure tone thresholds were contained within relatively rigidly defined limits to study the effect of age on four speech audiometric measures. Average pure tone thresholds from 250 through 8000 Hz did not differ by more than 6 dB across four age groups. Results revealed that all four speech audiometric measures used in evaluation showed some decline with age, in spite of the fact that degree of peripheral hearing loss did not differ

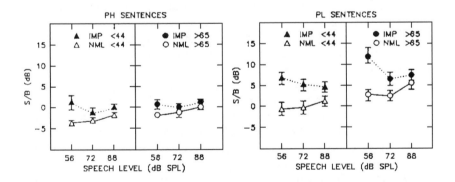

Figure 5–4. Signal-to-babble ratios needed for 50% recognition of sentence material in four groups of subjects: young normal (NML) and hearing-impaired (IMP) listeners (*left panels*) and older normal (NML) and hearing-impaired (IMP) listeners (*right panels*). (Redrawn with permission from " Effects of age and mild hearing loss in speech recognition in noise" by J. R. Dubno, D. D. Dirks, and D. E. Morgan, 1984, *Journal of the Acoustical Society of America, 76,* 87–96.)

substantially between groups. Jerger concluded from this study that there exists a progressive, age-related decline in performance on speech audiometric measures that cannot be explained by age-related change in hearing sensitivity.

Stach, Spretnjak, and Jerger (1990) evaluated subjects ranging in age from 50 to 93 years, matched for hearing loss on the basis of pure tone average. Results revealed that, despite equivalent peripheral hearing sensitivity loss across age groups, the prevalence of speech understanding difficulties still increased systematically with age. These results indicate that poor speech understanding cannot be explained solely as an artifact of peripheral sensitivity loss.

It has been proposed that individual differences in speech recognition capabilities of the elderly may result from impaired processes of the central auditory nervous system, a phenomenon commonly referred to as *central auditory processing disorder* (CAPD). Utilizing a variety of speech audiometric measures, CAPD has been found to be very prevalent among the elderly (Jerger, Jerger, Oliver, & Pirozzolo, 1989; Jerger, Oliver, & Pirozzolo, 1990; Rodriguez, DiSarno, & Hardiman, 1990; Stach et al., 1990).

Based on what we know about the peripheral hypothesis, it is reasonable to conclude that the presence of peripheral hearing loss may confound estimates of CAPD prevalence. For example, as Humes et al. (1992) previously noted, Jerger et al. (1990) estimated CAPD prevalence to be approximately 18% for a group of 53 listeners ranging in age from about 60 to 70 years. The prevalence estimate from this sample is much lower, however, than that obtained by Stach and colleagues (1990) over a similar age range, despite the fact that the same speech measures were employed in both studies. This study reported a prevalence estimate of 45% in the 60 to 64 age range and 58% for the 65 to 69 age range. It is important to note that all 53 listeners in the group studied by Jerger et al. (1990) had midfrequency pure tone averages less than 20 dB HL, whereas the amount of peripheral hearing loss was not controlled in the study by Stach and colleagues (1990). Thus, the elimination of the confounding influence of peripheral hearing loss in the 60 to 70 age range resulted in a significant decline in the estimated prevalence of CAPD.

Despite such findings, numerous investigators have reported an increased prevalence of CAPD among the elderly, with estimates ranging from approximately 20% to over 70% in this population. Although prevalence estimates are reduced when the confounding influence of peripheral hearing loss is eliminated (Humes et al., 1992), results suggest that at least some of the problems in speech understanding may be attributed to central auditory deficits.

In response to claims that deficits in speech understanding may be attributed to cognitive deficit, several investigators have addressed the role of cognitive ability in declining speech understanding with age. Jerger and colleagues (1989) reported that speech audiometric tests of central function were not necessarily related to cognitive disability (Jerger, Stach, Pruitt, Harper, & Kirby, 1989). Audiological data were analyzed from 23 patients with a neuropsychological diagnosis of dementia. Among the cognitive deficits found in these patients were those of memory, mental tracking and sequencing, and cognitive flexibility. Despite such deficits, 12 of the 23 subjects (52%) yielded speech audiometric results consistent with normal auditory processing ability.

In another study, Jerger et al. (1989) measured both auditory and cognitive status in 130 elderly subjects. Central auditory status was abnormal in the presence of normal cognitive function in 23% of subjects. Central auditory status was normal in the presence of cognitive deficit in 14% of subjects. Auditory processing ability and cognitive function were congruent in only 63% of subjects, indicating that the two measures were relatively independent. Rodriguez and colleagues (1990) supported this work. In a similar study, however, Jerger et al. (1991) evaluated 200 subjects ranging in age from 50 to 91 years. Analysis suggested that cognitive status did have a significant effect on speech recognition in the elderly. In this study, general cognitive status affected performance on two of five speech measures used to assess central auditory status.

Finally, in a series of studies by van Rooij and colleagues (1989, 1990, 1991), subjects were again evaluated using both auditory and cognitive measures. These investigators found that the majority of systematic variance in speech recognition performance could be explained by peripheral hearing loss. However, their results indicated that the balance of the systematic variance, although small in comparison, could be attributed to individual differences in cognitive function.

It is reasonable to hypothesize that age-related deficits in cognitive abilities might explain some of the age-related decline in speech understanding. However, in spite of known changes in cognitive function which occur as a consequence of normal aging, the effect of these changes on speech recognition remains controversial. Available data reveal that cognitive decline can occur without adversely affecting speech audiometric results. Likewise, a decline in speech understanding ability can occur in the absence of cognitive decline.

Earlier in this discussion three hypotheses were set forth concerning the decreased performance on speech understanding measures in elderly listeners. To date, there is no conclusive evidence that can implicate any one of these hypotheses as a single predictor of speech performance. Based on the aging literature, it is reasonable to conclude that the presence of peripheral hearing loss, changes in processing abilities along the central auditory pathways, as well as senescent changes in cognition interact to account for the reduced speech performance commonly found among elderly listeners. The extent to which each factor contributes to speech understanding in a given individual, however, is most likely variable.

Electrophysiological Measures

OTOACOUSTIC EMISSIONS Otoacoustic emissions (OAEs) are sounds produced by the ear which can be recorded within the ear canal. A substantial amount of research suggests that OAEs are produced by the motile activity of inner ear structures, specifically the outer hair cells (Brownell, 1990; Kim, 1984; Mountain, 1980; Zenner, 1986). Consequently, damage to outer hair cells due to excessive noise exposure, ototoxic drug treatment, or anoxia is associated with reduction or disappearance of OAEs (Kim, Molnar, & Matthews, 1980; Lonsbury-Martin, McCoy, Whitehead, & Martin, 1993; Schmeidt, 1986). If this is true in presbycusis, OAEs may provide information about physiological changes in auditory function associated with age.

There are two basic classes of OAEs, spontaneous and evoked. The primary distinction between the two has to do simply with whether or not a sound stimulus is required to elicit the OAE. Spontaneous emissions occur without stimulation, whereas evoked emissions require an acoustic stimulus to be generated. Several investigators have reported abnormal evoked OAEs (both transient-evoked and distortion-product) associated with advancing age, suggesting that clinical OAE measurements may be more accurately interpreted using age-adjusted normative values (Bonfils, Bertrand, & Uziel, 1988; Collet, Gartner, Moulin, & Morgan, 1990; Lonsbury-Martin, Cutler, & Martin, 1991; Stover & Norton, 1993). However, changes in the incidence and amplitude of OAEs in the elderly population are likely attributable to inner ear hair cell loss associated with age, as it is well established that hearing loss produces decreased OAE amplitude which is systematically related to degree of sensitivity loss (Kemp, Ryan, & Bray, 1990; Kimberley, Hernadi, Lee, & Brown, 1994; Nielsen, Popelka, Rasmussen, & Osterhammel, 1993). More recent research suggests that when the degree of peripheral hearing loss is adequately controlled, there is no direct effect of advanced age on OAEs, at least for distortion-product OAE measurement (Strouse, Ochs, & Hall, in press).

AUDITORY EVOKED POTENTIALS Auditory evoked potentials (AEPs) are typically used to identify and estimate hearing impairment in patients who cannot be tested using behavioral techniques or as special auditory tests in neuro-otologic diagnosis. AEP measurement involves the recording of gross electrical potentials representing the activity of hundreds or thousands of individual hair cells or nerve fibers within the auditory CNS. These tiny electrical potentials are usually recorded from remote locations on the surface of the head and require amplification and computer averaging of at least several hundred stimulus presentations to be visible. Resulting waveforms are identified in terms of their latency (time in which the response occurs following presentation of the stimulus) and amplitude (size of the waveform) characteristics.

Studies examining the effect of age on AEPs typically show increased latency values for all classes of evoked potential responses. Amplitude changes are somewhat more variable. The auditory brainstem response (ABR) is a measure of electrical activity evoked by very brief sounds originating from the auditory nerve and auditory portions of the brainstem. The resulting waveform generally consists of five to seven distinct bumps or waves which appear in the first 10 ms after the stimulus has been presented and represent electrical activity from different areas along auditory nerve and brainstem pathways. Thus, ABR is very useful in a wide variety of clinical applications, from assessment of the functional integrity of the auditory nerve and brainstem portions of the ascending auditory CNS, to assessment of hearing in infants or difficult-to-test patients.

Most investigations on ABR indicate a systematic increase in absolute latency values of approximately 0.2 msec for waves I, III, and V over the age range of 25 to 55 years (Jerger & Hall, 1980). Brewer (1987) and Ottaviani, Maurizi, D'Alatri, and Almadori (1991) have suggested that high frequency hearing loss may account in part for apparent age-related shifts in absolute latency values. In addition, the American Speech-Language-Hearing Association Working Group on Auditory Evoked Potential Measurement (1988) reported that hearing level at 4000 Hz may influence the absolute latency of selected waves. Because the majority of older adults exhibit some degree of peripheral hearing loss, latency increases associated with age as well as sensorineural hearing loss must be considered in waveform analysis. The amplitude of all ABR waves tends to decrease with advancing age, although, as with latency measurements, the specific contributions of aging and peripheral hearing loss are difficult to separate. It is likely that both factors are of clinical significance (Mitchell, Phillips, & Trune, 1989).

Although evoked potentials beyond the ABR are not as common in the assessment of the elderly hearing-impaired, age-related alterations in these later responses have been identified. The later responses represent electrical activity recorded from the upper brainstem and auditory cortical areas, and include the auditory middle latency response (AMLR), the auditory late response (ALR), and the P300 event-related response. They are so named according to the latency period in which they are generated following stimulus onset. The AMLR is believed to originate from the upper portions of the auditory brainstem, appears approximately 15 to 50 msec following stimulus onset, and consists of a series of positive and negative waveform components. AMLR values show similar latency effects as ABR, however amplitude values, particularly for the Pa component of the AMLR, tend to show a significant increase with advancing age (Lenzi, Chiarelli, & Sambataro, 1989; Woods & Clayworth, 1986). Following the AMLR along the latency continuum, the ALR appears at approximately 75 to 200 msec following presentation of the stimulus. This response is believed to originate from within areas of the auditory cortex. Latency and amplitude measures for the ALR reveal an increase in latency and a concomitant decrease in amplitude values with advancing age for N1, P2, and N2 waveform components (Callaway, 1975; Callaway & Halliday, 1973; Pfefferbaum, Ford, Roth, & Kopell, 1980). Finally, the P300 event-related potential is believed to be an index of higher level auditory processing and is often referred to as a "cognitive" potential. The P300 is generated from within the medial temporal lobe and, as the name implies, occurs in the electrical waveform approximately 300 msec following stimulus onset. Average normal P300 latency over the age range of 10 to 90 years steadily increases from 300 msec to 400 msec (a change of 1 to 1.5 msec/year), whereas amplitude decreases at an average rate of 0.2 µV per year (Goodin, Squires, Henderson, & Starr, 1979; Pfefferbaum, Ford, Wenegrat, Roth, & Kopell, 1984; Puce, Donnan, & Bladin, 1989). Unlike ABR, these later responses are generally unaffected by degree of peripheral hearing loss. Consequently, variations in latency and amplitude values as a function of age illustrate the need to compare obtained findings with normative data matched for age for accurate interpretation.

This section has reviewed audiological findings in the evaluation of elderly adults, ranging from the evaluation of middle ear function using acoustic immittance measures to the evaluation of subcortical and cortical areas associated with audition using auditory evoked potentials. A general conclusion is that nearly every measure of auditory function is affected to some degree by age or age-related hearing loss, thus highlighting the need for careful interpretation of test findings in the diagnosis of hearing problems of elderly patients. The final section of this chapter goes beyond anatomical and audiological findings and considers the effect of age-related hearing loss on the functional health status of elderly individuals.

FUNCTIONAL IMPACT OF HEARING LOSS IN THE ELDERLY

Self-assessment scales and questionnaires can provide an objective method for quantifying an individual's perception of communication difficulties, evaluating progress in rehabilitation, and identifying needs outside of the standard audiometric test battery. Examples include the Hearing Handicap Scale (High, Fairbanks, & Glorig, 1964), the Hearing Performance Inventory (Giolas, Owens, Lamb, & Schubert, 1979), Self-Assessment of Communication (Schow & Nerbonne, 1982), and the Hearing Handicap Inventory for the Elderly (Ventry & Weinstein, 1982). Such scales are communication-specific because the questions are weighted toward communication difficulties caused by hearing loss. Investigators who have used these scales to assess the functional impact of hearing loss on older individuals have repeatedly reported that hearing-impaired elders experience a wide variety of listening difficulties (Schow & Nerbonne, 1982; Ventry & Weinstein, 1982; Weinstein, 1985).

More recently, attempts have been made to assess the impact of hearing loss on more global measures of function such as functional health status and psychosocial well-being. As noted at the beginning of this chapter, hearing loss is thought to have a progressive impact on functional health status with increasing age. To illustrate such findings, Bess et al. (1989) analyzed the impact of hearing impairment in individuals over 65 years of age screened in primary care practices. Functional and psychosocial impairment was measured using the Sickness Impact Profile (SIP), a standardized questionnaire for assessing sickness-related dysfunction. The individual items are weighted and grouped into 12 subscales. The subscales include ambulation, mobility, body care/movement, social interaction, communication, alertness, emotional behavior, sleep/rest, eating, work, home management, and recreation/pastimes. In addition there are three main scales: physical (combining ambulation, mobility, and body care/movement), psychosocial (combining social interaction, communication, alertness, and emotional behavior), and overall (combining all 12 subscales). The higher the SIP score, the greater the functional impairment. The SIP has been shown to be a valid and reliable measure and has been used in many studies to measure sickness-related dysfunction (Bergner, Bobbitt, Carter, & Gilson, 1981; Bergner, Bobbitt, Pollard, Martin, & Gilson, 1976).

The results for persons with or without hearing impairment are shown in Figure 5–5. Hearing impairment is defined as (a) 40 dB HL at 1000 or 2000 Hz in both ears, or (b) 40 dB HL at 1000 or 2000 Hz in one ear (Ventry & Weinstein, 1983). The figure is divided into four panels, illustrating first the data for the summary indices (total scores) on the SIP scale, followed by the physical and psychosocial subscales, and then several other independent life quality measures. The open trian-

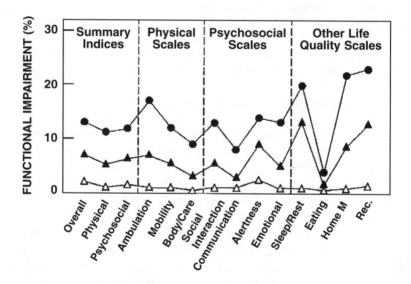

Figure 5–5. Mean scores obtained on various scales of the Sickness Impact Profile (SIP) for unimpaired young adults (*open triangles*), non-hearing-impaired elderly (*filled triangles*), and hearing-impaired elderly (*filled circles*). (Adapted from "Hearing impairment as a determinant of function in the elderly" by F. H. Bess, M. J. Lichtenstein, S. A. Logan, M. C. Burger, and E. C. Nelson, 1989, *Journal of the American Geriatric Society, 37,* 123–128.)

gles represent normative data for young adults. The average scores are seen to range between 2 and 3 for all subscales. The second set of data, represented by filled triangles, depicts the average scores obtained by the elderly individuals with no hearing impairment, as determined by the previous criteria. The perceived functional impairment for this subgroup is somewhat greater than that obtained for the normative data for young adults. Finally, the filled circles denote scores obtained by the hearing-impaired elderly. For this group, the average SIP scores for most subscales are seen to be higher than the SIP scores of the elderly subjects with normal hearing.

Bess et al. (1989) also examined the impact of varying degrees of hearing loss on functional health status. The unadjusted associations between degree of hearing impairment and the SIP scores are shown in Table 5–1. For the physical scale, the mean SIP score increases from 3.3 for those with no impairment to 18.9 among those with a loss of 41 dBHL or greater in the better ear. Similar results are seen for the psychosocial dimension, the overall dimension, and most of the subscales.

It is recognized that factors other than hearing loss can affect functional health status. Hence, Bess et al. (1989) used a stepwise multiple linear regression to adjust for baseline differences in age, race, sex, educational level, number of illnesses, presence of diabetes and ischemic heart disease, number of medications, near visual acuity, and mental status between the two groups. In this analysis, the score of each SIP scale served as the dependent variable. The regression coefficient is reported as a change in SIP score per change in hearing level, and these data are shown in Table 5–2. This table illustrates the change in SIP scores for the three main scales and their associated subscales, with an accompanying change in hearing level after controlling for case-mix differences and other confounding variables. The data in Table 5–2 depict the SIP score change with every 10 dB change in hearing level. That is, for the physical dimension, a SIP score change of 2.8 will occur with each 10 dB increase in hearing loss. For the psychosocial and overall scales, the SIP score changes are 2.0 and 1.3, respectively.

The data of Bess and colleagues are in agreement with earlier observations by Herbst (1983), who reported that age-associated hearing impairment was associated with such factors as poor general health, reduced mobility, reduction in interpersonal communications, depression, and reduced enjoyment of life. Taken together, these studies support that hearing loss is an important determinant of function in older persons. Consequently, efforts to improve the hearing of elderly patients could result in a significant and meaningful improvement in the quality of life of elderly individuals.

Table 5-1. Mean sickness impact profile (SIP) scores by level average decibel loss in the better ear.[a]

SIP Scale	0-16dB			17-25 dB			26-40 dB			> 41 dB		
	N	Mean	(SD)	N	Mean	(SD)	N	Mean	(SD)	N	Mean	(SD)
Ambulation[d]	46	4.8	(10.5)	53	5.4	(8.6)	38	15.9	(15.0)	16	25.4	(21.1)
Mobility[d]	46	3.3	(8.2)	53	4.2	(9.1)	38	7.5	(11.5)	16	22.6	(21.1)
Body care/Movement[d]	46	2.6	(5.2)	53	3.3	(7.2)	38	6.9	(9.1)	16	14.8	(14.1)
PHYSICAL DIMENSION[d]	46	3.3	(6.6)	53	4.0	(6.5)	38	9.1	(9.8)	16	18.9	(15.7)
Social Interaction[d]	46	4.6	(9.0)	53	6.6	(10.2)	38	8.8	(12.1)	16	20.2	(16.6)
Communication[b]	46	3.4	(7.5)	53	3.4	(7.0)	37	6.4	(10.6)	16	10.0	(13.9)
Alertness[b]	46	4.3	(8.7)	53	9.2	(18.5)	38	14.0	(21.0)	16	15.3	(20.6)
Emotional[c]	46	3.1	(6.4)	53	5.2	(12.5)	38	9.9	(15.9)	16	18.5	(26.3)
PSYCHOSOCIAL DIMENSION[d]	46	4.0	(6.9)	53	6.2	(10.2)	37	9.6	(12.1)	16	16.8	(16.1)
Sleep/Rest	46	12.0	(21.1)	53	14.2	(17.8)	38	18.8	(19.8)	16	27.2	(29.8)
Eating[c]	46	1.6	(3.3)	53	2.4	(4.2)	36	2.7	(4.3)	16	6.9	(9.9)
Work	11	15.4	(24.4)	14	14.2	(27.2)	8	16.5	(23.4)	2	52.7	(24.6)
Home Management[d]	46	6.1	(12.0)	53	9.5	(15.8)	38	20.0	(21.6)	16	31.3	(35.2)
Recreation/Pastimes[c]	46	11.7	(16.7)	53	12.4	(16.7)	36	22.1	(25.5)	16	29.7	(30.0)
OVERALL[c]	46	5.3	(7.6)	53	6.6	(8.8)	38	11.3	(12.1)	16	17.1	(14.8)

[a]Decibel loss averaged over 500, 1,000, and 2,000 Hz in the better ear.   [b]p<0.05   [c]p <0.01   [d]p <0.001

Table 5–2. Change in sickness impact profile (SIP) scores per 10-dB change in average decibel loss in the better ear.[a]

SIP Scale	Change per 10-dB loss		
	SIP change (Std err)	p value	Percent variance[b]
Ambulation	4.2 (0.7)	<0.001	27
Mobility	3.3 (0.7)	<0.001	21
Body Care/Movement	1.9 (0.4)	<0.001	10
PHYSICAL DIMENSION	2.8 (0.5)	<0.001	24
Social Interaction	2.7 (0.6)	<0.001	16
Communication		0.053	
Alertness		0.269	
Emotional	2.9 (0.8)	<0.001	7
PSYCHOSOCIAL DIMENSION	2.0 (0.6)	<0.001	8
Sleep/Rest	3.1 (1.1)	<0.01	4
Eating	1.0 (0.3)	<0.01	9
Work		0.11	
Home Management	4.9 (1.1)	<0.001	19
Recreation/Pastimes	2.7 (1.2)	<0.05	3
OVERALL	1.3 (0.6)	<0.02	5

[a]Changes associated with hearing levels adjusted for age, race, sex, education, number of medications, number of illnesses/conditions, near vision, and mental status.

[b]Percent variance is the amount of variance in the SIP scale attributed to hearing at the step when hearing entered the model.

SUMMARY

In this discussion, we have addressed changes in hearing with advancing age. It is estimated that one of every three individuals over the age of 65 years exhibits a significant hearing impairment. Although hearing loss is so common and many people can expect to develop some hearing loss in later life, few are aware of the meaning of hearing loss for everyday living and of the difficulties of people who experience hearing loss and old age at the same time.

In this chapter, we have focused on the pathophysiologic changes that occur throughout all levels of the auditory system and typical findings on specific tests of auditory function in the elderly listener.

Perhaps most important, the effect of hearing loss on the functional health status and psychosocial well-being of the elderly hearing-impaired has been reviewed.

REFERENCES

American Speech-Language-Hearing Association. (1988). The short latency auditory evoked potentials. *ASHA Audiologic Aging Group on Auditory Evoked Potential Measurement.* Rockville, MD: Working Group on Auditory Evoked Potential Measurement.

Belal, A. (1975). Presbycusis: Physiological or pathological. *Journal of Laryngology and Otology 14,* 1011–1025.

Bergman, M. (1971). Changes in hearing with age. *The Gerontologist, 11,* 148.

Bergner, M., Bobbitt, R. A., Carter, W. B., & Gilson, B. S. (1981). The sickness impact profile: Developments and final revision of a health status measure. *Medical Care 19,* 787-805.

Bergner, M., Bobbitt, R. A., Pollard, W. E., Martin, D. P., & Gilson, B. S. (1976). The sickness impact profile: Validation of a health status measure. *Medical Care, 14,* 57–67.

Bess, F. H., Lichtenstein, M. J., Logan, S. A., Burger, M. C., & Nelson, E. C. (1989). Hearing impairment as a determinant of function in the elderly. *Journal of the American Geriatric Society, 37,* 123–128.

Bonfils, P., Bertrand, Y., & Uziel A. (1988). Evoked otoacoustic emissions: Normative data and presbycusis. *Audiology, 27,* 27–35.

Brewer, C. (1987). Electrophysiologic measures. In H. G. Mueller & V. Geoffrey (Eds.), *Communication disorders in aging: Assessment and management* (pp. 334–381). Washington, DC: Gallaudet University Press.

Brody, H. (1955). Organization of the cerebral cortex: III. A study of aging in the human cerebral cortex. *Journal of Comparative Neurology, 102,* 511–556.

Brownell, W. E. (1990). Outer hair cell electromotility and otoacoustic emissions. *Ear and Hearing 11,* 82–92.

Callaway, E. (1975). *Brain electric potentials and individual psychological differences.* New York: Grune & Stratton.

Callaway, E., & Halliday, R. A. (1973). Evoked potential variability: Effects of age, amplitude and methods of measurement. *Electroencephalography and Clinical Neurophysiology 34,* 125–133.

Collet, L., Gartner, M., Moulin, A., & Morgan, A. (1990). Age-related changes in evoked otoacoustic emissions. *Annals of Otology, Rhinology, and Laryngology, 99,* 993–997.

Davis, A. (1983). The epidemiology of hearing disorders. In R. Hinchcliff (Ed.), *Hearing and balance in the elderly* (pp. 1–43). Edinburgh: Churchill Livingston.

Dubno, J. R., Dirks, D. D., & Morgan, D. E. (1984). Effects of age and mild hearing loss on speech recognition in noise. *Journal of the Acoustical Society of America, 76,* 87–96.

Feller, B. A. (1981). Prevalence of selected impairments: United States-1977. DHHS publication No. PHS 86-1588. *Vital and Health Statistics, Series 10,* No. 134. Washington, DC: National Health Center for Statistics.

Fisch, U., Dobozi, M., & Greig, D. (1972). Degenerative changes of the arterial vessels of the internal auditory meatus during the process of aging. *Acta Otolaryngologica, 73,* 259–266.

Giolas, T. G., Owens, E., Lamb, S. H., & Schubert, E. D. (1979). Hearing performance inventory. Journal of Speech and Hearing Disorders, 44, 169-195.

Goodhill, V. (1969). Bilateral malleal fixation and conductive presbycusis. *Archives of Otolaryngology, 90,* 107–112.

Goodin, D., Squires, K., Henderson, B., & Starr, A. (1979). An early event-related cortical potential. *Psychophysiology, 15,* 360–365.

Gordon-Salant, S. (1987). Basic hearing evaluation. In H. G. Mueller & V. C. Geoffrey (Eds.), *Communication disorders in aging* (pp. 301–333). Washington, DC: Gaulladet University Press.

Gordon-Salant, S. (1991). The audiologic assessment. In D. Ripich (Ed.), *Handbook of geriatric communication disorders* (pp. 301–333). Austin, TX: Pro-Ed.

Gussen, R. (1969). Plugging of vascular canals in the otic capsule. *Annals of Otology, Rhinology, and Laryngology, 78,* 1305–1315.

Hall, J. (1979). Effects of age and sex on static compliance. *Archives of Otolaryngology, 105,* 153–156.

Hall, J. (1982). Acoustic reflex amplitude. I. Effects of age and sex. *Audiology, 21,* 294–309.

Hansen, C. C., & Reske-Nielsen, E. (1965). Pathological studies in presbycusis. *Archives of Otolaryngology, 82,* 115–132.

Harless, E. L., & McConnell, F. E. (1982). Effects of hearing aid use on self-concept in older persons. *Journal of Speech and Hearing Disorders, 47,* 305–309.

Hawkins, J. E., & Johnsson, L. G. (1985). Otopathological chances associated with presbycusis. *Seminars in Hearing, 6,* 115–134.

Helfer, K. S., & Wilber, L. A. (1990). Hearing loss, aging, and speech perception in reverberation and noise. *Journal of Speech and Hearing Research, 33,* 149–155.

Herbst, K. G., & Humphrey, C. (1980). Hearing impairment and mental state in the elderly living at home. *British Medical Journal, 281,* 903–905.

Herbst, K. R. G. (1983). Psychosocial consequences of disorders of hearing in the elderly. In R. Hinchcliff (Ed.), *Hearing and balance in the elderly* (pp. 174–200). New York: Churchill Livingston.

High, W. S., Fairbanks, G., & Glorig, A. (1964). Scale for self-assessment of hearing handicap. *Journal of Speech and Hearing Disorders, 29,* 215–230.

Hull, R. H. (1980). Aural rehabilitation for the elderly. In R. Schow & M. A. Nerbonne (Eds.), *Introduction to aural rehabilitation* (pp. 311–348). Baltimore: University Park Press.

Humes, L. E., & Christopherson, L. (1991). Speech identification difficulties of hearing-impaired elderly persons. *Journal of Speech and Hearing Research, 34,* 686–693.

Humes, L., Christopherson, L., & Cokely, C. (1992). Central auditory processing disorders in the elderly: Fact or fiction? In J. Katz, N. Stecker, & D. Henderson. (Eds.), *Central auditory processing: A transdisciplinary view* (pp. 141–149). Chicago: Mosby-Year Book.

Jerger, J. (1992). Can age-related decline in speech understanding be explained by peripheral hearing loss? *Journal of the American Academy of Audiology, 3*, 33–38.

Jerger, J., & Hall, J. W. (1980). Effects of age and sex on auditory brainstem response (ABR). *Archives of Otolaryngology, 106*, 387–391.

Jerger, J., Jerger, S., & Mauldin, L. (1972). Studies in impedance audiometry. Normal and sensorineural ears. *Archives of Otolaryngology, 96*, 513–523.

Jerger, J., Jerger, S., & Pirozzolo, F. (1991). Correlational analysis of speech audiometric scores, hearing loss, age, and cognitive abilities in the elderly. *Ear and Hearing 12*, 103–109.

Jerger, J., Jerger, S., Oliver, T., & Pirozzolo, F. (1989). Speech understanding in the elderly. *Ear and Hearing, 10*, 79–89.

Jerger, J., Oliver, T., & Pirozzolo, T. (1990). Impact of central auditory processing disorder on the self-assessment of hearing handicap in the elderly. *Journal of the American Academy of Audiology, 1*, 75–80.

Jerger, J., Stach, B., Pruitt, J., Harper, R., & Kirby, H. (1989). Comments on "speech understanding and aging." *Journal of the Acoustical Society of America, 85*(3), 1352–1354.

Johnsson, L. G., & Hawkins, J. E. (1972). Vascular changes in the human inner ear associated with aging. *Annals of Otology, Rhinology, and Laryngology, 81*, 361–376.

Kemp, D. T., Ryan, S., & Bray, P. (1990). A guide to the effective use of otoacoustic emissions. *Ear and Hearing, 11*, 93–105.

Kim, D. O. (1984). Functional roles of the inner- and outer-hair-cell subsystems in the cochlea and brainstem. In C. I. Berlin (Ed.), *Hearing science: Recent advances* (pp. 239–249). San Diego: College-Hill Press.

Kim, D. O., Molnar, C. E., & Matthews, J. W. (1980). Cochlear mechanics: Nonlinear behavior in two-tones responses as reflected in cochlear nerve fiber responses and in ear canal pressure. *Journal of the Acoustical Society of America, 67*, 1704–1721.

Kimberley, B. P., Hernadi, I., Lee, A. M., & Brown, D. K. (1994). Predicting pure tone thresholds in normal and hearing-impaired ears with distortion product emission and age. *Ear and Hearing, 15*, 199–209.

Kirikae, I., Sato, T., & Shitara, T. (1964). A study of hearing in advanced age. *Laryngoscope, 74*, 205–220.

Krympotic-Nemanic, J. (1971). A new concept in the pathogenesis of presbycusis. *Archives of Otolaryngology, 93*, 161–166.

Lebo, C. P., & Reddell, R. C. (1992). The presbycusis component in occupational hearing loss. *Laryngoscope, 82*, 1399–1409.

Lenzi, A., Chiarelli, G., & Sambataro, G. (1989). Comparative study of middle-latency responses and auditory brainstem responses in elderly subjects. *Audiology, 28*, 144–151.

Lonsbury-Martin, B. L., Cutler, W. N., & Martin, G. K. (1991). Evidence for the influence of aging on distortion-product otoacoustic emissions in humans. *Journal of the Acoustical Society of America, 89*, 1749–1759.

Lonsbury-Martin, B. L., McCoy, M. J., Whitehead, M. L., & Martin, G. K. (1993). Clinical testing of distortion-product otoacoustic emissions. *Ear and Hearing, 1*, 11–22.

Makishima, K. (1978). Arteriolar sclerosis as a cause of presbycusis. *Otolaryngology, 86*, 322–326.

Maurer, F. J., & Rupp, R. R. (1979). *Hearing and aging: Tactics for intervention.* New York: Grune & Stratton.

Mitchell, C., Phillips, D. S., & Trune, D. R. (1989). Variables affecting the auditory brainstem response: Audiogram, age, gender and head size. *Hearing Research, 40*, 75–86.

Moss, A. J., & Parson, V. L. (1986). Current estimates from the National Interview Survey: United States-1985. DHHS publication No. PHS 86-1588. *Vital and Health Statistics, Series 10, No. 160.* Washington, DC: National Health Center for Statistics

Mountain, D. C . (1980). Changes in endolymphatic potential and crossed olivo-cochlear bundle stimulation alter cochlear mechanics. *Science, 210*, 71–72.

Mulrow, C. D., Aguilar, C., Endicott, J. E., Tuley, M. R., Valez, R., Charlip, W. S., Rhodes, M. C., Hill, J. A., & DeNino, L. A. (1990). Quality of life changes and hearing impairment: Results of a randomized trial. *Annals of Internal Medicine, 113*, 188–194.

Nadol, J. (1979). Electron microscope findings in presbycusic degeneration of the basal turn of the human cochlea. *Otolaryngology and Head and Neck Surgery, 87*, 818–836.

Nerbonne, M., Bliss, A., & Schow, R. (1978). Acoustic impedance values in the elderly. *Journal of the American Auditory Society, 4*, 57–59.

Nerbonne, M., Schow, R., & Gosset, F. (1976). *Prevalence of conductive pathology in a nursing home population* (Laboratory Research Reports). Pocatello: Idaho State University, Department of Speech Pathology and Audiology.

Nielsen, L. H., Popelka, G. R., Rasmussen, A. N., & Osterhammel, P. A. (1993). Clinical significance of probe-tone frequency ratio on distortion product otoacoustic emissions. *Scandinavian Audiology, 22*, 159–164.

Ottaviani, F., Maurizi, M., D'Alatri, L., & Almadori, G. (1991). Auditory brainstem response in the aged. *Acta Otolaryngologica, 476*(Suppl), 110–114.

Pfefferbaum, A., Ford, J. M., Roth, W. T., & Kopell, B. S. (1980). Age-related changes in auditory event-related potentials. *Electroencephalography and Clinical Neurophysiology, 49*, 266–276.

Pfefferbaum, A., Ford, J. M., Wenegrat, B. G., Roth, W. T., & Kopell, B. S. (1984). Clinical application of the P3 component of event-related potentials: I. Normal aging. *Electroencephalography and Clinical Neurophysiology, 59*, 85–103.

Puce, A., Donnan, G. A., & Bladin, P. F. (1989). Comparative effects of age on limbic and scalp P3. *Electroencephalography and Clinical Neurophysiology, 74*, 385–393.

Rasmussen, A. T. (1940). Studies of the VIIIth cranial nerve of man. *Laryngoscope, 50*, 67–83.

Rodriguez, G. P., DiSarno, N. J., & Hardiman, C. J. (1990). Central auditory processing in normal-hearing elderly adults. *Audiology, 29*, 85–92.

Rosenwasser, H. (1964). Otitic problems in the aged. *Geriatrics, 19*, 11–17.

Saunders, J. C., Dean, S. P., & Schneider, M. E. (1985). The anatomical consequences of acoustic energy: A review and tutorial. *Journal of the Acoustical Society of America, 78*, 833–860.

Schmiedt, R. A. (1986). Acoustic distortion in the ear canal. I. Cubic difference tones: Effect of acute noise injury. *Journal of the Acoustical Society of America, 79*, 1481–1490.

Schow, R. L., & Nerbonne, M. A. (1982). Communication screening profile: Use with elderly clients. *Ear and Hearing, 3*, 135–147.

Schuknecht, H. F. (1955). Presbycusis. *Laryngoscope, 65*, 407–419.

Schuknecht, H. F. (1964). Further observations on the pathology of presbycusis. *Archives of Otolaryngology, 80*, 369–382.

Schuknecht, H. F. (1974). *Pathology of the ear.* Cambridge, MA: Harvard University Press.

Spoendlin, H., & Schrott, A. (1989). Analysis of the human auditory nerve. *Hearing Research, 43*, 25–38.

Spoendlin, H., & Schrott, A. (1990). Quantitative evaluation of the human cochlear nerve. *Acta Otolaryngologica, 470*(Suppl), 61–70.

Stach, B. A., Spretnjak, M. L., & Jerger, J. (1990). The prevalence of central presbycusis in a clinical population. *Journal of the American Academy of Audiology, 1*, 109–115.

Stover, L., & Norton, S. J. (1993). The effects of aging on otoacoustic emissions. *Journal of the Acoustical Society of America, 94*, 2670–2681.

Strouse, A. L., Ochs, M. T., & Hall, J. W., III. Evidence against the influence of aging on distortion-product otoacoustic emissions. *Journal of the American Academy of Audiology, 7*, 339–345.

Tsai, H. K., Fong-Shyong, C., & Tsa-Jung, C. (1958). On the changes in ear size with age. *Journal of the Formosa Medical Association, 57*, 105–111.

van Rooij, J. C. G. M., & Plomp, R. (1990). Auditive and cognitive factors in speech perception by elderly listeners. II. Multivariate analyses. *Journal the Acoustical Society of America, 88*, 2611–2624.

van Rooij, J. C. G. M., & Plomp, R. (1991). Auditive and cognitive factors in speech perception by elderly listeners. III. *Journal of the Acoustical Society of America, 91*, 1028–1033.

van Rooij, J .C. G. M., Plomp, R., & Orbelek, J. F. (1989). Auditive and cognitive factors in speech perception by elderly listeners. I. Development of test battery. *Journal of the Acoustical Society of America, 86*, 1294–1309.

Ventry, I. M., & Weinstein, B. (1982). The hearing handicap inventory for the elderly: A new tool. *Ear and Hearing, 3*, 128–134.

Ventry, I. M., & Weinstein, B. (1983). Identification of elderly people with hearing problems. *Asha, 25*, 37–42.

Weinstein, B. E. (1985). *Hearing problems in the elderly: Identification and management.* New York: The Brookdale Institute on Aging and Adult Human Development, Columbia University.

Weinstein, B. E., & Amsell, L. (1986). Hearing loss and senile dementia in the institutionalized elderly. *Clinical Gerontologist, 4*, 3–15.

Woods, D. L., & Clayworth, C. C. (1986). Age-related changes in human middle latency auditory evoked potentials. *Electroencephalography and Clinical Neurophysiology, 65*, 297–303.

Working Group on Speech Understanding and Aging. (1988). Speech understanding and aging. *Journal of the Acoustical Society of America, 83*, 859–893.

Zenner, H. P. (1986). Motile responses in outer hair cells. *Hearing Research, 22*, 83–90.

6

Hearing Aids and Older Adults

Barbara E. Weinstein, Ph.D.

Introduction

Hearing aids are the intervention of choice for older adults with hearing impairments that are both disabling and handicapping. Recent advances in hearing aid technology have improved the effectiveness of hearing aid fittings in individuals with sensorineural hearing loss. The future holds even greater promise with the advent of programmable hearing instruments, which offer superior performance as compared with the conventional analog technology. Despite technological advances and the trend toward miniaturization, overall satisfaction with hearing aids and hearing aid sales has declined substantially (Kochkin, 1994). End-user satisfaction with hearing aids is critical if audiologists are to reach older adults who are potential candidates for amplification.

This chapter is organized to develop an understanding of the impact of aging on the hearing aid selection and fitting process. It begins with a review of the demographics of hearing aid use and proceeds to a discussion of the impact of aging on hearing aid selection. A brief overview of current hearing aid technologies and fitting strategies for use with older adults is offered. The chapter concludes with a review of data on the efficacy of hearing aids with older adults and some suggestions for promoting successful hearing aid use among older adults. This chapter's organization is based on the author's belief that most texts on hearing aids provide an understanding of the technological aspects of hearing instruments. The goal here is to enable the reader to apply the information on older adults to their working knowledge of hearing aids.

129

Demography of Hearing Aid Use

Of the 25.8 million Americans who have hearing difficulty, fewer than 23% use hearing instruments, representing a gap of more than 20 million people (Kochkin, 1992). Persons over 60 years of age represent the segment of the population most likely to use and benefit from hearing aids. According to results of the 1991 MarkeTrak III survey, hearing aid use varies as a function of age with 6.5% of hearing aid users between 18 to 34 years of age and 56.1% over 85 years of age (Kochkin, 1992). Interestingly, despite the increase in the aging population and improvements in technology, hearing aid penetration by age group has been remarkably stable over the past decade (Kochkin, 1992). Hearing instrument ownership is highly related to age, even when degree of hearing loss is considered. That is, older adults with severe self-reported hearing loss are more likely to purchase hearing instruments than younger adults with severe self-reported hearing loss. Similarly, older adults with mild self-reported hearing loss are more likely to purchase hearing aids than younger adults with comparable loss (Kochkin, 1992). It is of interest that the average age of new hearing aid use has not changed over the past few years. In 1989 the average age of new hearing aid users was 66, in 1990 it was 62.9 years, and in 1991 it was 68 years.

The typical hearing aid owner in the United States who purchased hearing aids in 1993 or 1994 was male (59%), 68 years of age, had a bilateral hearing loss (82%), and wore binaural hearing aids (Kochkin, 1994). Further, 59% of hearing aid users viewed their hearing loss as a problem most of the time, 76% had difficulty conversing in noise, 47% had a moderate self-reported hearing loss, 40% had a severe self-reported hearing loss, and 7% had a profound self-reported hearing loss (Kochkin, 1994). Sixty percent of hearing instrument owners were retired, whereas 51% of nonowners reported full-time employment (Kochkin, 1992). One other distinguishing factor between owners and nonowners is that 35% of owners were between 65 and 74 years of age versus 19% of nonowners. Similarly, 25% of owners were between 75 and 84 old years as compared to 8% of nonowners (Kochkin, 1992).

Despite the apparent age-related dependence of hearing aid use, the majority of older adults with hearing loss do not use hearing instruments. According to a variety of surveys, only 18 to 20% of older adults with hearing loss use hearing aids. According to the MarkeTrak III survey of 6,000 owners and nonowners, the majority of respondents cited stigma associated with hearing aid use as the most important reason for not purchasing a hearing instrument (Kochkin, 1992).

Interestingly, stigma was more of a deterrent for adults between 35 and 54 years of age than for adults over 55 years of age.

The following factors are additional deterrents to hearing aid use among elders: (a) a hearing aid represents public admission to a hearing loss, (b) hearing aids make people look old, (c) hearing aids make people look disabled, and (d) hearing aids are too embarrassing to wear (Kochkin, 1994). Fino, Bess, Lichtenstein, and Logan (1991) confirmed that hearing impaired elderly who elected not to pursue amplification believed that hearing aids were too conspicuous, too expensive, too noisy, and called attention to their hearing problem. It appears that the "stigma effect" is consistent across age groups: 47% of persons between 45 and 54 years of age and 43% of persons between 55 and 64 years of age reported it as the reason for not purchasing a hearing instrument (Kochkin, 1994). Once older adults commit to purchasing a hearing instrument, however, they no longer remain stigmatized by it. The latter is not the case for adults under 18 years of age. The majority continue to report feeling stigmatized by use of a hearing aid (Kochkin, 1994).

The Hearing Aid Selection and Fitting Process

The hearing aid fitting process should be seen in the context of a comprehensive audiological rehabilitation program. The responsibility of audiologists involved in audiological rehabilitation is to facilitate reduction of the communication disability and psychosocial handicap associated with a given hearing impairment via an acceptable intervention, such as hearing aids. The first step in the rehabilitation process is to describe the nature of the auditory impairment and its consequences, namely, the disability and the handicap. This will serve as the basis for identifying individuals who are likely to use and benefit from hearing aid technology and will help to establish a pretreatment performance baseline against which the outcome of the intervention can be judged. Having identified the candidate for a hearing aid, the next step is the hearing aid selection/fitting process wherein the audiologist takes the earmold impressions, decides on the most appropriate hearing aid style and/or type of technology, and selects the electroacoustic characteristics most likely to optimize performance. The fitting session is designed to verify that the electroacoustic response of the hearing aid meets the pre-established target. At the time of the hearing aid fitting, baseline information about the disability and handicap should be used to establish a set of rehabilitation goals and to design the rehabilitation program. The goals should be realistic, client driven, and adequately reinforced on completion of each phase of the intervention. Following the fitting, a period of accommodation takes place, typically 3 to 6 weeks, and the client returns for the postfitting to ensure response adequacy and to quantify the satisfaction and benefit derived from the hearing aid use. If post-hearing-aid-fitting data suggest that the individual is not deriving adequate benefit, then hearing aid modifications and a brief interval of counseling-oriented rehabilitation should be instituted. Counseling and follow-up procedures tend to increase the ranks of satisfied hearing aid users. A brief description of each aspect of the selection and fitting process follows.

Candidacy Issues

When deciding on candidacy for a hearing aid referral, the audiologist should give primacy to the needs of the elderly person. Keep in mind that older adults are motivated to purchase rehabilitation if it can help restore or maintain functional abilities, namely, the ability to independently perform activities of dailiy life (Ramsdell, 1990). Approaching a person from a functional perspective means analyzing the physiological or biological impairment in the context of the individual's social, psychological, and environmental milieu. Hence, candidacy for hearing aids should depend on the following five factors: (a) auditory, (b) physical, (c) sociological, (d) psychological, and (e) environmental. Table 6–1 summarizes the variables to consider in each of these categories.

Auditory

The goal of fitting hearing aids and accompanying audiological rehabilitation is to assist individuals in overcoming the disabling or handicapping effects of hearing impairment. The World Health Organization (WHO) disease response model provides a basis for understanding how

Table 6–1. Variables that influence hearing aid use among the elderly.

Auditory	Physical	Psychological	Sociologicalal	Environmental
Impairment	Manual dexterity	Motivation	Lifestyle	Safety needs
Disability	Physical health	Cognitive	Familial support	
Handicap	Visual status	Personality	Financial factors	

various components of disease or disorders interrelate (WHO, 1980). The WHO paradigm provides a systems approach to understanding how a pathology at the organ level (i.e., hearing impairment) generates a disability at the person level, which ultimately produces a handicap at the societal level. It can serve as a basis for determining hearing aid candidacy. According to the model, impairment is documented with an audiogram that details the extent of hearing loss for pure-tone and speech signals. Disability is the effect of impairment on the individual's specific auditory functioning in daily life. Handicap represents the social and emotional manifestations of impairment and disability. A given handicap affects the client with the condition, the family/caregiver, and often society. Handicap and disability are inferred from self-report questionnaires which seek to quantify perceptions of the extent of auditory and nonauditory problems associated with a given impairment (Cox & Alexander, 1995; Stephens & Hetu, 1991).

The impairment variable that figures most prominently in candidacy decisions is performance on physiological or behavioral measures of hearing status. The auditory variables audiologists consider when deciding on candidacy are listed in Table 6–1. Impairment measures include pure-tone air and bone conduction thresholds, loudness judgments, peripheral and central auditory processing, or speech recognition ability. Performance on these tests helps determines the need for medical intervention and assists in selection of a particular style of hearing instrument. Further, impairment measures serve as the basis for decisions related to the electroacoustic characteristics of the hearing aid rather than candidacy per se.

Performance on routine pure-tone and speech tests bears little relation to hearing aid benefit defined as the difference between aided and unaided self assessed psychosocial handicap (Newman, Jacobson, Hug, Weinstein, & Malinoff, 1991). Rather, severity of hearing impairment contributes to our understanding of the nature of benefit from hearing aids and hence can be used in establishing realistic expectations. For example, restoration of the ability to hear warning signals and environmental sounds is the primary benefit for older adults with profound hearing loss. In contrast, enhanced speech understanding in quiet and noise might be the advantage for persons with less severe hearing loss. Thus, armed with this information, persons with profound hearing impairment should be counseled regarding what they can realistically expect from their hearing instruments.

Suprathreshold hearing profiles and/or loudness growth measures are being used to select the SSPL-90 or maximum output of the hearing aid. These measures help ensure that the hearing aid response is tolerable in terms of the loudness of the amplified signal, shape the hearing aid's output function, and serve as the basis for decisions about the appropriate hearing aid circuitry. Finally, threshold data are used in conjunction with word recognition scores to decide on the hearing aid arrangement or ear to fit. Barring medical contraindication, clinical experience suggests that the only time a hearing aid should not be fit is when there is no measurable response to sound (e.g., profound loss), when word recognition ability is virtually nonexistent in a given ear, or in the presence of a central auditory processing disorder (CAPD). The latter has been shown to adversely affect hearing aid satisfaction and benefit (Jerger, Chmiel, Florin, Pirozzolo, & Wilson, 1996; Stach & Stoner, 1991). Older adults with postlingual bilateral severe-to-profound sensorineural hearing loss who cannot benefit from hearing aids or FM systems should be encouraged to pursue the possibility of cochlear implantation. Waltzman, Cohen, and Shapiro (1993) reported that the majority of older adults in their sample ($N = 20$) achieved improved word and sentence recognition with multichannel cochlear implants. Further, the implant was a significantly better aid to lipreading than conventional amplification.

Fino, Bess, and Lichtenstein (1991) were among the first investigators to demonstrate that hearing aid candidacy is directly linked to self-perceived hearing handicap. Specifically, they found that the extent of self-perceived hearing handicap on the 10-item screening version of the Hearing Handicap Inventory for the Elderly (HHIE-S) reliably distinguished between hearing aid use and nonuse. At each hearing level category, persons who obtained hearing aids were more handicapped than those who did not. Bess (1995) reported a score of 23 or greater on the HHIE-S to be indicative of need for a hearing aid. The average HHIE-S score of persons who did not pursue amplification was 9. Similarly, Newman, Jacobson, Hug, Weinstein, and Malinoff (1991) found that the average prefitting score on the HHIE-S for first-time users was approximately 18, irrespective of mean hearing level and word recognition scores. Swan and Gatehouse (1990) also noted that individuals with hearing impairment pursue hearing health care services because of hearing disabilities and handicaps that often do not correspond to degree of hearing impairment.

Encouragement from spouses and direction from medical professionals also influences the decision to pursue amplification. Kochkin (1993) considered the recommendations of the physician and the audiologist to be powerful predictors of a hearing aid purchase. He speculated that, given two individuals of comparable age and hearing level, the person to whom amplification is recommended is nearly eight times more likely to purchase a unit than the person who does not receive a recommendation. As people age 65 years and older on average visit a physician eight times a year, it is incumbent on audiologists to use medical education channels and physician education brochures to promote positive attitudes about the value of hearing aids. Primary care physicians and geriatricians are increasingly using the HHIE-S as a screening tool for identifying older adults who require audiology services.

Physical Factors

The primary physical variables that may influence hearing aid candidacy include visual status, manual dexterity, ear and ear canal variables, overall health, and mental status. Changes in vision inevitably accompany the aging process. Visual problems in older adults range from low vision to functional visual impairment (e.g., interference with activities of daily living) to blindness. Among those who are functionally visually impaired, 70% are 65 years of age and older. Visual problems that potentially impact on hearing aid candidacy and success include: (a) inability to focus on close objects; (b) difficulty discerning the difference between an object and its background; (c) difficulty seeing under conditions of poor lighting; (d) a filtering of the color spectrum which results in a loss of color sensitivity especially green, blue, and violet shades; (e) vulnerability to glare created by bright light shining into the eye; and (f) impaired visual acuity and accommodation interfering with speech-reading ability. The techniques listed in Table 6–2 can help overcome these difficulties and minimize the threats that visual problems pose to hearing aid candidacy and success. Chapter 3 contains more detailed information about visual changes that accompany the aging process.

In general, the high prevalence of visual problems in older adults is an important factor in favor of pursuing amplification in the form of hearing aids, assistive listening devices, or a cochlear implant. The severity and nature of the visual problem should influence hearing aid arrangement, hearing aid style, and type of signal processing. Binaural hearing aids may facilitate localization and are highly recommended when visual status is compromised. Similarly, noise cues take on increasing importance in persons who are visually impaired as availability of information about environmental sounds can promote a sense of safety and security. Finally, the role of speechreading as a supplement to audition takes on less and less importance as visual acuity becomes poorer than 20/70.

The primary otological considerations that pertain to candidacy relate to the earmold impression for in-the-ear (ITE) or the new genera-

Table 6–2. Solutions to visual problems which may interfere with maximal benefit from hearing aids and audiologic rehabilitation

Condition	Solution
Glare	1. Light should be even and from multiple sources to ensure adequate light levels without glare. 2. Curtains or blinds should be adjusted to diffuse sunlight and to prevent direct illumination. 3. Shiny surfaces, reflective fixtures, or waxed floors add to the problems created by glare and should be avoided.
Loss of color sensitivity	1. Contrast between colors and between an object and its background (e.g., dark image on a light surface) should be emphasized. 2. Colors used for identification and locating information should be contrasting, for example, as yellow and blue.
Slower light adaptation	1. Adequate time for adaptation to changes in illumination should be allowed. 2. Abrupt changes in light should be avoided.
Reduced visual activity	1. Large images and print sizes should be used on written instructions and when performing paper-pencil evaluations. 2. Lighting should be increased without increasing glare. 3. Eye contact should be established and the clinician positioned in the person's line of vision

tion of hearing instruments, namely, completely-in-the-canal (CIC) hearing aids which must be custom-made to fit and remain seated in the ear canal. Cerumen accumulation and impaction is a recurring problem for older adults, and the ear should be free of debris prior to making the earmold impression. Although it is within the audiologist's scope of practice to remove cerumen, the skin of the older adult's external auditory canal can be easily traumatized as it is sensitive to manipulation. Further, selected medical conditions prevalent among the elderly contraindicate cerumen management. These include, but are not limited to, diabetes, basal or squamous cell carcinoma, and autoimmune disease. Audiologists are encouraged to exercise good judgment before practicing cerumen management and are encouraged to refer the older adult to a physician for management and clearance when medical conditions warrant. State licensure law regarding scope of practice for audiologists should be consulted to determine whether it is permissible for an audiologists to practice cerumen management.

Prior to selecting a given hearing aid style, the audiologist should examine the shape and dimensions of the external canal to ensure compatibility with the features of the hearing aid. The presence of active infection, unusual growth, atresia, or stenosis of the external ear canal may preclude a canal or deep canal fitting. If an ear has been surgically altered, the decision to proceed with the fitting should be made in consultation with a physician. Further, inability to obtain a sufficiently deep impression contraindicates a CIC unit. Older adults with abnormal skin sensitivity in the area of the ear canal and persons experiencing excessive cerumen accumulation may not be candidates for microhearing instruments. Older adults with the tendency toward excessive accumulation of cerumen should be acquainted with options for controlling cerumen so that it does not interfere with the operation of hearing instruments. Options include an adhesive cerumen guard positioned at the end of the hearing aid or a brush and loop to clean the debris.

The miniaturization of hearing aid components has allowed reductions in the dimensions of hearing aids and decreases in the size of their controls. Older adults with manual dexterity problems, compromised wrist or finger mobility, reduced fine motor coordination, and/or diminished sense of touch should be encouraged to purchase hearing aids that they can manipulate, insert, remove, and adjust independently. Older adults with arthritic and/or rheumatoid disorders, paralysis, or developmental disabilities are most prone to movement impairments that may interfere with manipulation of hearing aid controls. Clinical experience suggests that the hearing aid selection process should include a dexterity check and an assessment of tactile sensation in the fingers to determine the style of hearing aid, the modifications, and the controls to be recommended.

Selected hearing aid manufacturers state specifically that individuals with manual dexterity problems and/or a lack of sensation in the fingers are not candidates for microhearing instruments. As clinical experience suggests that visual-motor coordination and touch recognition may affect successful use of amplification systems, audiologists are urged to experiment with formal and informal tests of dexterity and touch sensitivity. Formal measures are easily accessible through occupational or physical therapy departments or professionals. When formal measures of dexterity are not feasible, informal tests of touch sensitivity; wrist, hand, and finger motion; and dexterity should be pursued.

According to the data of Bess, Lichtenstein, and Logan (1989), hearing impairment and handicap are associated with the functional problems of poor general health, reduced mobility, and reduced interpersonal communication. Hearing aid interventions have been reported to improve the psychosocial correlates of hearing impairment leading to enhanced quality of life. Accordingly, when physical functional status appears to be reduced and independence potentially compromised, hearing status should be assessed and the possibility of audiological intervention pursued.

Dementia, an umbrella term encompassing several distinct subtypes, stands out as a health problem that may preclude hearing aid candidacy and success. In general, the more severe the dementing illness, the greater the cognitive decline and the less likely the individual is to use the hearing aid successfully. Auditory problems are prevalent among older adults in general and among persons with dementia in particular. Undetected moderately severe to severe sensorineural hearing loss both mimics and exacerbates the behavioral and cognitive signs of dementing illness. Personal hearing aids and assistive listening devices have been used successfully to facilitate the diagnosis of dementia. Further, personal or group hearing instruments represent a rehabilitative intervention that has the potential to help maintain the residual assets/strengths and relieve the emotional distress associated with the cognitive decline of dementia (Molloy & Lubinski, 1995).

Persons in advanced stages of dementia may not be candidates for first-time hearing aid use. They may (a) have difficulty locating their head to position the unit in the ear, (b) be unable to maintain and adjust the hearing aid, (c) be unable to position and reposition the hearing aid, and (d) be confused by the amplified noise. Hardwired assistive listening devices are ideal for these individuals, especially during intake, during rehabilitation, and in small group listening situations. Clinical experience suggests that experienced hearing aid users with more advanced dementia are more likely to adjust to and benefit from amplification than are new hearing aid users with comparable degrees of dementing illness. The audiologist is encouraged to explore the patient's mental status thoroughly prior to making a hearing aid recommendation and to monitor memory and cognitive function should a hearing aid be pursued.

Psychosocial Variables

The psychological variables that are considered potential determinants of hearing aid candidacy and benefit include, but are not limited to, motivational level of the patient and caregiver and attitude toward or expectations from hearing aid use. There is a lack of definitive data on the role of personality and psychological variables as determinants of hearing aid satisfaction and benefit (Bentler, Niebuhr, Getta, & Anderson, 1993; Chmiel & Jerger, 1994; Gatehouse, 1994). Motivation is one of the most important, yet least well understood factors that affects rehabilitation potential and candidacy (Kemp, 1990). It explains why behavior is initiated, why it persists, and why it is attenuated (Kemp, 1990). Motivation is a multivariate process that refers to self-directed behavior. It is defined according to the perception of: (a) what one wants from an intervention; (b) what one expects or believes can be achieved with a given intervention; (c) the relevance of the rewards associated with a given intervention; and (d) associated costs of pursuing an intervention (Kemp, 1990). Motivation to pursue intervention is optimal when an individual knows what he or she wants, expects it can be attained, and believes that the rewards are meaningful and occur at a reasonable cost. It is incumbent on the audiologist to understand the patient's motivations for pursuing a hearing aid to ensure that they are met.

The primary sociological variables to be considered when selecting candidates for hearing aids and a particular device relate to lifestyle and familial support. The audiologist must use formal or informal self-report questionnaires to explore engagement in physical activities, social interactions, and work-related activities. Responses to the inquiry may influence candidacy, the hearing aid features recommended, and the counseling process. Further, responses to the self-report can also guide the course of counseling once the hearing aid is recommended. For example, if the individual experiences only isolated listening difficulties, sporadic use of a hearing aid should be encouraged. Ultimately the new user will gradually come to understand the benefit of a hearing aid and increase its use in a number of situations. Similarly, if an individual is retired and is a musician by avocation, his or her listening needs and level of sophistication may dictate use of a programmable instrument. With regard to familial support, if an individual is relatively independent and does not wish to rely on a family member or a caregiver for hearing aid insertion or operation, then the most basic hearing instrument should be recommended. Older adults will most likely have an easier time adjusting and inserting an ITE than a canal or a CIC hearing aid. Similarly, ITE instruments are easier to manipulate and adjust than behind-the-ear units, accounting in part for their popularity.

The final sociological variable that influences the hearing aid selection process is financial considerations. Cost is often a factor in the decision to forego amplification. For individuals on a fixed income, $600 to $1,500 can be quite prohibitive for one unit. Newman and his colleagues (1993) reported that ability or inability to pay for hearing aids does not influence benefit. Economics may also influence the style of hearing aid recommended or the hearing aid arrangement (Bess, 1995; Kochkin, 1994). As older adults are at first surprised and at times put off by the cost of a monaural unit, audiologists are encouraged to explore potential candidates' financial positions to help guide them in their hearing aid recommendations.

Environmental Factors

According to Maslow's (1954) hierarchy of needs formulation, older adults will be motivated to pursue rehabilitative intervention if it is for a physical condition that compromises their safety at home or outside. For older persons who are hearing impaired and live alone, safety and security are of paramount importance. The inability to hear the smoke or fire alarm, the doorbell, a burglar alarm, or a car horn is a threat to safety posed by unremediated hearing loss. Hearing aids can help restore the role of hearing as an indicator of potential dangers in the distant environment. Older adults who ultimately do purchase hearing aid(s) should be encouraged to wear the unit at home, especially when alone, and when driving to ensure that warning signals are audible.

In summary, a host of audiological and nonaudiological variables combine to determine candidacy for and feasibility of hearing aid use. The audiologist must be mindful of all variables that will determine the appropriateness of a hearing aid for a given individual to ensure hearing aid satisfaction. After considering the variables influencing the decision to recommend hearing aids, the next step in the decision-making process is hearing aid selection and fitting.

Considerations in the Hearing Aid Selection, Fitting, and Verification Process

The goal of the hearing aid selection is to determine amplification requirements and a hearing aid arrangement that is electroacoustically, physically, and cosmetically acceptable. It is beyond the scope of this chapter to address in great depth strategies for selecting and verifying the hearing aid response for older adults. For the most part, the rules and strategies used with younger adults pertain to older adults. The philosophy governing all hearing aid fittings should be that electroacoustic characteristics should be selected that (a) maximize speech recognition, (b) provide good sound quality, and (c) provide amplification that is comfortable and compensates for the loss of loudness resulting from the impaired hearing (McCandless, 1994). Prior to selecting electroacoustic characteristics, the hearing aid style and arrangement must be mutually agreed upon.

A variety of hearing aid styles are available to the hearing impaired older adult. In 1994 approximately 1.6 million hearing instruments were sold. Custom ITE and ITC units were the most popular, with a small proportion of persons purchasing behind-the-ear (BTE) hearing aids. Specifically, from January to September 1994, 22.9% of hearing aids sold were BTEs, 41% were custom ITEs, 20% were ITCs, and 5.3% were CIC units (Hearing Instruments of America, [HIA] 1994). Programmable instruments represent only a small proportion (5%) of the market share, yet sales of these units increased dramatically in the third quarter of 1993 (HIA, 1994). Finally, only 29% of hearing instruments sold in 1993 to 1994 were to new users, down from 41% in 1991 and 53% in 1989 (Kochkin, 1994).

Until the 1980s, BTE hearing instruments were the most popular style. At present, they are the hearing aid aid of choice primarily for persons with severe-to-profound hearing impairment who require high-gain (50–70 dB), output limiting that lies between 120 to 142 dB SPL, and a strong telecoil. When electroacoustic flexibility and accessibility to direct audio input microphones are desirable, BTEs are recommended. Residents of nursing facilities with a history of hearing aid use may continue to use BTE hearing instruments despite the advent of ITE instruments.

Several companies have incorporated an FM receiver and a conventional hearing aid into a single BTE hearing aid case. The advantage of introducing an FM system is the improved signal-to-noise ratio achieved by bringing the microphone closer to the source of sound. Essentially, FM systems bridge the acoustical space between the sound source and the listener by eliminating the detrimental effects of distance, noise, and reverberation on speech perception (Ross, 1995b). The speaker's voice reaches the listener's ear directly without interference from noises in the environment and distance. The BTE/FM system can be used as a regular hearing aid, as an FM receiver bringing the signal directly to the user's ear, or as both an FM system and a hearing aid together. It is ideal when driving in a car, conversing in a noisy environment, at a lecture, or in a restaurant. Older adults with central auditory processing problems who no longer derive benefit from conventional hearing aids should be encouraged to avail themselves of this new technology, given the reported advantages derived from personal FM systems, which until recently have been worn on the body .

One additional point with regard to BTE units relates to the telecoil. A high power telecoil, which includes a preamplifier in the "T" coil circuit, should be recommended for persons with moderate-to-severe hearing loss to ensure compatibility with the telephone and with an ALD coupler. Inclusion of the preamplifier produces an amplified output nearly identical to that obtained with the microphone circuit (Ross, 1995b). Ross (1995b) recently reported on the availability of a waterproof

BTE unit developed in Japan. This arrangement in which the body assembly has been made watertight with rubber packing in the seams, may be ideal for older adults who have difficulty removing the ear-mold/hearing aid arrangement each time they take a shower, swim, or are caught outdoors in the rain.

The demand for smaller, less visible hearing aids coupled with miniaturization of hearing aid components has led to the expansion of the custom hearing aid market. Three categories of custom units are presently available to the consumer. These include ITC, ITE, and CIC hearing aids. Each is custom fitted to the contour of the ear, becoming less and less visible as the insertion point moves deeper into the ear canal. ITE units occupy the entire concha portion of the external ear, whereas ITC units terminate at the entrance to the external auditory meatus. Two categories of deep canal or CIC instruments are available. Category A, which includes most CICs, consists of hearing aids that have an ear tip that comes in contact with the second bend of the ear canal, but whose fitting does not involve making contact with the tympanic membrane. The only portion that is visible after insertion is the thin plastic removal cord. Category B includes deep-canal instruments whose fitting does include an impression-taking procedure in which the dispenser makes contact with the tympanic membrane (Kirkwood, 1994).

For the most part, the value of CICs has been theoretically rather than empirically based. The advantages of CICs over other custom instruments are displayed in Table 6–3 (Mueller, 1994). Investigators are currently attempting to validate the communicative and psychosocial benefits of CIC fittings. Results from a recent survey conducted by Ebinger, Holland, Holland, and Mueller (1995) revealed that, overall, CICs significantly reduced the proportion of listening difficulties experienced by older adults. The benefits experienced by older adults in reverberant conditions, background noise, and quiet were comparable to those perceived by a younger adult sample. Given the manual dexterity and vision problems that are so prevalent among older adults and the cosmetic and acoustic appeal of CICs, candidacy should be determined on an individual basis.

Older adults who insist on purchasing these units should have medical clearance to ensure that the ear canal and tympanic membrane are free of visible medical conditions, including abrasion, hematoma, dermatologic infections, or visible drainage. Further, if the bony canal appears to be high in vascularity, as is the case with some older adults, a deep canal fitting should be discouraged because of potential discomfort. The use of videootoscopy is encouraged with the elderly population, given the potential effects of aging on ear canal anatomy. Finally, older

Table 6–3. Potential advantages of completely-in-the-canal hearing aids.1

Advantages	Implications
No volume control wheel	Persons with manual dexterity problems will not have difficulty with volume control adjustments, as automatic gain control circuitry eliminates need for a volume control
Reduction of acoustic feedback	Less need for venting, positioned closer to the eardrum, leading to a securer fit
Reduction of occlusion effect	Rests in the bony portion of the canal, minimizing the echo and stuffiness associated with the occlusion effect
Ease of removal	A string extending from the faceplate is used for removal making it relatively easy to grasp
Reduced wind noise	The microphone is recessed in the ear canal so it is less affected by wind
Increased high frequency input	High frequency input to the microphone is increased because placement deep in the canal allows for natural acoustic effects of the concha and pinna to take place
Improved sound localization	Placement of the hearing aid microphone in the ear canal allows for more natural pinna effects, namely, improved sound localization
Telephone use	Using the telephone is comfortable, as the individual can easily place the telephone receiver against the ear. Also, little acoustic feedback is generated when using the phone because of microphone placement.

Source: Adapted from "Small Can Be Good Too" by G. Mueller, 1994, p. 11. *The Hearing Journal, 47.*

adults who ultimately purchase CICs should have extensive hearing aid orientation with a caregiver to ensure adequate insertion of the unit and proper battery insertion. The hearing aid should be clearly labeled with proper colors visible to the aging eye (e.g., right, left; top, bottom). Emphasizing the relative location of the removal cord can facilitate proper placement.

Manufacturers have recently introduced programmable hearing instruments available as BTE, ITE, or ITC units. In essence, programmable hearing aids employ digital technology to shape and manipulate a signal that has been amplified using analog technology (Radcliffe, 1991). Programmable or digitally controlled analog (DCA) hearing aids, as they are known in the hearing aid industry, have greater flexbility and a more extensive range over all of the traditional frequency and intensity controls than conventional analog devices (Radcliffe, 1991). In general, programmable instruments employ different circuit options to achieve a variety of sound qualities and performance characteristics. The vast majority of programmable instruments must be attached to an external programmer for adjustment of the electroacoustic characteristics. In 1994, 17 companies reportedly sold 9,014 ITE programmable aids and 15 companies reported selling 3,641 BTE programmable devices (HIA, 1994). According to Bray (1995), in 1995 there were 27 different brands of programmable hearing aids on the market.

Programmable instruments, which are capturing an increasingly large percentage of the hearing aid aid market (e.g., 10 to 12%), offer the user and the dispenser fitting flexibility. The electroacoustic response can be easily modified, the unit reprogrammed, and multiple hearing aid responses programmed into the memory of a single instrument. For example, hearing aid users have the ability to custom tailor the hearing instrument to their lifestyles, enabling them to benefit from amplification in situations in which a previous hearing aid was unusable. The dispenser can adjust the low frequencies, independently from the high frequencies depending on the hearing configuration and the nature of the input sound. A number of investigators have reported that programmable instruments provide considerable improvement in sound quality. Further, a number of reports have demonstrated improved speech understanding in noise in terms of overall intelligibility as well as ease of understanding. Further, subjective ratings of sound quality and performance in a variety of listening situations have been superior with programmable units versus more traditional personal hearing aids.

Programmable units will most likely play an important role in the hearing aid industry in the next decade and may be the option some older adults have been waiting for. As of this writing, a small number of "true digital" hearing aids are available; and they too are acknowledged to have excellent sound quality and improve the ability of the hearing impaired to function in a number of environments and listening conditions. In contrast to DCA devices, hearing aids that use digital circuitry for both the signal processing and the controlling functions are referred to as digital signal processing (DSP) hearing aids (Agnew, 1996). They too are attractive to older adults, especially those who can afford to purchase the technology.

Before recommending a programmable (DCA) or a true digital (DSP) hearing aid, be sure to consider the potential user's type of hearing impairment, hearing aid history, and comfort level with technology, before recommending a multimemory and/or multichannel hearing aid (Kuk, 1993). The majority of older adults first entering the hearing aid market may be overwhelmed by the variety and complexity of programmable units. Further, their listening needs may not demand the sophistication inherent in programmable units. As candidacy for programmable hearing instruments is determined primarily by occupational, social, or recreational listening needs, an in-depth needs assessment should be conducted to determine the appropriateness of a programmable instrument. The needs assessment should attempt to unravel the particular listening needs of the individual, the extent of communicative disability in each situations, and the psychosocial handicap attributable to the hearing loss. In addition, the individual's listening and technological sophistication, motivational level, availability for repeat visits, and experience with hearing aids should be established. Should the background history and audiometric profile justify the investment of time and money associated with use of a programmable hearing aid, the audiologist should review the options available and allow the candidate an opportunity to "interact with the device." The audiologist should review with the client the options that must be chosen and proceed to evaluate a few devices. The demands placed on the user should be kept to a minimum; however, the listening flexibility desired by the hearing impaired individual must be provided. Also, the candidate should be accompanied by a family member or caregiver each step of the way to facilitate adaptation to the unit.

When fitting a programmable instrument, always keep in mind that, for the older adult, the most important feature is the availability of a program that will assist him or her in the most difficult situations, namely, noisy environments and large group situations. Older adults may not feel comfortable "having responsibility" for a remote control and this may influence the choice of instrument. The client should have an opportunity to compare systems that use remote controls to those that do not. It is critical that the consumer have the opportunity to judge the different forms of processing with real-life listening materials. He or she should have an opportunity to manipulate the controls, and the audiologist should observe the ease or difficulty with which the individual approaches the task. Finally, older adults more and more are demanding objective justification or verification of the value of programmable instruments relative to their cost. Audiologists are urged to involve the consumer in every aspect of the dispensing and decision-making process. Self-assessment tools allow for comparison of perceived disability/handicap in an unaided condition with that experienced in the aided condition. Anecdotal reports suggest that consumers find this aspect of the fitting process clarifying because the benefits of programmable technology become more apparent.

Once the style of unit is chosen, agreement must be reached on the optimal hearing aid arrangement: monaural or binaural. Binaural amplification has been the fitting philosophy of choice because of theories that suggest a series of acoustic advantages. These advantages include improved localization, binaural summation, improved ability to understand speech in noise, ease of listening, and more natural/balanced sound. Recently, there has been a flurry of research reporting on auditory deprivation and recovery offered by binaural amplfication. The data of Silman, Gelfand, and Silverman (1984) suggest that, when speech recognition scores of subjects with bilateral sensorineural hearing loss who are fit monaurally are compared to those of a comparable group of subjects who are fit binaurally, speech recognition scores in the unaided ear of the monaurally aided group decline dramatically over a 4- to 5-year period. Most encouraging are reports that some patients who experience auditory deprivation effects experience clinically significant, albeit incomplete, recovery following use of binaural amplification. These findings have been replicated by a number of investigators on a variety of populations including older adults with presbycusis. The presence of late-onset auditory deprivation is a compelling reason to fit individuals binaurally.

Although quickly becoming the arrangement of choice among dispensers, binaural amplification may not be appropriate for older adults on a fixed income, for those with manual dexterity problems, persons with cognitive or emotional problems, or when binaural performance is impaired by the poorer ear because of the phenomenon of binaural interference (Jerger, Silman, Lew, & Chmiel, 1993). The latter is evident clinically when aided binaural speech recognition ability is significantly poorer than performance in the better aided ear. When financial considerations preclude binaural amplification, the possibility of alternating monaural amplfication should be explored to minimize the potential for auditory deprivation effects.

Selecting and Verifying the Hearing Aid Response

As of this writing, the majority of hearing aids purchased in the United States are custom ITE hearing aids and a large proportion of current ITE units are purchased from dispensers who rely on manufacturer-derived electroacoustic characteristics using threshold-based formulas (McCandless, 1994). Accordingly, the audiometric information sent to the manufacturer is a critical part of the selection process. In addition, the verification phase takes on greater importance. Prescriptive formulas used for selecting frequency-gain characteristics and setting the SSPL90 are typically based on threshold measures and suprathreshold judgments of comfort and discomfort at each ear. Threshold data assist in selecting desired real-ear gain/frequency response, whereas suprathreshold measures help set an SSPL90 that prevents the loudness discomfort associated with over-amplification (Vanderbilt/VA Hearing Aid Conference, 1990). Recently, clinicians and researchers have made a strong case for incorporating tests of loudness perception and/or loudness growth. Tests of loudness growth or tests that map loudness sensitivity are critical for selecting targets for nonlinear hearing devices and selecting special circuit options. To compensate for the loss of loudness resulting from impaired hearing, nonlinear hearing aids are becoming an industry standard. The International Hearing Aid Fitting Forum (IHAFF) (Mueller, 1994a) has recommended a protocol for selecting, fitting, and verifying the electroacoustic response of nonlinear hearing aids. Readers are encouraged to consider the IHAFF approach as well as the other formulas that have been introduced to assist in selecting and verifying the response of nonlinear hearing aids. As the protocols are lengthy and have not yet been validated, in terms of user reported benefit or satisfaction, they will not be incorporated in this chapter. Irrespective of the prescriptive formula or protocol used for selecting target responses, the response should be verified using some combination of real-ear measures, functional gain, speech materials, and subjective verification of sound quality or clarity.

The primary purpose of the fitting session is to verify, using measures of functional gain, insertion gain, and probe microphone measures, that prescribed gain/frequency response and output levels have been achieved. The electroacoustic characteristics necessary to achieve target gain and output levels should produce maximum speech recognition, sound quality, and clarity that are acceptable. The response of the hearing aid should be modified to satisfy the subjective report of the consumer. The consumer should be actively involved in this phase and be exposed to a variety of controlled sound inputs and loud environmental sounds to help the audiologist make the fine adjustments necessary for a comfortable and acceptable fitting (Vanderbilt/VA Hearing Aid Conference, 1990). This is especially important when fitting nonlinear amplification, multichannel, and noise reduction systems (McCandless, 1994).

THE POSTFITTING PROCESS

The 1990 Consensus Statement for "Recommended Components of a Hearing Aid Selection Procedure for Adults" suggested that verification strategies also incorporate the individual's perception of benefit obtained from amplification (Vanderbilt/VA Hearing Aid Conference, 1990). The subjective verification phase, commonly referred to as the postfitting visit, generally takes place 3 to 6 weeks after the fitting. The Office of Technology Assessment (1978) defined treatment efficacy as the "probability of benefit to individuals in a defined population from a medical technology applied for a given medical problem under ideal conditions of use" (p. 16). Hearing aid benefit is based on outcome measures that quantify the extent of improvement an individual experiences in selected situations (Montgomery, 1994). Benefit must be expressed with respect to a frame of reference and relative to a specific significance level. In the arena of audiological rehabilitation, treatment efficacy can be quantified in terms of the probability that individuals with a hearing impairment, disability, and/or handicap will benefit from hearing aids as determined by performance above a predetermined level on a reliable and valid outcome measure. The proliferation of disability and handicap questionnaires enables the clinician to objectively quantify treatment efficacy and the potential cost-benefit of a particular intervention (Hyde & Riko, 1994).

Available self-report disability and handicap questionnaires focus attention on what the patient tells the audiologist rather than on what audiometric test results suggest. Such data are beginning to demonstrate that, as criterion measures, self-report measures yield information on the ability of hearing aids to reduce the communicative disability and psychosocial handicap associated with hearing impairment in older adults. Table 6–4 describes the content of the more commonly used self-report instruments. The 25-item Hearing Handicap Inventory for the Elderly (HHIE) is the most widely used clinical tool for measuring self-

Table 6–4. Content of selected self-report instruments.

Scale	Content
Abbreviated Profile of Hearing Aid Benefit (APHAB)	Four subscales: ease of communication, background noise, aversiveness of sound, and reverberant conditions
Hearing Handicap Inventory for the Elderly (HHIE)	Two subscales: Emotional and social/situational
Hearing Aid Performance Inventory (HAPI)	Hearing aid benefit in a variety of daily listening situations

reported outcomes with hearing aids in adults. It is a reliable and valid instrument that allows measurement of benefit in the handicap domain quickly and efficiently. The HHIE is a self-administered questionnaire that enables the clinician to quantify the emotional (13 items) and social/situational (12 items) problems associated with hearing loss in older adults. A "no" response to an item scores 0, a "sometimes" scores 2, and a "yes" scores 4. Scores for the HHIE range from 0 to 100, with higher values representing greater perceived handicap. The HHIE was shortened from the full version (25-items) to a 10-item screening tool for which sensitivity and specificity values have been determined to be adequate (Newman, Weinstein, Jacobson, & Hug, 1992; Ventry & Weinstein, 1982). The 95% confidence interval (or critical difference value) associated with the HHIE is 18.7, whereas the 95% confidence interval for the HHIE-S is 10.

The Abbreviated Profile of Hearing Aid Benefit (APHAB) and the shortened version of the Hearing Aid Performance Inventory (HAPI) have been used with elderly individuals to demonstrate change in auditory disability following an interval of hearing aid use (Cox & Alexander, 1995; Schum, 1992). The shortened version of the HAPI consists of 38 items that assess speech understanding in quiet, noise, and situations that are low in redundancy (Schum, 1992). Norms for the APHAB and HAPI scales are based on responses obtained at one sitting, with the respondent comparing aided hearing to the unaided condition. It is preferable for older adults completing these questionnaires to rate their unaided hearing ability at the time of the audiological evaluation or hearing aid fitting. At the post-fitting assessment they should judge their aided speech understanding. This separation in time will most likely be less demanding for older adults and will likely increase the validity of their responses.

Using the HHIE-S or the HHIE as a gold standard, the following conclusions can be drawn from a large series of studies conducted on older adults: (a) beneficial treatment effects from hearing aids emerge as early as 6 weeks after the initiation of treatment and are most pronounced in the handicap domain; (b) the benefit from hearing aids can be demonstrated as early as 3 weeks after the initial fitting; (c) the benefit of hearing aids is demonstrable and sustainable in the handicap domain throughout a 1-year period; (4) a period of accomodation or adaptation to the hearing aid response tends to take place in selected individuals over time requiring the need for short-, medium- and long-term follow-up to monitor psychosocial benefit over time; and (5) a brief interval of counseling based audiologic rehabilitation, communication training, and/or simple hearing aid modifications can promote hearing aid benefit among older adults who initially do not realize benefit from their hearing aids (Abrams, Chisolm, Guerreiro, & Ritterman, 1992; Mulrow, 1990; Taylor, 1993). Further, from available program evaluation data, the majority (70 to 80%) of older adults derive significant psychosocial benefits from hearing aids. Finally, data from a limited number of available studies suggest that, when older adults who previously enjoyed considerable benefit from hearing aids begin to experience difficulty with their devices, the audiologist should monitor hearing levels and, more importantly, assess their central auditory processing abilities. The latter tend to contribute to speech understanding difficulties with and without hearing aids, compromising previously experienced benefit. For these individuals, FM systems have proven more helpful than hearing aids, although these systems are not yet considered an acceptable alternative, given their large size (Jerger, Chmiel, Florin, Pirozzolo, & Wilson, 1996).

Audiologic and Nonaudiologic Correlates of Hearing Aid Benefit

A variety of studies conducted in different settings have revealed that, with the exception of central auditory processing ability, audiometric data bear little relationship to hearing aid benefit. Newman, Jacobson, Hug, Weinstein, and Malinoff (1991) reported that severity of hearing loss and degree of word-recognition ability did not influence absolute perceived handicap on the HHIE-S, nor did they bear a relation to benefit from hearing aids. Mulrow and her colleagues (1992) and Taylor (1993) also found that improvement in audibility for pure-tone signals or functional gain values did not correlate with hearing aid benefit (i.e., change in score on HHIE following hearing aid fitting) perceived by older adults. The findings at Abrams, Chisolm, Guerreiro, and Ritterman (1992) that aided speech recognition performance using the CUNY Nonsense Syllable Test did not correlate with benefit on the HHIE confirmed the lack of relation between basic audiometric and self-report data.

One myth surrounding hearing aids is that older adults use their hearing aids less consistently and derive less benefit from hearing aids than do younger adults. Recent studies have demonstrated that this conclusion cannot be substantiated empirically. Bender and Mueller (1984) compared younger and older adults in subjective judgments of hearing aid use, satisfaction, and benefit. After 1 year of hearing aid use, the responses of older adults were comparable to those of younger adults. In fact, the vast majority of older adults reported more than a moderate degree of benefit and satisfaction with amplification. Kochkin (1992) also reported that there were no statistically significant differences by age group in overall mean satisfaction ratings. Ebinger et al., (1995) found that older and younger adults reported comparable benefit in the disability domain from CIC hearing aids. Specifically, according to responses to the APHAB, the percentage of aided problems in various listening conditions was comparable for older and younger adults. Further, the CIC units reduced the percent of listening problems experienced by older and younger adults to below the 50th percentile of the norms established by Cox and Alexander (1995). Finally, Primeau (1997) reported that older and younger adults were comparable in the magnitude of perceived benefit in the psychosocial domain which emerged on the HHIE/HHIA.

In summary, available data indicate that older adults derive significant short- and long-term benefit and satisfaction from hearing aids. Age does not appear to be a deterrent to successful hearing aid use as evidenced by the finding that hearing instrument satisfaction is comparable for younger and older adults (Kochkin, 1992). In fact, according to a series of studies using the HHIE, 70–80% of older adults appear to experience significant reductions in psychosocial handicap associated with hearing aid use. The major factor that may mitigate against a successful fitting is the presence of a central auditory processing disorder. This group of individuals may benefit from other devices such as FM systems that help to overcome the debilitating effect of noise and distance on speech understanding. (See Chapter 7 for an in-depth discussion of assistive listening devices.) Despite the impressive results older adults are obtaining with hearing aids, the high cost of hearing aids continues to deter potential candidates from pursuing amplification. Cost-effectiveness estimates generated by Mulrow and her colleagues (1990) suggest that, when the cost of a hearing evaluation, hearing aid selection, and fitting is compared with the functional and quality of life benefits of amplification, hearing aids actually represent an inexpensive intervention for the amount of benefit gained. These data should be used by audiologists to convey the value of hearing aids.

Counseling and Follow-up Procedures

Postpurchase satisfaction depends in large part on the extent to which the performance of and everyday function with the hearing aid(s) conforms to the consumer's expectations. If performance exceeds expectations, the customer will be satisfied; if performance falls short of expectations, the customer will be dissatisfied. Thus, it behooves the audiologist to devote considerable time to counseling the patient about the amplification device and how best to cope with the consequences of acquired hearing impairment. Audiologists should adopt a problem-and emotion-focused approach to rehabilitation that is natural rather than contrived (Schum, 1994). When possible, counseling sessions should be short-term, brief, and include the consumer and a family member or close friend. The former is critical for compliance, and the latter is critical for carryover of information into everyday life.

Counseling sessions should be client-driven and based on formal or informal exploration of perceived problems and needs. This approach empowers the client to take responsibility for the rehabilitation process. Further, assertiveness, or a tendency to assume responsibility for or control over the rehabilitative process, tends to be associated with better rehabilitative outcomes (Kemp, 1994). As noted previously, self-report measures that quantify hearing aid benefit in the disability and handicap domains can be invaluable. Further, responses to satisfaction scales that quantify problems relating to the hearing instrument can guide the discussion about the device per se. Each session should incorporate a problem-focused discussion relating to the hearing instrument and an emotion-focused discussion relating to adjustment to the hearing loss. Counseling sessions should begin with a review of the client's device management skills and some form of listening check to verify that the hearing instrument is functioning properly. Input should be sought regarding use patterns and concerns that have arisen. Modifications in the hearing instrument should take place at the beginning of each session. Finally, for rehabilitative efforts to be successful, the audiologist must establish a good working relationship with the hearing impaired elder and members of his or her social support system.

The problem-focused portion of the counseling session should emphasize the amplification system, how to best use amplification, and the limitations inherent in amplification systems. When discussing the hearing aid, it is important to emphasize what a hearing aid can and cannot provide for a individual who is hearing impaired (Schum, 1994). Ample time should be devoted to resolving device-related inconveniences and practicing insertion, removal, and manipulation of the hearing aid. When demonstrating use of the hearing aid(s), accommodations should be made for the visually impaired by ensuring adequate illumination and visual contrast and using surfaces with minimal glare. Make optical enlarging devices available to enable older adults to see the markings on the hearing aid. Also, make sure that older adults repeatedly demonstrate and practice hearing aid/battery insertion and removal and have the opportunity to adjust the various controls.

The emotion-focused segment should attempt to resolve or restore some of the disadvantages posed by the impairment and disability.

Every attempt should be made to promote independence, improve functioning, and restore enjoyment of the routine activities of daily living. The rehabilitation literature suggests that improvement in these areas goes a long way toward promoting life satisfaction and enhancing self-esteem (Kemp, 1990). Modifying attitudes regarding the stigma associated with hearing aid use and demonstrating the value of hearing aids to the consumer should be the focus. Negative attitudes of family members can serve as a deterrent to acceptance of hearing loss and hearing aid use, and thus their attitudes should be examined and remedied when appropriate. Further, strategies for facilitating coping and adaptation to acquired hearing impairment should be offered. Communication strategies and strategies for manipulating the environment to enhance speech understanding can facilitate adjustment to hearing loss and a hearing aid. If the client appears to have difficulty in specific situations that could be remedied with assistive listening devices, the availability and variety of systems should be discussed with an opportunity for hands-on experience. Chapter 7 offers a more in-depth discussion of assistive listening devices.

At the conclusion of counseling (3 to 6 weeks preferably), the self-assessment scales(s) administered at the initial session should be read-ministered and the responses compared. The final session is the appropriate time to share the profile that emerges and compare final responses to those obtained at the first session. The apparent benefit that emerges should be reviewed so that the consumer and family member can have objective verification of the value of the hearing instrument. These data can serve to address the increasingly important issue of accountability in health care.

The audiologist must consider the total person when instituting any form of audiological intervention, given the multiple stresses associated with aging. Clinicians should operate from the perspective that many older persons have complex problems of a physical, psychological, and social nature that will influence the treatment approach and outcome. In light of the individual variables that characterize older adults, one cannot predict what each of these stresses will be. Thus, the audiologist must have at his or her disposal a means of assessing and perhaps minimizing the effects of those variables on audiological management. Selected cognitive changes associated with the aging process are the stressors most likely to have the most profound influence on the course and success of audiological rehabilitation. The impact of aging on the capacity to learn, on memory, on reaction time, and on coping strategies should be kept in mind to enable audiologists to more effectively treat the older hearing impaired adult.

The ability to perform new tasks and flexibility of learning style undergo some decline with age. Further, older people tend to learn more slowly than do their younger counterparts; thus, it takes more trials for a particular skill to be acquired (Bienfeld, 1990). Older adults tend to require more time to integrate newly learned information into their daily routine (Davis, 1990). To compensate for this and possible declines in reaction time, the clinician should routinely allow time for the older adult to fully process information prior to demanding a response. Further, older adults tend to be vulnerable to distracting events, which can interfere with their level of concentration. Thus, visual and auditory distractions should be removed from the room where counseling and instructional sessions are conducted.

Aging also may have an impact on sensory, primary, or secondary memory. As time does not permit assessment of each, the clinician should consider practicing the following when counseling the older adult regarding hearing aid use. First, the individual must register the instructions in order to remember what has been said. Thus, the clinician must make sure that the client has heard what was said and has seen what was demonstrated. The clinician should provide cues that will help the individual to remember what he or she has learned. The clinician should make sure to allow adequate time for storage of new information. Ample opportunity should be provided for practicing what has been recommended, and the individual should demonstrate his or her understanding of the instructions or new information. Reinforcement should be provided as a way of motivating the individual to store and later retrieve the new information. It is helpful to provide suggestions for storage of new information into memory to facilitate later retrieval. The activities should be kept relevant and meaningful so that they can be integrated into the individual's knowledge base. Finally, as ability to learn orally presented material, as opposed to written material, declines in persons over 70 of age, it is important to write down the instructions to ensure carryover. These factors can make a difference in the outcome with hearing aids and should be considered when fitting older adults with hearing aids. Table 6–5 contains tips to be shared with the new hearing aid user to facilitate adjustment.

SUMMARY

Hearing aids are the intervention of choice for older adults with late onset sensorineural hearing loss. Older adults derive dramatic benefit from hearing aids in the communicative and psychosocial domains of

Table 6–5. Helpful hints for adjusting to hearing aids.

■ Allow yourself time to adjust to hearing aids.

■ Take advantage of services offered by the audiologist.

■ Do not become discouraged if the hearing aid does not restore hearing to normal—return to the audiologist for reassurance and counseling about realistic expectations. Understand that hearing aids WILL NOT restore hearing capabilities to normal.

■ Allow time to adjust—hearing aids do require time for adaptation and to attain maximum performance potential.

■ Gradually adjust to loud incoming signals by first using the hearing aid in quiet and in small groups, later moving to larger, less favorable listening situations.

■ Understand your audiogram in terms of the particular speech sounds and words which may be problematic. This will help you make sense of some of the misunderstandings that are likely to occur.

■ Understand that hearing aids will not filter out all background noise and that certain listening environments will continue to present a significant listening challenge.

■ Tell people that you have a hearing loss and ask for repetition if the speech of others is unclear.

■ Participate in group hearing aid orientation programs as a supplement to individual hearing aid follow-up appointments.

---

function. Unfortunately, the stigma associated with hearing aid use in older adults continues to thwart decisions regarding hearing aid purchase. Audiologists must concentrate their efforts on dispelling the myths surrounding hearing aid use and benefit, and work closely with physicians and other health professionals to encourage a trial period with hearing aids. Anecdotal reports suggest that, once older adults have positive communication experiences with hearing aids, they tend to embrace the technology. It is important to emphasize that the hearing aid industry is undergoing significant technological advances, and adults who previously were not candidates should reconsider hearing aids as an option. The positive experiences of older adults in terms of enhanced quality of life is testimony to their value among the large and growing population of older individuals who are hearing impaired.

References

Abrams, H., Chisolm, T., Guerreiro, S., & Ritterman, S. (1992). The effects of intervention strategy on self-perception of hearing handicap. *Ear and Hearing, 13*, 371–377.

Agnew, J. (1996). Hearing aid adjustments through potentiometer and switch options. In M. Valente (Ed.), *Hearing aids: Standards, options and limitations.* New York: Thieme Medical Publishers.

American Speech-Language-Hearing-Association. (1994). *Audiology Update, 13,* 17.

Bender, D., & Mueller, H. G. (1984). Factors influencing the decision to obtain amplification. *Asha, 26,* 120.

Bentler, R. (1994). Future trends in verification strategies. In M. Valente (Ed.), *Strategies for selecting and verifying hearing aid fitting* (pp. 343–346). New York: Thieme Medical Publishers.

Bentler, R., Niebuhr, D., Getta, J., & Anderson, C. (1993). Longitudinal study of hearing aid effectiveness. II: Subjective measures. *Journal of Speech and Hearing Research, 36,* 820–831.

Bess, F. (1995). Applications of the Hearing Handicap Inventory for the Elderly—Screening version (HHIE-S). *The Hearing Journal, 48,* 51–57.

Bess, F., Lichtenstein, M., & Logan, S. (1989). Hearing impairment as a determinant of function in the elderly. *Journal of the American Geriatrics Society 37,* 123–128.

Bienfeld, D. (1990). Psychology of aging. In D. Bienfeld (Ed.), Clinical geropsychiatry (3rd ed.) Baltimore: Williams & Wilkins.

Chmiel, R., & Jerger, J. (1994, April). *Impact of hearing aid on the quality of life of hearing impaired elderly.* Poster session presented at the annual meeting of the American Academy of Audiology.

Chmiel, R., & Jerger, J. (1995). Quantifying improvement with amplification. *Ear and Hearing, 16,* 166–175.

Cox, R. (1995, April). IHAFF. Paper presented at the annual meeting of the American Academy of Audiology, Dallas, TX.

Cox, R., & Alexander, G. (1995). The abbreviated profile of hearing aid benefit. *Ear and Hearing, 16,* 176–186.

Ebinger, K., Holland, S., Holland, J., & Mueller, G. (1995, April). *Using the APHAB to assess benefit from CIC hearing aids.* Poster session presented at the Annual Meeting of the American Academy of Audiology, Dallas, TX.

Fino, M., Bess, F. , Lichtenstein, M., & Logan, S. (1991). Factors differentiating elderly hearing aid wearers and non-wearers. *Hearing Instruments, 43,* 6–10.

Gatehouse, S. (1994). Components and determinants of hearing aid benefit. *Journal of the American Academy of Audiology, 15,* 30–49.

Hartke, R. (1991). The aging process: Cognition, personality and coping. In R. Hartke (Ed.), *Psychological aspects of geriatric rehabilitation.* Gaithersburg, MD: Aspen Publications.

Hearing Instruments Association. (1994). Washington, DC: Author

Hyde, A., & Riko, B. (1994). A decision-analytic approach to audiological rehabilitation. In J. P. Gagne & N. T. Murray (Eds.), Research in audiological rehabilitation: Current trends and future directions. *Journal Academy of Rehabilitative Audiology, 27*(Suppl.), 337–375.

Jerger, J., Chmiel, R., Florin, E., Pirozzolo, F., & Wilson, N. (1996). Comparison of conventional amplification and assistive listening devices in elderly persons. *Ear and Hearing, 17*, 490–504.

Jerger, J., Silman, S., Lew, H., & Chmiel, R. (1993). Case studies in binaural interference: Converging evidence from behavioral and electrophysiologic measures. *Journal of the American Academy of Audiology, 4*, 122–131.

Kemp, B. (1990). The psychosocial context or geriatric rehabilitation. In K. Kemp, K. Brummel-Smith, & J. Ramsdell (Eds.), *Geriatric rehabilitation*, (pp. 41–61.) Boston: Little, Brown and Co.

Killion, M., Staab, W., & Preves, D. (1990). Classifying automatic signal processors. *Hearing Instruments, 41*, 24–26.

Kirkwood, D. (1994). *Hearing Journal Report, 47*, 7–8.

Kochkin, S. (1992). Market Trak III: Higher hearing aid sales don't signal better market penetration. *The Hearing Journal, 45*, 47–54.

Kochkin, S. (1993). MarkeTrak III: The billion dollar opportunity in the hearing instruments market. *The Hearing Journal, 46*, 35–38.

Kochkin, S. (1994). Optimizing the emerging market for completely-in-the-canal instruments. *The Hearing Journal, 47*, 1–6.

Kochkin, S. (1997). MarkeTrak IV norms: Subjective measures of satisfaction and benefit: Establishing norms. In B. Weinstein, (Ed.), *Seminars in Hearing, 18*, 37–48.

Kuk, F. (1993). Clinical consideration in fitting a multimemory hearing aid. *American Journal of Audiology, 2*, 23–27.

Malinoff, R., & Weinstein, B. (1989). Measurement of hearing aid benefit in the elderly. *Ear and Hearing, 10*, 354–356.

Maslow, A. (1954). *Motivation and personality*. New York: Harper and Row.

McCandless, G. (1994). Overview and rationale of threshold based hearing aid selection procedures. In M. Valente (Ed.)., *Strategies for selecting and verifying hearing aid fittings* (pp. 1–19), New York, NY: Thieme-Medical Publishers.

McCarthy, P., Montgomery, A., & Mueller, G. (1990). Decision making in rehabilitative audiology. *Journal of the American Academy of Audiology, 1*, 23–30.

Molloy, D., & Lubinski, R. (1995). Dementia: Impact and clinical perspectives. In R. Lubinski (Ed.), *Dementia and communication* (pp. 2–22), San Diego: Singular Publishing Group.

Montgomery, A. (1994). Treatment efficacy in adult audiological rehabilitation. In J. P. Gagne & N. T. Murray (Eds.), Research in audiological rehabilitation: Current trends and future directions. *Journal of the Academy of Rehabilitative Audiology, 27*(Suppl.), 317–337.

Mueller, G. (1994a). Getting ready for the IHAFF protocol. *The Hearing Journal, 47*, 46–48.

Mueller, G. (1994b). Small can be good too! *The Hearing Journal, 47*, 11.

Mueller, G., & Killion, M. (1990). An easy method for calculating the articulation index. *Hearing Journal, 43*, 14–17.

Mulrow, C., Auilar, C., Endicott, J., Tuley, M., Velez, R., Charlip, W., Rhodes, M., Hill, J., & Denino, L. (1990). Quality of life changes and hearing impairment: Results of a randomized trial. *Annals of Internal Medicine, 113,* 188–194.

Mulrow, C., Michael, T., & Aguilar, C. (1992). Correlates of successful hearing aid use in older adults. *Ear and Hearing, 13,* 108–113.

Mulrow, C., Tuley, M., & Aguilar, C. (1992). Sustained benefit of hearing aids. *Journal of Speech and Hearing Research, 35,* 1402–1405.

Nerbonne, M., Christman, W., & Fleschner, C. (1995, April). *Comparing objective and subjective measures of hearing aid benefit.* Poster presentation at the 1995 Convention of the American Academy of Audiolgy, Dallas, TX.

Newman, C., Hug, G., Wharton, G., & Jacobson, G. (1993). The influence of hearing aid cost on perceived benefit in older adults. *Ear and Hearing, 14,* 285–289.

Newman, C., Jacobson, G., Hug, G., Weinstein, B., & Malinoff, R. (1991). Practical method for quantifying hearing aid benefit in older adults. *Journal of the American Academy of Audiology, 2,* 70–75.

Newman, C., & Weinstein, B. (1988). The Hearing Handicap Inventory for the Elderly as a measure of hearing aid benefit. *Ear and Hearing, 9,* 81–85.

Office of Technology Assessment. (1978). Assessing the efficacy and safety of medical technologies. (OTA Rep. No. 11–75). Washington, DC: Congress of the United States, Office of Technology Assessment.

Olswang, L., Thompson, R., Warren, S., & Minghetti, N. (1990). *Treatment efficacy research in communication disorders.* Rockville, MD: American Speech-Language-Hearing Foundation.

Primeau, R. (1997). Hearing aid benefit in adults and older adults. In B. Weinstein (Ed.), *Seminars in Hearing, 18,* 29–36.

Radcliffe, D. (1991). Programmable hearing aids: Digital control comes to analog amplification. *The Hearing Journal, 44,* 9–12.

Ramsdell, J. (1990). A rehabilitation orientation in the workup of general medical problems. In B. Kemp, K. Brummel-Smith, & J. Ramsdell (Eds.), *Geriatric rehabilitation.* (pp. 23–41). Boston: College-Hill Press.

Ross, M. (1995a). Developments in research and technology. *SHHH, 16,* 32–34.

Ross, M. (1995b). Developments in technology. *SHHH, 16,* 25–26.

Schum, D. (1992). Validation of self-assessment scales as outcome measures in hearing aid fitting. *Seminars in Hearing, 14,* 326–337.

Schum, D. (1994). Personal adjustment counseling. *Journal of the American Academy of Audiology, 27,* 223–237.

Silman, S., Gelfand, S., & Silverman, C. (1984). Late onset auditory deprivation: Effects of monaural versus binaural aids. *Journal of the Acoustical Society of America, 76,* 1357–1362.

Stach, B. (1990). Hearing aid amplification and central processing disorders. In R. E. Sandlin (Ed.), *Handbook of hearing aid amplification: Vol. II. Clinical considerations and fitting practices.* Austin, TX: Singular Publishing Group.

Stach, B., & Stoner, R (1991). Sensory aids for the hearing-impaired elderly. In D. Ripich (Ed.), *Handbook of geriatric communicaiton disorders.* Austin, TX: PRO-ED.

Stephens, S., & Hetu, R. (1991). Impairment, disability and handicap in audiology: Towards a consensus. *Audiology, 30*, 185–200.

Swan, I., & Gatehouse, S. (1990). Factors influencing consultation for management of hearing disability. *British Journal of Audiology, 24*, 155–160.

Taylor, K. (1993). Self-perceived and audiometric evaluations of hearing aid benefit in the elderly. *Ear and Hearing, 14*, 390–395.

Vanderbilt/VA Hearing Aid Conference 1990 Consensus Statement: Recommended components of a hearing aid selection procedure for adults. In G. Studebaker, F. Bess, & L. Beck (Eds.), *The Vanderbilt Hearing Aid Report II*. Maryland: York Press.

Ventry, I., & Weinstein, B. (1982). The Hearing Handicap Inventory for the Elderly: A new tool. *Ear and Hearing, 3*, 128–134.

Waltzman, S., Cohen, N., & Shapiro, B. (1993). The benefits of cochlear implantation in the geriatric population. *Otolaryngology—Head and Neck Surgery, 108*, 329–333.

World Health Organization. (1980). *International classification of impairments, disabilities and handicaps (ICIDH)*. Geneva: author.

7

Assistive Listening Devices for the Elderly

M. Kathleen Pichora-Fuller, Ph.D.

INTRODUCTION

The assistive listening technology that may be useful for seniors is merely a subset of the assistive listening technology that may be useful for hard of hearing individuals of any age (for reviews see Compton, 1993; Garstecki, 1994; Montano, 1994). Some technology that is useful to younger adults may be prohibitively complex or unmanageable for elderly individuals. Nevertheless, it is not so much that the technology used to assist the elderly differs from that used to assist younger adults, but more that there is an age-related difference in some of the factors governing how the technology is chosen, how it is incorporated into service delivery programs, and how it is used by seniors themselves. This chapter describes various assistive listening devices (ALDs) within the context of a health promotion approach to the planning of hearing accessibility programs for seniors living in the community and in institutions. It is argued that there needs to be a paradigm shift away from the provision of traditional audiological rehabilitation to individuals toward the development of hearing accessibility programs for communities or groups of hard of hearing listeners. A facility or service is "accessible" if conditions exist that allow it to be utilized by a person who is disabled to the same extent that it is utilized by the general public. To accomplish the paradigm shift, audiologists must learn to work in a reconfigured team that consists of consumer and community groups, new commercial partners who design and market ALDs, new interdisciplinary professional partners such as acoustical engineers who design acoustical environments, and electrical or biomedical engineers who design ALDs (Pichora-Fuller, 1994; Robards-Armstrong & Stone, 1994). On an organizational level, many different professional associations, consumer groups, manufacturers, and distributors are concerned with hearing accessibility (see Resource List at the end of the chapter.) In the future, it will become increasingly important for these various organizations and their individual members to coordinate efforts to achieve the common goal of hearing accessibility.

Within the health promotion approach, programs target a combination of changes in behavior and changes in the environment that are conducive to the promotion of well-defined health goals. The well-defined health goal of interest here is hearing accessibility for seniors. Traditional audiological rehabilitation has focused on the evaluation of the needs and abilities of the hard of hearing individual in a clinical, laboratory-like context and has sought to change the behaviors of the individual, who is largely viewed as an isolated entity. In contrast, hearing accessibility programs employing a population-based health promotion approach would be more ecological (see Jennings & Head, 1994; Pichora-Fuller & Robertson, 1994, in press). Such programs would address the aspirations, needs, and abilities of targeted groups of listeners within the context of specific communication activities with specific groups of communication partners in specific communication environments. Solutions would entail behavioral changes on the part of the hard of hearing individuals and/or their communication partners as well as changes to the physical and social environment. Behavioral changes would include the use of appropriate amplification, personal assistive technology, and communication strategies. Factors that predispose, enable, and reinforce changes in behavior related to the use of ALDs would be emphasized. Environmental changes would include the use of institutional assistive technology, modifications to the physical environment and the provision of the necessary support by professionals and by society in general. This chapter describes available assistive listening technology; and in addition, by adopting a health promotion perspective, it provides a framework for the planning, implementation, and evaluation of hearing accessibility programs.

APPLYING A HEALTH PROMOTION MODEL
TO ACHIEVE HEARING ACCESSIBILITY

A simple definition of health promotion is "the combination of educational and environmental supports for actions and conditions of living conducive to health" (Green & Kreuter, 1991, p. 4). One of the most widely applied models of health promotion is Green and Kreuter's 1991 PRECEDE-PROCEED model (see Figure 7–1). Their model is generic and adaptable enough to be applied to any sector of health care. Therefore, it can readily be applied to the planning and evaluation of hearing accessibility programs that incorporate assistive listening technology. Two important aspects of the model are that (a) before implementing a pro-

Precede

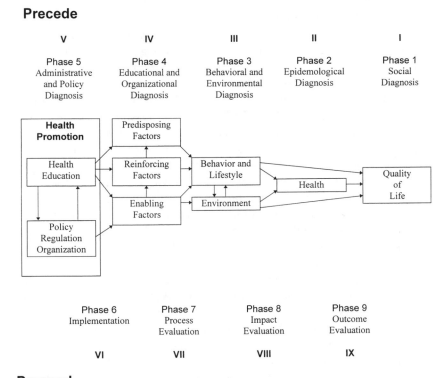

V	IV	III	II	I
Phase 5 Administrative and Policy Diagnosis	Phase 4 Educational and Organizational Diagnosis	Phase 3 Behavioral and Environmental Diagnosis	Phase 2 Epidemological Diagnosis	Phase 1 Social Diagnosis

Phase 6 Implementation	Phase 7 Process Evaluation	Phase 8 Impact Evaluation	Phase 9 Outcome Evaluation
VI	VII	VIII	IX

Proceed

Figure 7–1. Overview of the PRECEDE-PROCEED health promotion program planning and evaluation model. Note that the arrows illustrate some possible relationships between components of the models; however, the absence of arrows does not preclude the possibility that other relationships between the components might exist. (Adapted from *Health Promotion Planning: An Educational and Environmental Approach* by L. W. Green and M. W. Kreuter, 1991, p. 24, Mountain View, CA: Mayfield, with permission.)

gram, a rigorous program planning exercise needs to be conducted (PRECEDE), and (b) implementation of the program and its evaluation will naturally circle back (PROCEED) to the factors that shaped the design of the program during the planning process.

As shown in Figure 7–1, PRECEDE begins in Phase 1 with a *social diagnosis* in which the program planner assesses the quality of life issues that are important to the targeted community. Typically, these issues are identified through a study of the social and economic needs and aspirations of the members of the community (e.g., comfort, self-esteem, happiness, achievement, performance). During Phase 2, the *epidemiological diagnosis*, the program planner attempts to map the social goals or problems defined by the community in Phase 1 onto specific health goals. Typically, the planner considers existing demographic or clinical data concerning potentially relevant health issues (e.g., physiological measures of health problems, indicators of disability, risk patterns, prevalence of disease). In Phase 3, the *behavioral and environmental diagnosis*, the planner creates an inventory of all of the behavioral and environmental factors that might be linked to the health issues of greatest concern. In Phase 4, the *educational and organizational diagnosis*, the planner categorizes the inventory of potentially linked factors into those that predispose, enable, or reinforce behavioral and environmental changes that will result in the achievement of the health and, ultimately, the quality of life goals. Predisposing factors include knowledge, attitudes, beliefs, values, and perceptions that relate to a targeted change. Enabling factors are skills, resources, or barriers that relate to a targeted change. Reinforcing factors are rewards and feedback following a targeted change that support its continuation. This analysis culminates in the planner prioritizing the factors according to their relative importance to the program goals and the relative likelihood that change will be realized. Factors that are important and highly likely to result in targeted changes are given the highest priority. In Phase 5, the *administrative and policy diagnosis*, the planner reconciles program plans with policy and resource limitations. Planning then PROCEEDs to program *implementation* in Phase 6. Implementation entails the selection of strategies and methods, staff allocation, and the commencement of program organizational processes. Phases 7, 8, and 9 concern the *evaluation of program process, impact,* and *outcome,* respectively. These final three evaluation phases circle back to the planning done in the PRECEDE phases to determine if the objectives and criteria set out during planning are successfully met by the program.

ASSESSING HEARING ACCESSIBILITY NEEDS
IN TERMS OF QUALITY OF LIFE ISSUES

In Phase 1 of the PRECEDE-PROCEED model, the social diagnosis phase, program planning, begins by considering the quality of life issues of concern to the targeted community. Within the context of the quality of life and health issues that are identified in the initial phase of program planning, we may well discover that hearing accessibility is an implicit health concern even though it may not be an explicit health concern. So, for example, seniors may say that they have trouble "getting around." A quality of life issue such as "getting around" likely maps onto a variety of health issues, one of which might be hearing loss, or, more to the point, lack of hearing accessibility. For example, we might find that seniors have trouble getting around because they cannot hear on the telephone when they are trying to arrange for special needs transportation or because they cannot understand the directions that are given to them by bus drivers or information agents employed by public transportation systems. Seniors may not readily volunteer that they need an ALD for the telephone; rather they would tell us that they feel trapped at home and they might elaborate that they feel that they cannot call the transportation service for the handicapped with confidence. Hearing loss may be the root of these particular problems, although the seniors may not directly identify hearing loss as a major concern or the direct source of their problem.

One reason why hearing may not be stated as an explicit concern, even though it may be apparent as an implicit concern, is that people with presbycusis typically have lost their hearing slowly over the course of aging. They are likely to be unaware of the extent of their hearing impairment or perhaps even that they have a hearing impairment or that hearing health care options are available (Garstecki, 1990). Traditionally, we have asked questions directly about whether or not people have trouble hearing or about how hearing loss affects them in one situation or another. In a study of how people attribute difficulty in understanding conversation to problem sources, it was found that only about 3% of the problem sources that were generated specifically made reference to impairments of hearing or vision (Pichora-Fuller & Kirson, 1994). Consistent with these findings, in the clinic we often hear hard of hearing individuals say that their problem is not so much that they cannot hear or understand, but rather that they find it tiring or effortful to listen or that they do not enjoy listening. Within the health promotion framework, where we ask directly about daily living and indirectly determine if loss of hearing may be a health factor that contributes to handicap, we are more likely to define program goals that are meaningful. From the point of view of improving quality of life, assistive listening technology may be incorporated into a program in an effort to relieve stress or fatigue or to increase the enjoyment of listening in the everyday life activities of seniors.

The health promotion approach, which begins with an appraisal of quality of life issues, contrasts with the usual perspective of rehabilitative audiologists, which begins with an appraisal of perceptual impairment (see also McKellin, 1994). In recent years, audiologists have become increasingly aware of the importance of the trio of concepts that have been defined by the World Health Organization (WHO, 1993): handicap, disability, and impairment (for reviews Giolas, 1990; Hyde & Riko, 1994; Schow & Gatehouse, 1990; see Stephens & Hétu, 1991). Impairment is defined as a physical, physiological, or anatomical loss or abnormality of function (e.g., loss of ability to detect sound); *disability* is defined as the loss or reduction of normal ability resulting from impairment (e.g., a disability related to difficulty perceiving speech); *handicap* is defined as the detrimental effect that a disability has on an individual's life, especially on the activities or roles he or she normally performs. It is interesting that most discussions of these concepts by audiologists begin with impairment, map impairment onto disability, and then map disability onto handicap. Within the health promotion framework, we would begin with handicap or quality of life issues (What difficulties do seniors encounter in their everyday lives?), and then we would try to translate those difficulties into more specific disabilities or particular health issues (What component behaviors, such as understanding speech on the telephone, do they have trouble performing?), and finally we might identify related impairments (Does impaired hearing account for some of the relevant disabilities?).

DETERMINING THE NEED FOR A HEARING ACCESSIBILITY PROGRAM

In Phase 2, the epidemiological diagnosis, the program planner gathers relevant health, illness, or disability data and associated demographic data. These data are used to estimate how many people are eligible and how many are likely to participate in a program. For the purposes of planning a model program for seniors living in residential care facilities, relevant data might be that as many as 90% of institutionalized elderly have a hearing loss (Hull & Griffin, 1989). Therefore, we might expect that most senior residents in care facilities might benefit from a hearing accessibility program. Other relevant data might be that, for seniors living in institutions, less than 15% have normal cognitive function, 67% have dementia, and the remainder have cognitive deficits other than dementia (Canadian Study of Health and Aging Working Group, 1994). Based on these population data, we might expect that few residents would be able to engage in the self-initiated behaviors that would be required in some kinds of programs. The planned accessibility program would be designed with an expected targeted audience in mind. For example, in a program targeting the 15% of the institutional residents who are hearing impaired but not cognitively impaired, it would be reasonable to expect the active participation of residents. In contrast, in a program targeting all hearing impaired residents regardless of their cognitive status, it would be reasonable to emphasize solutions that do not require the active participation of residents, such as training communication partners or modifying the environment. Population data can be useful in guiding the initial phases of program planning for residents of a specific institution, and such data will also be important later when policymakers consider the feasibility of implementing programs on a more widespread basis. Nevertheless, the program planner will still need to gather specific information about the characteristics of the specific subgroup for whom the program is being planned. For example, the hearing and cognitive status of the residents of a specific institution will probably need to be assessed. Additionally, for the targeted group, the program planner might need to find out what communication situations (activities and environments) are important to program participants in their everyday life at the institution and whether or not they encounter difficulties in those important situations (see Pichora-Fuller & Robertson, 1994). Finally, the program planner might gather data that would help in determining the level of performance to be targeted by an accessibility program.

SETTING OBJECTIVES FOR CHANGES IN BEHAVIOR

Phase 3 of the PRECEDE-PROCEED model is concerned with the identification of the behavioral and environmental changes that will be targeted by the program. This phase is central to the present chapter.

Listeners' Behaviors

To achieve hearing accessibility, the listener must adopt new behaviors. Obviously, many seniors with hearing loss will be candidates for amplification, and many new behaviors will be learned as they become competent hearing aid users (see Chapter 6). As described in Chapter 5, in addition to age-related peripheral hearing loss, many seniors will also suffer from central auditory processing and/or cognitive deficits that will affect their ability to understand spoken language, especially when the listening conditions are noisy, as they often are in everyday life (see Committee on Hearing, Bioacoustics and Biomechanics, Working Group on Speech Understanding and Aging [CHABA], 1988; Crandell, Henoch, & Dunkerson, 1991; Grimes, 1995; Helfer, 1991; Willott, 1991).

Hearing aids are beneficial in ideal listening conditions, such as when a single, familiar talker is speaking clearly on a familiar topic in a quiet place where there are no competing distractions. However, in everyday life, listening conditions are often less than ideal. For example, imagine a dinner party scenario where there could be a number of unfamiliar talkers (the neighbors of the daughter of a senior), with unclear speech (partly because they are talking while eating), who are rapidly alternating turns on a number of rapidly changing topics (some of which are unfamiliar), while background music is playing, and there are competing distractions (misbehaving grandchildren). In noisy listening conditions, hearing aids will be of limited benefit (Plomp, 1978). In addition, many seniors with good hearing, who are not candidates for hearing aids, have little difficulty in ideal listening situations, but they experience difficulty in nonideal listening conditions such as the one depicted in the dinner party scenario (see CHABA, 1988; Willott, 1991). In contrast to hearing aids, assistive listening technology can be extremely useful in adverse listening conditions, at least to the extent that ALDs will enhance the signal-to-noise ratio (S:N). Assistive listening technology may be used instead of or in conjunction with a hearing aid. Because assistive technology is effective in improving the S:N, it is also of potential benefit to seniors with no clinically significant pure-tone threshold elevation.

To become a successful user of assistive listening technology, the individual will need to learn when and how to use the equipment and how to maintain it. Along with acquiring new skills, successful ALD users will usually also need to modify their attitudes and self-image, becoming comfortable with the idea that they are using a piece of technology that will be even more conspicuous and less familiar than a conventional hearing aid. Many of the changes in the listeners' behaviors will be directly related to their use of specific pieces of equipment. The types of ALDs and changes in behavior directly related to their use are described first and then other behaviors less directly related to the use of specific equipment are described.

ALDs and Behaviors Specific to the Use of Equipment

ALDs can be categorized according to the situation where the technology is used: (a) telephone devices, (b) television devices, (c) room systems, (d) nonconventional hearing aids, and (e) alerting devices (see also Montano, 1994). In all of these situations there is a sound source, there is transmission of the signal through an environment or medium, and there is delivery of the signal to the receiver. Within each category of ALDs, there are devices that differ in terms of how the acoustical signal is transmitted and delivered. Like hearing aids, some ALDs amplify the acoustical signal. If the wanted acoustical signal is transmitted in a noisy environment, the amplifying device will pick up both the wanted signal and unwanted background noise. Furthermore, if the signal is transmitted in a large room or a room with hard walls, the signal will be distorted by reverberation (for a discussion of the consequences of this to the elderly, see Plomp & Duquesnoy, 1980). To achieve transmission of a signal through a noisy or reverberant (echoic) environment, without it being distorted by reverberation, and without interference from unwanted background noise, it is advantageous to convert the acoustical signal to a nonacoustical signal, such as a magnetic, infrared, or FM signal. Such nonacoustical signals can be transmitted free of the adverse acoustical affects of noise and reverberation. Once the signal is successfully transmitted to the position of the listener, it can then be reconverted into an acoustical signal to be delivered to the listener. Most listeners, even those who do not require amplification, would benefit from the use of a device that preserves S:N in adverse listening conditions. In such conditions, seniors who wear hearing aids or need amplification would benefit from a device that both preserves S:N and amplifies. For those whose residual hearing is insufficient for them to be able to identify acoustical signals, other devices can be used that deliver a visual or tactual signal as a substitute for the acoustical signal. The application of these methods of transmitting and delivering signals will be illustrated in the following generic descriptions of some of the more common types of ALDs that are available for use in each of the situation-specific categories. Details regarding specific products can be obtained from manufacturers and distributors of ALDs (see Resource List).

Note that the term *communication aid* predates the term *assistive listening device* (Riko, Cummings, & Alberti, 1979). The term *rehabilitative technology for the hearing impaired* is considered by some to be more appropriate than the term *assistive listening device* because some devices employ visual or tactile representations of acoustical signals such that the message receiver is no longer required to listen (Montano, 1994). I have chosen to apply the term *assistive listening device* to all of the technology discussed in this chapter, including devices that use visual or tactile modes of signal delivery, for three reasons: (1) the purpose of the devices is to assist people who would otherwise experience difficulty listening; (2) ALDs may be used by individuals, especially older individuals listening in adverse environments, even though they are not considered to have clinically significant hearing impairments; and (3) other chapters in this book describe devices whose purpose is to assist individuals who would otherwise have difficulty seeing or speaking or using language to communicate.

TELEPHONE DEVICES. By far the most widely used and popular ALD is an amplifier that is built into the telephone handset and operated by a simple volume control. When the listener adjusts the volume control, the sound level of the signal is varied. In many localities, customers are able to trade in their regular handset for one with an amplifier, either for free or for a small cost, if they rent equipment from the telephone company. Handset amplifiers may also be bought by individuals who purchase rather than rent their telephone, although handset amplifiers are not an option on all telephones. It is also possible to purchase portable telephone amplifiers that attach to the receiver of the telephone handset.

In addition to emitting a sound signal, telephone receivers also emit an electromagnetic signal that can be picked up by a magnetic induction coil such as the telecoil operated by the telephone switch (T-switch) on a hearing aid. Individuals who wear a behind-the-ear hearing aid and wish to use their T-switch with the telephone need to be instructed on how to use the equipment. They will need to realize that it is necessary to hold the telephone to the case of the hearing aid where the telecoil is located. It would be incorrect to hold the phone to the ear as is done by people without hearing aids or to hold the phone to the hearing aid microphone as is done by some hearing aid users who do not have a T-switch on their hearing aid. They will also need to readjust the volume of the hearing aid to achieve a comfortable level for telephone listening when the T-switch is used. It should be noted that one reason for these readjustments is that the characteristics of the hearing aid when it picks up a magnetic signal through the telecoil are usually not the same as when it picks an acoustic signal through the hearing aid microphone.

For the early telephone receivers, the electromagnetic signal was simply a by-product of the telephone. In the early 1980s there was a wave of protest from hard of hearing consumers who used the hearing aid T-switch for telephone listening because innovations in telephone engineering during the 1970s virtually eliminated the electromagnetic by-product that they had come to rely on (Pichora-Fuller, 1981). Subsequently, the electromagnetic properties of the phone receiver were restored to enable use of the T-switch. In many localities the modified receivers are now mandatory on public telephone company equipment. Nevertheless, some older equipment may not be T-switch compatible, and seniors who have not updated equipment obtained in the 1970s or early 1980s may encounter difficulties when they try to use a hearing aid T-switch for telephone listening. In determining whether or not a receiver on rented telephone company equipment is T-switch compatible, it may be useful to check the color of the receiver by looking through the holes in the earpiece of the handset: The early compatible receivers are silver or gold in color, the later incompatible receivers are black, and the more recent modified T-switch compatible receivers are red. Alternatively, to determine whether or not a telephone receiver will be adequate for T-switch operation, a person could simply listen through a hearing aid set on the T-switch, or a magnetic field tester (Assistive Listening Device Systems, Inc., 1993) could be used to quantify the level of electromagnetic output of the phone and to compare the measured level to a criterion value. In circumstances in which the telephone does not produce a sufficient electromagnetic signal to allow the operation of a hearing aid telecoil, a portable converting device may be strapped onto the telephone as a temporary solution. The converting device picks up the acoustical signal from the telephone and converts it into an electromagnetic signal that may be delivered to a telecoil. This type of converting device may be useful for T-switch users when they travel in countries where the telephone receivers are not T-switch compatible.

In addition to simply amplifying the telephone message, the S:N may be enhanced when a hearing aid set on the T-switch is used for telephone listening. Because the microphone of the hearing aid is usually turned off when the T-switch is turned on, the electromagnetic signal is picked up but the acoustic signal is not, thereby eliminating interference by unwanted background noise from the environment. Many individuals with severe hearing loss choose to use a combination of devices on the telephone so that they can achieve a sufficient level of amplification and also benefit from an enhanced S:N. A common option is to combine a hearing aid set on the T-switch with a handset or portable amplifier. This combination is advantageous because when the acoustical signal is boosted by the amplifier, the accompanying electromagnetic signal is also boosted (Pichora-Fuller, 1981). It is important to carefully consider the potential use of the T-switch when a hearing aid is purchased because not all hearing aids feature a T-switch. In addition to telephone use, the hearing aid T-switch permits the use of many other ALDs that rely on electromagnetic signal transmission.

For those who have insufficient residual hearing to hear amplified telephone signals, visual presentation of telephone messages is widely used. A TT (text telephone), also sometimes called a TDD (telephone device for the deaf), allows the sender to type a message; the typed message is relayed and picked up by a TT terminal at the other end which displays the typed message. It is increasingly common for government offices and agencies to have telephone lines dedicated to TT use. Telephone communication between TT users and people without TT access is now available through message-relay services operated by telephone companies. In this situation, a telephone company operator receives a message typed by the TT user, then reads it aloud to the person who does not have a TT. In turn, the person who does not have a TT speaks a message and the operator types the message which is relayed as text to the TT user. It is also increasingly popular for people with hearing loss to use Fax (facsimile) machines and electronic mail if they require or prefer visual message transmission.

TELEVISION DEVICES. Hearing aid microphones are primarily intended to pick up sound from distances of up to about 8 feet (the typical distance between conversational partners). Those who wear hearing aids to watch TV but sit farther away than 8 feet may find that the signal is not sufficiently amplified. In addition, the greater the distance between the TV and the viewer, the more likely it is that there will be reverberation (echo) as the TV signal is acoustically transmitted across the room, and the viewer will be more likely to hear other noise sources in the room that will compete with the TV signal. A frequent complaint of family members is that hard of hearing people turn up the volume on the TV to an unpleasantly high level. Although amplifying the TV signal may improve the S:N, nonacoustic methods of signal transmission across the room will be even more effective in improving the S:N. Listeners may benefit from having extension loudspeakers deliver the TV sound signal at a position close to where they are sitting, or by using radios with TV band stations that can be placed nearby. In effect, these solutions allow the listener to put his or her ear close to the loudspeaker, thereby reducing the adverse effects of room acoustics and improving S:N. Alternatively, viewers may chose to wear earphones with volume controls for each ear or to connect their hearing aid to the TV by direct audio-input (a wire connected to the TV plugs into the hearing aid). The TV connections for earphones or direct audio-input can be wired so that viewers without hearing difficulties may hear the signal from the regular TV loudspeaker. Another method by which hearing aid wearers may choose to enhance the S:N that does not wire them directly to the TV is to use a magnetic loop to the TV. The loop (a wire) plugs into the TV at one end and the rest of its length is distributed around the room so that it is close to the listeners who wish to use it. The loop emits an electromagnetic signal that can be picked up by any listener wearing a hearing aid set on the T-switch. Those who do not have a hearing aid with a telecoil can pick up the signal through a headset receiver with a telecoil.

Other popular devices that can be used to transmit the TV sound signal by nonacoustic methods are frequency modulation (FM) and infrared (IR) systems. FM signals are transmitted like FM radio signals, and IR signals are transmitted as infrared light waves. FM and IR signals are not subject to interference from other sources of acoustic noise in the room or to room effects such as reverberation. In either the FM or IR systems, a transmitter unit is coupled to the TV (either by direct wiring or by microphone pick-up at the TV loudspeaker). The transmitter transduces the acoustical or electrical signal that is picked up from the TV and transmits it through the room as either an FM or an IR signal. The viewer wears an appropriate receiver that picks up the signal and transduces it back into an acoustical signal. The acoustical signal is delivered from the receiver unit to the viewer, who may choose to use one of a variety of possible headsets, direct audio-input, or magnetic loop coupling to a hearing aid with a telecoil.

Individuals with insufficient residual hearing to be able to understand TV programs may benefit from captioning, which has become widespread over the last two decades. A written version of what is said is added like a subtitle along the bottom of the TV image (TV listings indicate which shows are captioned by using a code or symbol such as "CC" for closed captioning). To see the captions, the viewer must have a decoder that is either attached or built into the TV.

ROOM SYSTEMS. In large public rooms, the talker and listener can be separated by greater distances. Therefore, loss of signal intensity over distance and the adverse effects of increased noise and reverberation are even more challenging for hard of hearing listeners in these situations, even for seniors with clinically normal audiograms (Nábelek & Robinson, 1982). Amplification of the signal through regular public address or sound reinforcing systems may be beneficial, although it has also been found that such systems sometimes create even more distortion of the signal (B. McKinnon, personal communication, 1996). For the same reasons that were described in the section on TV devices, it will usually be more beneficial to use a personal loop or an FM or IR system that uses a nonacoustical mode to transmit the signal across the room from the source to the listener.

The choice of which room system to use will depend on the nature of the activity and the room, with privacy and susceptibility to interference from unwanted sources being important issues (Laszlo, 1994). A major disadvantage of loop or FM systems is that there may be leakage from one room to the next. When an FM system is used in one room, it may be isolated from an FM system in the next room if the two systems are set to different channels. Success in isolating loop systems will depend on the strength of the electromagnetic signals they emit and the distance between the loops and the receivers. Furthermore, leakage makes it impossible to prevent eavesdropping. To overcome this problem, secure or private coding of FM signals is now being developed (C. Laszlo, personal communication, 1995). In the meantime, IR technology is the solution of choice to overcome leakage from room to room and to ensure privacy. IR systems are also less susceptible to interference from unwanted sources. Loops are susceptible to interference from other sources of electromagnetic interference (e.g., power lines or even computers). Because IR transmission employs a light signal, the transmission will not travel beyond the walls of a room. Also, new IR technologies have been developed that are not subject to interference from some light sources such as sunlight (C. Laszlo, personal communication, 1995).

For individuals who must rely on vision to understand what is said in large rooms, on-line captioning devices are often indispensable. Portable computers and software similar to familiar word-processing software have been adapted to facilitate on-line captioning. A captionist types what is said and the typed message is displayed on a second computer monitor that is positioned so that it can be seen by a hearing-impaired viewer. Alternatively, the typed message can be projected on a TV monitor or by an overhead projector-computer interface device so that a large number of hearing-impaired viewers may read the captions. If it is sufficient for the captionist to relay only the gist of what is being said, then a good dictatypist can act as the captionist. However, if it is important that the message be transcribed verbatim, a court reporter may be required to act as the captionist. It is also possible for prepared texts (e.g., sermons) to be uploaded from disk and simply scrolled on the screen, thereby making on-line typing unnecessary.

NONCONVENTIONAL HEARING AIDS. Nonconventional hearing aids or one-to-one communicators are a must in the tool-kit of those working with elderly individuals, especially when hearing aids are not available (lost or broken) or prohibitively complex, unmanageable, or too costly to be recommended. These devices pick up the speech signal by microphone and the signal is then delivered to the listener by a headphone.

The transmission between the microphone and the headphone may be accomplished by hard-wiring, loop, FM, or IR. The types of transmission are similar to what has been described for TV viewing or for listening in large rooms. One difference is that nonconventional hearing aids are used to assist one-to-one conversation; and therefore, their purpose is less to overcome distance and adverse room acoustics and more to provide amplification in conditions in which personal hearing aids cannot be used for one reason or another.

ALERTING DEVICES. This category of devices usually substitutes a visual or sometimes a tactile signal for an acoustical signal. Such devices are invaluable to seniors who would not otherwise be able to hear the ring of the telephone, the doorbell, the alarm clock, or the fire alarm. Such devices may be vital to ensure the safety and security of seniors. In care facilities, because so many residents would not hear a knock at the door, it becomes acceptable for visitors to enter rooms without the resident's permission and the expectation of privacy is abandoned. Alerting devices may be important in restoring a sense of privacy and control, especially for seniors living in care facilities.

Use of Compensatory Communication Behaviors

Although ALDs are invaluable for solving many problems of hearing accessibility, devices will not offer solutions in all circumstances and they will not restore communication function to normal. Communication will inevitably still fail some of the time. Users of ALDs, like users of hearing aids, must be trained to employ communication strategies that will allow them to optimize their performance when using ALDs and to successfully cope when the device fails either partially or totally.

Training programs have been developed to enable hard of hearing persons to communicate more effectively when using the telephone. For example, a useful strategy for a hard of hearing telephone user might be to repeat information so that the message sender can reply "yes" or "no" to verify that the information was heard correctly. Some training programs conducted by rehabilitative audiologists feature the use of telephone training devices that can simulate good and bad telephone lines. This kind of equipment can be used to construct practice sessions in which the ALD user is trained to use communication strategies to prevent and repair breakdowns in communication that might occur during telephone conversations (see Castle, 1978; Erber, 1985). It can also be used to evaluate various ALDs for a potential user of telephone devices (Hanusaik, Benguerel, & Laszlo, 1992) or to familiarize the telephone ALD user or potential user with the correct method of using the ALD and/or hearing aid with the telephone.

Similar to the approach used in training users of telephone devices, the idea of using simulations of more realistic listening conditions has also been employed by some rehabilitative audiologists who have been interested in developing the communication strategies of consumers who wish to use other kinds of assistive technology (see Fellendorf, 1982; Garstecki, 1988, 1994; Pichora-Fuller, 1985; Pichora-Fuller, Corbin, Riko, & Alberti, 1983; Riko et al., 1979). In clinics where audiologists offer rehabilitation services featuring ALDs, it is typical for such training to be conducted in specially designed rooms (other than sound-attenuating booths) that duplicate conditions like those that might be encountered in everyday life. Consumers can watch television using devices, experience listening with various room systems, or test alerting or other ALDs. Rather than just talking about these devices, it is important for rehabilitative audiologists to be able to evaluate devices with a potential user and to undertake hands-on training using actual devices in conditions that are as realistic as possible. In some instances, rather than in-clinic therapy, on-site consultation and therapy may be provided (see Jennings & Head, 1994). Such on-site work may be far more valuable than clinic-based work for seniors, especially for those who reside in homes for the aged. Sharing of experiences and mutual support among members of consumer groups may also play an invaluable role in providing consumers with concrete examples of how others are using ALDs in their everyday lives. These experiences can be shared in person or through other media such as books, videotapes, newsletters and journals, or even the internet (see Resource List).

Communication Partners' Behaviors

Traditional audiological rehabilitation has focused on services delivered to the hard of hearing individual. However, some rehabilitative audiologists have realized the importance of involving communication partners (see Erdman, 1993), and even training the primary communication partners (usually family members or nurses) in communication therapy (see Erber, 1988). Clearly, because ALDs are so unfamiliar to the general public, and especially because many elderly individuals will need considerable support in adjusting to the idea and the practical requirements of using ALDs, it is crucial that their primary communication partners cooperate and support the venture. Communication partners should understand the compatibilities and limitations of ALDs, and they should understand under what conditions ALDs should be used. Furthermore, partners may need to be able to help the hard of hearing person to put the device on and adjust it, or possibly to trouble-shoot problems. When FM or IR systems or nonconventional hearing aids are used, the involvement of communication partners is essential because they will need to operate the transmitting portion of the equipment. Communication partners also need to know how to modify their behaviors, employ helpful communication strategies, and support the behavioral changes that their hard of hearing partners are trying to make. Indeed, given the important relationship between communication and social interaction, instead of trying to assist hard of hearing elderly individuals to remain independent and not become dependent, we should actually be trying to assist them to remain successfully interdependent, at least insofar as it is important for them to achieve continued contact and communication with members of their social network (Janzen, 1995). Furthermore, the members of the social network of a hard of hearing person may experience reduced quality of life because of the hearing accessibility problems encountered by their partners during activities in which they participate together. Therefore, in a hearing accessibility program, communication partners are also called upon to change their behaviors.

Use of Personal Assistive Technology

Communication partners will need to learn new behaviors and to modify old behaviors to facilitate the use of personal ALDs. The following examples illustrate how the behaviors of partners might be changed to accommodate the use of specific types of ALDs. The partners of users of TT or telephone message relay services are obviously required either to own and operate a piece of transmitting equipment and/or to use special telephone company services. Less obviously, partners of T-switch users may need to learn to allow time for their hard of hearing partner to adjust the hearing aid for telephone use. The choice of an appropriate TV device will depend on whether or not the hard of hearing person wishes to watch TV alone or with partners and on whether or not the partners have good hearing. If a partner with good hearing wishes to watch TV with a hard of hearing partner, an appropriate device will be an ALD that amplifies and transmits the signal to the hard of hearing person without altering the regular transmission of the TV signal to the partner who has good hearing. Furthermore, the choice of an ALD for TV viewing will depend on the degree of conversational interaction that the partners wish to have while they are watching TV together. If partners wish to converse while watching TV, then the hard of hearing person must opt for an ALD that does not enhance the TV signal at the cost of cutting off ability to hear conversation. For example, hearing aid wearers may wish to use an audio-input ALD that can operate without interfering with the regular operation of the hearing aid microphone. As pointed out earlier, the success of room systems (loop, FM, IR) and one-to-one communicators or nonconventional hearing aids directly depends on the cooperation of the partner because the partner must wear or operate the transmitting portion of these devices during conversation. Many hard of hearing individuals who are willing to consider using personal ALDs reject options that place demands on partners because they do not wish to impose on or embarrass their partners. Therefore, to allow the widest range of choice of ALDs, an accessibility program would need to involve partners who are willing to adopt new behaviors.

Use of Compensatory Communication Strategies

Just as hard of hearing people must learn communication strategies that, when employed in conjunction with ALDs, will allow them to prevent or at least to repair communication breakdowns, so must their communication partners. Partners will benefit from training in the use of appropriate behaviors while using an ALD (e.g., proper use of a microphone) and also from training in the use of compensatory communication strategies (e.g., breaking a complex idea into short phrases or slowing the rate of speech). When the elderly hard of hearing person is mentally or physically unable to assume responsibility for making communication succeed, it is critical to train communication partners to modify their communication behaviors.

Therapies directed at training communication partners in communication strategies have been described (Erber, 1988, 1994a). Communication therapy involving partners has been successfully implemented in clinical practice (e.g., Feldbreugge, 1994), although such therapy is not widespread. One reason for the success of this kind of therapy is that partners are not passive receivers of knowledge; they actively practice new communication behaviors. Whereas it is common to distribute written materials describing hints for communicating with a hard of hearing person, these materials are frequently insufficient to trigger the desired changes in everyday behaviors. For partners to succeed in changing their behaviors, it is extremely useful for them to have an opportunity to practice and to receive support and guidance when they are learning how to improve their behaviors. Such guided practice is facilitated by the use of a hearing-loss simulator (HELOS), which allows the partner to experience what it might be like for a hard of hearing person to try to engage in conversation (Erber, 1988). HELOS is also used to train the partner to produce clearer speech and more easily understandable messages. In these therapy sessions, the clinician sits in for the hard of hearing person (the clinician listens to the speech of the partner after it has been processed by HELOS) and provides explicit feedback to the talker about what communication techniques have or have not been used successfully.

SETTING OBJECTIVES FOR CHANGES IN THE ENVIRONMENT

Phase 3 of the health promotion model is also concerned with the environmental changes that must accompany behavioral changes. At least four aspects of environmental change are important in a hearing accessibility program: (1) the adoption of institutional ALDs in public areas, (2) the modification of the physical (acoustic, light, electromagnetic) properties of rooms, (3) raising awareness of relevant properties of the environment, and (4) the evolution of the social environment.

Use of Institutional Technology

Hard of hearing individuals may purchase personal ALDs for home use or even for use at some public events. Nevertheless, most hard of hearing people attending public events will require ALDs that must be provided by the facility or institution. This is especially likely to be the case at public events that attract elderly participants because the majority of these participants will likely find that such events are not hearing accessible unless ALDs are used. It is the moral and often the legal responsibility of the management to offer ALDs that are appropriate to the event and meet the specific needs of the participants (for discussions on the Americans with Disabilities Act of 1990, see Garstecki, 1993; Spahr, 1992; see also Health and Welfare Canada, 1988). In general, institutional or public ALDs are similar or identical to the personal ALDs described earlier in this chapter. The following examples illustrate how ALDs may be used in public places.

Telephone Devices

Public phones are now regularly equipped with handset amplifiers. Many public services (e.g., police stations, hospitals) also offer TT lines. Business transactions (e.g., services of travel agents, insurance agents, home renovators) are routinely accomplished by fax for all customers, including hard of hearing customers. Information services (e.g., libraries, government offices) are now often accessible by electronic mail. The telecommunications field is perhaps the most truly hearing accessible of all sectors in society, and this kind of remote communication is potentially extremely important for the elderly who may live alone and/or be homebound.

Television Devices

Although we may think that TV viewing is primarily a private, home-based activity, in fact, TV (including videotapes) may be viewed by groups who are living in institutional facilities such as homes for the aged, or by groups participating in community-based activities such as public meetings. This medium is also a feature of places such as airports, waiting rooms in offices, sports bars, and museums. In all cases, these public purpose TVs should be hearing accessible. Probably the most common choice of ALD in these situations is a loop and a choice of tele-coil receivers. Captioning is another common choice.

Room Systems

Institutional room system ALDs such as loops, or FM and IR systems, are ideal for achieving hearing accessibility in public places such as the-aters, places of worship, conference or lecture halls, and auditoriums. In large rooms such as these, even seniors with normal audiograms often find listening difficult, because noise levels are high, reverberation times are long, and large distances separate listeners from the source of the signal. Many public facilities have installed one or more room systems, and most rent or lend compatible receivers to participants. Ideally, stan-dards for this equipment should be adopted so that hard of hearing par-ticipants can purchase personal receivers for use at a variety of public events, thereby relieving public facilities of the need to provide receiv-ing as well as transmitting equipment (for a discussion about the need for standards and universality, see Laszlo, 1994).

Nonconventional Hearing Aids

Nonconventional hearing aids, or one-to-one communicators, are invalu-able in situations where a hard of hearing person does not have an ade-quate hearing aid (e.g., the person may not own a hearing aid, there may have been a sudden change in hearing that has rendered a hearing aid inadequate, or the person's hearing aid may be missing or broken). There are many situations where service providers might find a one-to-one communicator useful (e.g., a fireman responding to an emergency call, a nurse doing triage at the emergency department of a hospital, a social worker interviewing a new resident at a home for the aged, or a speech-language pathologist testing a new client in an Alzheimer's assessment clinic). Furthermore, without the assistance of an ALD, the workers in the examples just described would be likely to raise their voices, resulting in vocal stress in the talker, annoyance to others in the vicinity, and violations of the privacy of the hard of hearing person.

Alerting Devices

Devices to alert hard of hearing seniors to emergency conditions (e.g., flashing lights that signal that a smoke detector has been activated) are an important example of the need for ALDs in public places. If the hearing abilities of a population in a facility are known, then audible warning signals can be chosen (Hétu & Tran Quoc, 1994; Tran Quoc, Hétu, & Laroche, 1992). Otherwise, visual signals must be substituted when warning signals are not audible to the targeted population.

Modification of Physical Environment

The acoustical, visual, and electromagnetic properties of the physical environment must be considered when ALDs are used (see Chapter 10).

Acoustical Environment

Because noise and reverberation present major obstacles to hearing accessibility, S:N enhancement is an important function of most ALDs. Nevertheless, ALDs are not perfectly successful in overcoming all acoustical obstacles. The reduction of noise and reverberation in the environment is an important part of the solution to many hearing accessibility problems. Modification of the acoustical environment will result in greater success when ALDs are used. It is even possible that, if communication environments are made sufficiently quiet, ALDs might not be required. Especially in communication environments where groups of elderly individuals participate and many participants need an ALD because the acoustical conditions are adverse, in the long run, it would be cost-effective to improve the acoustical conditions so that ALDs would not be required by so many people. The view that building quieter environments would be a better method of accomplishing hearing accessibility than would be distributing good, but imperfect and costly, ALDs to large numbers of seniors is akin to the argument that reducing industrial noise would be a superior method of eliminating noise-induced hearing loss than would be distributing ear protection to large numbers of workers. Just as it was never considered realistic for industry to totally eliminate noise as a hazard, it is probably equally unrealistic to expect that architects and acoustical engineers could design and build rooms to be totally hearing accessible. Nevertheless, improvements in room acoustics would certainly increase the ease of achieving hearing accessibility. Recent efforts concerning approaches to the modification of the environment to achieve hearing accessibility were discussed at special sessions on the topic of hearing accessibility that were held at the annual meeting of the Canadian Acoustical Association in Ottawa in October 1994 (see *Canadian Acoustics*, 22(3), 73–86) and at the 129th Meeting of the Acoustical Society of America held in Washington, D.C., in May 1995 (see Journal of the Acoustical Society of America, 97, 3261–3263). We can expect that in the future architectural standards will be developed that will result in the building of quieter communication environments, which will be more hearing accessible for seniors.

Visual Environment

The importance of the visual environment is less obvious, but also important, in relation to the ease of achieving hearing accessibility. Many hard of hearing elderly individuals will experience failing vision in conjunction with failing hearing (see Chapter 3), yet many will continue to rely heavily on speechreading and visual information to supplement audition (Erber, 1994b). In particular, we should not forget how important it is for the face of a talker to be well lit so that the ALD user will be able to speechread while listening with an ALD. It is interesting to note that, in addition to enhancing the reception of speech sound, the use of some ALDs, especially one-to-one communicators, may also improve comprehension because their use encourages the maintenance of eye contact during conversations, with a resulting increase in the ability of elderly listeners to speechread and to maintain attention during conversation.

Electromagnetic Environment

ALDs that incorporate a loop that picks up an electromagnetic transmission of the signal are subject to electromagnetic interference. Many hard of hearing individuals who use loops encounter problems in locations where there are architectural features or other technologies that produce strong electromagnetic fields. Computers and power lines are examples of sources of such interference. Over the years, problems due to electromagnetic interference have frequently puzzled hard of hearing people and their audiologists. Unaware of the presence of electromagnetic interference in a situation, rather than attributing problems with the performance of ALDs to a hostile environment, consumers and professionals alike tended to assume that the devices were unreliable. Such puzzles may be resolved with use of a magnetic field tester (Assistive Listening Device Systems, Inc., 1993) or with the assistance of engineers or consultants who are able to measure electromagnetic fields and recommend modifications to overcome high levels of electromagnetic interference that undermine the use of ALDs (see McKinnon, 1994).

Awareness of the Environment

Those who are unaware of the acoustical, visual, and electromagnetic properties of their environment and how these properties may affect their ability to communicate must be made aware if they are to fully understand which ALDs and communication strategies will or will not work in particular circumstances. At an institutional level, those planning hearing accessibility programs featuring ALDs would be well served by having acoustical and electromagnetic evaluations conducted by qualified personnel before making decisions about the selection of ALDs. At an individual level, an important goal of therapy is to enhance awareness of the environment as it relates to communication. Such awareness of the environment is necessary for individuals to be able to engage in the kinds of problem-solving that are taught during therapy. Knowledge of the effects of the environment on communication will guide the individual in selecting a physical location for communication (the living room over the kitchen at a friend's home; a small restaurant with carpet and upholstered furniture over a large open restaurant with wooden tables and floor surfaces), selecting a position within a room (sitting with a window at one's back so that sunlight falls on the face of the talker sitting across the table), and eliminating unnecessary and unwanted sources of noise (closing the door of a meeting room to eliminate hallway noise, or turning off a computer in an office to eliminate electromagnetic interference).

The Social Environment

It was argued earlier in this chapter that it is important for both hard of hearing individuals and their regular communication partners to change their communication behaviors when they begin to use ALDs.

However, hard of hearing people also interact with a multitude of strangers when they participate in public events or use public services. It follows that the public at large, and personnel employed by public institutions and commercial retailers in particular, need to be educated, trained, and sensitized so that they will adopt communication behaviors and attitudes that foster hearing accessibility (for a discussion of hearing impairment seen from a cultural perspective, see McKellin, 1994). New codes of behavior must be established to accompany new technology. Further discussion of how this might be done is offered in the section in this chapter on administrative and policy considerations.

PROMOTING CHANGES IN BEHAVIOR AND THE ENVIRONMENT

Phase 4 of the PRECEDE-PROCEED model, the educational and organizational diagnosis, is concerned with setting priorities among the potential changes in behavior or in the environment that may be targeted by the program. In this phase we also analyze the conditions under which the targeted changes are likely to be achieved. The decision to try an ALD and the selection of an appropriate device are necessary but not sufficient conditions for the success of a person with an ALD. Before an ALD can be used effectively, the hard of hearing person may need technical assistance to have the ALD installed, and he or she will certainly need to be trained to operate the device, to troubleshoot problems encountered in its operation, and to complement its use with appropriate communication strategies. These issues are akin to those surrounding the selection, evaluation, and fitting of hearing aids; however, for ALDs no standard procedures or practices have yet been developed and accepted (Laszlo, 1994). It is apparent that, despite the availability of very useful technology, hard of hearing people who seem to be candidates for the technology do not necessarily use it (Unger, 1994). Human rather than technological obstacles present the greatest challenge to those developing hearing accessibility programs. To ensure that hard of hearing seniors take advantage of ALDs, it is imperative that we discover the factors that predispose, enable, and reinforce them to become and remain users of ALDs (see also Noh, Gagné, & Kaspar, 1994). In the absence of any hard evidence as to what these factors are, we can only speculate about what some likely factors might be. These factors can be prioritized after an appraisal of which factors are most important to the goals of the program and which factors are the most changeable.

Factors That Predispose People to Use ALDs

Many factors are likely to predispose the use of ALDs by hard of hearing people, their communication partners, or institutions. Four examples of interrelated predisposing factors are (a) increasing consumer knowledge about ALDs, (b) creating a well developed delivery system for ALDs, (c) increasing the availability and acceptance of ALDs in public places, and (d) increasing the acceptance of ALDs by communication partners. There is no doubt that consumer education to increase awareness of ALD options is necessary because consumers will never try ALDs if they are not aware that there are such devices. Often even hard of hearing individuals who are long-time, regular hearing aid users lack knowledge of the ALDs that might be useful to them. Although there are various well developed hearing aid delivery systems in the world, there are only poorly developed systems for delivering ALDs. Furthermore, ALD delivery systems have not been combined with existing hearing aid delivery systems; otherwise, hearing aid users would be better informed about ALDs. Sometimes these individuals have invented their own ALDs, and they are almost always delighted to learn of and are then eager to try commercial ALDs. Others may be more reluctant to try something new even if they know about ALD options. The development of an ALD delivery system and an increase in the availability of ALDs will help to increase public awareness of ALDs. In addition, especially for those who are reluctant to become users of ALDs, increasing the availability of ALDs in public places is likely to promote and predispose the adoption of ALDs. Just as many individuals reject hearing aids because of the stigma associated with them, many will feel even more uncomfortable using less familiar ALD technology, especially in public places. We can expect that the widespread availability and acceptance of the use of ALDs in public places will help to change the stigma associated with such technology, thereby predisposing more people to use it. Furthermore, the acceptance of ALDs by communication partners, both familiar partners and strangers, will be necessary to predispose hard of hearing people to use ALDs (for a similar finding with regard to hearing aid use see Getty & Hétu, 1994).

Factors That Enable People to Use ALDs

Two examples of enabling factors are (1) creation of a well developed delivery system and (2) provision of funding for ALDs. It is clear that a system for delivering ALDs must be developed if we are to enable the use of ALDs by those who are predisposed to use them. The creation of a well developed delivery system, therefore, serves as both a predisposing and an enabling factor. Such a delivery system would include not only a way of selling products, but also the establishment of standards and procedures that could be used in selecting and evaluating ALDs for individuals and institutions. It would also include the provision of the accompanying training or consultation that is necessary to support the appropriate implementation and maintenance of ALDs. Recruiting the assistance of engineers and architects within this delivery system also seems likely to be necessary if we are to optimize the use of ALDs. Another obvious enabling factor is the funding of ALDs so that they can be purchased by seniors and/or by institutions serving seniors, especially as these individuals and institutions may have limited budgets. A related economic issue is how the ALD delivery system will be funded (for a discussion of financial issues, see Chapter 13). Note that funding serves as an enabling factor, although it is not considered to be a predisposing factor.

Factors That Reinforce the Use of ALDs

Four examples of reinforcing factors are: (a) increased acceptance of ALDs by partners, (b) provision of ongoing communication training, (c) provision of ongoing technical support, and (d) building of a consumer feedback mechanism into the delivery system that is developed. The acceptance and support of ALDs by familiar communication partners and by other members of society will reinforce the use of ALDs. This factor, therefore, serves both as a predisposing and a reinforcing factor. Continued training in the use of communication strategies that can be employed to achieve communication success will alleviate frustration with the necessarily imperfect performance of ALDs in some situations. Ongoing technical support and consulting from engineers will alleviate frustrations due to malfunctioning equipment or hostile environments that interfere with the proper functioning of ALDs. Perhaps most important, ALD use is likely to be reinforced if a feedback mechanism is established so that consumer comments about and reactions to ALDs can be communicated to institutions providing ALDs, deliverers of ALDs, and manufacturers of ALDs. Hard of hearing consumer groups will be invaluable in this feedback cycle.

ADMINISTRATIVE AND POLICY CONSIDERATIONS

Phase 5 of the PRECEDE-PROCEED model is concerned with administrative and policy issues related to the program. It is obvious that, at least at the present time, most ALD technology is very unfamiliar to hard of hearing people and to the public at large—vastly more unfamiliar than conventional hearing aids. Unlike hearing aids, there are no standard clinical procedures for selecting or evaluating ALDs, nor are there even manufacturers' standards that would protect consumers from purchasing poorly made products (Laszlo, 1994). As described previously, the development of effective ALD delivery systems would serve to predispose, enable, and reinforce the use of ALDs. Just as hearing aid delivery systems have developed in various localities, various ALD delivery systems are also likely to be developed (Montano, 1994; Vaughn, Lightfoot, & Arnold, 1981). The form that such systems will take will be influenced by administrative and policy decisions and sometimes even by legislation such as the Americans with Disabilities Act (Garstecki, 1993; Spahr, 1992). Local administrative and policy decisions will also guide the planning, implementation, and evaluation of hearing accessibility programs for seniors. Most important, the necessary technical and human resources will need to be secured if hearing accessibility programs are to be implemented (see also Chapter 13).

IMPLEMENTING A HEARING ACCESSIBILITY PROGRAM

Phase 6 of the PRECEDE-PROCEED model begins to double back on the planning phases as the program is implemented. Having worked through the model thus far, the hearing accessibility program planner has arrived at a statement of the quality of life issues of importance to the targeted community of hard of hearing elders. The important quality of life or handicap issues are mapped onto particular health or disability and impairment issues that become the overall goals of hearing accessibility programs. To accomplish the overall hearing accessibility goals of the program, specific goals are set based on the subsequent phases of planning in which the planner identifies an inventory of relevant changes in the specific behaviors of hard of hearing people and their regular communication partners and changes in the specific aspects of the physical and social environment. Prior to implementing the program, the inventory of potential changes in behavior and the environment is reviewed to determine a short list of changes that are likely to be realized and that are considered to be important to the goal. Next, the planner sets detailed goals as to who will achieve what level of hearing accessibility in what time frame. An example goal might be that all residents who wish to attend chapel at a home for the aged will be able to use an FM system (with assistance if necessary) and will be totally satisfied with their ability to understand services within 6 months after an FM system has been installed and the training of residents and staff in its use has begun. Finally, guided by the detailed goals, with the required and available resources identified, and the required administrative and organizational support recruited, the program can be implemented.

EVALUATING A HEARING ACCESSIBILITY PROGRAM

Phases 7, 8, and 9 of the PRECEDE-PROCEED model concern the evaluation of the program. After carefully planning a hearing accessibility program, program evaluation is accomplished by circling back to determine if the goals have been accomplished. Phase 7 is concerned with process evaluation, where the process being evaluated refers to the strategies and immediate objectives of the program, such as the specific improvements in the provision of health services, resources, or education that were formulated in Phase 4. Process evaluation can take the form of quality assurance, peer review, or critical examination of the implementation of program procedures and protocols. An example of one component of a process evaluation for an accessibility program for seniors living in a home for the aged might be an audit of the nursing charts to verify that all seniors have been informed about the installation of a new FM system in the chapel and about how it could be used if they were interested in trying it.

Phase 8 is concerned with impact evaluation, where the impact being evaluated refers to the intermediate outcomes of the program, such as the specific increases in professional, public, and institutional awareness and action that were formulated in Phase 3. Impact evaluations can take the form of tests of knowledge or skill acquisition or studies of cost-effectiveness. An example of one component of an impact evaluation might be a follow-up interview with a sample of the seniors to determine if they had attempted and were successful in using a new FM system.

Phase 9 is concerned with outcome evaluation, where the outcome being evaluated refers to the more long-term objectives formulated in Phases 1 and 2 regarding how the program would change quality of life. An outcome evaluation can take the form of a large-scale cost-effectiveness study (Pichora-Fuller & Robertson, in press). An example of one component of an outcome evaluation might be to determine if, after the residents had become accustomed to using an FM system, they were more satisfied with their ability to understand and participate in services in the chapel. The ultimate verdict on whether or not the program is a success will depend on the criteria for success that are adopted. The criteria for program success can be defined using a variety of standards of acceptability, including historical, scientific, normative, compromise, or arbitrary standards (see Green & Kreuter, 1991, for further discussion). Given the newness of hearing accessibility programs and the absence of standards, most standards for program success at the present time are likely to be compromise standards that emerge from a consensus of the opinions of practitioners, administrators, and hard of hearing consumers.

SUMMARY

Over the last two decades there has been an increase in the availability of ALDs; nevertheless, we are still in the early stages of developing hearing accessibility programs that incorporate these ALDs. Furthermore, systems to deliver ALDs are still not well established. ALDs are potentially extremely useful for seniors in a number of everyday situations, especially for those who do not use hearing aids because they do not have more than a mild degree of hearing impairment, because they do not derive adequate benefit from hearing aids in noisy situations, or because they are physically or mentally unable to handle a hearing aid. Older adults may benefit from a subset of the same technology that is useful to younger adults, with the primary age-related difference being not so much the technology itself but rather how ALDs are incorporated into programs for seniors. ALDs must be incorporated into hearing accessibility programs that are designed in response to the quality of life concerns of seniors in a context-specific or ecological fashion. The PRE-CEDE-PROCEED model of health promotion (Green & Kreuter, 1991) provides a useful conceptual framework within which more ecological hearing accessibility programs featuring ALDs can be planned, implemented, and evaluated. Hearing accessibility programs for seniors developed using this model will likely succeed for many reasons: (a) they will focus on needs and aspirations that are of importance to the targeted community; (b) they will emphasize the need for changes in behavior beyond the initial acquisition of new technology; (c) they will emphasize prerequisite changes in the behaviors of communication partners (familiar partners, the general public, health care practitioners, and others serving the public) rather than only changes in the behaviors of hard of hearing seniors; (d) they will stress the need for environmental changes in conjunction with behavioral changes; and (e) they will prioritize factors that not only enable, but also predispose and reinforce, changes that are important to the achievement of the goals of the program. It is reasonable to expect seniors, who stand to benefit from the use of ALDs, to be able to achieve significant improvements in the quality of their life only if the use of ALDs is placed within this larger context.

ACKNOWLEDGMENTS

I would like to thank Lisa Dillon for compiling the list of resources. I would also like to thank Arlene Carson, Lawrence Green, Noelle Lamb, and Charles Laszlo for their helpful comments on the manuscript.

RESOURCE LIST

Associations and Consumer Groups

Advocacy Resource Center for the Handicapped (ARCH)
40 Orchard View Blvd., Suite 255
Toronto, ON CANADA M4R 1B9
416-482-1254 (TTY)
416-482-8255 (Voice)
416-482-2981 (Fax)

Alexander Graham Bell Association for the Deaf
3417 Volta Place, N.W.
Washington, DC 20007
202-337-5220

American Academy of Audiology (AAA)
c/o Dr. Northern
University of Colorado Health Science Center
P.O. Box 210
4200 E. 9th St.
Denver, CO 80262
303-394-7856

American Association for Retired Persons (AARP)
1909 K St., N.W.
Washington, DC 20049

American Deafness and Rehabilitation Association (ADARA)
P.O. Box 251554
Little Rock, AR 72225
501-868-8850 (Voice/TTY)
501-868-8812 (Fax)

American Speech-Language-Hearing Association (ASHA)
10801 Rockville Pike
Rockville, MD 20852
Consumer Help Line: 800-638-8255

American Tinnitus Association (ATA)
P.O. Box 5
Portland, OR 97207-0005

Better Hearing Institute (BHI)
P.O. Box 1840
Washington, DC 20013
800-EAR-WELL

Canadian Acoustical Association (CAA)
P.O. Box 1351 Station "F"
Toronto, ON CANADA M4Y 2V9

Canadian Association of Speech Language Pathologists and Audiologists (CASLPA)
130 Albert St. Suite 2006
Ottawa, ON CANADA K1P 5G4
613-567-9968 (Voice)
613-567-2859 (Fax)

Canadian Association of the Deaf (CAD)
2435 Holly Lane, Suite 205
Ottawa, ON CANADA K1V 7P2
613-526-4785 (TTY/voice)
613-526-4718 (Fax)

Canadian Deafened Persons Association
Box 449, 205 Hiram St.
Bracebridge, ON CANADA P1L 1T7
705-689-8415

Canadian Hard of Hearing Association (CHHA)
2435 Holly Lane, Suite 205
Ottawa, ON CANADA K1V 7P2
613-526-2692 (TTY)
613-526-1584 (Voice)
613-526-4718 (Fax)

Canadian Hearing Society (CHS)
271 Spadina Road
Toronto, ON CANADA M5R 2V3
416-964-9595 (Voice)
416-964-0023 (TTY)
416-964-2066 (Fax)

Canadian International Hearing Services
Contact: Gordon Kerr
54 Strathburn Blvd.,
Weston, ON CANADA M9M 2K7
416-743-9755 (Voice)
416-743-1232 (Fax)

Coalition of Provincial Organizations of the Handicapped (COPOH)
926-294 Portage Ave.
Winnipeg, MB CANADA R3C 0B9
204-947-0303 (TTY/Voice)
204-942-4625 (Fax)

Council on Assistive Devices and Listening Systems (COALS, Inc.)
c/o Felldendorf Associates, Inc.
P.O. Box 32227
Washington, DC 20007

Hear You Are, Inc. (HYAI)
4 Musconetcong Ave.
Stanhope, NJ 07874
201-347-7662

House Ear Institute
2100 West 3rd St.
Los Angeles, CA 90057
213-483-4431

International Association for Augmentative and Alternative Communication (ISAAC)
P.O. Box 1762, Station R,
Toronto, ON CANADA M4G 4A3

National Advisory Council on Aging (NACA)
Ottawa, ON CANADA
613-957-1968

National Association for the Deaf (NAD)
814 Thayer Ave.
Silver Spring, MD 20910-4500
301-587-1788
301-587-1789 (TTY)
301-587-1791 (Fax)

National Association for Hearing and Speech Action (NAHSA)
10801 Rockville Pike
Rockville, MD 20852
800-638-8255

National Captioning Institute, Inc.
1900 Gallows Rd.
Vienna, VA 22182
703-917-7600

National Counsel of Senior Citizens
1331 F Street, N.W.
Washington, DC 20004-1171
202-347-8800

National Hearing Aid Society (NHAS)
20361 Middlebelt Road
Livonia, MI 48152
Consumer Help Line: 800-521-5247

National Information Center on Deafness (NICD)
Gallaudet University
800 Florida Ave., N.E.
Washington, DC 20002
202-651-5051

Rehabilitation International
25 East 21st St.
New York, NY 10010
212-505-0871 (Fax)
212-420-1500 (Voice)
212-420-1752 (TTY)

Self Help for Hard of Hearing People (SHHH)
7910 Woodmount Ave., Suite 1200,
Bethesda, MD 20814
301-657-2248 (Voice)
301-657-2249 (TTY)
301-913-9413 (Fax)

Tinnitus Association of Canada
23 Ellis Park Road
Toronto, ON CANADA M6S 2V4
416-762-1490

Manufacturers and Distributors

Accessibility Communication Product Center
14250 Clayton Rd.
Ballwin, MO 63011
800-233-1222

Assistive Listening Device Systems Inc. (ALDS)
#2-11220 Voyageur Way
Richmond, BC CANADA V6X 3E1
604-270-7751 (Voice-TTY)
604-270-6308 (Fax)

Crestwood Co.
6625 N. Sidney Place
Milwaukee, WI 53209-3259
414-352-5678

D. J. Technical Sales, Ltd.
2647 Kingsway
Vancouver, BC CANADA V5R 5H4
604-436-2694

HARC Mercantile, Inc.
P.O. Box 3055
Kalamazoo, MI 49003-3055
800-445-9968

National Captioning Institute (NCI)
5203 Leesburg Pike
Falls Church, VA 22041

Phonak Hearing Instruments
7895 Tranmere Dr., Suite 207
Mississauga, ON CANADA L5S 1V9
905-677-1167
905-677-7536 (Fax)
800-867-1167

Phonic Ear
250 Camino Alto,
Mill Valley, CA 94941
800-772-3374

Phonic Ear Ltd. (Canadian Distributor)
10-7475 Kimbel Street
Mississauga, ON CANADA L5S 1E7
1-800-387-3158
905-677-3231
416-677-7760 (Fax)

Radio Shack Special Needs Catalog
Department 88-A-393
300 1 Tandy Center
Ft. Worth, TX 76102

Sennheiser (Canada) Inc.
221 Labrosse,
Pointe-Claire, PQ CANADA H9R 1A3
514-426-3013 (Voice)
514-426-3953 (Fax)
800-463-3013 (Toll free fax)

Telex Hearing Instruments
P.O. Box 1488, Stn. B
3510 Mainway Dr.
Burlington, ON CANADA L7P 4C5
416-335-3744
800-263-6392

Williams Sound Corp.
Assistive Listening Products
Minnetoka, MN 55345-5997

Zygo Industries, Inc
P.O. Box 1008
Portland, OR 97207-1008
800-234-6006
503-684-6006

Zygo Rehabtek, Inc.
Lynn Valley, P.O. Box 16040
North Vancouver, BC CANADA V7J 3S9
800-663-1633
604-876-1314 (Fax)

Your local telephone company

Your local hospital or medical clinic department of audiology or department of speech and hearing

Newsletters and Journals

Abilities
Box 527, Station P
Toronto, ON CANADA M5S 2T1

Augmentative and Alternative Communication
Decker Periodicals Inc.
One James St. South,
P.O. Box 620, L.C.D. 1,
Hamilton, ON CANADA L8N 3K7

Focus
Canadian Standards Association
178 Rexdale Boulevard
Rexdale, ON CANADA M9W 1R3

IFHOH Journal
International Federation of Hard of Hearing People
Teldersstraat 7, NL-8265 WS Kampen
The Netherlands
Phone: 05202-15463

Journal of the Academy of Rehabilitative Audiology
Monograph Supplement, Vol. XXVII, 1994
Chapter 7: Assistive Devices for the Hearing-Impaired
Dean C. Garstecki

Listen/Écoute
2435 Holly Lane Suite 205
Ottawa, ON K1V 7P2
613-526-1584 (Voice)
613-526-2692 (TTY)
613-526-4718 (Fax)
1-800-263-8068 (Toll Free)

Rehabilitation Digest
Canadian Rehabilitation Council for the Disabled
45 Sheppard Ave. East, Suite 801
Toronto, ON CANADA M2N 5W9
416-250-7490 (Voice/TTY)
416-229-1371 (Fax)

Soundwaves
Dahlberg Hearing Systems Ltd.
P.O. Box 9022
Kitchener, ON CANADA N2G 4J3

Transition
c/o BC Coalition of People with Disabilities (BCCPD)
204-456 West Broadway
Vancouver, BC CANADA V5Y 1R3

Vibrations
Information Services: The Canadian Hearing Society
271 Spadina Road
Toronto, ON CANADA M5R 2V3

Texts

Assistive Devices: Doorway to Independence, 1989
Cynthia L. Compton
Washington, DC
Gallaudet University Press

Coping with Hearing Loss and Hearing Aids, 1992
(Coping with Aging Series)
Debra A. Shimon
San Diego, California, Singular Publishing Group, Inc.

Video Tapes

Assistive Devices: Doorway to Independence
produced by Gallaudet University

World Wide Web Sites

Name: Deaf Gopher WWW
http://web.cal.msu.edu/deaf/deafintro.html

Name: Center for Assessment and Demographic Studies
http://www.gallaudet.edu/~teallen/cads.html

Name: Society and Culture: Disabilities
http://www.yahoo.com/Society_and_Culture/Disabilities

Name: Economy: Organizations: Public Interest Groups: Disabilities
http://www.yahoo.com/Economy/Organizations/
Public_Interest_Groups/Disabilities

Name: Cornucopia of Disability Information gopher
gopher://val-dor.cc.buffalo.edu

Name: A variety of disability gophers
gopher://val- dor.cc.buffalo.edu/11/ .bulletin.boards/.gopher

USENET Newsgroups

alt.support.tinnitus
misc.handicap

REFERENCES

Assistive Listening Device Systems, Inc. (1993). Magnatel™, Magnetic Field Tester. *ALDS product sheet.* Richmond, BC, Canada: ALDS, Inc.

Canadian Study of Health and Aging Working Group. (1994). Canadian Study of Health and Aging: Study methods and prevalence of dementia. *Canadian Medical Association Journal, 150,* 899–914.

Castle, D. L. (1978). Telephone communication for the hearing impaired: Methods and equipment. *Journal of the Academy of Rehabilitative Audiology, 11,* 91–104.

Committee on Hearing, Bioacoustics and Biomechanics, Working Group on Speech Understanding and Aging (CHABA). (1988). Speech understanding and aging. *Journal of the Acoustical Society of America, 83,* 859–895.

Compton, C. L. (1993). Assistive technology for deaf and hard of hearing people. In J. G. Alpiner & P. A. McCarthy (Eds.), *Rehabilitation audiology: Children and adults* (2nd ed., pp. 441–469). Baltimore: Williams & Wilkins.

Crandell, C. C., Henoch, M. A., & Dunkerson, K. A. (1991). A review of speech perception and aging: Some implications for aural rehabilitation. *Journal of the Academy of Rehabilitative Audiology, 24,* 121–132.

Erber, N. P. (1985). *Telephone communication and hearing impairment.* San Diego: College-Hill Press.

Erber, N. P. (1988). *Communication therapy for hearing-impaired adults.* Abbotsford, Australia: Clavis.

Erber, N. P. (1994a). Conversation as therapy for older adults in residential care: The case for intervention. *European Journal of Disorders of Communication, 29,* 269–278.

Erber, N. P. (1994b, March–April). Perception of facial cues by adults with low vision. *Journal of Visual Impairment and Blindness,* pp. 171–175.

Erdman, S. A. (1993). Counseling hearing-impaired adults. In J. G. Alpiner & P. A. McCarthy (Eds.), *Rehabilitation audiology: Children and adults* (2nd ed., pp. 374–416). Baltimore: Williams & Wilkins.

Fellendorf, G. W. (1982). A model demonstration center of assistive devices for hearing-impaired people. *Journal of the Academy of Rehabilitative Audiology, 15,* 70–82.

Feldbreugge, W. (1994). *Evaluation of communication therapy as aural rehabilitation.* Unpublished master's thesis, University of British Columbia, Canada.

Garstecki, D. (1988). Considerations in selecting assistive devices for hearing-impaired adults. *Journal of the Academy of Rehabilitative Audiology, 21,* 153–157.

Garstecki, D. (1990). Hearing health knowledge of aging adults. *Journal of the Academy of Rehabilitative Audiology, 22,* 79–88.

Garstecki, D. (1993). Rehabilitative audiologists and the hearing-impaired population: Continuing and new relationships. In J. G. Alpiner & P. A. McCarthy (Eds.), *Rehabilitation audiology: Children and adults* (2nd ed., pp. 17–34). Baltimore: Williams & Wilkins.

Garstecki, D. (1994). Assistive devices for the hearing-impaired. *Journal of the Academy of Rehabilitative Audiology,* (Suppl. 27), 113–132.

Getty, L., & Hétu, R. (1994). Is there a culture of hard of hearing workers? *Journal of Speech-Language Pathology and Audiology, 18,* 267–270.

Giolas, T. (1990). The measurement of hearing handicap revisited: A 20-year perspective. *Ear and Hearing, 11*(Suppl.), 2S–5S.

Green, L. W., & Kreuter, M. W. (1991). *Health promotion planning: An educational and environmental approach* (2nd ed.). Mountain View, CA: Mayfield.

Grimes, A. (1995). Auditory changes. In R. Lubinski (Ed.), *Communication and dementia* (pp. 47–69). San Diego, CA: Singular Publishing Group.

Hanusaik, L., Benguerel, A.-P., & Laszlo, C. (1992). User performance with inductively coupled amplifying telephones. *Journal of Speech-Language Pathology and Audiology, 16,* 45–52.

Health & Welfare Canada. (1988). *Acquired hearing impairment in the adult: Report of a task force convened by the Health Services Directorate,* Health Services and Promotion Branch. Supply and Services Canada: Ottawa, Ontario, Canada.

Helfer, K. S. (1991). Everyday speech understanding by older listeners. *Journal of the Academy of Rehabilitative Audiology, 24,* 17–34.

Hétu, R., & Tran Quoc, H. (1994). Validation of masked threshold predictions among people with sensorineural hearing loss. *Canadian Acoustics, 22,* 83–84.

Hull, R., & Griffin, K. M. (1989). *Communication disorders in aging.* Newbury Park, CA: Sage.

Hyde, M. L., & Riko, K. (1994). A decision-analytic approach to audiological rehabilitation. *Journal of the Academy of Rehabilitative Audiology,* (Suppl. 27), 337–374.

Janzen, H. (1995). *Meanings of hearing loss in the elderly.* Unpublished doctoral dissertation. University of British Columbia, Vancouver, Canada.

Jennings, M. B., & Head, B. G. (1994). Development of an ecological audiologic rehabilitation program in a home-for-the-aged. *Journal of the Academy of Rehabilitative Audiology, 27,* 73–88.

Laszlo, C. (1994). Engineering aspects of assistive device technologies for hard of hearing and deaf people. *Canadian Acoustics, 22*(3), 77–78.

McKellin, W. (1994). Hearing and listening: Audiology, hearing and hearing impairment in everyday life. *Journal of Speech-Language Pathology and Audiology, 18,* 212–219.

McKinnon, B. (1994). Electromagnetic interference in a hearing aid T-coil application. *Canadian Acoustics, 22,* 77.

Montano, J. (1994). Rehabilitation technology for the hearing impaired. In J. Katz (Ed.), *Handbook of clinical audiology* (4th ed., pp. 638–649). Baltimore: Williams & Wilkins.

Nábelek, A. K., & Robinson, P. K. (1982). Monaural and binaural perception in reverberation for listeners of various ages. *Journal of the Acoustical Society of America, 71,* 1242–1248.

Noh, S., Gagné, J.-P., & Kaspar, V. (1994). Models of health behaviors and compliance: Applications to audiological rehabilitation research. *Journal of the Academy of Rehabilitative Audiology,* (Suppl. 27), 375–389.

Pichora-Fuller, M. K. (1981). The use of telephone amplifying devices by the hearing–impaired. *Journal of Otolaryngology, 10,* 210–218.

Pichora-Fuller, M. K. (1985). The aural rehabilitation program. *Audiology in Practice, 2,* 3–5.

Pichora-Fuller, M. K. (1994). Introduction to the special issue on the psychosocial impact of hearing loss in everyday life: An anthropological view. *Journal of Speech-Language Pathology and Audiology, 18,* 209–211.

Pichora-Fuller, M. K., Corbin, H., Riko, K., & Alberti, P. W. (1983). A review of current approaches to aural rehabilitation. *International Rehabilitation Medicine, 5,* 58–66.

Pichora-Fuller, M. K., & Kirson, S. R. (1994). How the allocation of cognitive resources may alter handicap. *Journal of Speech-Language Pathology and Audiology, 18,* 223–234.

Pichora-Fuller, M. K., & Robertson, L. F. (1994). Hard of hearing residents in a home for the aged. *Journal of Speech-Language Pathology and Audiology, 18,* 278–288.

Pichora-Fuller, M. K., & Robertson, L.F. (in press). Planning and evaluation of a hearing rehabilitation program in a home for the aged. *Journal of Speech-Language Pathology and Audiology.*

Plomp, R. (1978). Auditory handicap of hearing impairment and the limited benefit of hearing aids. *Journal of the Acoustical Society of America, 63,* 533–548.

Plomp, R., & Duquesnoy, A. J. (1980). Room acoustics for the aged. *Journal of the Acoustical Society of America, 68,* 1616–1621.

Riko, K., Cummings, F., & Alberti, P. W. (1979). The role of communication aids in the rehabilitation of hearing impairment. *Journal of Otolaryngology, 8,* 13–19.

Robards-Armstrong, C., & Stone, H. (1994). Research in audiological rehabilitation: Current trends and future directions, the consumer's perspective. *Journal of the Academy of Rehabilitative Audiology,* (Suppl. 27), 25–46.

Schow, R., & Gatehouse, S. (1990). Fundamental issues in self-assessment of hearing. *Ear and Hearing, 11*(Suppl.), 6S–16S.

Spahr, F. T. (Ed.). (1992). Americans with Disabilities Act: The dream . . . An accessible America. *Asha, 34.*

Stephens, D., & Hétu, R. (1991). Impairment, disability and handicap in audiology: Towards a consensus. *Audiology, 30,* 185–200.

Tran Quoc, H., Hétu, R., & Laroche, C. (1992). Computerized assessment and prediction of the audibility of sound warning signals for normal and hearing impaired individuals. In M. Mattila & W. Karwowski (Eds.), *Computer applications in ergonomics, Occupational safety and health.* (pp. 105–112). North Holland: Elsevier Science Publishers.

Unger, S. (1994). Industry's inability to develop and market technology to counter hearing handicaps. *Journal of Speech-Language Pathology and Audiology, 18,* 243–247.

Vaughn, G. R., Lightfoot, R. K., & Arnold, L. C. (1981). Alternative listening devices and delivery systems for audiologic habilitation of hearing-impaired persons. *Journal of the Academy of Rehabilitative Audiology, 14,* 62–77.

Willott, J. (1991). *Aging and the auditory system: Anatomy, physiology, and psychophysics.* San Diego, CA: Singular Publishing Group.

World Health Organization (WHO). (1993). *International classification of impairments, disabilities and handicaps.* Geneva: Author.

8

Assistive Communication Technology for Elders with Cognitive and Language Disabilities

Kathryn L. Garrett, Ph.D.
Kathryn M. Yorkston, Ph.D.

INTRODUCTION

Williams (1989) informed an audience of professionals involved in the rehabilitation of acquired communication disorders that "what virtually every older person with disabling conditions wants most is restoration, to the maximum degree possible, of her/his independence, autonomy, ability to choose and live her/his own life preferences" (p. 77). Assistive communication technology is one means of helping elders to achieve these goals.

This chapter and the next provide an introduction to the application of assistive communication technology for elders. An overview of communication disorders in the elderly is presented in this chapter, and assistive technology intervention strategies for elders with cognitive and language disabilities are discussed. The following chapter targets elders with acquired motor speech disorders and apraxia. In each section, the type of elders who may use the technology and their specific communication needs are described, and some examples of available technology are provided. The authors also discuss the training and partner support

203

required for successful implementation of communication technology with elders.

Relevant Definitions

Assistive technology is a general term applied to devices that enhance the independence or level of function of individuals with disability. Public Law 100–407 defines an assistive technology device as:

> Any item, piece of equipment or product system whether acquired commerically, off the shelf, modified, or customized that is used to increase or improve functional capabilities of individuals with disabilities. (Cook & Hussey, 1995, p. 5)

In the area of communication, "light tech" assistive communication technologies involve minimal electronic, computerized, or mechanical components. They assist elders to compensate for communication problems encountered in daily living. For example, persons with hand weakness may use a built-up handle or grip for a pencil to write. Assistive communication technology also includes "high tech" solutions, such as computer-based communication systems that provide spoken output, printed output, and adaptive computer access for individuals with a variety of motor impairments. Both light tech and high tech solutions to a variety of communication challenges among the elderly will be offered.

Interventions in these chapters also will be presented in terms of their function. Some interventions, such as electronic speech devices for persons with motor speech disorders, serve as a substitute for an impaired modality, or channel, of communication. Other interventions are discussed in terms of their potential to enhance the quality of elders' communication interactions.

The authors of these chapters want to emphasize that the strategies presented may not be appropriate for a given individual; the intent of the technical descriptions is to offer examples of potentially successful interventions for elders in general.

AN OVERVIEW OF COMMUNICATION DISORDERS IN THE ELDERLY

A Model of Expressive Communication Disorders

For most of us, speaking understandably and in well-formulated utterances is an effortless process. Although it may appear to be easy, speaking demands proficiency in a number of underlying processes represented schematically in Figure 8–1. First, an idea is created. At this stage, the meaning or intent of the communication act is established. The idea must then be translated into sound sequences that form the words of spoken language. The words in turn are sequenced in a particular order according to the grammatical rules of the language. Finally, the words and phrases must be translated into intricate patterns of movement by which speech is produced. In other words, a motor plan is developed which instructs the muscles of speech when, how far, and with what speed and force to move. Speech movements involve the muscles of breathing which provide the energy source for speech, the muscles of the vocal folds which provide the sound source, and muscles of the soft palate, tongue, lips, and jaw which precisely shape speech sounds.

In summary, expressive communication consists of a number of processes including cognition, language, motor planning, and speech execution. Each of these processes is necessary for normal communication, and when one of them is damaged by neurologic disease or injury, a distinctive communication disorder will emerge. Specific terms have been applied to breakdowns at each level of the expressive communica-

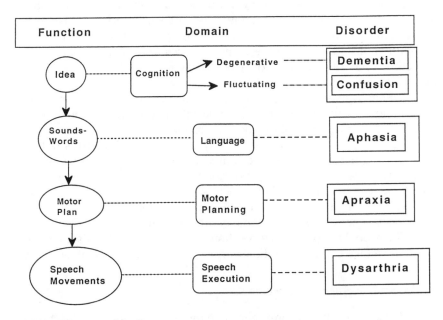

Figure 8–1. Model of expressive communication.

tion process. If the cognitive process of generating ideas is disrupted, the disorders of dementia or confusion may occur. The term *dementia* is typically used for degenerative disorders, whereas *confusion* is used in cases of transient or reversible conditions. *Aphasia* refers to disruption of the language processes. When motor planning is impaired, the communication diagnosis is *apraxia* of speech. Finally, when the execution of speech movements is disrupted, the term *dysarthria* is applied.

Assistive Communication Technology and the Elderly: What Can/Should We Enhance?

Assistive communication technology can be pursued for two reasons: to substitute for an impaired communication modality, or because the elderly communicator wishes to enhance the quality of communication interactions.

Modality-Specific Enhancements

When elderly persons acquire some diseases or conditions, they may lose control of one or more modalities, or channels, of communication. Speech may become impaired, or writing may not be possible through manual means. Technology can sometimes provide an acceptable replacement. For example, many communication devices use electronic speech output to substitute for impaired speech. Interventionists can design alternate means for persons with limited hand control to access computers or appliances in the home. Devices that store messages can sometimes aid the memory of a person who has difficulty recalling appointments or names and addresses.

Persons who design technical interventions to substitute for damaged communication modalities must often take into account changes in the disability across time. Some of the disease processes that cause communication disorders, such as dementia or amyotrophic lateral sclerosis (ALS), have a declining course. Other acquired disorders may improve across time, such as some stroke-related disabilities. Fluctuating courses of disability are seen in some conditions such as Parkinson's disease, particularly when medication levels subside. Still other disorders maintain a flat profile of change across time (e.g., some brain stem cerebrovascular accidents [CVAs]). Modality-specific interventions for persons with disorders of aging must take into account these varying options for course of recovery.

Sociocommunicative Enhancements

Light (1988) described a comprehensive model of communication function that conceptualized communication as more than the process of conveying words and sentences. According to her model, the purpose of a communication act can be categorized into the following four functions: (a) needs and wants; (b) information exchange; (c) maintenance of social etiquette; and (d) social closeness. Light's basic premise is that although interventionists may focus on reestablishing an individual's ability to convey information essential to his or her physical well-being (e.g., medical needs, food requests in a restaurant), most adults spend a significant amount of time communicating to establish social closeness or to "glue" their interactions via the devices of social etiquette. This distinction may be particularly true for the elderly.

NEEDS AND WANTS. Accurate and timely communication of needs and wants is a significant need of the elderly. They need to communicate information about medical needs, particularly if they have a chronic disorder such as diabetes or high blood pressure. At times this requires an elderly individual to communicate quickly and accurately in emergency situations (e.g., "I'm feeling dizzy; maybe it's my blood pressure"). On other occasions, the elderly communicator can request specific treatments or medications in less pressured transactions (e.g., pharmacy, doctor's office). Acquisition of a disorder of communication can affect an elderly person's ability to convey this information specifically and efficiently.

SOCIAL INTERACTION. Tamir (1979) noted that quality communication interactions are essential for elders to cope with the ongoing changes in their lives. However, in the face of acquired communication disorders, facilitation of interaction may not be prioritized as a treatment goal for several reasons. First, partners may perceive that the communication of needs and wants in a medical setting is the most pressing issue. Second, contrary to our general impressions that "conversing is easy," social interaction requires an individual to use a wide variety of complex skills, including dynamic receptive and expressive language processing, information retrieval, and pragmatic nuances. This function of communication may simply be more difficult for our communication-impaired elders than we typically think. As Buzolich and Wiemann (1988) observed, "Conversation is so much a part of our everyday experiences that most people take its execution for granted" [p. 3]. Finally, adapting technology to augment communication interactions is relatively complex for elders with social interaction challenges. The pragmatic aspects of communication must be considered. For example, assistive communication technology should help the elderly communicator to organize information around topics, engage in dynamic communication exchanges with partners, and repair communication breakdowns when they inevitably occur. The vocabulary and operational sequencing for such functions can be fairly complex, and many potential users of "off-the-shelf" technology (e.g., laptop computers) may not have the cognitive flexibility to use systems in a dynamic and situationally appropriate manner. This chapter introduces many light tech options that can potentially enrich interactions while not exhausting the cognitive resources of elders.

It is also essential that communication strategies imposed on communicatively impaired older adults acknowledge their life roles and experiences. As Tamir (1979) and Boden and Bielby (1986) noted, older adults occupy much of their social interaction time consolidating their life stories by reminiscing with peers and reviewing important life events. They also may continue to give advice or share personal information with their children. In the community, they conduct business or discuss current events. The assistive technology interventions in this chapter were designed to assist older adults to participate in meaningful life activities and roles such as these once again. (For further discussion of the value of communication to elders, see Chapter 1.)

The following sections of this chapter introduce assistive communication technology options and associated training issues for elders with dementia and confusion or aphasia.

DEMENTIA AND CONFUSION

Compensation for cognitive impairment is an increasingly urgent area of concern for those serving a population of elders. A number of reasons exist for this urgency. First, a large number of elders exhibit either dementia (a progressive, irreversible deterioration) or acute confusion (a potentially reversible disorder primarily of attention and orientation). The most common cause of chronic progressive dementia is Alzheimer's disease (Molloy & Lubinski, 1995). It has been estimated that 10.3% of individuals over age 65 have probable Alzheimer's disease (Evans et al., 1989). Prevalence rates are strongly associated with age with an estimated 47.2% of individuals over 85 years who exhibit characteristics of the disease. Both of these disorders impose important limitations on independence in elders. They can also create the potential for further complications such as social isolation, depression, and further physical injuries.

Descriptions

Dementia

Dementia is a general term for mental deterioration that includes loss of memory and intellectual functioning as well as changes in behavior, mood, and personality. It is a relatively common clinical syndrome among elderly individuals. Dementia can be characterized by deterioration so severe that it impairs an individual's ability to work and perform functional activities (Molloy & Lubinski, 1995). At least three of the following areas of function must be impaired to warrant a diagnosis of dementia: cognition, memory, language, visuospatial skills, and emotion or personality (Cummings & Benson, 1983).

Although there are many causes of dementia, by far the most common causes are Alzheimer's disease and multi-infarct dementia. Dementia associated with Alzheimer's disease is characterized by a gradual onset and slow, steady decline in a variety of functions over time. The natural course of multi-infarct dementia may be somewhat different in that it is characterized by abrupt onset and a stairstep pattern of deterioration. Currently there is no cure for either type of dementia. The progressive course of dementia has implications for the selection of technology. Because improvement is not expected to occur and learning ability may be severely compromised, simple, intuitive technologies are usually the most appropriate.

Confusion

Acute confusional state is a term applied to sudden changes in mental status and is characterized by deficits in attention, irrelevant or rambling speech, and other cognitive deficits (Johnson, 1990). Patients may be hyperactive (restless and screaming) or hypoactive (quiet, inactive and stuporous). Confused individuals have difficulty understanding their environment and remaining oriented to time and place. Patients with postoperative confusion report anxiety and feelings of being crazy or lost. Neelon (1990) reported:

> Confusion is a terrible feeling, a feeling of being lost in the most basic sense. The markers, maps, cues and senses used to orient oneself to the immediate environment are not recognizable. This applies to what one sees, hears, and feels. The person searches for something that makes sense, that he or she can anchor thoughts or actions to. Sitting up, getting up, and walking are anchoring responses. Using hands to touch one's own body, fingering objects, and "calling out" reflect a searching for something that is meaningful to the individual. (p. 579)

Confusion may also arise from other, nonsurgical causes, including trauma to the brain, CVAs, infection, and administration of a large number and variety of drugs (Stewart, 1992). These conditions typically result in diffuse or generalized damage to the brain. Elders are particular-

ly vulnerable to acute confusional states, and it is estimated that confusion occurs in 20 to 25% of hospitalized elderly patients (Johnson, 1990;
Rockwood, 1989).

Unlike most types of dementia, an acute confusional state is often transient. The first course of treatment is to manage the underlying condition
(e.g., to decrease infection or eliminate medications). Additional treatment
can consist of providing appropriate fluid and electrolytes, allaying the
patient's fear and agitation through the use of simple, repetitive instructions
and orientation cues, and limiting the use of physical restraints.

Characteristics of the Communication Deficits

Dementia

Table 8–1 contains a description of the communication characteristics of
individuals with dementia. Often the communication disorder is termed
"language of generalized intellectual impairment." In this disorder, language and cognition are equally impaired, and elders experience more
pronounced problems in unfamiliar or complex activities. Bayles (1984)
described changes in communication as the disease progressed. In the
early stages of language disturbance, problems are not likely to be
noticed in casual conversation. Although persons with early-stage
dementia may digress from the topic, they continue to follow the rules
of grammar and word selection. In the middle stages of dementia, language impairment is apparent and conversation is vague, empty, and
often irrelevant. Language becomes egocentric. Individuals in middle-
stage dementia may not be able to generate sequences of meaningfully
related ideas. In late-stage dementia, language impairment is severe
across all modalities. Individuals at this stage may be mute or produce
bizarre, nonsensical utterances. All aspects of language are affected at
this stage of the disease.

Confusion

A review of Table 8–1 suggests that language of confusion is characterized by reduced recognition, and understanding of and responsiveness
to the environment. Language output is a window into the elder's
underlying cognitive ability. Because thinking is muddled in acute confusional states, language may also be disconnected and incoherent.
Provision of structure often assists the confused individual; therefore
open-ended tasks such as conversing may be more difficult for confused
patients than more structured tasks such as naming pictures.

Table 8-1. Description of communication characteristics in dementia, confusion, and aphasia.

Dementia: Language of generalized intellectual impairment is characterized by:

- deterioration of performance on more difficult language tasks;
- reduced efficiency in all modes;
- greater impairment in language tasks requiring better retention, closer attention, and powers of abstraction and generalization;
- degree of language impairment roughly proportionate to deterioration of other mental function.

Confusion: Language of confusion is associated with impairment of language accompanying neurologic conditions, often traumatically induced. It is characterized by:

- reduced recognition and understanding of and responsiveness to the environment, faulty memory, unclear thinking, and disorientation in time and space;
- structured language events that are usually normal and responses that utilize correct syntax;
- irrelevance and confabulation in open-ended language situations.

Aphasia: Aphasia is an impairment, due to brain damage, of the capacity to interpret and formulate language symbols. It is characterized by:

- a multimodal loss or reduction in decoding conventional meaningful linguistic elements (morphemes and larger syntactic units);
- a disproportionate level of impairment relative to impairment of other intellectual functions;
- reduced availability of vocabulary, reduced efficiency in applying syntactic rules, reduced auditory retention span, and impaired efficiency in input and output channel selection, and is not attributable to dementia, sensory loss, or motor dysfunction.

Sources: Adapted with permission from "Neuropathologies of Speech and Language: An Introduction to Patient Management" by R. T. Wertz in D. F. Johns (Ed.), *Clinical Management of Neurogenic Communicative Disorders* (p. 2), 1985, Boston: Little, Brown.

Interventions

Modality-Specific Interventions

Because dementia and confusion affect the deepest internal language and memory processes of elders, assistive devices cannot simply provide a substitute modality for their impaired expressive communication. Although, at end stages, the speech of persons with dementia or confusion is sometimes described as unintelligible, this breakdown is primarily one of thinking and reasoning, not the motor execution of sounds and words. Because at present it is impossible to replace faulty memory and reasoning, it may be more helpful to focus on ways for the person with dementia or confusion to participate in meaningful interactions throughout the stages of the disease process via assistive technology.

Sociocommunicative Interventions

NEEDS AND WANTS. The following assistive device adaptations may allow the person with dementia or confusion some increases in independence with regard to communicating needs and wants.

1. *Getting attention/signaling emergencies*
   It is imperative that persons with dementia or confusion signal their need for assistance in a manner that requires the least amount of planning, problem solving, or motor activity possible. It is also helpful to use call systems that are visible and meaningful to these individuals, unlike some of the wall-plate call signals often used in care facilities.

   Self-contained signaling devices. The BIGmack™ device (AbleNet, Inc.) consists of a large, colored plastic plate switch covering a single message digitized speech unit. The clinician or health care provider first records a message ("Please come here; I need your help") into the device that the user then activates by touching the plate. Care providers are then taught to place the call device in a visible, easily accessible location whenever the person with dementia or confusion is left alone (e.g., on a tray table by the bed; on the end table in the lounge). A self-contained signaling device also can be very appropriate in the home where built-in call systems, such as those found in a hospital, are not available.

   Modifications to wall call systems. Persons with dementia or confusion frequently cannot locate the thumb-press or squeeze bulb switches that are commonly used to activate nurse-call systems in care facilities or hospitals. Additionally, they may forget the purpose of the switch, particularly because there is no externally visible association between the object (the call switch) and the potentially delayed outcome (assistance with an activity of daily living). It may be appropriate to replace the standard call switches with an enlarged, tripod-type plate switch. This type of switch can be modified to be more representative of the act of requesting assistance by taping a photograph of a familiar nurse or another associational symbol (colored fabric, texture) to its surface. The caregivers must then teach the elder with dementia to "touch the picture when you need a nurse" and provide a timely response to this request in the early stages of training.

Community emergency-call systems. Many communities and hospitals now standardly issue radio-transmitter systems that relay through the phone lines into a central emergency response system for persons who may need a rapid means of calling for emergency help. The person with emergency needs presses a button worn on a chain around the neck or encased in a plastic "wristwatch." This activation then initiates an automatic call to a hospital liaison, who attempts to call the individual on the telephone to confirm the emergency. If no one responds via telephone, an emergency response team is immediately dispatched to the person's home. This type of system may be the most appropriate for individuals who continue to live in their homes without a companion and who have acute medical needs in addition to dementia.

2. *Identification aids*
   Individuals with dementia or confusion may be unreliable when relating factual or biographical information, particularly when they are in an unfamiliar environment. In the case of individuals who may wander from their home or facility, it is essential that identifying information be present on their person. Most identification aids are light technology devices such as wrist bracelet or necklace identification tags. Some of these identification aids contain embedded microchips or metal components that set off an alarm system when the individual leaves the premises.

3. *Timers/activity signalers*
   Lynch (1995) noted that the capacity to remember to carry out a prior instruction or appointment requires memory for events that will occur in the future. This cognitive skill is impaired early in the course of many dementias. Lynch

suggested that the use of external memory devices may be more valid than attempting to restore memory. Some of the following signaling devices may be appropriate for persons with dementia.

Talking alarm clocks. Several commercially available portable alarm clocks now incorporate digitized speech so that the time or the wake-up call can be announced in a natural-sounding voice. For the person with dementia, the automatic alarm announcer can be set to signal important events that occur at the same time on a daily basis, such as eating dinner, taking medications, or receiving visits from family.

Beeping electronic wristwatches. Similarly, inexpensive digital wristwatches that signal events or hourly changes by beeping can be purchased for elders with tendencies to forget future tasks.

Light/music timers. Commercially available AC appliance timers can also be used by individuals with memory problems. The timer is set to turn on the appliance (lamp with pastel light bulb, radio) just prior to the critical time for the activity.

In the preceding approaches, the person with early-stage dementia might require a partner to construct a verbal association (e.g., "Oh, the pink light went on; must be time for your bridge club") until she or he becomes familiar with the meaning of the cue. The next three strategies provide more explicit verbal reminders for persons with memory challenges.

Neuropage. Hersh and Treadgold (1994) created an electronic pager system called Neuropage™ (Hersh & Treadgold, Inc). This system allows prestored reminders to be transmitted from a computer storage system directly to a personal receiver. The message is signaled by a flashing light, a vibration, or an auditory signal. The individual then reads the reminder from a screen on the receiver. The developers reported several examples of increased functional recall, such as remembering therapy times, taking along keys, and completing household chores following introduction of the Neuropage™ system. The hospital system (including a base computer and individual receivers) has recently been modified for home and individual use.

Automated answering service. For individuals who have the capacity to live independently but who experience occasional lapses in memory regarding medications or appointments, a commercial answering service can call and personally remind them to complete these activities. Reminder calls can be scheduled well in advance. Estimated costs for an answering service to call once or twice daily ranges from $10 to $20 per month in the midwestern United States.

Intercom. For individuals in care facilities with intercom systems wired to each room, personal reminders could also be transmitted directly to the individual on a prescheduled basis.

4. *Memory aids for facts and lists*

   For persons with early-stage dementia who begin to have difficulty retrieving rote information such as grocery items, phone numbers, names, or addresses, Lynch (1995) described other electronic memory devices. The Voice It Personal Note Recorder™ (Voice It Technologies, Inc.) is a small, portable device that allows an individual to record and play back messages or reminders. Buttons with picture symbols allow the user to access the record, play, erase, and rewind functions. The user is signaled that a message is waiting by a flashing light. This device can be clipped to a pocket or belt or attached to a metal surface via a magnet. It costs approximately $50 to $110.

   The Voice Organizer™ (Voice Powered Technology International, Inc.) recognizes and records up to 100 names, 400 telephone numbers, 99 notes, and 99 reminders. The user can store this information in his or her own voice, enter key words or a description, and then access the entire message by stating these logical descriptors. The device costs approximately $200.

5. *Environmental organizers*

   Light tech options frequently assist elders with dementia or confusion to make sense of their routines or environment. Wall charts containing schedules or safety precautions can be posted and reviewed by attendants. Planning phone call times in advance with family members and posting this information can sometimes alleviate anxiety regarding contact with loved ones. Color-coding door signs to rooms and placing a correspondingly colored sticker on the elders' wheelchairs or walkers can sometimes help them locate their rooms more independently. Leseth and Meader (1995) described a strategy of placing a vase of red flowers on the dining table of an elderly woman with dementia; she reportedly learned to locate her dining area with no assistance most of the time. (See Chapters 10 and 11 for more information on environmental technologies.)

6. *Instructional*

Because persons with dementia or confusion may experience memory breakdowns for the specific details or sequence of steps involved in daily activities, such as taking medication or doing a small load of laundry, visual instructions may be of assistance. To provide the maximum degree of support, instructions should consist of highly visible or familiar information (e.g., photos of the elder completing the activity) or consist of immediately recognizable spoken messages. (See the discussion of affordance theory in Chapter 10 for more details on this topic.)

Voice output augmentative devices. Simple, inexpensive digitized voice output augmentative systems such as the Hawk™ (Adamlab), AlphaTalker™ (Prentke Romich Company), Message Mate™ (Words +, Inc.,), Macaw™ (Zygo Industries, Inc.), or the SpeakEasy™ (AbleNet, Inc.) can be used to store spoken sequences for activities of daily living. For example, to complete a load of laundry, the first "row" of eight messages could consist of (1) choose all light or all dark clothing, (2) put them in a basket , (3) put the basket by the washer and load the clothes, (4) set the dial to warm for dark and hot for white, (5) put in 1 scoop of detergent, (6) close the lid, (7) push the start button, (8) set the egg timer for 30 minutes. The second row could consist of messages pertaining to drying the clothes, and the third row to folding and sorting. The person with early-stage forgetfulness could initially be assisted to review the messages and then complete the activity sequence until mastering the use of this type of reminder system.

Visual reminder charts. Wall charts or posters, printed clearly in large letters or meaningful symbols, can sometimes be effective in assisting elders to complete step-by-step

tasks. Older persons with mild confusion or early dementia can refer to a simple printed outline to assist
them in completing simple "chores" such as watering
plants, or activities of daily living such as brushing teeth
or grooming. Care must be taken to choose important information and to not clutter all available wall space.

SOCIAL INTERACTION/PARTICIPATION. The primary purpose of other
assistive technology interventions for elders with dementia or confusion
is to improve their participation in communication interactions.

1. *Personality/biographic introducers*
   Many persons with dementia are ultimately placed in
   institutional care, particularly in the later stages of the disease. Opportunities for rich social interactions tend to be
   sparse in most facilities (Carstenson & Erickson, 1986;
   Hutchinson & Jensen, 1980; Lubinski, 1981). In part, this
   may be because individuals with advanced dementia
   have difficulty remembering or narrating their work or
   personal accomplishments in detail. Although many families attempt to enrich the care setting by posting photographs of important family members or placing favorite
   keepsakes on a shelf, most caregiver interactions focus on
   determining the immediate physical needs of the individual. If caregivers do engage in social interactions with the
   person with dementia, they choose superficial topics that
   typically do little to evoke the meaningful life memories of
   the individual. The following technology-based interventions may assist in building a stronger, shared interpersonal context beyond day-to-day activities.

   "Electronic Scrapbook." The simple, digitized voice output
   devices with large message squares listed earlier (e.g.,
   AlphaTalker™) can serve as a mechanical "scrapbook."
   Pictures from a favorite vacation, retirement dinner, trea-
   sured family holiday, or of family pets can be placed on the
   message squares. The clinician or other selected narrator
   then stores a message beneath the square by speaking into
   the system's microphone. Messages pertaining to a series of
   pictures from a family vacation are illustrated in Figure 8–2.
   The person with dementia or confusion could learn to activate these messages in structured, conversation-sharing
   activities with caregivers or in recreational activities.

In 1992 we went to Hawaii 🌴 🍍	We stayed in a bungalow 🏠 on the beach	My wife liked to wake up 🔲 early ☼	and look for shells..🦀..she found 100 s!!!
I'll never forget the jeep trip up the *VOLCANO!*	We ate in many nice restaurants 🍴	They even got me to try the hula ≈ 🌴	It was a wonderful trip, but we were glad to be home 🏠

Figure 8–2. Electronic scrapbook overlay for social closeness activities.

Narrated stories on tape recorder or videotape/relay systems. Family members can audio- or videotape stories of favorite, memorable occasions and mail or bring them to care facilities. Staff can play these tapes for the elder with dementia during leisure time. Sometimes loop tapes (i.e., the self-repeating tapes found in answering machines) are preferable for listening activities if the person with dementia or confusion becomes upset when a nonrepeating tape stops. Elders with dementia can sometimes access tapes more readily via simple relay technology. In this approach, a large, colored plate switch can be hooked into a tape recorder or relay unit such as the PowerLink 2 Control Unit™ (Ablenet, Inc.). This same type of technology could be used for videotape playback as well.

Memorabilia box. Leseth and Meader (1995) placed items that reminded an elderly woman with dementia of special personal events or activities in an attractive box. Examples of items included business papers, coins, and sewing scraps. When this individual became agitated or confused, family members reviewed these familiar items with her, subsequently decreasing her agitated behaviors. (See the discussion in Chapter 11 of memory facilitating environments for more information on this topic.)

2. *Memory activities with old movies and songs*
   Viewing nostalgic movies on videotape and listening to reprise versions of songs from earlier decades can serve as conversation starters for persons with dementia. This activity may be appropriate for individuals or for small groups, both supervised and during independent leisure time.

3. *Memory books and wallets*
   Bourgeois (1992) recommended constructing memory wallets for persons with dementia and other memory impairments. She showed that persons with dementia communicate more understandable, on-topic comments when provided with important pictures or mementos of their past.

APHASIA

Description

Aphasia refers to language disorders resulting from damage to specific areas of the brain, usually the left cortical hemisphere. Aphasia results in a loss of ability to use language to communicate, comprehend, or exchange thoughts and feelings (Chapey, 1994).

Wertz (1985) described three essential features of aphasia (see Table 8–1). First, persons with aphasia typically demonstrate impairments across all modalities of language, including speaking, understanding, gesturing, reading, and writing. Although all modalities are frequently not affected to the same extent, deficits are typically present to some degree in all modalities. This means that interventionists cannot simply substitute training in one modality (gestures, for example) for speech. The second element of Wertz's (1985) description is that language impairment is more pronounced than deterioration of other functions such as motor skills or cognition. This means that elders with aphasia can often rely upon their knowledge of the world, memory, and reasoning ability to compensate for difficulty manipulating language. Finally, Wertz noted that aphasia is not typically due to dementia, sensory loss, or motor impairment.

The most common cause of aphasia is stroke or CVA. A stroke occurs when one of the following happens: (a) the blood vessels of the brain are blocked and parts of the brain do not receive sufficient oxygen or (b) a blood vessel in the brain ruptures and causes bleeding in the brain. The second most common cause of aphasia is trauma to the left hemisphere (e.g., falls, blunt injury). Brain tumors and infections also cause a small proportion of the cases of aphasia.

Aphasia resulting from stroke is a sudden-onset disorder. Although there is a period of recovery that may last many months, most agree that the greatest amount of physical recovery occurs within the first 6 months after onset. Following this period of physical recovery, aphasia is typically considered to have a stable condition unless other neurologic events occur. Although our ability to predict the long-term outcome for individuals with aphasia is limited, a number of factors have been used to estimate prognosis (Wertz, 1985). Younger individuals make better recovery than older individuals. The type and severity of the aphasia also has prognostic implications. For example, mild aphasia without significant auditory comprehension deficits or apraxia of speech is a positive prognostic indicator. Individuals who are in the early stages of recovery are more likely to improve than individuals who are many years post-stroke.

Characteristics of the Communication Deficits

The pattern and severity of speaking, listening, reading, and writing impairments in individuals with aphasia vary widely due to differences in size and location of the brain damage and time since the stroke. When considering assistive communication strategies, it is useful to categorize individuals with aphasia based on their profiles of competencies, challenges, and needs. Garrett and Beukelman (1992) described such a categorization system:

The *Basic Choice Communicator* describes individuals who have overall difficulty mapping language to ideas. Basic Choice Communicators have difficulty conveying ideas through any language modality. They seldom initiate, even by gesturing or vocalizing. Because they are so limited in their ability to process multistep information, complex communication devices are not appropriate. Basic Choice Communicators do benefit from context, however. In familiar routines, they tend to comprehend more. They sometimes communicate at an automatic level. Interventions for this category of communicators may be limited to simple strategies to increase meaningful social interaction and the communication of wants and needs.

The *Controlled Situation Communicator* describes persons with aphasia that do process linguistic information but only in controlled doses. They attempt to initiate communication, but they break down before completing a message successfully. Many of these individuals understand more than they can say. They can frequently recognize choices, presented in writing or aloud, and can confirm their preferred answer. They are attuned to the social routines of the day, and are quick to remind care providers when they are late for an appointment. Like the Basic Choice Communicators, complex communication systems are extremely difficult for this group of individuals to use.

The *Comprehensive Communicator* describes individuals who have many residual communication skills. Most of these individuals can communicate verbally in some situations. Many of them gesture or pantomime to convey precise meanings. Some persons write words or word fragments at times. Comprehensive Communicators are noted for their efforts to search for other means to convey a message when their initial attempts are inadequate. They wish to communicate about a variety of topics with a variety of partners. Some Comprehensive Communicators can learn to use complex communication systems containing prestored vocabulary. Typically, goals for comprehensive communicators consist of consolidating and using appropriate strategies in various communication situations.

The *Augmented Input Communicator* describes persons with aphasia who do not comprehend all verbal information presented to them through the auditory channel. These individuals typically need some form of visual supplementation (writing, gestures) or additional context to help them process the spoken messages of their partners. Assistive devices for this group are best utilized by the aphasic person's communication partner.

The *Specific Needs Communicator* describes individuals with aphasia who have communication needs that are not necessarily a result of impairment of a particular process or modality. Rather, their communication needs are derived from the interaction of their language impairment with their lifestyle. For example, individuals with mild aphasia may manage most of the communication challenges they encounter in daily life but experience breakdowns when trying to recite numbers aloud. Other persons with aphasia may manage communication of needs and wants in face-to-face situations but struggle when talking on the telephone. Still others face challenges in unique personal situations that require use of specific vocabulary, such as placing bets at the horse races.

Interventions

The careful application of technology to the preceding groups of communicators can supplement the functional and social communication of persons with all types of aphasia.

Modality-Specific Interventions

Because persons with aphasia have disrupted symbolic language skills in all modalities, it is seldom possible for them to use complex assistive communication devices to attain their previous level of fluency. The following sections therefore give examples of more specific applications of assistive technology to certain types of aphasic communicators.

Sociocommunicative Interventions

NEEDS AND WANTS. This communication function has received the most attention from interventionists. Although it is critical for persons with aphasia from all the previous categories to request and receive basic items related to their care and comfort, many persons with aphasia ultimately manage most basic needs themselves or via familiar caregivers. Instead, challenges arise in highly unique and personal situations (indicating a specific bus stop, expressing concerns about family finances). Possible approaches for managing specific communication needs follow:

1. *Getting attention/signaling emergencies*
   Interventions for getting attention and signaling emergencies should be as simple as possible. Many of the suggestions described earlier for the person with dementia (e.g., buzzers, single message voice output devices, Life-Line) should be relevant. An additional suggestion for supported phone transactions is described here:

   Voice output device—phone overlay. Simple 8- to 32-message voice output devices (e.g., Hawk™, AlphaTalker™) can store a limited number of messages appropriate for telephone use. Examples of messages include: "Hello, this is (name)," "I need you to come over," "EMERGENCY," "today or tomorrow," "RIGHT NOW," "Call the doctor," "I need help with . . . ," "MEDICAL," "shopping," "the bills," "housework," "YES," "NO," "I'm fine." The facilitator can place these messages on an overlay; the user then activates the voice by pressing the message square. It is important to practice telephone skills with the person with aphasia. It may be useful to write out a "script" or hypothetical dialogue sequence of the phone call and role play until the individual is comfortable completing a call. The facilitator can also write out the operational steps of the call (looking up the address, how to dial, etc.) It may also be important to teach regular callers to ask questions in the same sequence each time they call so that the person with aphasia does not become confused. This intervention may be most appropriate for Controlled Situation Communicators, Comprehensive Communicators, and Specific Needs Communicators. (See Chapter 12 on telephone technology for additional information on this topic.)

2. *Basic requests*

Object choices. Even if persons with aphasia successfully obtain the attention of a caregiver, they frequently fail to convey their needs. Basic Choice Communicators might communicate their needs more effectively if partners provide them with choices represented by familiar objects. For example, the caregiver could present a blanket and a pillow to the person's visual field, label these choices aloud ("Do you need a blanket to keep warm? . . . or a pillow for your head?") and then pause and wait for the communicator to look at or point to his or her choice. It may be possible to transition some communicators from indicating choices via real objects to picture representations of objects after consistent associations have been established.

Written choices. For persons in the second category of aphasic communicators, the Controlled Situation Communicators, partners can likewise generate a series of choices by writing them on a tablet or erasable slate (Garrett & Beukelman, 1995). For example, if partners wish to find out which hobbies the person wants to participate in during recreation time, they could say and write the following:

"What would you like to do in recreation time, Nell?" [Writes and says aloud]:

- GARDENING
- SEWING
- PUZZLES
- CERAMICS

The partner would then wait for the person with aphasia to point to his or her answer. This strategy frequently is more productive than engaging in "Twenty Questions" or waiting for the person with aphasia to generate the response.

Rating scales. In this variation of the written choices strategy to facilitate communication of basic requests, partners can confirm the individual's degree of need, amount of pain, or priority level by providing a rating scale with 3 to 5 intervals and clearly marked endpoints. The person with aphasia points to the numbered interval to communicate a qualitative response (see Figure 8–3).

Prestored message boards or overlays on electronic devices. For persons who can use stored messages, such as those from the Comprehensive Communicator category, it may be useful to anticipate basic needs and represent them on a simple communication board, a voice output device where all options are displayed, or in a communication notebook with a highly visible needs page. Extensive training using role-playing and scripting is recommended to assist persons with aphasia to communicate their needs independently in real situations.

3. *Complex home or community needs*

When some persons with aphasia transition from the rehabilitation or care facility to supervised living situations or to home, their communication needs may become

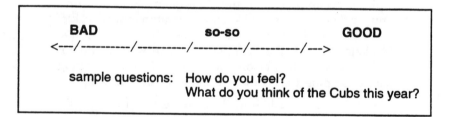

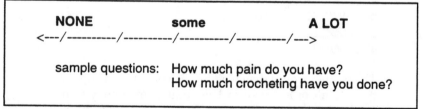

Figure 8–3. Rating scale response alternatives.

even more specific (Comprehensive Communicators, Specific Needs Communicators). For instance, Garrett, Beukelman, and Low (1989) described one gentleman who, as he gained more independence, wished to travel to various locations around town by bus. He could convey some information verbally, but was typically inefficient and was not always successful with unfamiliar partners. He learned to use a small notebook containing phrases needed to take a cab or bus, lists of important locations, paper for writing and drawing, a first letter spelling card, and lists of key phrases for the race track. With training, he became an adept multimodal communicator in a variety of situations important to him.

4. *Accurate comprehension of environmental information*

Some individuals with aphasia cannot meet their needs because they do not adequately understand spoken information. These persons may not comprehend instructions from their therapists or general conversations (Augmented Input Communicators). The technique of "augmenting input" (Garrett & Beukelman, 1992) requires partners to generate key words or phrases for this type of communicator. Devices that can assist the partner to complete this simple accommodation include: erasable slates, pen and paper, or notebook computers.

SOCIAL INTERACTION/PARTICIPATION. It is important to choose assistive technology for elders with aphasia that is flexible enough to accommodate the dynamic nature of social interactions. Many of the following strategies are a combination of light technology, specific uses of high technology, and partner-based interventions.

1. *Conversation*

Written Choice Conversation. Earlier, the strategy of partners generating written choices to assist elders with aphasia to communicate basic needs was described. The principle of choice-making can also be applied to conversational interactions via a more expanded strategy called Written Choice Conversation (Garrett & Beukelman, 1995). The partner facilitates interactions by generating a series of written choices that may help the aphasic communicator answer questions or comment in the course of the conversation. For example, if the partner asks: "Who do you think will win the election this year? A Republican or a Democrat?" the person with aphasia can point to the written choice that corresponds with his or her answer. In this extended application of the written choice strategy, the partner makes the technique "conversational" by then generating a follow-up question such as "How much will he/she win by, a lot or a little?" and again writes out possible responses. The partner with aphasia can then answer these genuine conversational questions by pointing to the choices or points on the rating scale. Although partners frequently choose to generate choices via pen-and-paper or erasable slate devices, typing devices with large screens and clear graphic output may be preferable for some individuals, particularly if they wish to print any of the discussion for later use. This strategy is most effective for persons from the Controlled Situation Communicator category.

Augmented Input. This strategy can be used to facilitate conversations as well as communication of specific needs as described earlier. Partners should write key words or gesture when they perceive an elder having difficulty comprehending a conversation. Light technology options (paper and pen, erasable slates) are most commonly used, although laptop computers with easy-to-read screens also may be helpful. This strategy is extremely helpful when persons with aphasia cannot follow topic changes or highly specific instructions.

Scripted exchanges. Simple voice output technology (see the devices listed previously) can be used to help persons with limited expressive output and an inability to use multimodal systems participate in structured conversations. First, a social script denoting the turns for the partner and aphasic communicator is constructed and printed. The script is designed to allow the person with aphasia an opportunity to not only answer questions, but also to comment, share news, and initiate questions. The aphasic communicator's turns are then represented on the message squares of the voice output device. A novel partner enters the situation, and the person with aphasia is encouraged to follow the script and activate the messages at the appropriate moment. These facilitator cues are faded, and the person with aphasia is encouraged to convey conversational messages as independently as possible to a variety of partners. This strategy was designed to transition Controlled Situation Communicators to more independent levels of communication instead of being an end-goal of the therapy process.

Topic initiator/turn regulator systems. New software is currently under development to allow persons with a variety of communication disorders to select topics, plan relevant messages, and then insert turn-regulating devices ("So, go ahead") and remarks into a dynamic exchange. Talk: About™ (Don Johnston, Inc.) is a computer-based program with these features; its usefulness for elders with aphasia bears investigation.

2. *Storytelling*

Storytelling is a means for adults to review their lives. Assistive devices can provide opportunities for persons with aphasia to participate once again in this important interaction. The person with aphasia and familiar partners can identify important or recurring stories and then generate the sequence of messages needed to complete the story structure. Story components are stored on individual message squares of a voice-output augmentative system. Each story message is then represented with a meaningful picture symbol and/or written key words. Persons with aphasia, even those with severely limited communication skills, can typically learn to activate the story messages, wait for the spoken output, and then activate the next message in the sequence. Electronically stored stories can serve as a catalyst for interaction if partners are then encouraged to respond and comment about the story frames. Successful storytelling interventions have been described by Fried-Oken (1995) and Stuart (personal communication, 1994). (See the previous section on electronic scrapbooks for persons with dementia and Figure 8–2 for additional illustrations of this concept.)

3. *Game-playing*

Stuart (1995) described an activity-specific AAC intervention for a 73-year-old gentleman who best fit the category of controlled situation communicator. This gentleman had not shown any aptitude for initiating communication with a series of mini-boards containing needs-based questions or personally relevant comments. He was unable to use a complex communication system containing an unlimited number of words or sentences. The clinician then targeted comments (e.g., "You got two more points than me") and requests (e.g., "I need another card") for playing checkers or cards. These messages were stored on a simple voice output system with preprogrammed phrases for numbers and card suits (Vocaid™, Texas Instruments). Eventually, the gentleman began utilizing the Vocaid to request a specific number of cards or to comment on how many points he had scored in a true game-playing interaction.

IMPLEMENTATION ISSUES

An Emphasis on Competence

Many traditional approaches to the treatment of dementia and aphasia focus on remediating the individual's communication *deficits*. The preceding interventions were designed to simultaneously acknowledge the elder's preserved *competencies*. For example, reminiscing activities can capitalize on remote memories, which in turn may improve social interaction and language. Representing place names with a map or family names with a family tree allows the person with aphasia to draw upon preserved visual recognition skills. Most persons with dementia, confusion, or aphasia have a rich history of personal experiences and successful communication that can be tapped when developing interventions.

An Emphasis on Partners

Clearly, some flexibility in the typical routine of caring for persons with dementia or confusion is needed to promote higher quality interactions. Partners may require special training to implement the strategies described. They may need to participate in self-evaluation and simulation activities to better understand the communication dilemmas of elders with confusion or dementia. They may need technical training to operate some of the systems described above. It will be important to include caregivers on strategy development teams so that interventions are customized and practical for all participants.

Similarly, the most successful communication interventions for persons with aphasia involve partners who have mastered appropriate strategies and who learn to provide communication opportunities in the midst of rapidly flowing interactions. It is critical for interventionists to include family members, health care workers, recreation directors, and friends of the elder with aphasia in therapy sessions. Some strategies and activities for training partners are suggested in Garrett and Beukelman (1992).

Restructuring Environments

The physical environment of the person with dementia, confusion, or aphasia may need to be redesigned to allow for maximum social interaction. Lubinski (1995) pointed out that elders with dementia may have little choice or control over their physical environment. To provide true opportunities for social interaction, it is important to personalize the living space of elders with acquired communication disorders. This may require some accommodation or restructuring of rules that protect the confidentiality of nursing home residents. It may also mean that all persons responsible for building maintenance be involved in decisions with regard to placement of visual materials and equipment. Family members of persons who live at home may want to make communication systems and memory books consistently available. Reducing confusion in the home environment is essential. (See Chapter 11 for more infomration on environmental manipulation.)

Providing Meaningful Opportunities for Communication

Elders with dementia or aphasia must continue to be included in activities that are of interest to them and that allow them to participate in meaningful life roles. Immersion in activities such as reminiscing about the "good old days," discussing the college choices of grandchildren, choosing the seeds for next year's garden, attending makeup demonstrations, going to the horse track, and participating in tribal ceremonies, among others, will yield many opportunities for communication. Hopefully, as elders, team, and family members strive for increased quality of life, these opportunities can be provided with minimal effort and with an end result of improved social interaction for all.

SUMMARY

Dementia, confusion, and aphasia are acquired neurological disorders that can impair the communication of elders. This chapter reviews the medical and communication characteristics of dementia, confusion, and aphasia (see Table 8–1 for a summary).

Although individuals with these disorders differ significantly with regard to their residual challenges and capabilities, assistive communication technology often can be manipulated in creative ways to improve their participation in meaningful communication activities. All groups can be served by assistive communication technology that addresses both wants and needs as well as sociocommunicative interaction. Some interventions consist of complex, or high, technology, whereas others rely primarily on easily assembled light technology components. The technology-based approaches that have been described in this chapter for each of these groups is summarized in Table 8–2.

Table 8–2. Summary of assistive technology applications for elders with cognitive or language impairment.

Diagnosis	Dementia	Confusion	Aphasia
Cause	Alzheimer's disease Multiple strokes	Trauma, stroke, infection, multi-drug therapy	Stroke
Natural course	Progressive	Fluctuating	Improving with later stabilization
Types of problems	Loss of memory and intellectual functioning Changes in behavior, mood, and personality	Deficits in thinking and orientation	Reduced ability to speak, listen, read, and write
Examples of assistive technology	Attention getting, emergency signaling Identification aids Timer or activity signalers Memo systems and list makers Environmental organizers Instructional aids Biographic introducers Memory activities Memory books and wallets	Attention getting devices Basic physical need requests Home and community communication systems Comprehension enhancers Conversion enhancers Storytelling Game-playing	

Identification of essential technology is only the first step, however. Successful interventions for elders also require an integrated knowledge of the individual, participation of partners, and some degree of environmental restructuring. Finally, those who serve elders with acquired communication disorders must be prepared for the inevitable reality of change. It is critical that facilitators adapt to changes in technology, individual functioning, or environmental challenges to continue to provide integrative technology-based communication interventions for elders with dementia, confusion, or aphasia.

RESOURCES

Associations

Academy of Neurologic Disorders and Sciences (ANCDS)
1250 24th St, N.W., Suite 300
Washington, DC 20037
(202) 467-2787

Alzheimer's Disease and Related Disorders Association
919 North Michigan Avenue, Suite 1000
Chicago, IL 60611-1676

American Speech-Language-Hearing Association
10801 Rockville Pike
Rockville, MD 20852
(301) 897-5700

International Society for Augmentative and Alternative Communication (ISAAC)
ISAAC Secretariat
P.O. Box 1762, Station R
Toronto, Ontario
M4G 4A3, Canada

National Aphasia Association
P.O. Box 1887
Murray Hill Station
New York, NY 10156-0611

Manufacturers

AbleNet, Inc.
1081 Tenth Ave. S.E.
Minneapolis, MN 55414-1312
1-800-322-0956

Adamlab, Inc.
Wayne RESA
33500 Van Born Road
Wayne, MI 48184
(313) 467-1415

Don Johnston, Inc.
1000 N. Rand Rd. Bldg. 115
P.O. Box 639
Wauconda, IL 60084-0639
1-800-999-4660

Hersh & Treadgold, Inc.
6657 Camelia Drive
San Jose, CA 95120
(408) 997-7017

Prentke Romich Company
1022 Heyl Rd.
Wooster, OH 44691
1-800-262-1933

Texas Instruments, Inc.
Dallas, TX
(214) 995-2011

Voice It Technologies, Inc.
2643 Midpoint Drive
Fort Collins, CO 80525
(303) 221-1705

Voice Powered Technology International, Inc.
19725 Sherman Way
Canoga Park, CA 91306
1-800-998-2200

Words +, Inc.
40015 Sierra Highway
Building B-145
Palmdale, CA 93550
1-800-869-8521

Zygo Industries, Inc.
PO Box 1008
Portland, OR 97207-1008
1-800-234-6006

REFERENCES

Bayles, K. A. (1984). Language and dementia. In A. Holland (Ed.), *Language disorders in adults* (pp. 209–244). San Diego, CA: College-Hill Press.

Boden, D., & Bielby, D. (l986). The way it was: Topical organization in elderly conversation. *Language & Communication, 6,* 73–89.

Bourgeois, M. (1992). Evaluating memory wallets in conversations with persons with dementia. *Journal of Speech and Hearing Research, 35,* 1344–1367.

Buzolich, M., & Wiemann, J. (1988). Turn-taking in atypical conversations: The case of the speaker/augmented communicator dyad. *Journal of Speech and Hearing Research, 31,* 3–18.

Carstensen, L., & Erickson, R. (1986). Enhancing the social environments of elderly nursing home residents: Are high rates of interaction enough? *Journal of Applied Behavior Analysis, 19,* 349–355.

Chapey, R. (1994). Introduction to language intervention strategies in adult aphasia. In R. Chapey (Ed.), *Language intervention strategies in adult aphasia* (pp. 3–26). Baltimore: Williams & Wilkins.

Cook, A. M., & Hussey, S. M. (1995). *Assistive technologies: Principles and practice.* St. Louis: Mosby.

Cummings, J. L., & Benson, D. F. (1983). *Dementia: A clinical approach.* Boston: Butterworth.

Evans, D., Funkenstein, H., Albert, M., Scherr, P., Cook, N., Chown, M., Hebert, L., Hennekens, C., & Taylor., J. (1989). Prevalence of Alzheimer's disease in a community population of older persons. *Journal of American Medical Association, 263,* 2447–2449.

Fried-Oken, M. (1995). Story telling as an augmentative communication approach for a man with severe apraxia of speech and expressive aphasia. *ASHA AAC Special Interest Division Newsletter, 4,* 3–4.

Garrett, K., & Beukelman, D. (1992). Augmentative and alternative communication approaches for persons with severe aphasia. In K. Yorkston (Ed.),

Augmentative communication in the acute medical setting. Tucson, AZ: Communication Skill Builders.

Garrett, K., & Beukelman, D. (1995). Changes in the interaction patterns of an individual with severe aphasia given three types of partner support. In M. Lemme (Ed.), *Clinical aphasiology, 23,* 237–251. Austin, TX: Pro-Ed.

Garrett, K., Beukelman, D., & Low, D. (1989). A comprehensive augmentative communication system for an adult with Broca's aphasia. *Augmentative and Alternative Communication, 5,* 55–61.

Hersh, N., & Treadgold, L. (1994). NeuroPage: The rehabilitation of memory dysfunction by prosthetic memory and cueing. *NeuroRehabilitation, 4,* 187–197.

Hutchinson, J., & Jensen, M. (1980) A pragmatic evaluation of discourse communication in normal and senile elderly in a nursing home. In L. Obler & M. Albert (Eds.), *Language and communication in the elderly: Clinical, therapeutic and experimental issues* (pp. 59–73). Lexington, MA: Lexington Books.

Johnson, J. C. (1990). Delirium in the elderly. *Emergency Medicine Clinics of North America, 8,* 255–265.

Leseth, L., & Meader, L. (1995). Utilizing an AAC system to maximize receptive and expressive communication skills of a person with Alzheimer's Disease. *ASHA AAC Special Interest Division Newsletter, 4,* 7–9.

Light, J. (1988). Interaction involving individuals using augmentative and alternative communication systems: State of the art and future directions. *Augmentative and Alternative Communication, 4,* 66–82.

Lubinski, R. (1981). Language and aging: An environmental approach to intervention. *Topics in language disorders, 14,* 89–97.

Lubinski, R. (Ed.). (1995). *Dementia and communication.* San Diego: Singular Publishing Group.

Lynch, W. (1995). You must remember this: Assistive devices for memory impairment. *Journal of Head Trauma Rehabilitation, 10,* 94–97.

Molloy, D. W., & Lubinski, R. (1995). Dementia: Impact and clinical perspectives. In R. Lubinski (Ed.), *Dementia and communication* (pp. 2–21). San Diego, CA: Singular Publishing Group.

Neelon, V. J. (1990). Postoperative confusion. *Critical care nursing clinics of North America, 2,* 579–587.

Rockwood, K. (1989). Acute confusion in elderly medical patients. *Journal of the American Geriatrics Society, 37,* 150–154.

Stewart, R. B. (1992). Acute confusional states in older adults and the role of polypharmacy. *Annual Review of Public Health, 13,* 415–430.

Stuart, S. (1995). Expanding communicative participation using augmentative and alternative communication within a game playing activity for a man with severe aphasia. *ASHA AAC Special Interest Division Newsletter, 4,* 9–11.

Tamir, L. (1979). *Communication and the aging process.* New York: Pergamon Press.

Wertz, R. (1985). Neuropathologies of speech and language: An introduction to patient management. In D. F. Johns (Ed.), *Clinical management of neurogenic communicative disorders* (p. 2). Boston: Little Brown.

Williams, T. (1989). Teamwork for the problems of aging. *ASHA, 31,* 77.

9

Assistive Communication Technology for Elders with Motor Speech Disability

Kathryn M. Yorkston, Ph.D.
Kathryn L. Garrett, Ph.D.

INTRODUCTION

"Two characteristics distinguish humans from other species: technology and language" (Edwards, 1991, p. 2). These two human characteristics come into clear focus in the management of elders with acquired motor speech disorders. With these individuals, language and the drive to communicate may be unaffected, but the execution of intricate sequences of movements required for normal speech is impaired. Many strides have been made in using assistive technology to compensate for motor problems; however, many clinical challenges still exist.

This chapter reviews four important groups of adults with acquired motor speech disorders—individuals with *locked-in syndrome*, *amyotrophic lateral sclerosis* (ALS), *Parkinson's disease*, and *apraxia of speech and aphasia*. Although these groups share some important features such as an adult onset and a motor impairment, they vary in some important respects that affect application of assistive technology. The natural courses of these disorders also vary. Some disorders may have associated problems such as impaired cognition or language that complicate rehabilitation efforts. We have selected each of these disorders for presentation here because of their frequency of occurrence and because each represents a different type of impairment. Therefore, the assistive technology needs of each group will vary. The following section includes a definition of each disorder, common causes, natural course, and speech characteristics. Typical assistive technology interventions and associated training issues are also presented.

LOCKED-IN SYNDROME

Description

Locked-in syndrome refers to a constellation of symptoms including paralysis of the arms, legs, and muscles of the oral structures. These symptoms have an enormous impact on communication. Severe dysarthria along with limited movement of the hand and head is common. Vertical eye gaze and upper eyelid movement are the only movements preserved in some individuals with locked-in syndrome (Plum & Posner, 1966). The term is a descriptive one suggesting literally "a mind locked inside the body" (Mauss-Clum, Cole, McCort, & Eifler, 1991). Cerebrovascular disease and basilar artery stroke are the most common causes of locked-in syndrome. The most typical site of lesion is in the brainstem. The second most frequent cause of the syndrome is trauma to the brainstem (Keane, 1986). Here the damage is caused by either direct trauma or trauma followed by hemorrhage.

In the early stages of the disorder, patients may not be able to breathe on their own and therefore require mechanical ventilation. Studies of electrical activity of the cortex show that higher brain function remains relatively intact; thus, cognition is not a factor limiting communication. Visual impairment may be present, but symptoms may fluctuate. Visual difficulties including blurring, visual field cuts, double vision, figure-ground discrimination difficulty, and reduced acuity are a challenge when attempting to develop assistive communication technologies.

The typical course of locked-in syndrome is a sudden onset from either a stroke or trauma followed by a period of gradual recovery and later stabilization. Although this is a relatively rare condition, the literature has reported outcomes for groups of patients who have been followed for many years (Culp & Ladtkow, 1992; Haig, Katz, & Sahgal, 1987; Katz, Haig, Clark, & DiPaola, 1992; McCusker, Rudick, Honch, & Griggs, 1982; Patterson & Grabois, 1986). In a series of 29 individuals with locked-in syndrome, the 5-year survival rate was 81%; most were cared for in their own homes at follow-up (Katz et al., 1992). Katz and his colleagues stated that ethical decisions about intervention and access to assistive technology must be made with the statistics about long-term survival in mind.

Culp and Ladtkow (1992) followed 16 individuals with locked-in syndrome for management of communication problems. All remained nonambulatory at follow-up, and many (44%) continued to experience visual impairment. In terms of communication function, most (75%) did not regain functional speech, needing instead to rely on assistive communication devices. In summary, the natural course of this disorder is characterized by the sudden onset of profound motor impairment that improves over time, but does not return to normal. Thus, long-term management is required. Critical to this management is the development of a reliable means of communication (Katz et al., 1992; Patterson & Grabois, 1986).

Characteristics of the Communication Deficits

Severe dysarthria is the primary communication deficit associated with locked-in syndrome. The speech characteristics are due to muscular weakness and reduced muscle tone. These motor disorders limit the speed, range, and accuracy of speech movements. All components of the speech production mechanism are affected. Respiratory muscles are weak, as are muscles responsible for movement of the vocal folds. Individuals with profound dysarthria are often unable to produce any voice. As recovery occurs, the voice may be reduced in loudness and breathy. Muscles of the soft palate are also impaired. The lack of ability to close off the mouth from the nose results in hypernasality. Individuals with severe impairment of the soft palate may not be able to build up pressure in the oral cavity and thus are unable to produce many of the consonant sounds. In summary, the classical features of the speech of individuals with severe weakness are a reduced loudness level, hypernasal speech, and imprecise production of consonants. Taken together, these features frequently make speech both exhausting for the speaker to produce and difficult for the listener to understand.

Intervention

Culp and Ladtkow (1992) introduced an approach for the staging of communication intervention based on four phases.

Initial Assessment

During the initial assessment stage, individuals with locked-in syndrome are profoundly impaired, medically fragile, and may be dependent on mechanical ventilation for breathing. They typically are highly susceptible to fatigue, and symptoms, especially visual problems, may fluctuate. Intervention at this stage involves providing the patient and family with information, assessing basic skills, and developing a reliable, nonfatiguing yes/no response.

In order to establish a yes/no system, caregivers should be instructed to record any observable movement attempt (Culp & Ladtkow, 1992). Later, in structured clinical trials, the facilitator can evaluate whether the person with locked-in syndrome can reliably answer yes/no questions by consciously making one or more of these movements. Examples of movements that have been used to establish a reliable yes/no response include:

> Eyebrows up for "yes," eyes closed for "no";
> One squeeze/blink for "yes," two quick blinks for "no";
> Eye gaze upward for "yes," eye gaze downward for "no";
> Licking lips for "yes," pursing lips for "no"; or,
> Thumb up for "yes," thumb inserted into fist for "no."

After the yes/no response system is established, it is important to inform nursing staff and family members of the system so that communication is consistent. It may be useful to post a simple chart describing the signals above the patient's bed.

Early Intervention

During the early intervention stage, individuals may tolerate slightly more active participation. Reliable signaling systems may be established, but profound motor impairment continues to limit both speech and access to complex assistive communication systems. During this phase, it is important to provide access to the nurse call system and to some means of getting attention. The following systems may be helpful for communication of frequently occurring or unique messages.

SCANNING. Scanning involves use of a single, controlled motor response (e.g., head move, eye gaze, finger lift) to trigger presentation of desired symbols, words, or whole messages. The target items are typically presented one at a time, and the person who communicates by scanning then uses the motor response to indicate when the desired choice has been presented. In *partner-dependent scanning* a partner holds the display (frequently an alphabet board) and asks the communicator to signal when his or her target is reached, given the following questions: (1) Is it in this row? (pointing to consecutive rows); (2) Is it in this position? (pointing to consecutive spaces in the row). In this manner, the communicator can spell out messages letter-by-letter or choose from a set of key phrases, such as "I need a drink" or "I need to be turned." In *electronic scanning*, the communicator hits a switch placed close to a reliable body movement (head switch, finger switch, knee switch). This in turn activates a light on an electronic device or computer that then scans through rows and columns of symbols. The communicator typically hits a switch a second time and sometimes a third time to stop the scanning light at the desired item. On some assistive communication devices, the selected message is then spoken aloud via a speech synthesizer. At times, because persons with locked-in syndrome have visual processing problems, the device scans each selection aloud via the speech synthesizer rather than using electronic light scanning. Training on simple scanning systems can begin in the early to middle-stages of recovery from locked-in syndrome. Readers are referred to more comprehensive sources of information regarding assistive technology such as Buekelman and Mirenda (1992) or Cook and Hussey (1995) for a detailed discussion of scanning approaches.

EYE-POINTING TO A COMMUNICATION BOARD. Another communication strategy used for some persons with locked-in syndrome is eye-pointing to a communication display. In this approach, the partner stands behind a communication board that typically has the middle section removed so that both persons can see each other through the middle of the board. A communication display consisting of letters, words, or complete messages is placed in the corners and midsections of the resulting "frame." This same display, in reverse order, is also placed on the partner's side of the communication board frame. Letters and words are printed in a font size large enough for easy reading. When the person with locked-in syndrome wishes to communicate, the partner holds the board in a mutually visible position and watches the eye movements of the person. If the partner can guess the message or the letter, the communicator then confirms or rejects the partner's guess by using the previously established yes/no signals. Communication boards for eye-pointing often have multiple overlays, one containing emergency messages and another representing the letters of the alphabet for unique messages.

Formal Assessment

After the patient's medical condition has stabilized, formal and in-depth assessment of communication needs, language skills, and motor function can take place. Recommendation of specific assistive communication devices can then be made. These systems may be complex, multipurpose devices capable of storing messages, generating unique messages, and displaying, printing, or "speaking" these messages. In the series of cases followed by Culp and Ladtkow (1992), 50% of the cases were able to use a single-finger or light pointer to access these communication systems. Others developed switch activation using visual or auditory scanning methods. Even those who regained functional natural speech ability needed to use technology as a means of written communication.

Ongoing Intervention

Individuals with locked-in syndrome may live in extended care facilities or in the home setting. If electronic assistive communication devices are in place, it is critical to identify an "advocate," or an individual who has the day to day responsibility for maintaining the system. These responsibilities include recharging the battery, changing the printer paper, and adding new vocabulary. He or she also must instruct people new to the environment about the various modes of communication used by the person with locked-in syndrome. Because of the long-term support needed, the advocate plays a vital role in communication.

Implementation Issues

Issues critical to the management of individuals with locked-in syndrome vary with the stage of the disorder. Initially, persons with locked-in syndrome are medically fragile and in the process of accommodating psychologically to the sudden onset of profound disability. These factors dictate management approaches. Perhaps the best way to appreciate the issues being faced by individuals with locked-in syndrome is through a personal account. In his book, *To the Edge and Back* (1991), J. H. Montgomery recounted his recovery from a brainstem stroke. Mr. Montgomery was a 50-year-old engineer at the time of this stroke. Initially, he was dependent on a ventilator for breathing. He expressed his concerns and fears related to this technology:

> I detested that machine, as it would normally have a regular inhale/exhale sequence, but every so often (5 minutes or less) it would break the cycle and not inhale for me for maybe close on eight seconds! Of course I had no other supply of air and being an engineering designer, I came to the conclusion that this thing wasn't worth the paper it was designed on and might soon expire, bringing me with it. That didn't exactly do anything to boost my confidence in its design or designer! On top of it all, I couldn't tell anyone it had me worried sick. I looked at it often and figured it

could be made for $100 tops. It was small enough to be held in the hand and I thought: "There is the price of my life." However, I wasn't on it too long and I heaved a (mental) sigh of relief when I was taken off it. (p. 59)

Later he described the frustration of suddenly being unable to communication. The lack of communication was made particularly distressing during a period of personal and medical crisis:

> In this day and age of modern communication devices, it comes as a shock when one finds that they have no means of communicating with the world that exists even outside their own brain. A terrible feeling of imprisonment endures when one can only lie on their back and stare at a particular spot on the ceiling during the hours that they are awake. Sleep when it comes, is brief at best, as the mind is in continuous never ending turmoil, full of questions that can't be asked, answers that can't be given. (p. 63)

Following the initial medical crisis, he summarized his feeling about his first simple communication system, a yes-no response system.

> As soon as they knew that I could differentiate between "yes" and "no," and that the stroke had not affected my mental balance, as far as they could tell anyway, a communication link was formed, "once for yes, twice for no!" It is difficult to describe the feeling I had just then. Happiness? Joy? Inappropriate words! I had felt as if I had been under a great internal pressure, and my family had "cracked open" a valve just a little and the pressure reduced and I know I was relieved. (p. 65)

After being weaned from the ventilator, this individual was faced with the realization that his speech disorder might be permanent:

> I was a fairly fluid speaker and was known to have "the gift of the gab" as they say in Ireland, and to wake up and find that one cannot talk for some unknown reason, is quite traumatic. To learn that it is not entirely due to a hopefully temporary medical device in the throat comes as a further shock. (p. 87)

This personal account highlights the long-term management needed by individuals with locked-in syndrome. Rehabilitation efforts cannot occur "all at once." Early in the recovery process, staff must make a concerted effort to establish a basic communication system. Providing staff with information about the intact cognitive and language skills should ensure appropriate verbal interactions with and around the patient. It is also critical for an intervention team or teams to follow the patient until a permanent, comprehensive communication system is developed. This may take weeks or months of problem-solving regarding issues such as seating and positioning, vision, motor access, scanning instruction, and taking an inventory of important messages. This type of team intervention effort must be staged over time to accommodate the medical, social, psychological, and financial needs of the patient and family.

AMYOTROPHIC LATERAL SCLEROSIS

Description

Amyotrophic lateral sclerosis (ALS) or Lou Gehrig's disease is a rapidly progressive, degenerative disease involving the motor neurons of the brain and spinal cord. At this time, both the cause and cure are unknown. Symptoms may involve the arms and legs (spinal symptoms) or muscles of the speech production mechanisms (bulbar symptoms). The underlying motor problems may be weakness, or spasticity (increased muscle tone and lack of fine control), or both, depending on the stage of the disease.

ALS is considered a relentlessly progressive disease with the average age of onset in the mid 50s. Although individuals vary in the rate at which motor symptoms increase, the rate of deterioration is strikingly linear for an individual (Caroscio, Mulvihill, Sterling, & Abrams, 1987; Pradas et al., 1993). In long-term follow-up studies, approximately one-third of individuals with ALS exhibit rapid change (progression to a terminal stage in less than 2 years), whereas approximately one-fifth show slow progression (Appel, Stewart, Smith, & Appel, 1987). Survival durations can be predicted on the basis of a number of factors, including (a) age—those with early onset survive longer than those with onsets later in life (Eisen, Schulzer, MacNeil, Pant, & Mak, 1993), (b) type of initial symptoms—those with spinal onset survive longer than those with early speech and swallowing symptoms (Rosen, 1978), (c) pulmonary status—respiratory complications are the usual cause of death, and (d) psychological factors—those with high psychological well-being survive longer than those in psychological distress (McDonald, Wiedenfeld, Hillel, Carpenter, & Walter, 1994).

Characteristics of the Communication Deficits

The dysarthria or motor speech impairment associated with ALS has features associated with both spasticity and weakness. For about one-third of individuals with ALS, dysarthria is among the first symptoms of the disease. For others, it appears later in the disease. The characteristics of mild dysarthria in ALS are variable depending on whether spasticity or weakness predominates. With mild spasticity, the voice may sound strained or strangled and articulation may be somewhat imprecise. With mild weakness, the voice may sound breathy and articulatory movements may be slightly slow. The features of moderate dysarthria in ALS include grossly defective articulation of both consonants and vowels, laborious and extremely slow speaking rate, marked hypernasality, vocal harshness, and strained-strangled voice quality. Severe dysarthria in ALS is characterized by profound weakness, lack of oral movement, and reduced ability to produce voice. For individuals with severe dysarthria in ALS, natural speech may no longer be a functional means of communication.

Intervention

Loss of the ability to communicate, or even the prospect of that loss, is among the most distressing aspects of ALS. Basic communication functions, such as the expression of wants and needs, may not be affected unless dysarthria is severe. However, maintaining social closeness may be difficult at any stage of communication impairment. Maintenance of communication is essential to preserve some sense of control for individuals with ALS.

Individuals with ALS progress through a series of predictable stages of speech change. Table 9–1 contains a description of the stages of speech progression in ALS. In the following section, these stages will be used to describe assistive technology intervention. A complete description of behavior intervention for speech and management of swallowing in ALS can be found elsewhere (Yorkston, Miller, & Strand, 1995).

Stage I: Normal Speech Processes

For individuals at this stage, speech is functionally normal. However, assistive technology may be appropriate for some individuals whose initial symptoms involve the hands and arms. Severe weakness in the upper extremities may make handwriting or typing difficult. These indi-

Table 9–1. The Speech Scale from the ALS Severity Scale.

STAGE I: NORMAL SPEECH PROCESSES
Patient may deny any difficulty speaking. In other cases, only the patient or spouse notices that speech has changed. Patient maintains normal rate and volume.

STAGE II: DETECTABLE SPEECH DISTURBANCE
Speech changes are noted by others, especially during fatigue or stress. Speech remains easily understood.

STAGE III: BEHAVIORAL MODIFICATIONS
Speaking rate is much slower than normal. The speaker repeats specific words in adverse listening situations and may limit the complexity or length of messages.

STAGE IV: USE OF AUGMENTATIVE COMMUNICATION
Intelligibility problems need to be resolved by writing or a spokesperson. The speaker may initiate communication nonvocally.

STAGE V: LOSS OF USEFUL SPEECH
Speakers may not use vocal inflection to express emotion, affirmation, or negation.

Source: From *Management of speech and swallowing disorders in degenerative disease.* by K. M. Yorkston, R. M. Miller, and E. A. Strand, 1995. Tucson, AZ: Communication Skill Builders. Adapted with permission.

viduals may benefit from a variety of devices ranging from light tech solutions such as built-up pencils and portable typing systems to high tech computer systems with alternative means of access. These alternative means of access may involve voice recognition, modified keyboards, or single switch activation.

Stage II: Detectable Speech Disturbance

For individuals at this stage, speech changes are noticeable and tend to worsen with fatigue or stress. Although speech remains intelligible, many individuals complain that speech is effortful. The following are some assistive technology devices that may be beneficial.

VOICE AMPLIFICATION SYSTEMS. The muscles of respiration provide the energy source for speech. If these muscles are weak, as is frequently the case in ALS, speaking at normal loudness levels may be fatiguing. Portable speech amplification systems are available to assist speakers to increase their loudness levels. Candidates for such devices typically have a weak voice but adequate oral articulation. These systems may be battery powered and portable or located in a particular setting such as a meeting room where they will be used.

HEARING AMPLIFICATION FOR PARTNERS. Because ALS typically occurs in elders, hearing loss in spouses of people with ALS is not uncommon. Even individuals with mild hearing loss may experience difficulty understanding dysarthric speech when others do not. Therefore, assistive technology includes devices such as hearing aids for frequent communication partners of individuals with ALS. Hearing aids may also be needed by the individual with ALS.

Stage III: Behavioral Modifications

Individuals at this stage are experiencing some reduction in speech intelligibility, especially in difficult listening conditions such as noisy environments or where distances are involved. At this stage, natural speech may continue to be functional in most communication situations. However, in difficult communication environments, with unfamiliar partners, or when resolving communication breakdowns, assistive communication systems may be needed as a backup for natural speech. Handwriting and systems that generate printed output represent highly understandable modes of communication for these difficult situations. A number of hand-held, battery powered typing devices are available.

Stage IV: Use of Augmentative Communication

Individuals at this stage of progression must rely on assistive communication devices, either as their primary means of communication or to supplement natural speech when it is not understood. Most individuals at this stage use a number of different approaches to communication, depending on the situation, the communication partner, and the communication task. Typically, the goal of intervention is to meet the following needs of the individuals with ALS: alerting signal (personal and public), face-to-face communication (with familiar and unfamiliar partners), breakdown resolution techniques (with familiar and unfamiliar partners), independent telephone use, and letter/memo preparation. Again, the types of assistive technology available to these individuals ranges from light tech approaches such as handwriting to high tech approaches involving single switch access and synthesized speech output. High tech approaches have been extremely helpful to individuals with ALS because they are able to compensate for deterioration in motor function. For example, an individual with ALS may use a succession of access devices including a standard keyboard (first with touch typing and later with single finger typing), a single switch activated by finger or head movements, and finally, a highly sensitive switch placed on the forehead and activated by raising the eyebrow. The selection of these switches is dependent upon a reliable and nonfatiguing movement site.

ALPHABET SUPPLEMENTATION. This is a technique where speakers point to the first letter of each word as they say the word (Yorkston, Beukelman, & Bell, 1988). It provides individuals who are difficult to understand with a number of benefits. In addition to slowing their speech and separating words, the technique provides the partner with the first letter of the target word so that guessing is easier. Individuals with ALS usually wish to use natural speech for as long as possible. This technique allows them to do so in many cases when unassisted natural speech would no longer be understandable. Thus, alphabet supplementation is a transitional technique that may bridge the gap between total reliance on natural speech and exclusive use of an assistive communication device.

ALERTING SYSTEMS. Some individuals with ALS are not able to produce a voice loud enough to call someone in another room. These individuals may benefit from devices such as buzzers or baby monitors that transmit signals to distant locations within the home. See Chapter 11 for additional options for attention getting and emergency messages.

TELEPHONE COMMUNICATION. The perceived need for telephone communication varies greatly among people with ALS. When telephone communication is needed, various means of access are available. Some individuals use loop tapes for predictable messages or for messages that summon aid. Others use augmentative systems with synthesized speech output for telephone communication. See Chapter 8 for more details of such systems. In some locations, telephone companies provide teletype (TTY) devices that can be used to relay messages through an operator. When using the device, the individual with ALS types a message, and the operator relays the message to the person being called. Thus, the person receiving the call does not need to use a TTY device. See Chapter 12 for further discussion of telephones.

PORTABLE WRITING SYSTEMS. Portable writing systems fall into two broad categories—paper and pencil systems and the small hand-held typing systems that print messages. It has been our experience that people with ALS who have the hand function to hold a pencil and write prefer to do so rather than using a portable typing system.

MULTIPURPOSE SYSTEMS. A number of computer-based multipurpose assistive communication systems are currently commercially available.

We will not review these systems in detail because technology is changing so rapidly that today's systems will no doubt be replaced by more efficient and effective ones in the near future. These systems have a number of common features including multiple ways of accessing the device (e.g., keyboards or switches), message storage, and multiple output (e.g., printed messages and synthesized speech). Although individuals with ALS typically have good reading and spelling skills, training in the technical aspects of electronic communication devices is necessary.

Stage V: Loss of Useful Speech

Individuals at this stage are no longer able to use natural speech as a functional means of communication and, therefore, must rely on assistive communication devices and techniques. In addition to the communication systems described earlier, the following types of assistive technology may be implemented with individuals who have lost the use of natural speech.

YES/NO RESPONSE SYSTEMS. Establishing a nonfatiguing and reliable means of indicating yes or no is an essential component of communication. Yes/no systems often involve identification of a reliable motor response. Natural gestures such as head nods are preferred, but when this is not possible, eye movements may serve as a signal. As with all novel communication systems, training of communication partners is needed to ensure successful implementation.

EYE-GAZE SYSTEMS. Because eye gaze is usually preserved in individuals with ALS, eye pointing or eye gaze can frequently be used as a selection technique when head and hand movements are no longer functional. Letters or messages are displayed on a large Plexiglas board. Partners identify messages by watching the user's gaze. Again, client and partner training is needed for this unique means of communication. For a more complete description of selection techniques and strategies for use see Beukelman and Mirenda (1992) and Goossens and Crain (1987).

COMMUNICATION FOR PATIENTS ON VENTILATORS. Respiratory complications are common in end-stage ALS. A number of communication options are available to individuals who are ventilator dependent and have good oral movement (see Mitsuda, Baarslag-Benson, Hazel, & Therriault, 1992; Manzano et al., 1993; Tippett & Siebens, 1991). Unfortunately, many individuals on ventilators also exhibit severe dysarthria. Therefore, use of natural speech via a modified tracheotomy tube or electrolarynx is not possible. These individuals will benefit most from one of the assistive communication systems described earlier.

Implementation Issues

Yorkston et al. (1995) summarized the philosophy and principles that guide clinical management decisions for individuals with ALS. The first of these principles is early intervention. Managing the assistive technology needs of individuals with end-stage ALS is extremely difficult. Although the needs of individuals at this stage are urgent, intervention is often inadequate. Individuals with ALS and their families may be unable to make informed decisions during times of crisis. Lack of time and energy may hinder implementation. Early intervention allows the team to provide information at a pace at which patients and families can assimilate it. Early intervention also allows for the gradual introduction of technology, usually beginning with light tech solutions for specific communication needs. Gradually, more comprehensive and perhaps more technologically sophisticated solutions can be adopted.

The second principle of intervention is to focus on communication function rather than on the speech impairment. Because of the relentlessly progressive nature of the disorder, intervention with the goal of stabilizing the speech impairment will not succeed. On the other hand, if the goal is to maintain communicative function, assistive technology can be successful. The third issue faced in planning intervention for individuals with ALS is acknowledgment of the emotional and psychosocial aspects of the disease. Individuals with ALS and their families are making many decisions related to technology. Multiple decisions about wheelchairs, beds, vans, aspirators, ventilators, as well as communication devices may be overwhelming, especially if these decisions are delayed until a point of crisis.

The final principle is to intervene at critical periods. The goal of intervention is to intervene promptly and briefly at critical points when the individual's capabilities have changed and communication needs are not being met. One of the most important periods of intervention is when natural speech is no longer sufficient to meet the individual's needs. At this point, alternative means of communication must be identified and implemented. Promptness in meeting these needs is essential.

PARKINSON'S DISEASE

Description

Parkinson's disease is a common, slowly progressive disease of elders. The occurrence of the disease increases with increasing age. Estimates suggest that 1% of the population over the age of 60 years exhibits the disease (Hull, 1970). Parkinson's disease is the result of deterioration in an area of the brain called the basal ganglia. Specifically, levels of an important neurotransmitter, dopamine, are reduced. The essential problem in Parkinson's disease is the inability to automatically execute learned motor plans (Marsden, 1984). Three motor symptoms are classically seen in the disease. The first is a resting tremor that occurs at a rate of 3 to 6 per second and is reduced during activity or sleep. The second is bradykinesia, which literally means slowness of movement, but more specifically, is an inability to initiate or to perform voluntary movement sequences. Because of bradykinesia, individuals with Parkinson's disease will have reduced levels of a variety of automatic movements including eye blinks, expressive gestures of the hands and face, arm swings during walking, and swallowing of saliva. The third classic symptom is rigidity or increase in muscle tone that is present more or less constantly throughout a movement.

Parkinson's disease is not considered fatal. However, the disease is associated with a variety of functional limitations. Scales such as the Hoehn and Yahr Functional Rating Scale (1967) serve as a general index of severity of the disease. The scale consists of 5 stages and ranges from mild, unilateral symptoms to severe disability and complete dependence. The rate of progression varies from person to person (Marttila & Rinne, 1991). During the last 20 years, drug management has significantly decreased the symptoms of individuals with Parkinson's disease. See Duvoisin (1991) for an excellent discussion of advances in pharmacological interventions.

Many individuals with Parkinson's disease experience problems not directly attributable to motor impairment. These include depression, cognitive changes, and subtle changes in language. Estimates of occurrence of depression range from 40 to 90% of the parkinsonian population (Mayeux, Williams, Stern, & Cote, 1984). Diagnosis of depression is difficult because of other parkinsonian symptoms such as masklike face and changes in cognition. Estimates of the occurrence of cognitive changes in individuals with Parkinson's disease also vary extensively from conservative figures of 15% (Levin, Tomer, & Rey, 1992) to 70% (Cummings, 1988). The following specific cognitive deficits have been identified in Parkinson's disease (Levin et al., 1992):

Failure to initiate activities spontaneously

Inability to develop a successful approach to problem solving

Impaired and slowed memory

Impaired visuospatial perception

Impaired concept formation

Poor word-list generation

Impaired set shifting

Reduced rate of information processing.

Knowledge of the presence, type, and extent of cognitive changes is critical for planning appropriate intervention. Cognitive changes are typically more pronounced in later stages of the disease. Unfortunately, this is the period when assistive communication technology is more likely to be needed. In terms of language impairment, individuals with Parkinson's disease may differ from nondisabled peers on a number of language-related measures, including comprehension and spontaneous language production (Cummings, Darkins, Mendez, Hill, & Benson, 1988; Grossman et al., 1991; Illes, Metter, Hanson, & Iritani 1988).

Characteristics of the Communication Deficits

Dysarthria is common especially in the later stages of Parkinson's disease. In a large survey of individuals with the disease, 70% reported that speech and voice were worse than prior to disease onset (Hartelius & Svensson, 1994). The dysarthria associated with Parkinson's disease results from reduced range of movement. Listeners hear the features of monotonous pitch and loudness, reduced stress, and short phrases. Variable speaking rate, short rushes of speech, and imprecise consonants may also be reflective of the reduced range of speech movements. Voice changes, including breathiness, voice harshness, and low pitch, may be the result of rigidity of the vocal mechanism. Often individuals with Parkinson's disease do not appreciate how difficult it is to understand their speech or how quiet their speech may be. Instructions by a spouse to "speak up" are often not followed and may lead to frustration for both the speaker and the listener.

The features of dysarthria change as severity increases. In mild dysarthria, changes in voice may be the only symptom. These changes may include reduced loudness, breathy or weak voice, reduced pitch flexibility, and an unsteady, hoarse, or rough voice. In moderate dysarthria, there may be a reduction in speech intelligibility in certain situations. In addition to the changes in voice, moderate dysarthria is characterized by a decreased ability to produce consonants and vowels. Some speakers may pause inappropriately, others may speak too rapidly. In severe dysarthria, natural speech may not be a functional means of communication. Some persons with Parkinson's disease cannot initiate voice. For others, speech is produced in short unintelligible bursts. Still others may freeze in the middle of an utterance and be unable to continue. If there are associated cognitive problems, language production may be sparse and infrequent.

Intervention

Problems with Handwriting

The bradykinesia and rigidity associated with Parkinson's disease may result in reduced movement. If the hands and arms are affected, a condition termed micrographia, small handwriting, may be present. Some individuals with Parkinson's disease may benefit from portable typing devices to supplement handwriting. Because of reduced range of movement, small keyboards are usually preferred. Individuals with prominent tremor may need to use a stabilizing bar or keyguard to dampen the tremor. Portable writing devices may also be useful for individuals with severe dysarthria.

Moderate Dysarthria

DELAYED AUDITORY FEEDBACK (DAF). Many individuals with Parkinson's disease speak very rapidly. Their rate in combination with a reduced loudness level makes speech difficult to understand. For some, use of a DAF device may be helpful. Speakers wear this portable device which consists of a microphone, a pocket-sized delay unit/battery, and earphones. The unit delays speech a fraction of a second, which then has the effect of slowing the individual's speaking rate. A number of reports describing successful application of DAF devises are available (Adams, 1994; Downie, Low, & Lindsay, 1981; Hanson & Metter, 1983).

VOICE AMPLIFIERS. Portable voice amplifiers may also be useful for some individuals with Parkinson's disease. They are most effective for speakers who can produce voice consistently, but whose loudness is reduced. Voice amplifiers are typically not satisfactory for those with severe vocal initiation difficulties.

Severe Dysarthria

PACING BOARDS. Pacing boards are simple devices consisting of a series of colored squares separated by ridges (Helm, 1979). The speaker touches one square while saying each word, thus bringing an automatic act under voluntary control. The effectiveness of pacing boards is reduced if movement patterns become overlearned and the individual increases his or her tapping rate.

ALPHABET SUPPLEMENTATION. For individuals with Parkinson's disease this technique (described earlier in this chapter) slows their rapid speaking rate and provides the communication partner with the first letter of each word. In contrast with pacing boards, the technique requires unique selection of movements, and thus cannot be overlearned. The technique may also be helpful for individuals with vocal initiation problems.

Implementation Issues

Parkinson's disease is a slowly progressive disease in which severe speech impairment may not occur until late in its course. Implementation of assistive technology in this population is challenging for a number of reasons. The first is that cognitive decline may occur in addition to the motor impairment. When the speech impairment is severe enough to limit function, cognitive decline may limit learning and use of assistive technology. The second challenge relates to fluctuating symptoms. The severity of speech may vary from hour to hour depending on how long ago the last medication was taken. Long-term use of antiparkinsonian medications tends to worsen the fluctuation of symptoms. Finally, individuals with Parkinson's disease are not always good at judging when their speech is being understood and when listeners are having difficulty. Therefore, well-informed communication partners who can support the patient in the use of assistive technology are necessary.

APRAXIA OF SPEECH AND APHASIA

Description

Apraxia of speech is considered a motor speech disorder. Unlike dysarthria, which affects the execution of speech movements, apraxia of speech is an impairment in the planning of movement sequences. Wertz (1985) defines apraxia as a disruption in the capacity to program the positioning of speech muscles. This disruption prevents the sequencing of muscle movements for speech. It occurs without significant weakness, slowness, or incoordination of these muscles when the speakers are performing automatic acts. In apraxia of speech, the muscles of speech appear to be capable of normal function because they are normal in nonspeech movements such as chewing and eating. In its pure form, when it is not complicated by severe aphasia, an appropriate message appears to have been formulated but it is either difficult to enact the planned message, or the perceptual characteristics of the sounds that emerge are not what is intended (Duffy, 1995).

The most common cause of apraxia of speech is stroke, although it may also occur in individuals with tumors or focal trauma. The common characteristic of these conditions is that they affect isolated areas in the dominant hemisphere that are involved in motor speech programming.

Because apraxia of speech is commonly caused by stroke, the typical course is one of sudden onset followed by a period of recovery and later stabilization. Prognostic indicators are similar for aphasia and apraxia of speech. That is, the most important period of recovery occurs within the first 6 months after onset. Younger individuals and individuals with less severe impairment are thought to make better recovery.

Characteristics of the Communication Deficits

Like other adult-onset, expressive communication problems, the severity of apraxia of speech varies along a continuum. Individuals with mild apraxia of speech may complain that "speech doesn't come out right." These individuals may speak slowly to prevent errors. As severity of the disorder increases, articulatory errors increase in frequency. Individuals with severe apraxia of speech may have only a limited repertoire of speech sounds. Some of these utterances may be highly automatic, for example, phrases such as "okay," "well," and "my oh my." The articulatory errors may be so severe that speakers are unable to even imitate simple words correctly. Unfortunately, severe apraxia of speech is usually accompanied by severe aphasia and nonverbal oral apraxia (difficulty performing voluntary movements of the oral structures such as puckering the lips). Assistive communication technology may benefit individuals at a range of severity levels. In some cases it supplements speech; in others it replaces speech. Rehabilitation efforts with these individuals are challenging not only because of the severity of the impairment but also because of concomitant problems such as aphasia.

Intervention

The following are some approaches to intervention that have been used with individuals with severe apraxia of speech (Yorkston & Waugh, 1989).

Augmented Responses

At times a combination of apraxia of speech, limb apraxia, and aphasia makes it impossible for an individual to respond using natural speech or gestures. For these individuals, a voice output communication device with a small number of preselected responses may help them to indicate choices, such as "yes," "no," "good," "bad," and so on. Candidates for this approach typically exhibit severe apraxia of speech complicated by limb apraxia, aphasia, or both. They often will be unreliable in responding to simple yes/no questions with natural speech or gestures. This failure to respond is often attributed to poor auditory comprehension skills, but may also be due, at least in part, to their inability to formulate an adequate gestural or verbal response.

Comprehensive Communication Approaches

Comprehensive communication approaches are multicomponent assistive communication devices designed for individuals who wish to "go anywhere and say anything" (Beukelman & Garrett, 1988; Garrett & Beukelman, 1992). Such systems usually contain a number of components, including natural speech; a communication book or board for communicating basic needs, personal interests, names of people and locations, among other things; a spelling system; a drawing system (Lyon, 1995); a gestural system; and a well-instructed partner. Candidates for this type of intervention are individuals whose high communicative drive places them in a large number of different communication situations. They may have some natural speech, some identifiable gestures, some spelling and drawing skills, but none of these areas are strong enough to carry the full burden of communication. Their comprehension skills and world knowledge far exceed their expressive abilities. See Chapter 8 for a more complete discussion of such systems with aphasic individuals.

Approaches for Specific Situations

Persons with apraxia and mild aphasia typically continue to communicate in highly specific, personal situations such as going to ball games, playing cards, or using public transportation. They may require any or all of the following components in their communication system:

TOPIC SELECTION. At times, it is helpful to preprint a list of common or preferred topics in a notebook or in a high technology system. Examples include about me/personal history, current events, gossip, politics, vacations, friends and family, movies, and sports. The person with apraxia can then introduce a novel topic or indicate when a topic will shift by pointing to or selecting one of these items.

SPECIFIC VOCABULARY. It is frequently helpful to select specific vocabulary that pertains to each topic in advance. Several options are available for organizing this vocabulary. Items can be arranged categorically, so that all family names or preferred food items are stored on the same page. They can be organized thematically or situationally, so that all words or messages needed for a given situation can be found on a single page (e.g., *Baseball*:I want a ticket for the cheap seats/box seats; Where's the restroom?; I need a bag of peanuts/ice cream bar/hot dog; Good/Average/Lousy game; He should have hit hard/bunted/ grounded/stolen base/waited for the next pitch). Other information is depicted best in a visual format (e.g., locating towns in the state on an outline map, scales to represent opinions, a timeline to represent the chronology of events from the person's life, a family tree). The person with apraxia of speech can then point to this vocabulary if he or she cannot say the words or phrases. At times, this prestored vocabulary helps trigger a more accurate production of the spoken word.

CONTROL PHRASES. It may also be beneficial for the person with apraxia to have access to conversational control phrases. Printed phrases such as "Please don't guess"; "I'll describe it"; "I'll point to the first letter"; "It's not that important—forget it" may allow the person with apraxia to regulate the conversation even when he or she cannot do so verbally.

ALPHABET SUPPLEMENTATION/FIRST LETTER CUEING. Persons with apraxia may also learn to cue their partners regarding the specific word by pointing to its first letter. This strategy is particularly helpful if the word production is approximate but not perfect. This type of application of an alphabet board differs from use by Parkinson's disease patients because it is not used to pace the communicator but rather to cue the partner.

Implementation Issues

Historically, the field of augmentative communication has developed from a number of diverse viewpoints including use of language/word boards for individuals with cerebral palsy and typing or environmental control systems for individuals who used natural speech but who were severely physically disabled. Thus, early work benefited individuals with motor impairment and good literacy skills. A number of trends have been identified that contribute to our increasing ability to serve individuals with severe apraxia and aphasia (Yorkston & Waugh, 1989). The first of these trends is changing technology that provides devices with speech output that do not require spontaneous spelling skills. Other trends include a broadened view of communication competence that suggests that social contact as well as communication of basic needs must be considered. Finally, there is a growing appreciation of the need to develop multicomponent assistive communication systems. A variety of system or system components are used to meet an array of different needs.

SUMMARY

Motor speech disorders are one of the types of expressive communication disorders that may occur in elders. Although communication may be profoundly affected by degenerative diseases such as ALS or Parkinson's disease, or by stroke, communication function need not be lost. Assistive technology can be used by even those with the most profound movement problems. This chapter has reviewed the medical and speech characteristics of four groups and has described the types of technology that may be useful to them (see Table 9–2 for a summary).

Although these disorders differ greatly in symptoms, natural course, and associated problems, a number of themes are consistent across the various groups. First, intervention must take a broad view of communication that includes both the expression of basic wants and needs and the maintenance of social contact. Second, a wide range of assistive devices may be useful in meeting the communication needs of elders. In other words, both light tech and high tech approaches may serve important functions in the overall communication plan. Third, communication abilities and assistive technology needs change over time in all of the populations reviewed in this chapter. Therefore, rehabilitation efforts are not concluded when a device is selected. Rather, long-term follow-up is needed for individuals with both progressive and recovering disease courses. Finally, appropriate assistive technology intervention must be based on a thorough knowledge of the individuals with the severe communication disorder. This knowledge includes an understanding of the effects of aging on function in the areas of cognition, hearing and vision, and on an the understanding of underlying nature of the disorder, typical symptoms, and likely natural course. In addition, those providing services to individuals with severe disabilities must understand the skills and communication needs of their clients. This basic information will continue to be required as the assistive communication systems become more effective and efficient with continuing advances in technology.

Table 9–2. Summary of assistive technology applications for elders with acquired motor speech disorders.

	Locked-in Syndrome	Amyotrophic Lateral Sclerosis	Parkinson's Disease	Apraxia of Speech
Cause	Stroke or trauma	Unknown	Depletion of dopamine	Stroke, tumor, or trauma
Natural course	Recovering or stable	Rapidly progressive	Slowly progressive	Recovering or stable
Type of motor problems	Weakness	Weakness and spasticity	Tremor, bradykinesia, and rigidity	Disruption of motor planning
Associated problems	Medical fragility	Accommodation to a rapidly progressive course	Cognitive decline in late stages	Aphasia
Examples of assistive technology	■ Yes/no signal ■ Call system ■ Auditory scanning system ■ Direct selection or scanning multicomponent device	■ Portable writing systems ■ Voice amplifiers ■ Hearing aids for partners ■ Alphabet boards ■ Alerting systems ■ Telephone communication ■ Multipurpose systems ■ Eye-gaze systems	■ Portable writing systems ■ DAF ■ Voice amplifiers ■ Alphabet pacing boards	■ Augmented response systems ■ Comprehensive communication systems ■ Systems for specific situations

RESOURCES

Academy of Neurologic Disorders and Sciences (ANCDS)
1250 24th St N.W., Suite 300
Washington, DC 20037
(202) 467-2787

American Speech-Language-Hearing Association
10801 Rockville Pike
Rockville, MD 20852
(301) 897-5700

Amyotrophic Lateral Sclerosis Society of America
21021 Ventura Boulevard, Suite 321
Woodland Hills, CA 91364

International Society for Augmentative and Alternative Communication (ISAAC)
ISAAC Secretariat
P.O. Box 1762, Station R
Toronto, Ontario
M4G 4A3, Canada

National Aphasia Association
P.O. Box 1887
Murray Hill Station
New York, NY 10156-0611

National Organization for Apraxia and Dyspraxia
c/o Vicci Hazelwood
32507 Cervin Circle
Temecula, CA 92592

National Parkinson's Disease Foundation
1501 N.W. 9th Avenue
Miami, FL 33136

REFERENCES

Adams, S. G. (1994). Accelerating speech in a case of hypokinetic dysarthria: Descriptions and treatment. In J. A. Till, K. M. Yorkston, & D. R. Beukelman (Eds.), *Motor speech disorders: Advances in assessment and treatment* (pp. 213–228). Baltimore: Paul H. Brookes Publishing.

Appel, V., Stewart, S. S., Smith, G., & Appel, S. H. (1987). A rating scale for amyotrophic lateral sclerosis: Description and preliminary experience. *Annual of Neurology, 22,* 328–333.

Beukelman, D., & Garrett, K. (1988). Augmentative communication for adults with acquired severe communication disorders. *Augmentative and Alternative Communication, 4,* 104–121.

Beukelman, D. R., & Mirenda, P. (1992). *Augmentative and alternative communication: Management of severe communication disorders in children and adults.* Baltimore, MD: Paul H. Brookes Publishing.

Caroscio, J. T., Mulvihill, M. N., Sterling, R., & Abrams, B. (1987). Amyotrophic lateral sclerosis: Its natural history. *Neurologic Clinics, 5,* 1–8.

Cook, A. M., & Hussey, S. M. (1995). *Assistive technologies: Principles and practice.* St. Louis: Mosby.

Culp, D., & Ladtkow, M. C. (1992). Locked-in syndrome and augmentative communication. In K. M. Yorkston (Ed.), *Augmentative communication in the medical setting.* Tucson: Communication Skill Builders.

Cummings, J. (1988). Intellectual impairment in Parkinson's disease: Clinical, pathologic, and biochemical correlates. *Journal Geriatric Psychiatry Neurology, 1,* 24–36.

Cummings, J. L., Darkins, A., Mendez, M., Hill, M. A., & Benson, D. F. (1988). Alzheimer's disease and Parkinson's disease: Comparison of speech and language alterations. *Neurology, 38,* 680–684.

Downie, A. W., Low, J. M., & Lindsay, D. D. (1981). Speech disorders in parkinsonism: Usefulness of delayed auditory feedback in selected cases. British *Journal of Disorders of Communication, 16,* 135–139.

Duffy, J. R. (1995). *Motor speech disorders: Substrates, differential diagnosis, and management.* St. Louis: Mosby.

Duvoisin, R. C. (1991). *Parkinson's disease: A guide for patient and family* (3rd ed). New York: Raven Press.

Edwards, A. D. N. (1991). *Speech synthesis: Technology for disabled people.* London: Paul Chapman Publishing Ltd.

Eisen, A., Schulzer, M., MacNeil, M., Pant, B., & Mak, E. (1993). Duration of amyotrophic lateral sclerosis is age dependent. *Muscle Nerve, 16,* 27–32.

Garrett, K., & Beukelman, D. (1992). Augmentative communication in aphasia. In K. M. Yorkston (Ed.), *Augmentative communication in the medical setting* (pp. 245–338). Tucson: Communication Skill Builders.

Goossens, C., & Crain, S. (1987). Overview of nonelectronic eye-gaze communication technique. *Augmentative and alternative communication, 3,* 77–89.

Grossman, M., Carvell, S., Gollomp, S., Stern, M. B., Vernon, G., & Hurtig, H. I. (1991). Sentence comprehension and praxia deficits in Parkinson's disease. *Neurology, 41,* 1620–1626.

Haig, A. J., Katz, R. T., & Sahgal, V. (1987). Mortality and complications of the locked-in syndrome. *Archives of Physical Medicine and Rehabilitation, 68,* 24–27.

Hanson, W., & Metter, E. (1983). DAF speech rate modification in Parkinson's disease: A report of two cases. In W. Berry (Ed.), *Clinical dysarthria* (pp. 231–254). Austin, TX: Pro-Ed.

Hartelius, L., & Svensson, P. (1994). Speech and swallowing symptoms associated with Parkinson's disease and multiple sclerosis: A survey. *Folia Phoniatrica et Logopaedica, 46,* 9–17.

Helm, N. (1979). Management of palilallia with a pacing board. *Journal of Speech and Hearing Disorders, 44,* 350–353.

Hoehn, M. M., & Yahr, M. D. (1967). Parkinsonism: Onset, progression and mortality. *Neurology, 17,* 427–442.

Hull, J. T. (1970). The prevalence and incidence of Parkinson's disease. *Geriatrics, 25,* 128–133.

Illes, J., Metter, E. J., Hanson, W. R., & Iritani, S. (1988). Language production in Parkinson's disease: Acoustic and linguistic considerations. *Brain and Language, 33,* 146–160.

Katz, R. T., Haig, A. J., Clark, B. B., & DiPaola, R. J. (1992). Long-term survival, prognosis, and life-care planning for 29 patients with chronic locked-in syndrome. *Archives of Physical Medicine and Rehabilitation, 73,* 403–408.

Keane, J. R. (1986). Locked-in syndrome after head and neck trauma. *Neurology, 36,* 80–82.

Levin, B. E., Tomer, R., & Rey, G. J. (1992). Cognitive impairments in Parkinson's disease. *Neurologic Clinics, 10,* 471–481.

Lyon, J. G. (1995). Drawing: Its value as a communication aid for adults with aphasia. *Aphasiology, 9,* 33–50.

Manzano, J. L., Lubillo, S., Henríquez, D., Martín, J. C., Pérez, M. C., & Wilson, D. J. (1993). Verbal communication of ventilator-dependent patients. *Critical Care Medicine, 21,* 512–517.

Marsden, C. D. (1984). The pathophysiology of movement disorders. *Neurologic Clinics, 2,* 435–459.

Marttila, R., & Rinne, U. (1991). Progression and survival in Parkinson's disease. *Acta Neurologica Scandinavia, 136* (Suppl.), 24–28.

Mauss-Clum, N., Cole, M., McCort, T., & Eifler, D. (1991). Locked-in syndrome: A team approach. *Journal of Neuroscience Nursing., 23,* 273–285.

Mayeux, R., Williams, J. B. W., Stern, Y., & Cote, L. (1984). Depression and Parkinson's disease. In R. G. Hassler & J. F. Christ (Eds.), *Advances in neurology.* New York: Raven Press.

McCusker, E. A., Rudick, R. A., Honch, G. W., & Griggs, R. C. (1982). Recovery from the "locked-in" syndrome. *Archives of Neurology, 39,* 145–147.

McDonald, E. R., Wiedenfeld, S. A., Hillel, A., Carpenter, C. L., & Walter, R. A. (1994). Survival in amyotrophic lateral sclerosis: The role of psychological factors. *Archives of Neurology, 51,* 17–23.

Mitsuda, P. M., Baarslag-Benson, R., Hazel, K., & Therriault, T. M. (1992). Augmentative communication in intensive and acute care settings. In K. M. Yorkston (Ed.), *Augmentative communication in the medical setting.* Tucson, AZ: Communication Skill Builders.

Montgomery, J. H. (1991). *To the edge and back.* (Available from Glenrose Rehabilitation Hospital 10230–111 Avenue, Edmonton, Canada.)

Patterson, J. R., & Grabois, M. (1986). Locked-in syndrome: A review of 139 cases. *Stroke, 17,* 758–764.

Plum, F., & Posner, J. B. (1966). *The diagnosis of stupor and coma.* Philadelphia: F. A. Davis.

Pradas, J., Finison, L., Andres, P. L., Thornell, B., Hollander, D., & Munsat, T. L. (1993). The natural history of amyotrophic lateral sclerosis and the use of natural history control in therapeutic trials. *Neurology, 43,* 751–755.

Rosen, A. (1978). Amyotrophic lateral sclerosis: Clinical features and prognosis. *Archives of Neurology, 35,* 638–642.

Tippett, D. C., & Siebens, A. A. (1991). Using ventilators for speaking and swallowing. *Dysphagia, 6,* 94–99.

Wertz, R. T. (1985). Neuropathologies of speech and language: An introduction to patient management. In D. F. Johns (Ed.), *Clinical management of neurogenic communicative disorders.* Boston: Little, Brown.

Yorkston, K. M., & Waugh, P. F. (1989). Use of augmentative communication devices with apractic individuals. In P. Square-Storer (Ed.), *Apraxia of speech.* London: Taylor & Francis.

Yorkston, K. M., Beukelman, D. R., & Bell, K. R. (1988). *Clinical management of dysarthric speakers* . Austin, TX: Pro-Ed.

Yorkston, K. M., Miller, R. M., & Strand, E. A. (1995). *Management of speech and swallowing disorders in degenerative disease.* Tucson, AZ: Communication Skill Builders.

10

Architecture as a Communication Medium

Edward Steinfeld, Arch.D.

INTRODUCTION

It is unusual to find a chapter on architecture in a book concerned with communication technologies. However, for more than 30 years it has been clear that the physical environment is used as a form of nonverbal communication. Since the 1960s there has been extensive research on issues of environment and human behavior. Two of the most important early books on the subject were E. T. Hall's *The Hidden Dimension* (1966) and Robert Sommer's *Personal Space* (1969). Social gerontologists were some of the first researchers to give attention to these issues, most notably in a book edited by Leon Pastalan and Daniel Carson called *The Spatial Behavior of Older People* (1970). Much has been written over the last 30 years, and it is impossible to give all the literature justice in the space of one chapter. Thus, this contribution focuses on identifying the role of the physical environment as a medium for communications during old age and on providing a conceptual framework for practice. Selected key findings of research will be discussed where they have a significant bearing on the work of communications therapists and others interested in facilitating effective communication with elders.

Importance of Environment

The multidiscliplinary field of environment and behavior studies has devoted attention to many aspects of the interaction between people and their physical world. At least three perspectives that have relevance in communication have emerged from this research:

1. The environment as an information field.
2. The environment as a prosthetic device.
3. The environment as an extension of self.

As an information field, the environment provides information about the world to individuals. As a prosthetic device, it assists individuals in understanding events, making decisions, and taking appropriate action. As an extension of self, it communicates information about the social status of individuals and groups and helps to structure the social relations through which the self develops.

Underlying this chapter are two propositions. First, the environment can be viewed as a type of assistive technology that compensates for age-related losses. Through enabling environmental design, we can help older people retain as much independence as possible. Second, the physical environment can be viewed as the spatialization of social relations in late adulthood. That is, in addition to being a communication device, the physical world structures and organizes the social relations of older people. In this way it serves, much like mass media, as a means through which the experience of aging itself is reproduced in our culture.

Many theorists have proposed that environmental design is basically a search for a "good fit" between individuals and their surroundings. Lawton and Nahemow (1973) proposed the Environmental Docility Hypothesis to describe the fit between person and environment in old age (see Figure 10–1). This model is based on adaptation level theory. Good fit is conceived as a match between adaptive capacity and environmental demand. As the demands of an environment increase or adaptive capacity decreases, the individual's performance declines in effectiveness. If abilities or environmental support improves, more effective performance results. People with limited adaptive capacity are more sensitive to environmental demand. They are the ones who are most vulnerable to environmental overload or underload. The Environmental Docility Hypothesis recognizes that there can be two types of misfits between individuals and environment. The first occurs when demand exceeds adaptive capacity. This produces the stress of overload. The second is caused when the demands of an environment produce too little challenge for an individual; this results in understimulation.

An important aspect of the model with particular relevance to the rehabilitation and design fields is the proposition that adaptive capacity

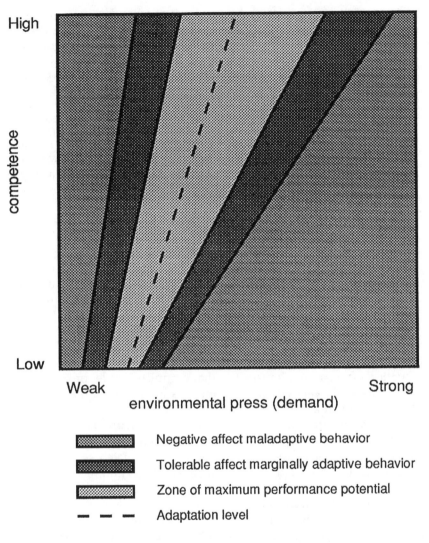

Figure 10–1. Environmental Docility Hypothesis.

can be altered for better or worse, through both environmental and social interventions. Thus, for example, individuals who experience little challenge in their physical world, or are provided with services on which they become dependent, may lose capacity to respond to the full range of challenges within their potential. Therapy has an important role in good fit. It is a means to improve adaptive capacity or restore it to previous levels through learning new skills or relearning lost skills.

There are also social implications to the model. Individuals who find themselves in a situation where environmental demands exceed their ability to cope will demonstrate incompetent behavior. Not only will other people in their social world perceive that incompetence, but they may internalize it as well.

Social status and self-concept are tied to social and personal expectations related to aging. Pastalan (1990, p. 98) proposed that several status passages occur in late adulthood. From a cultural perspective, most of these have negative connotations and can be conceptualized as "losses." There are losses of social roles due to retirement and the roles of parent and spouse. There are losses that occur with widowhood and the weakening of social networks due to deaths or migrations of friends and relatives. There is the loss of physical function due to physiological change. There may be losses of independence or function due to disability and health problems. Although many older people have substantial discretionary income, for others, retirement and/or widowhood bring a significant loss of economic status. The significant status passages associated with aging demand psychological adjustment from the individual. Much has been written about this process and there are several theories about what constitutes successful adjustment to old age. It is sufficient here to acknowledge that the process is, essentially, a continuation of the search for identity that occupies people for their entire lives. This search takes on new meaning as we approach the end of life (Erikson, 1968, pp. 85–87).

Environmental change is often associated with status passages. These changes may be small scale, such as the deterioration of one's home due to deferred maintenance, or large scale, such as relocation to a retirement home or a move to a different geographic region. Environmental changes can be involuntary or voluntary. In whatever form, they represent changes in social status and/or identity. Involuntary changes are not viewed positively. To the individual, they are threats to an established identity and can also be reflections of aging as a social construction, for example, when children move their parents to a nursing home. Voluntary changes, on the other hand, are conscious efforts to change or maintain identity and thus can be understood as part of the presentation of self (e.g., Goffman, 1972, pp. 234–244).

It is important to note that chronological age is not necessarily consistent with biological or social aging. Individuals within the population experience biological and social aging at vastly different rates. Thus, these status passages do not occur neatly along a preordained timetable. Individual differences mean that each person has a unique aging career and relationship with his or her physical world. Although there are many similarities in experience across the older population, there are just as many differences between individuals. Rehabilitation practitioners should learn to pay close attention to these differences and avoid letting stereotypes of aging mask the specific needs of each client.

THE ENVIRONMENT AS AN INFORMATION FIELD

Perception is a continuous information processing activity. The environment is a field from which the individual samples and selects significant information on which attention is then focused. Through selective attention, the individual constructs a "figure" distinct from the "ground" of secondary information. Most theorists today agree that our knowledge of the environment is significantly affected by the degree to which we construct reality as we search for and select relevant data from the information field around us (e.g., Kaplan & Kaplan, 1982).

Two aspects of this process are particularly important in understanding how the environment functions as a communications medium in old age: (a) the accuracy with which key information is perceived and (b) access to information.

Accuracy

In general, the sensory and cognitive losses associated with aging make it more difficult for older people to perceive information in the world. Important information can be considered as a type of signal. We can conceptualize the process of perceiving such information as a task in "signal detection." The degree to which a signal is detected from its background is a function of the strength of the signal, the individual's ability to perceive it, and its relationship to the information field within which it is embedded (Sanders & McKormick, 1993, p. 62). Three types of errors can result in the loss of signal detection. First, the perceiver can miss important information. An example is an inability to perceive an exit sign on a throughway or a street sign at an intersection. The second type of error is misinterpretation of the signal. For example, thinking that an ideogram on a restroom door represents a man when it actually represents a woman. Third, one may perceive a signal when there is none, for example, thinking that a crosswalk sign has changed to "walk" when it has not.

Clarifying the environment includes careful modulation of signal strength or exposure, the background noise level, and the relationship between the signal and its background. Older people who have experienced significant sensory reception losses (for most, this occurs about the age of 75) need such clarification to ensure satisfactory signal detection. This is the basis for many of the recommendations found in guidebooks on design for older people such as increased type size on signs and high contrast between signs and their backgrounds. In these guidelines, emphasis is often placed on increasing the strength of the signal, for example, larger type size. It should be noted that control of background elements, such as the reduction of glare from uncontrolled reflections or the reduction of noise from reverberations from air conditioning machinery, can be just as effective as increasing signal strength. In fact, increasing the signal strength without controlling noise can often result in a more detrimental situation than keeping signal strength low. This is most obvious where light levels are doubled but reflective surfaces are not eliminated. The resulting "disability glare" can create even more serious problems for older people than lower light levels. A similar problem occurs when hearing aid amplification systems boost noise as much as the sound signal.

Increasing the exposure of a signal is another very effective technique for making signals more detectable. For example, signage can be relocated so that it is more directly in the field of view (e.g., overhead) and more than one presentation of important information can be provided through "redundant cueing" (Cohen & Weisman, 1991, p. 56). This technique uses more than one sense modality to facilitate perception of signals. It provides alternative presentations for those who may have limitations in vision or hearing.

Access to Information

Visual exposure of important information in environmental design has significance far beyond signal detection. Norman (1988, p. 17) pointed out that hiding information about the functions of products leads to great difficulties in their use. One of the best examples is the design of computer software. The function of some screen icons is not apparent unless one has been instructed in what they mean. Pull-down menus, on the other hand, provide a high level of information on the commands that is accessible at any time. The principle of "making things visible" (Norman, 1988, p. 17) is a general design principle that has relevance for architectural and interior design for older people as well as product design. It is particularly relevant for designing places used by people who have cognitive impairments. Recommendations for design and modification of facilities for people with dementia emphasize visual exposure. For example, in a guidebook on home modifications for people with dementia, Pynoos, Cohen, and Lucas (1988) suggested putting a picture of a toilet on the outside of a bathroom door to support wayfinding and continence.

In conventional wisdom, physical environments are usually conceived as stable and static. But, our experience of the physical world as we move through it is actually quite dynamic and results in rapidly shifting information flows. It is very difficult to construct representations of these information flows because they are so complex. Benedikt (1979) developed a method using the concept of "isovist" to describe the environment as a field of information with different levels of visual access to the observer. Figure 10–2 shows the basic idea behind the isovist concept. The line of sight from the individual to an object within view is the "isovist." From any point in space, an individual has access to information that is not hidden by occluding surfaces. This forms the field of view. By laying out isovists on a plan of a space, it is possible to measure the degree of visual access from any one point in terms of area, bounding surface perimeter, or other calculable geometric properties. As one passes through space, the information field unfolds, new information becomes accessible, and previously accessible information is hidden.

People generally scan the environment around them so that the visual field to which they pay attention is not necessarily only within a limited angle of view. Moreover, visual exposure to others is an important factor in social relations. Lack of good sight lines when talking can eliminate people from a conversation. Lack of good exposure to formal or informal activities will reduce participation in them. From the perspective of self-concept, reduced exposure can result in isolation or loss of self-esteem. Consider the individual whose chair at the end of a long table limits eye contact with others and is ignored whenever he or she tries to speak. Archea (1984) demonstrated that social use of space is related to levels of visual access and exposure. For example, older people in a nursing home will congregate at points that have a high level of visual access, such as the nurses' station. People seeking intimacy and solitude will search out and find those places that have a low level of visual exposure.

Because of reduced sensory reception abilities and lower mobility (decreased ability to scan and move around in space), older people need a higher degree of visual access to obtain the same level of information about a setting or social relations than younger people. Indeed, guidelines for the design of facilities for older people with disabilities (Cohen & Weisman, 1991) usually include many suggestions that emphasize increasing the visual "permeability" of space, that is, providing more

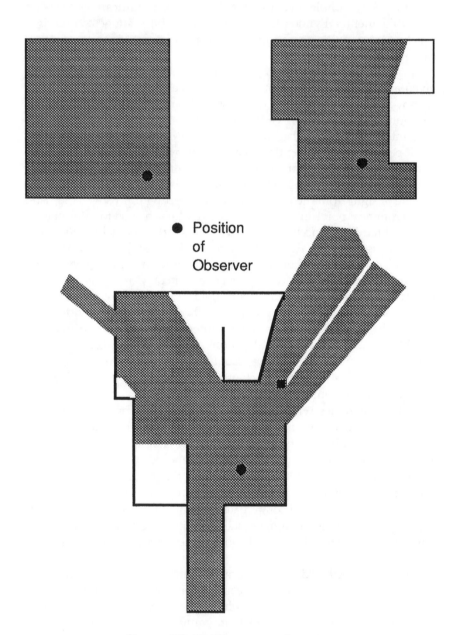

Figure 10–2. The concept of isovists.

visual access to important spaces. Likewise, the complementary need for privacy is well understood and such guidelines also emphasize its importance. Permeability helps older persons improve their knowledge of the social as well as physical environment. With more exposure, they are more likely to participate in social interaction, make fewer mistakes, and thus have a better self-image. Privacy allows individuals to control their degree of exposure based on their own desires at any moment. Without physical means to obtain privacy individuals may use reserve as a means to withdraw. Thus, too much exposure is maladaptive.

Many problems in the design of facilities for older people result from poor levels of visual access and exposure of resident activities. Code requirements often restrict the creation of more permeable buildings. The function of space in terms of visual access and exposure is well understood by building code writers. However, they usually focus on different goals than social integration. Thus, for efficiency in supervision, building codes for long-term care facilities often require a nursing unit station to be located at a point where it provides visual access to the doorways of all patient rooms. Maximum distances from nursing stations to the farthest room are also mandated. This severely restricts the options for floor plans and privacy. Other code requirements limit visual permeability indirectly. For example, many fire codes prohibit open areas off corridors beyond very minimum sizes and large glass areas in fire-rated partitions. Thus, the goals of regulators and management are at odds with the communication needs of residents. When management and regulators are primarily concerned with supervision and fire safety to the point where options for privacy and intimacy are too limited, the result is often an environment that optimizes control to the detriment of privacy, social contact, and orientation for the residents.

Although the isovist concept can be a very helpful analytical tool, it has some limitations. Existing research on isovists has not progressed beyond visual modality nor does it account for the three-dimensional qualities of space such as two-story spaces. Although it is still far from perfect, the concept is very useful at an intuitive level to understand a basic principle in design of space for older people. By improving visual access to important information, the user's knowledge about activities and resources in a building can remain at high levels even though sensory reception and mobility have decreased. High levels of visual exposure for social gathering places will increase their use. And, providing places with low levels of visual exposure will support intimacy and solitude, a necessary ingredient for developing a positive self-concept.

THE ENVIRONMENT AS A PROSTHETIC DEVICE

As an information field, the environment acts indirectly on communication. It is up to the individual to act on the information received. However, the environment also plays a more direct role in support of communication in its prosthetic function. The use of the environment for support in comprehension, making decisions, and taking appropriate action depends heavily on the how well people understand the functions of space and the objects in it.

Affordances

Affordances are properties of objects and spaces that communicate functions (Norman (1988). An example of an affordance is the handle of a hammer. The handle's length, width, and shape all are properties that *afford* gripping. Affordances are critical for ensuring the demonstration of competence in use of the physical world. Nothing is more embarrassing, for example, than being unable to operate an everyday product that should be easy to use. For example, Norman cites doors that provide no clue as to how they should be opened, particularly when equipped with the ubiquitous horizontal "panic bar" which does not indicate which side of the door to push.

One of the most familiar recommendations for improving the use of an environment by older people is to replace doorknobs with lever handles. Although it is true that lever handles are much easier for people with arthritic hands to use, they also are a significant improvement in the *affordance* of door opening. The doorknob gives no clue as to which way it should be turned to open the latch. The lever handle, on the other hand, clearly should be operated by pushing down. Although it may seem trivial, the provision of affordances like this example can help individuals with cognitive impairments to make effective use of space around them. In one of our research studies, an older woman who had suffered a stroke was videotaped as she tried to open over 20 different doors. She had significant difficulty, to the point of almost giving up, in determining which way some doors should open. In one case, she tried five or six times to pull a door toward her when it should have been pushed. She also had difficulty determining which way to turn doorknobs. Each one of the doors that she tested operated in a slightly different way. Some had door knobs; others had push plates or pull handles; some she entered from the right; others from the left; some had self-closing devices and no latches; others had latches and required manual closing. Because of this complexity, she found the environment to be quite unpredictable and became confused. Yet, she was perfectly capable of operating any of the doors. When she guessed correctly, she had no difficulty.

Doors are a good example to demonstrate how affordances can be improved. The trim on the frame of the door and the hinge location provide information on the direction of door swing but not many people are aware of these features, particularly when lighting conditions are poor or eyesight is failing. The slight differences between push and pull slides are not usually easy to see. The use of instruction signs (e.g., "push" or "pull"), pushplates, or kickplates can indicate which way a door should be opened. Better lighting and hinge and frame colors that contrast with the door can improve the understanding of door opening direction. Standardization of door function can also be effective. For example, all doors leading out of rooms could swing out.

Sometimes an otherwise well designed product or space can be inconvenient and unsafe because it lacks strong affordances. For example, the water faucet in my kitchen (Figure 10–3) is designed to be very

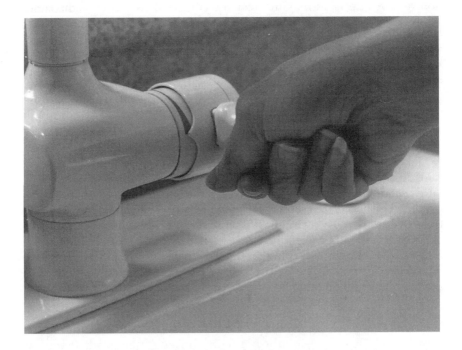

Figure 10–3. Water faucet.

easy to grip; it can be adjusted without twisting the wrist but it has an unusual method of operation. There are symbols on the control that show the direction for adjusting the water from hot to cold (blue for cold and red for hot.) The wedge shape indicates temperature. But most people would not associate these symbols with the function of the lever. Moreover, the handle moves to the right for increased flow and to the left to shut off. Typical single lever faucets move to the left for hot water and to the right for cold; and upward movement is usually associated with increasing flow. Thus, although this faucet has been designed for easy use by arthritic hands, it has not been designed for easy use from a cognitive perspective. The operation method should have been consistent with the common conceptual model of faucet operation.

Another example of poor affordance is poor spatial mapping of range burner controls. Many ranges have controls all in a row but the burners themselves are arranged in a square pattern. Controls arranged in the same spatial pattern provide an affordance for remembering which control adjusts which burner.

Many products do not provide enough feedback to help an older person know the status of operation. Feedback is essential when operation requires decision-making over the course of use. One of the best examples is the electric range that provides little information about whether burners are on or off when the temperature is set to low levels. The position of the knob on the burner control can sometimes be helpful, but for the individual with poor vision it is not usually sufficient. Some cooktops have warning lights indicating that a burner has been turned on. The new halogen burners, however, glow bright red when they have been turned on, no matter what temperature is selected.

Another good example of the importance of feedback is the tea kettle. My father (about age 85 at the time) once came to visit and decided to make himself some tea. At the time, we used a pot to boil water for tea. It made only a quiet rattling sound when it reached the boiling point. My father sat down in the living room to read the paper while waiting for his water to boil and dozed off. When we came home, the pot had melted on the stove burner! The burner was shorted, and it had almost caused a major fire. My father explained that he had a kettle that whistled. He never had a problem "sleeping on the job" in his own home because the whistle woke him up. The lack of the piercing whistle actually caused the accident. It is unlikely that he would have slept through it.

Cognitive Demand

Declines in central nervous system function are associated with normal aging and, of course, are exacerbated by dementia. These losses reduce the ability of an individual to react quickly, process large amounts of information, and complete evaluation and decision-making tasks in a reasonable time. Reduced ability to perform cognitive tasks essentially lowers the threshold of cognitive overload. This is not unlike the same condition that younger people encounter when demands for interpretation, evaluation, and decision-making are so great that they cannot keep up. The task of flying a high-speed aircraft, for example, would tax all but a few younger adults. For the older person however, cognitive overload can be reached in the course of many everyday tasks.

Adaptations to cognitive overload include pacing exposure to the information load, selective attention, and reliance on experience. By pacing, or acting slowly, an individual is reducing the amount of information that needs to be processed at one time to a tolerable level. This characteristic behavior, which is called cautiousness, is often observed among older people when crossing streets, driving, using busy buildings such as airport terminals, and making decisions at automatic teller machines or other automated devices. Although older people without dementia can generally perform cognitive tasks as well as people who are younger, they often need much more time to do so and have much greater difficulty giving attention to more than one thing at a time. The environment, then, can set the stage for cognitive performance in two ways: by keeping the cognitive load required to perform in any situation manageable and by reducing time pressures associated with completing any activity.

In the course of everyday events, everyone selects what is most important from all the information available. The older person adapts by narrowing the range of information that is given attention even further. A good example of this phenomenon was presented at a Human Factors and Ergonomics Society Symposium on the Older Driver in 1994. An occupational therapist who trains older people to improve driving skills described her experience riding with an older woman during driver education sessions compared to the woman's performance when taking the actual road test for a license. During the training session, a number of drivers followed each other through a course on city streets. During the actual exam however, each person was on his or her own. There was no one to follow. In the training session, when, she was able to follow the lead of the trainee in the car in front of her, this particular driver performed well At her exam, she had no one to use as a guide and was unable to pass the test.

Reliance on experience can be a successful adaptation strategy as long as the environment is familiar. Decrements in performance of everyday tasks are most noticeable in unfamiliar environments. In the familiar world of home and local community, an individual with cognitive problems may be able to function quite well by relying on the stability of the environment and habitual patterns of action. One research group that studied older drivers found that they performed much better within their familiar "home range" than they did in unfamiliar territory (Pastalan, Merrill, & Pomerantz, 1975). As another example, it is not uncommon for someone who has been placed in a nursing home to have a sharp and rapid decline in function. Family members often observe that the relocation occurred "just in time." An alternative explanation for the change of behavior could easily be the inability of the elder to utilize habitual patterns of action to accomplish everyday tasks. In a home that one has lived in for 30 or 40 years, there is no need to stop and think about where the bathroom is or how a door works. In the new environment, the same individual must expend a considerable amount of effort to learn how things work and where they are. During the early stages of relocation, many mistakes and apparently incompetent behavior may be evident. In fact, individuals may become overwhelmed by the increased cognitive load and give up doing many things that they did before as an adaptation strategy. New arrivals may need support and assistance to learn new behaviors.

Apparent incompetence in cognitive tasks is most evident where the instability of the environment is high, where attention must be given to multiple sources of information for successful performance, and where decision-making must take place under pressure.

There are many sources of environmental instability. It can occur when an individual is forced to relocate from one living setting to another, such as moving from one nursing home to another or even from one floor to another. It may also be caused by unpredictable events such as unannounced change in bus routes or schedules. Because physical environments are relatively stable, changes in the physical structure of a place are unusual, but when they occur they can become quite disorienting. An example of a physically unstable environment is a house that is deteriorating due to deferred maintenance or a neighborhood that has encountered significant increases in traffic.

In the course of everyday events, we encounter many tasks that require divided attention. The most obvious example is driving. Less obvious, but just as important for safety, is the task of walking up and down a stairway. Research has demonstrated that the visual environment of a stairway is just as significant for safe traversal as the configuration of the stairs or presence of a handrail (e.g., Carson, Archea, Margulis, & Carson, 1978; Templer, 1992). To ensure safe use, the physical features of a stairway have to be clarified (as discussed previously) and the environment structured so that objects in the general field do not distract attention away from those things that are critical for maintaining balance and a proper gait. Most falls usually occur near the top and bottom of the stairway during or immediately after mounting and before dismounting (Templer, 1992). Detailed studies of stairway accidents have demonstrated that the isovist field often expands abruptly at these locations, rapidly increasing the amount of information within view. This happens when walls or ceilings terminate near the end or beginning of their stair turn. This is also the location where the stairway user must change gait to accommodate mounting or dismounting. The result can be distraction and divided attention and, therefore, more missteps.

Crossing streets is also known to be far more dangerous to the older individual than it is to younger adults (e.g., Carp, 1971) because of the need to pay attention to many sources of information at one time and the inherent instability of the environment (moving traffic). Research has identified a characteristic hesitation on the part of the older person prior to crossing at an intersection (Wilson & Grayson, 1980). In fact, sometimes older persons will wait through a whole cycle of light changes before they venture out into the street. There is so much information to process at intersections that it exceeds their cognitive capacity. By pacing themselves carefully, they are able to identify all the potential threats and develop an effective safe strategy for crossing before putting themselves at risk.

Decision-making under time pressure is a particularly difficult problem for the older person with cognitive deficits because the adaptation strategy of cautiousness will not work when a narrow time frame for action is set for a task. It becomes even more difficult when there are social pressures from others in the surroundings to perform quickly.

Countermeasures

Many environmental countermeasures can be used to compensate for age-related cognitive impairments. Essentially, these countermeasures can be seen as prosthetic devices that aid in overcoming the deficits of information processing. They include those that have direct benefit by improving the accuracy and speed of sensory reception and reducing the demand for action.

One set of countermeasures focuses on the organization of space. The presence of orientation edges in which an individual is abruptly confronted with a large increase in the perceptual field should be reduced to a minimum or eliminated. A slow transition can be made through "previews" of the scene ahead or a gradual unfolding of the view. Time constraints can be expanded by stretching out decision-making points in space. Reducing the number of activities that take place at one point in time is particularly effective in bringing the cognitive load within manageable limits. For example, the entrance to a theater, transportation terminal, or theme park can be designed so that a ticket purchase can be made at one location along a path and the point at which a decision is made about which way to proceed can be set far enough away to allow preparation for that decision.

Instability of the environment is a major source of stress for older people. Although reducing physical changes is desirable as a strategy for improving stability of the environment, such changes are often the result of outside influences that are beyound anyone's control. For example, residents of long-term care facilities often have to relocate from one building to another when a new facility is built. Individuals may need relocation from independent living to a long-term care facility because of declines in health. Pastalan and Boursetom (1975) demonstrated that preparing residents for nursing home relocation with pre-move site visits can significantly reduce stress to the point that mortality is reduced after the move. Hunt and Pastalan (1987) demonstrated how a simulation method using models and slides can provide even more information about the new building than site visits. This suggests an important role for the communication therapist in relocation planning. Professionals in the rehabilitation fields can also represent the older person's interests in community planning. An emphasis on maintaining familiar patterns of use and important orientation landmarks should be goals of such activities.

Emergencies caused by fires, violence, or natural disasters are examples of unusual events that affect the stability of an environment. Older people are particularly vulnerable to extraordinary events such as these that usually come without warning. In addition to the unusual quality of the event itself, emergencies are often accompanied by rapid changes in the physical environment. There are many examples of older people suffering death or severe injury because they had difficulty adapting to the emergency conditions. Two maladaptive responses to emergencies are putting oneself at risk and "negative panic" or inaction.

Studies of emergency behavior show that an immediate reaction to an emergency is often movement toward someone or something that is personally significant (Archea, 1993; Sime, 1985). Sime (1985) described how parents in a nightclub of an entertainment complex immediately moved toward the location where they had left their children when a fire erupted. Fire investigation reports include descriptions of how people who have already been evacuated from a burning building go back into their apartment or room to retrieve important objects like medications (e.g., Willey, 1973). Archea (1993) described similar responses to earthquakes. Some individuals he interviewed moved to protect valuable possessions or loved ones in other rooms of the home. This movement toward something of personal significance often puts a person at greater risk than alternative courses of action and thus appears irrational. Seen from the perspective of the individual however, this type of behavior can be viewed as an attempt to maintain stability in a very uncertain world.

A common response of older people to emergencies is inaction. In several building fires in facilities for older people, many residents who perished apparently did not attempt to leave (e.g., Willey, 1973). In aircraft accidents there are also examples of older people who remained in their seats only to perish (e.g., National Transportation and Safety Board, 1973). Apparently when faced with so much uncertainty, the cognitive load becomes overwhelming and doing nothing appears to be the only course of action that is tolerable. By staying put, the individual may hope to ride out the storm and wait until some sense can be made of the environment. Thus, decision-making will be easier.

Two types of countermeasures can be used to overcome the great information overload caused by emergency situations. First, good preparation through consumer information and practice drills can help to speed response and aid decision-making during the emergency event. Second, environmental design that exposes the best path of refuge to everyday experience will make it easier for people to make a right decision during an emergency. For example, buildings designed as one long corridor usually have an elevator tower in the center and emergency stairways at either end. The residents of the building use the elevator every day, maybe several times, and become used to exiting and entering at the center. They rarely, if ever, use the stairways. But, in an emergency, they must alter their pattern of movement to the opposite direction, away from the center of the building, in order to reach the emergency stairways. They may not even know where the stairways are. Locating emergency exits along paths used for everyday circulation reduces the complexity of the emergency evacuation task because the path of travel will be the same and the residents' cognitive map will already include the location of exits.

THE ENVIRONMENT AS AN EXTENSION OF SELF

The physical environment can be viewed as the medium through which individuals construct their presentation of self to others in their social network and social world. The social perception of others is also influenced by environmental factors. Three key environmental features that play a role in the formation of identity are spatial organization, personalization of the environment, and the regulation of boundaries between an individual or social group and others.

Spatial Organization

Spatial syntax is a term coined by Hillier and Hanson (1984) to describe the organization of space in social terms. They developed a representation system for diagramming this organization. This system makes it possible to compare the social properties of buildings using graphic and quantitative methods. Figure 10–4 shows the spatial syntax of two floor plans diagrammed as a justified graph. The circle with the cross at the bottom indicates the outside. Each circle in the graph represents a space and each line link represents a connection between them (e.g., a doorway). Although the plans are relatively similar, two very different spatial structures can be clearly seen in the diagrams, a tree-like structure (Figure 10–4A) and a ring-like structure (Figure 10–4B). Tree-like buildings have a high degree of control over access from one space to another or to the outside. In ring-like buildings, there is less control because there are more alternative paths to the same destination. Each level of the graph represents one step into the structure of the building. Deep buildings have many steps between the outside and the deepest space. Shallow buildings have few steps. Thus, deep buildings are less well integrated with the community than shallow buildings; they put more social distance between inhabitants and others.

Hillier and Hanson (1984) argued that spatial syntax describes the inherent social qualities of a building. For example, ring-like buildings provide the potential for a higher degree of social integration among inhabitants and shallow buildings reduce the barriers between inhabitants and the community. Through cross-cultural analyses and comparisons of different building types, they demonstrated how the purposes of buildings and cultural values toward use of space lead to construction of buildings with different spatial syntaxes. Most buildings are combinations of tree-like and ring-like structures and have a very complex spatial syntax. Thus, to simplify comparison, Hillier and Hanson (1984) devised mathematical formulae for computing the degree of social integration and social control inherent in any floor plan.

Spatial syntax is valuable for uncovering the social implications of architectural plans. Hillier and Hanson (1984) categorized inhabitants as either "residents," those who control access to the space, or "visitors,"

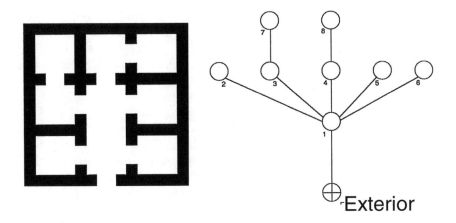

A. Tree-Like Structure

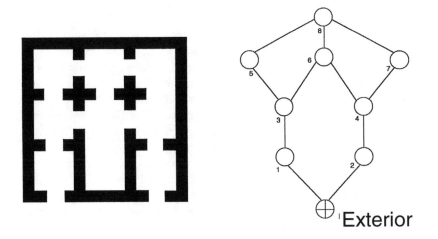

B. Ring-Like Structure

Figure 10–4. Spatial syntax. **A.** Tree-like structure. **B.** Ring-like structure. (Adapted from *The Social Logic of Space* by B. Hillier and J. Hanson, 1994. Cambridge: Cambridge University Press.)

those who are subservient in the social hierarchy to the residents and have only temporary access to spaces. In most buildings, residents can be found deep within the spatial structure, that is, at the top of the justified graph (when the outside is at the bottom). In some buildings, however, which they termed "reversed buildings," visitors can be found deep within the structure. This is the case with most institutional buildings like prisons or hospitals. In such buildings, there is a high degree of control over the "visitors," for example, prisoners or patients. Institutional buildings also tend to have highly tree-like structures that reflect the extensive levels of control inherent in such organizations.

The spatial organization of buildings, then, communicates status and the nature of social relations in a place. This is no accident but rather the result of purposeful planning to make space meet certain social goals. Hillier and Hanson (1984) argued that the spatial organization of a building embodies the social relations that take place there and the social intent is, in turn, reproduced by the building form as it structures the relationships between the inhabitants. The spatial organization essentially supports or deters various types of social relations between inhabitants. Thus, it plays a major role in communication patterns among visitors and residents, between both groups, and with the outside world.

Relocation from a residence to an age-segregated apartment building or long-term care facility is a change in status from "resident" to "visitor." The spatial syntax of most homes is relatively shallow compared to those of age-segregated apartment buildings. The spatial syntax of most long-term care facilities is far deeper than the apartment building. Thus, the spatial integration of the residents into the community is therefore far lower in an apartment building or long-term care facility than in their homes. The difference in spatial syntax between a typical community dwelling and an institution has profound implications for maintaining social ties with other people in individuals' social networks and their own social world. The age-segregated apartment building or institution, because of its relative isolation from the community, becomes a social world of its own. This is evident by different norms of dress, language, and other aspects of behavior. Because of the inherent difference in spatial syntax, community integration is difficult to achieve in the typical institutional environment without significant social support systems.

The change in status from "resident" to "visitor" can also be interpreted as a change from being a recognized member of a social network to being a "stranger." Matthews (1979) demonstrated the impact of the "stranger" role in facilities for older people. She showed how transformation of status from stranger to resident is linked to the shift from categorical knowing (e.g., an older person) to personal knowing (e.g., a person who is old). This transition can be very difficult. Building design plays an important role in helping new residents construct their identities as members of the new community by facilitating face to face contact.

Proximity of dwelling units, both in terms of direct physical distance and circulation pattern, has a significant impact on who will become friends (e.g., Friedman, 1966). The role of proximity is particularly significant in homogeneous communities like age-segregated housing where all the residents share common experiences related to their stage in life. Two examples of how proximity plays a major role in friendship formation are the location of amenities like mailboxes and laundries and the relationship of social gathering spaces to circulation paths.

The mailbox and laundry are like wells and stream banks in preindustrial settlements. All residents come to pick up their mail every day and do their laundry once a week; thus, these spaces have the potential of bringing residents into face to face contact. Experience has shown that the creation of social spaces adjacent to mailboxes can create important social contact opportunities, transforming what is essentially a functional space into an important social gathering area. A similar transformation can take place with laundry facilities. It is important to note that an attractive and comfortable environment is required in the social space for it to succeed; for example, isolation of noise and odor in the machine room of the laundry and a good view.

The level of exposure a space receives is often related to its location in the spatial syntax diagram of the building. Generally, for people who are relatively mobile, spaces that are shallow in the diagram will be more successful social gathering places than spaces that are deep within it; for people who are less able, social gathering places are more successful when located deep within the diagram. Thus, lounges on the top floors of high rise apartment buildings will be less likely to attract people than those that are on the first floor close to the entrance; skilled nursing facilities need a variety of "social spaces" including some immediately outside bedrooms. Spaces that are part of ring-like networks will also receive more exposure. An entire building may be tree-like but sections of it can have a localized ring-like structure. Spaces that serve to connect many branches of a tree-like structure will receive a great deal of exposure. These are spaces like race-track corridors that link many other spaces or large open areas onto which many other spaces open up (e.g., central gathering spaces). Designers of facilities for people with dementia have planned in "wandering paths" for residents that pass by or through areas with different uses and different views (e.g., Cohen & Weisman, 1991). The idea is that wandering is a form of self-stimulation. The race-track corridor exposes the restless wanderers to a variety of alternative activities that might engage their energies. At the least, a wandering path increases the stimulation level and makes wandering appear more purposeful than the back-and-forth pacing often observed in dead end corridors.

The degree of visual access within public spaces also plays an important role in how well these spaces will attract residents (Howell et al., 1976). Spaces with interior windows and large open doorways provide a preview and high level of visual access. They will be more effective than those that are hidden from view and those that, upon crossing the entry threshold, have an abrupt increase in exposure to others. The latter puts people on the spot, subject to a high degree of obligation once the threshold is crossed. The former provides more evaluation time before making a decision to enter the space. Entry can take place with better preparation and more control over the presentation of self.

Personalization

The dwelling is a primary site for the presentation of self (Steinfeld, 1981). From a communications' perspective, an individual's home can be "read" to uncover important aspects of the inhabitant's personality. Howell and Epp (1978) studied how furniture and personal possessions are displayed in apartments of older people. They found that important pieces of furniture were put on display even when they resulted in cramped conditions within small apartments. Residents created display areas and walls. Displays and important pieces of furniture were arranged to provide the highest degree of exposure from the entry of the apartment. It was not uncommon for people who moved into new age-segregated apartment buildings to buy new furniture because it was deemed more appropriate than the old and worn furniture from the house they had left.

I have noted previously (Steinfeld 1981) that many of the displays older people create in their apartments memorialize certain extremely important aspects of an individual's identity. For example, one woman I visited had an alcove with a spare bed set up exactly as it had been when used by a long-dead only child. Another woman had an elaborate display of her extensive collection of thimbles. A third had a display of wood pieces taken from the property of her ancestral home when she left it to relocate to an age-segregated building. The lack of a display and the absence of a carefully constructed presentation of self can also be highly informative. For example, I once visited an apartment inhabited by a single man who had never been married. It had nothing in it except a TV set, a table, a chair, and a bed. The furniture was set up in a fan-like arrangement focused on the TV. After getting to know this man, I learned he had very few interests other than watching TV; most of his time prior to moving to the senior citizens' apartment building had been spent hanging out in bars. Housekeeping style, from the obsessively neat to the slovenly and cluttered, may also provide important clues to an individual's sense of self, but no research has been completed on this subject as yet.

Moving out of one's longtime residence, particularly if it is owned, is a significant challenge to self-identity. Homeowner status has a particularly important meaning to the older person. Individuals have a need to compensate for the loss of the home. In addition, relocation involves a transition from "stranger" to "resident." Personalizing the dwelling is a means to reconstruct one's identity. There are many design features and facility management policies that support personalization of the dwelling space. One of the most important is having enough space to make displays and arrange furniture appropriately. Another is having the freedom to decorate and select one's own furniture. A third is being able to alter the outside of the dwelling, be it an apartment or a room in a nursing home, to provide a display of identity oriented toward the "public."

Displays of identity on the outside of dwelling spaces are perhaps the most interesting for the communications therapist and others interested in facilitating communication of elders. The tendency of management is to avoid giving residents the freedom to decorate the outside of their dwelling space because they believe that the result could be "messy" and "in bad taste." However, the freedom, or lack thereof, to personalize the outside boundary of dwelling space can be interpreted as a symbol of the value given to individuals within the "community." The activity of personalization in itself can be a means to encourage meaningful social interaction and ease the transition into the community. Residents and management can work together to develop shared community norms. If done properly, this will build a healthy social milieu and improve relations between tenants and management. Communication therapists have an important role to play as facilitators of this process.

The options for personalization encompass a continuum from a standard signboard displaying the name of an individual to the freedom to select interior design options and decorate the entire entry to the dwelling space. In between, there are many other possibilities: a personalized sign reflecting the identity of the inhabitants (e.g., color and style preferences); color and style choices for doors and door frames; a display board or box to provide a more elaborate presentation (e.g., ethnic symbols, identification with sports teams, memorabilia), a niche or shelf in the hallway within which individuals can mount a display; an interior window that can be decorated with curtains, plants, and knick-knacks. Even in long-term care facilities there are methods that can be used to improve the presentation of self to the outside world. The therapist can help convince the management that personalization is an important issue in the design of a building and also develop a program that involves residents in constructing displays. Direct work with individual residents can be a meaningful focus of communications therapy.

Boundary Regulation

Although personalization is very important in the presentation of self, identity ultimately is defined by our relationships with other people. The physical environment plays a major role in direct social interaction by providing a context for regulating boundaries between the individual and others. Altman and Chemers (1980) described territoriality, personal space behavior, and privacy behavior as three aspects of the boundary regulation process. They viewed privacy as the key to understanding the goals of the process. Privacy is selective control of access to the self (Altman, 1975). Through privacy behaviors, individuals can both open up and close off communications with others. Thus, privacy is a dialectical process. Sometimes, a high level of social contact is desirable and other times it is not. Autonomy and choice in establishing a spatial boundary between one's self and others will determine how easy it is for individuals to optimize their social interaction. Through a cross-cultural analysis, Altman (1975) demonstrated that privacy behavior takes place regardless of the physical support for it. If there is no physical means to obtain privacy, individuals use dress, posture, or social mechanisms to control access to the self. For example, reserve and withdrawal from social encounters are common responses to lack of privacy.

At the level of personal space behavior, furniture arrangements play a major role in facilitating face to face interaction. Much research (Altman, 1975) has demonstrated how interpersonal communication is supported by "societopetal" seating arrangements and discouraged by "sociofugal" arrangements (Hall, 1969). Corner seating, where individuals can have direct eye contact without maintaining an uncomfortable body posture is far better at promoting interaction than shoulder-to-shoulder seating arrangements. Round and square tables promote more equality in social intercourse, whereas long rectangular tables tend to favor the dominant position at the head.

Social interaction distance plays an important part as well, particularly for older people. DeLong (1970) demonstrated how social interaction distances that are common among the general population do not apply to older people. The distances used for intimate, personal, and social interaction sets tend to get compressed because of the "physiological screen" of aging. Because older persons cannot see facial expressions or hear speech as easily, they tend to get closer to compensate for the loss of sensory input. It is not uncommon for an older person to hold on to the arm of another individual while talking to them. They are not just seeking physical support. Holding onto the arm of another ensures that the other person will stay within sensory range. Thus, appropriate social interaction distances among older people in the United States are more like the close interaction distances that are common among people who live around the Mediterranean. DeLong observed that younger staff in an institution often misread the older person's desire for close contact as a desire for intimacy and, at the same time, the residents misinterpreted the staff's desire to maintain culturally normative interactive distances as unfriendliness and lack of interest in their welfare. Rehabilitation professionals working with older people should be aware of these differences and avoid slipping into proxemic sets that can be misinterpreted by their clients. Communications therapists can help other staff understand the need to adjust interaction distances to accommodate failing senses. Furniture selection also is related to interaction distances. Large, bulky furniture creates a spatial barrier by increasing face to face differences. Lightweight, easy to move (but still stable) furniture allows residents to adjust furniture arrangements to their needs.

Boundary regulation is particularly important in long-term care settings. The status passage of "resident" to "visitor" is accompanied by significant losses of control over the environment as compared to living in one's own home or apartment. Thus, maintaining a sense of personal territory through which to achieve control over space and privacy is much more difficult. The physical environment can provide a great deal of support for meeting territorial and privacy needs.

Traditional nursing home bedroom design is based primarily on efficiency of space utilization. The typical two-bed room creates significant conflicts in the use of territory. Individuals in the window location have a preferable territory because they obtain control over the window space, the corner area, and the view, and their territory is not violated when their roommate goes to the bathroom or someone enters or exits the room (see Figure 10–5A). The residents with beds near the corridor have fewer resources and control. In addition, neither resident has a closet for personal possessions within his or her territory. Although private rooms are preferable because they provide the highest level of territorial control and privacy, the conventional double room can be im-

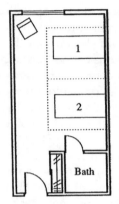
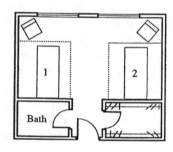

A. Territorial Conflicts and Poor Privacy   **B.** Improved Plan

Figure 10–5. Double room plans. **A.** Territorial conflicts and poor privacy. **B.** Improved plan.

proved. Figure 10–5B shows a double room in which each person has his or her own distinct territory and neither person's territory is invaded in the course of normal use. A room like this provides a clear demarcation of individual territories. Individuals can maintain their possessions with a higher degree of control, there is privacy for conversation with guests, and modesty is easy to maintain.

In an institutional environment there are limited opportunities to obtain solitude and intimacy. Yet solitude is an important resource for maintaining a positive self-identity (e.g., Pastalan, 1970). It is the nature of an institution to sacrifice solitude and intimacy for the visual and physical access needed for caregiving and supervision. But, whenever possible, institutions should strive to maintain the highest level of privacy, that is, the choice to be alone or with a significant other when desired and to avoid intrusion. For example, for residents who are capable, lockable toilet rooms are desirable. Individual bedrooms are preferable because they allow intimate interactions and solitude to take place in culturally normative settings. Some people, however, may benefit more from sharing a room. Increased contact with others can be beneficial in promoting culturally normative behavior through social pressure and expectations. Some nursing staff argue that it improves continence, for example. Clearly, for people who are prone to being socially withdrawn, sharing a room can improve their level of social engagement.

Private rooms, however, do not necessarily decrease social interaction overall. It appears that the relationship of room to public space is more critical. Lawton and Charon (1968) demonstrated that the combination of a private room with a shared social space immediately outside actually increases social interaction because it interposes a semipublic area between the private rooms and the public corridor. This space is conducive to hanging out and engaging passers-by in social interaction. It serves as a common ground for two or three individuals without requiring a commitment or obligation for intimacy that entering a bedroom space does. Essentially, positioning oneself in a semi-public area designed for social interaction signals to others that one is open to contact but does not connote an obligation for intimacy. The provision of a continuum of public, semipublic, and private territory allows the individual to adjust his or her level of contact to the needs and desires of the moment and thus facilitates more extensive use of space in the institution. Without all the options in this continuum, there is a tendency to avoid using public space (no semipublic space) or to practice reserve (no private space.)

SUMMARY

This chapter introduces key concepts, issues, and findings from environment-behavior theory and research that can help communications therapists and others to understand how the physical environment serves as a communications media. The two key ideas presented in this chapter are that the physical environment is a type of communication technology and that the physical world is an integral part of social relations. By designing the environment to facilitate sensory reception and cognition, a better fit between the capabilities of older people and the demands of their life space can be achieved. The definition of "good fit" between environment and person in late adulthood is complex. The Environmental Docility Model demonstrates that, for each person, the needs are different, and they change over time. It is just as important to avoid dependency and understimulation as it is to prevent incompetence and information overload. The status passages associated with old age provide the basis for understanding how the environment contributes to the quest for a meaningful identity late in life. Interventions should focus on helping to compensate for the losses that these status passages represent. From these basic ideas, three goals for designing supportive environments for older people emerge.

The first overall goal is to ensure that significant information can be perceived within the general information field. The principles of signal detection theory can be used for guidance. Design should be focused on clarifying the environment by carefully constructing an appropriate balance of emphasis between the foreground (significant) and background world. This may involve increasing signal strength, eliminating noise, and redundant cueing. Providing access to necessary information is another principle and is particularly important for people with cognitive impairments. Consideration must be given to the dynamic aspects of information search. Older people need greater permeability to understand the world around them because their sensory reception abilities are less acute and their energy reserves and mobility are more restricted. The concept of isovist can be useful in understanding the dynamic aspects of information fields.

The second goal in developing a supportive environment is to ensure that cognition is facilitated. Environmental designers should make the environment function as a prosthetic device for evaluation, understanding, and action. One important principle is to ensure that objects and spaces communicate strong affordances. In this way, it will be obvious how things are supposed to work. A second principle is to ensure that the cognitive load presented by environments is adjusted to the capabilities of the individual users. In general, older people need to have reduced cognitive loads to function at the same level. Several methods can be used to design environments that reduce cognitive load. They include clarification of the environment, using familiar models, spatial mappings, avoiding instability in the physical world, reducing distractions that lead to divided attention, and providing gradual transitions instead of abrupt orientation edges. In addition to design, preparation for particularly stressful events such as residential relocation and emergencies is also important for avoiding overload conditions.

The third goal is to provide an environment that facilitates the presentation of self and positive social perceptions of the older person. This can be achieved through spatial organization, personalization, and boundary regulation. Spatial syntax provides a way to represent buildings as social structures. Inherent properties of these structures affect the social perception and social interaction of inhabitants. From a communications' perspective, a basic principle of spatial organization for older people is to provide a physical structure that facilitates social integration with the outside community and within the residential community itself. In particular, this structure should help new residents overcome the difficult transitional stage of "stranger" or "newcomer." The use of proximity and circulation to increase the probability of face to face contact and a spatial syntax that increases exposure of gathering places can both be effective. A second principle is providing opportunities for personalization. This allows individuals to project a positive image of themselves to others in their social world. A third principle, facilitating personal space and territorial and privacy behavior, ensures that the quality of social encounters will be high.

Communication therapists and others interested in facilitating communications with elders have several roles to play in the environmental design and management process. First, rehabilitation therapists, can be informed advocates for design that supports improved use of the environment and social relations for older people. Second, therapists should be aware of the functions of objects and spaces as they relate to the process of service delivery. This will help them provide better service to their clients by arranging the immediate environment where service takes place in the best possible way. Third, the process of environmental design can be a powerful arena for facilitating communication among older people and between the residents and managers of facilities. In short, design can be therapy and therapy can be design. For example, the preparation for relocation, training for emergencies, and the process of personalization provide opportunities for therapists to deliver services at the individual and the group level. Reduction of stress, preservation of life, and the presentation of self are meaningful activities that can motivate and engage almost any person, regardless of their level of function. The environment, then, is a communications medium that presents many opportunities and challenges for the therapist.

Much research needs to be completed on this topic. In particular, the concepts of isovists and spatial syntax have potentially great significance for understanding the relationship of design to communications in general. The properties of spaces that encourage social interaction are well known, but it would be very useful to study the impact of code-mandated spatial arrangements on the information field. The spatial syntax model could be particularly useful in understanding how the properties of architectural plans facilitate and deter communications. Such research could focus on communications between residents, residents and staff, and residents and their families. Research should put more emphasis on the presentation of self as both an outcome variable and as a modifying variable affecting indicators of well being. For example, the input of personalization should be examined to test whether or not it facilitates improved self-concept and also to examine if it has an impact on morale and health. Empirical evidence demonstrating the psychological and physical benefits of personalization could help the long-term care industry make it a greater priority. Finally, there is a need to establish how the environment communicates information about residents to staff and the public at large. A medical director of a long-term care facility recently told me that he believed staff treat residents more humanely when their rooms are personalized because they are then aware that the residents have a past. If corroborated by research, such findings could be very valuable in promoting better quality of care.

REFERENCES

Altman, I. (1975). *The environment and social behavior.* Monterey: Brooks/Cole.

Altman, I., & Chemers, M. (1980). *Culture and environment.* Belmont: Wadsworth.

Archea, J. (1984). *Visual access and exposure: An architectural basis for interpersonal behavior.* Unpublished doctoral dissertation, Pennsylvania State University, State College.

Archea, J. (1993). *The path to refuge.* Unpublished manuscript, Department of Architecture, SUNY/Buffalo.

Benedikt, M. L. (1979). To take hold of space: Isovists and isovist fields. *Environment and Planning B.*

Carp, F. M. (1971). Walking as a means of transportation for retired people. *Gerontologist, 11,* 104–111.

Carson, D., Archea, J., Margulis, S., & Carson, F. (1978). *Safety on stairs.* Report to National Bureau of Standards. Washington, DC.

Cohen, U., & Weisman G. D. (1991). *Holding on to home: Designing environments for people with dementia.* Baltimore: Johns Hopkins University Press.

DeLong, A. J. (1970). The micro-spatial structure of the older person: Some implications of planning the social and spatial environment. In L. Pastalan & D. Carson (Eds.), *Spatial behavior of older people* (pp. 68–87). Ann Arbor: University of Michigan Institute of Gerontology.

Erikson, E. (1968). Generativity and ego integrity. In B. Neugarten (Ed.), *Middle age and aging* (pp. 85–87). Chicago: University of Chicago Press.

Friedman, E. (1966). Spatial proximity and social interaction in a home for the aged. *Journal of Gerontology, 21,* 566–570.

Goffman, E. (1972). The presentation of self to others. In J. Manis & B. Meltzer (Eds.), *Symbolic interaction: A reader in social psychology* (pp. 234–244). Boston: Allyn and Bacon.

Hall, E. T. (1969). *The hidden dimension.* Garden City, NJ: Doubleday.

Hillier, B., & Hanson, J. (1984). *The social logic of space.* Cambridge: Cambridge University Press.

Howell S., Albright, C., Ebbe, K., & Reizenstein, J. (1976). *Shared spaces in housing for the elderly.* Boston: Department of Architecture, Massachusetts Institute of Technology.

Howell S., & Epp, G. (1978). *Private space: Habitability of apartments for the elderly.* Boston: Department of Architecture, Massachusetts Institute of Technology.

Hunt, M. E., & Pastalan, L. (1987). Easing relocation: An environmental learning process. In V. Regnier & J. Pynoos (Eds.), *Housing the aged: Design directives and policy considerations.* New York: Elsevier Science.

Kaplan, S., & Kaplan, R. (1982). *Cognition and environment.* New York: Praeger Publishers.

Lawton, M. P., Liebowitz, B., & Charon, H. (1968). *Physical structure and the behavior of senile patients following ward remodeling.* Philadelphia: Philadelphia Geriatric Center.

Lawton. M., & Nahemow, L. (1973). Ecology and the aging process. In C. Eisdorfer & M. Powell Lawton (Eds), *The psychology of adult development and aging.* (pp. 619–674). Washington DC: American Psychological Association.

Matthews, S. H. (1979). *The social world of old women.* Beverly Hills, CA: Sage Publications.

National Transportation and Safety Board. (1973). *Aircraft Accident Report. North Central Airlines, Inc. DC–9–31. N954N. and Delta Air Lines, Inc., CV–880, N8807E, at O'Hare Interational Airport, Chicago, Illinois, December 20, 1972.* (NTSB-AAR–73–15) Washington, DC: Author.

Norman, D. A. (1988). *The design of everyday things.* New York: Bantam Doubleday Dell Publishing Group.

Pastalan, L. A. (1970). Privacy as an expression of human territoriality. In L. Pastalan & D. Carson, (Eds.), *Spatial behavior of older people* (pp. 88–101). Ann Arbor: University of Michigan Institute of Gerontology-Wayne State University.

Pastalan, L., & Bourestom, N. (1975). *Forced relocation: Setting, staff and patient effects.* Report to National Institute of Mental Health.Ann Arbor: University of Michigan Press.

Pastalan, L., & Carlson, D. (1970). *Spatial behavior of older people.* Ann Arbor: University of Michigan Institute of Gerontology-Wayne State University.

Pastalan, L., Merrill, J., & Pomerantz, B. (1975). *Street and highway environments for the older driver.* Ann Arbor: University of Michigan Institute of Gerontology.

Pynoos, J., Cohen, E., & Lucas C. (1988). *The caring home booklet: Environmental coping strategies for Alzheimer's caregivers.* Los Angeles: Andrus Gerontology Center, University of Southern California.

Regnier, V., & Pynoos, J., (Eds.). (1987). *Housing the aged.* New York: Elsevier Science.

Sanders, M. S., & McKormick, E. J. (1993). *Human factors in engineering and design.* New York: McGraw Hill.

Sime, J. (1985). Movement toward the familiar: Person and place affiliation in a fire entrapment setting. *Environment and Behavior, 17, 697–724.*

Sommer, R. (1969). *Personal space: The behavioral basis of design.* Englewood Cliffs, NJ: Prentice-Hall.

Steinfeld, E. (1981). The place of old age: The meaning of housing for old people. In J. Duncan, (Ed.), *Housing and identity* (pp. 198–246). London: Croom Helm.

Steinfeld, E. (1992). Toward artificial users. In Y. Kalay (Ed.), *Evaluating and predicting design performance* (pp. 328-346). New York: John Wiley & Sons.

Steinfeld, E., & Mullick, A. (1990). Universal design: The case of the hand. *Innovation: The Journal of the Industrial Designers Society of America.*

Templer, J. (1992). *The staircase: Studies of hazards, falls, and safer design.* Cambridge, MA: MIT Press.

Willey, A. E. (1972). Fire: Baptist Towers housing for the elderly. *Fire Journal and Fire Technology.* Boston: National Fire Protection Association (SPP–47).

Wilson, D. G., & Grayson, G. B. (1980). *Age-related differences in the road crossing behavior of adult pedestrians.* Crownthrone, UK: Transport and Road Research Laboratory.

11

Communication Technology and Safety

Mariana Newton, Ph.D.

INTRODUCTION

Life is risky! A combination of risk factors from the natural and man-made environment (exogenous) and from one's own ever-changing physical, cognitive, and social characteristics (endogenous) jeopardizes one's safety. Physical or personal safety becomes an increasingly important and complex issue for elders and their caregivers. An environment considered safe when an individual is 30 years old may pose potential risks for the same person at 80 years of age. During that 50-year period, the home may have undergone numerous planned and unplanned modifications in structure and design that now challenge the elder with vision, hearing, or cognitive difficulties. Even minor changes in the environment and mild sensory or cognitive impairments may compound risk and engender feelings of insecurity and anxiety among elders and their caregivers. Informal caregivers are likely to be less supportive of elders' independent living when they perceive an imbalance in the number and degree of risk factors and the ability of the elder to cope with them effectively. Safety may contribute to a decision to relocate elders to safe, albeit less familiar, less desirable, and more costly residential or institutional environments.

This chapter explores the relationship between safety for elders and communication strategies and technologies. It has two basic premises. The first is that safety is a primary concern for elders living independently in the community, for those who need some degree of formal or informal support to remain there, and for those who require relocation to some form of long-term care. Reduction of safety risks enhances quality of life for elders, their families, and other caregivers. The second premise of the chapter is that those interested in communication technology for elders have a new role in assessing the safety of elders and suggesting strategies to address their safety needs. Those strategies include simple to sophisticated technologies that will create a better balance between the safety challenges of the environment and the abilities of the elder.

This chapter begins with a discussion of safety risks related to the aging process and then moves to an exploration of assessment issues and possible interventions. The chapter ends with a discussion of the need to educate families and formal caregivers in strategies and technologies to reduce safety risks. It also includes a list of resources for various types of technologies.

SAFETY RISKS AND HAZARDS

Ninety-five percent of persons over the age of 65 years and 80% of those over the age of 80 years live at home. The incidence of home accidents is high among older persons. Common accident sites in the home are the bathroom, bedroom, kitchen, and stairs, with stairs being the most hazardous area (Christenson, 1990). Elders are at risk of falling, incurring shock or poisoning, being lost, and being burned. Minimizing safety risks for elders at home requires an understanding of age-related sensory and cognitive changes.

Age-Related Sensory and Cognitive Changes

Presbycusis, the loss of hearing related to aging, occurs in at least 35–50% of persons over 65 years of age. It includes both acuity and perceptual difficulties. Of particular concern is the decrease in ability to hear high-frequency sounds and to discriminate speech particularly when presented in a degraded format.

Environmental sounds of high frequency and intensity carry messages to alert people to potentially hazardous changes in their environment. Older persons with high-frequency hearing loss may not hear warning signals, for example, sirens, smoke alarms, doorbells, or telephone rings. Even if the elders can just detect warning sounds, they may hear them as faint noises, not loud or long enough to signal danger and prompt an appropriate response. Moreover, elders who are hearing-impaired may erroneously perceive common environmental sounds, confusing, for example, a fire siren with a ringing telephone.

Elders who are hearing impaired also may have difficulty with speech discrimination and processing. Discrimination problems cause errors in reception of spoken messages. Distortion complicates listening situations when directional or safety messages are amplified and delivered through a speaker. When tinnitus (ringing in the ears) accompanies presbycusis, perceptual difficulties are even greater. Some elders may have further difficulty with messages spoken at a rapid rate. General slowing of the nervous system in persons of advanced age compounds the difficulties experienced even by young people. Messages spoken at a slower rate afford longer cognitive-linguistic processing time and, hence, greater listening and comprehension accuracy.

Visual acuity and perceptual changes also occur in persons of advanced age. Approximately 90% of older persons need prescription lenses and up to 20% of those over the age of 80 years are unable to see well enough to read a newspaper, even with corrective lenses (Abrams & Berkow, 1990). Reduced visual acuity makes small print on signs, labels, instructions, and notices difficult to see and read. These written messages, even if presented in larger letters, may be difficult for the person who is visually impaired to see from a distance. The older person who must strain to see labels, instructions, and warnings may ignore them or give up reading messages entirely. Although refraining from reading may reduce the elder's frustration with print, missing or misreading the messages increases safety risks. (See Chapters 3 and 4 for further discussion of vision difficulties of elders.)

Older people need two to three times more light to see clearly. Inadequate lighting makes it difficult to see where one is going, to avoid obstacles, and to notice and read signage designed to advise and warn.

As is true with hearing, discrimination problems often accompany visual acuity deficits. Poor visual discrimination reduces accuracy in reading labels on faucets, stoves, foods, poisons, and so forth. Moreover, shiny surfaces can complicate visual discrimination by producing glare, poor figure-ground contrast, and reverse contrast (white on black versus black on white).

Some older people experience visual field and depth perception problems. Changes in walking surface levels (e.g., steps, curbs, thresholds, ramps, holes) and surface textures (e.g., gravel, slippery surfaces, pebbles, carpet) are difficult for elderly people to see. Corrective lenses, particularly bifocal and trifocal lenses, may cause perceptual confusion as the line of sight changes with head and eye position. Elders' inability to discern distances between themselves and other people or objects may precipitate some automobile and falling accidents. For example, elders may not accurately perceive the relative distance of cars and their relative speed. They may misjudge their distance from furniture or misread signs located at an angle or peripheral to the center of their visual field.

Many elders have elevated taste thresholds, particularly for salt. Perhaps even more significant regarding safety, however, is the decline of smell sensitivity with age. Peak performance for smell occurs from age 30 to 60 and declines significantly in those over age 70. Declines in both taste and olfactory sensitivity are probably the cause of complaints by elders that food lacks flavor. Changes in taste sensation may also be related to the disproportionate number of accidental poisoning cases involving persons who are elderly each year (Doty & Shuman, 1984).

Many people notice cognitive-linguistic changes in themselves as they age. They complain of such symptoms as memory loss, word-retrieval difficulties, and confusion in complex linguistic exchanges. Further, nearly 4 million older Americans experience severe symptoms of progressive dementia; over half of those have probable dementia of the Alzheimer type (DAT; Butler, 1990). Recent memory loss, inability to learn and retain new information, and deterioration of semantic-episodic language are all characteristic of early stages. In later stages, people with DAT have increased difficulty with activities of daily living, impaired judgment, and greater risk for falling. Behavioral disorganization is also characteristic in DAT. Typical indicators of this disorder include getting lost, wandering, and ineffective use of normal environmental and social cues. Any one of these difficulties can challenge elders' safety. Taken together, the cognitive-linguistic changes in older people, particularly those with DAT, greatly compromise safety.

The most commonly observed behavioral change related to aging is a general slowing phenomenon—biologically, psychologically, and socially. Examples include slower detection and recognition of stimuli, slower central processing, and slower movement. In tests of response speed, elders are inclined to sacrifice speed for accuracy, exacerbating the perception of slowness. This natural choice might seem adventitious for safety in that inaccuracies are more risk-laden than slowness. However, slowness prompted by fear and cautiousness may create additional safety risks. Age-related changes in the neuromotor systems are complex, involving numerous, interrelated neural circuits and feedback loops. Slowing in nerve conduction and decreased sensitivity of sensory receptors (vision, balance, and somesthetic) may cause errors in motor programming, particularly in timing and sequencing. In some cases, these programming errors may result in aberrant motor responses, including falls (Scheibel, 1985).

In summary, sensory, cognitive, and response system changes impair older persons' communication efficiency, thereby compromising their safety. Consideration of age-related changes in the ability of elders to receive sensory signals, interpret sensory information, and respond appropriately is important in developing strategies to prevent or repair communication breakdowns and, thereby, improve safety.

FACILITATING SAFETY WITH COMMUNICATION TECHNOLOGY

Types of Desirable Changes

Some communication technologies address personal needs for improved hearing, vision, and speech. Improved receptive and expressive communication will certainly have a positive impact on the safety of the individual. Technology that enhances the environments in which the older person functions will also contribute to increased safety.

Certain environmental areas are particularly conducive to communication. For example, social communication often accompanies dining. Small seating areas prompt visiting, and private living spaces meet the needs for more intimate communication. Group activities and joint routines in homes, daycare centers, community programs, and churches stimulate communication. Consequently, these areas are important spaces in which assistive communication may be helpful.

In congregate living arrangements and gathering places, shared facilities require messaging to direct participants to locations and activities. These environments may be less familiar to residents than their homes. Hence, assistive communication strategies are useful in facilitating wayfinding, minimizing confusion, guiding participation, and promoting a sense of security.

General Principles

The goal of applying assistive communication technology is to increase safety, and consequently, the independence of elders by bridging the gap between functional limitations and the requirements for safety (Gitlin, Levine, & Geiger, 1993). Some auditory, visual, and multimodality measures (a) increase the strength and duration and (b) reduce the complexity of communication messages. Consequently, these measures enhance the alerting value of the message and stimulate a more appropriate, safer response. Several general principles apply to the selection of aids and devices.

Esthetics

The institutional appearance of some assistive devices (e.g., grab bars, reachers) has caused many older persons to resist their use. Potential users will, more often than not, reject devices that symbolize disability or incompetence. Devices that signal cleverness, capability, and convenience are more acceptable. Augmentations of existing technology need to be as home-like as possible. Those that are unobtrusive and blended with decor and function are less likely to be confusing. Augmentation of familiar messages is preferable to alternative messages. (See the discussion in Chapter 10 for further elaboration of this topic.)

Accessibility

The accessibility of safety technology permits or enhances interface between the user and the technology. That interface may be sensory, cognitive, or physical. To facilitate visual accessibility, signs must be large enough to be seen from a distance and easily distinguished from their background. Auditory accessibility increases when (a) elders can easily use personal assistive hearing devices, (b) sounds are directly available to the elder at a comfortable listening level, and (c) background sounds are eliminated or reduced. Uncluttered messages and the use of common, well-known symbols enhance cognitive accessibility. For physical accessibility, switches or other devices need to be located in places that an older person can find and reach easily and manipulate accurately.

Multimodality and Flexibility

Most people do not have equal capability in all modalities. Such inequalities become exaggerated in the elderly because of loss of capability in one or more modalities. More efficient function occurs when the elder uses two or more modalities together. Each enhances the function of the others. Moreover, in environments where technology may be facilitative to more than one older person, each with different needs, using several strategies at once is advantageous.

The use of several sensory modalities for cueing provides the same information in several different ways. Some people will be able to follow a sign. Others will recognize a color code or another distinctive symbol. Symbols can suggest a response, as in lines to be followed or footsteps outlining a pathway. Still others may need verbal or auditory cueing along with visual stimuli.

Several mechanisms for responding communicatively will accommodate changing needs of individuals and varying needs in group situations. For example, voice, touch, or infrared remote devices can be used to activate environmental controls. Some people may achieve greater accuracy in communication by using several input devices to a computer (e.g., voice, keyboard, touchpad, mouse, joystick). Multiple computer output modalities (screen and print) are in common use. The advantages for accuracy and speed apply to all users, regardless of age. Elders who experience loss of speed and accuracy consider multiple output modalities to be part of a "safety net."

Because elders and their environments are in a constant state of change, flexible technologies provide greater options and choices. Flexible technologies are adaptable to the changing needs of the consumer and the environment. For example, a flexible technology provides increasing support for manipulation and control. Further, it can provide redundant or amplified information displays to meet varied user or environment demands.

Easy Maintenance

Technology is more useful and acceptable if the older user can maintain it with minimal expense. For example, battery replacement in hearing aids is a formidable obstacle to some users. Batteries are small, difficult to manipulate and position, and add expense. Returning devices to the manufacturer for calibration or repair may be a major project for some older people and may appear to be more trouble than it is worth.

Cost-Effectiveness

Affordability varies with income and need, but many older people are retired and live on fixed incomes or Social Security. Moreover, the present cohort of old-old persons (85+ years), whose needs for safety-related technology may be greatest, are products of several world wars and the economic depression of the 1930s. These experiences have shaped their views regarding cautious, conservative resource management. Thus, low initial and maintenance costs make safety technology more acceptable.

In addition, the cost-benefit ratio or the functional benefit as perceived by the user must be considered. The results of using the technology must be sufficiently valuable to justify the cost. The benefits are likely to be more valuable if they are related to safety in pleasurable activities and those activities critical to or symbolic of independent living. For example, communications for safety in automobiles (e.g., multimodality warning systems and infrared controlled locking, lighting, and alarm systems) are generally highly valued relative to their cost.

Safety Assessment

The environment influences the determination of individual needs. Some environments might be very safe for an older person who has good hearing, vision, coordination, and mobility. These environments, however, may be unsafe for an older person who moves slowly and has cataracts that obscure vision. Other environments would be unsafe for anyone, young or old. Still other environments might not be optimal, but in ways that are relatively unimportant to the person who lives there. Analysis of elders' access to the environment, response patterns, and error patterns will help to identify problem areas and specific needs for assistive technology.

Several assessment instruments, or strategies, address safety hazards and risks in living environments. The U.S. Consumer Products Safety Commission developed the Home Safety Checklist (1985). It is easy to administer and facilitates the reporting of information to the elderly and their caregivers and the measurement of change over time (Rubenstein, 1990).

Tideiksaar (1986) developed a home assessment program for fall hazards. This program helps to identify the area of the household in which a hazard exists, suggests corrections, and gives a rationale for the risk reduction expected.

Although these inventories are helpful, they are limited in their usefulness. These instruments address factors in the physical environment but not the mismatches between the demands of the environment and the capabilities of the older person. A multidisciplinary, comprehensive, and functional assessment and periodic reassessment are necessary to determine the changing needs of older individuals in specific environments. Such assessments facilitate care planning and the choice of technology applications (Czaja, 1993; Rubenstein, 1990). The assessment would analyze the functional requirements of home tasks, environmental demands, and capabilities of the older person. Consideration would also be given to those safety aspects of greatest concern to the older persons and the family (Czaja, 1993; Fretwell, 1990; Kane, 1993). Further, safety technologies and strategies must be identified and matched to the elders' needs and the environments within which they function. Adaptive equipment that does not match with individual needs will increase the likelihood of nonuse (Gitlin et al., 1993).

Data for the assessment can be obtained in several ways, including interviews with elders and those in their support network. Interview questions might focus on (a) health concerns, (b) difficult activities, (c) situations where help was solicited, and (d) tasks that the elder wishes to do more easily, independently, or accurately. Further, elders often devise their own strategies for safety and independence, and accounts of these will yield important information about awareness of safety, motivation, and ingenuity. Moreover, the ideas generated out of need may be the best solutions for that individual and possibly applicable to others.

Assessment also includes data gathered by directly observing elders engaged in activities of daily living in their natural environment. Typical tasks include preparing and eating food, answering the telephone, controlling the television, negotiating steps, and getting things out of reach. Tasks that cannot be observed because of privacy or time limitations can be role-played or observed and reported by family members or other caregivers.

Several aspects of the interaction and the older person's behavior deserve special attention during the observation. Evidence of sensory processing (accuracy and speed) and comprehension of observer's comments and requests can be recorded. Documentation of the following response attributes will be helpful: (a) presence and type of overt planning strategies; (b) inclusion or omission of critical parts of the task; (c) the sequence in which parts of the task are attempted and completed; (d) revisions in sequence; (e) task maintenance; (f) compensatory or coping strategies; and (g) rate and accuracy of responses.

The introduction of some stress is also desirable. Although some stress may improve performance, safety may be compromised by stressful conditions or feelings. Time pressure is particularly problematic because of the generalized slowing of responses in older people. Moreover, older people sometimes take even more time to do something to assure accuracy. The objective in introducing stress is to determine the threshold between helpful and counterproductive stress.

Time stress can be gently introduced into the observation with remarks such as "Our time together today is running out so we'd better hurry with this," or "It's getting late. We'll do this one quickly." In some instances, more direct time stress may be useful. An older person who is at safety risk because of slowness might be asked to do the task again as fast as possible, even if mistakes occur. This may yield a higher error rate, but would reveal the types of errors and their safety implications when stress negatively affects performance.

Application of Specific Technologies

Warning and Signaling

A wide variety of warning systems are available to detect hazards and hence provide opportunity to escape danger. Table 11–1 lists the major

Table 11-1. Assistive technology for safety.

Assistive Technology	Function
Detectors emitting loud long sounds; bright, flashing lights; strong vibrations	Increases signal strength and duration; multimodality warning
LED and digitized signals	Informs location, direction of movement, speed, operation, special instructions
Visual and voice door openings	Facilitates identification of outside source
Intercom systems	Increase loudness; permit communication between rooms
Carpeting, padded vinyl flooring	Reduces signal-to-noise ratios; facilitates auditory discrimination
Halogen lights	Increases brightness, visibility
Emergency lights	Provide light when AC power fails
Motion-sensitive lights	Activate light by motion in area
Large signs with simple messages or iconic symbols on white or yellow backgrounds	Increase signal strength; aids visual notice and process
Nonverbal symbols, irridescent paint, tapes, arrows, colors	Facilitate notice, recognition of hazards, guide, direct, instruct
Schedule boards, boxes	Cue time for activities
Location signals	Identify location of wearer; facilitate finding wearer
Computer software	Provides synthesized or digitized speech output, environmental control, schedules/calendars, information management
Home Assisted Nursing Care (HANC)	Monitors health status in home; computer-assisted health data management
Med-Alert jewelry	Informs unfamiliar helpers of special medical needs
Scotchlite, Refexlite reflective garments	Warn motorists of pedestrian presence
Programmable telephones and automatic dialers	Reduce memory requirements for dialing
Cordless telephones	Facilitate telephone use for mobility limited persons
Cellular telephones	Provide accessible telephone communication away from home

(continued)

Assistive Technology	*Function*
Assistive listening devices	Decrease function distance between speaker and listener; aid hearing impaired
Voice-activated telephone	Aids telephone use by physically restricted persons
RELAY	Facilitates communication between persons with unmatched capabilities
911 (National Emergency Telephone Number)	Summons help from police, fire department, ambulance
Lifeline	Summons help from caregiver or support network

types and functions of these technologies. Information about specific items can also be found in the resource list at the back of this chapter. The following sections describe some of the more common technologies.

Elders more easily hear warning sounds that have a significant low-frequency component and that are longer and louder than usual. Multimodality alarms that couple such auditory signals with bright, flashing xenon strobe lights are useful for those with severe hearing and visual impairments. Some of these multimodality alarms may also include a body-worn vibrotactile receiver.

Some signal technologies convey less urgency than alarms. Elevators, for example, usually have visual indicators of the level where the elevator is stopped. Tactile (Braille) signage in elevators is used by visually impaired elders who are familiar with these symbols. New technology includes an auditory signal using synthesized or digitized speech to announce the floor as the elevator arrives. The multimodality signal is safer because it allows elders to simultaneously hear the location and keep their vision focused on monitoring changing floor thresholds, surfaces, and obstacles upon exit.

Doorbells are commonly used by all, but usually only provide an auditory signal. For persons who are hearing impaired a doorbell that is augmented with a flashing light is helpful. Devices that permit both visual examination and voice contact with persons on the other side of a locked door maintain the security afforded by a solid door. Of course, they must be located at an appropriate height for easy, effective access.

Intercom systems at front doors provide only an auditory signal and may be expensive. However, intercom communication within a home may be helpful in sending and receiving messages without having to go up and down stairs, a major safety risk to older people.

Radio and television provide safety warning messages related to weather, traffic, products, and services. Closed captioning is a valuable augmentation technology for those with hearing loss. New television receivers now have built-in closed captioning capability (CCTV). For older sets, closed captioning receivers can be attached. Assistive listening devices are also helpful, for both safety and enjoyment. Auditory signals are picked up by a microphone near the speakers and converted to an infrared or frequency-modulated (FM) signal, which is transmitted to a wireless receiver worn by the user and coupled to a headset or hearing aid. (See Chapter 7 for additional information on personal and environmental assistive listening devices.)

Some general modifications in the environment will enhance both auditory and visual warning signals. Carpeting reduces the signal-to-noise ratio, making alarms and speech easier to discriminate. The use of padded vinyl flooring in bathrooms may be more serviceable, reduces reflected noise, and helps prevent injury in case of falls.

Analogous to background and reflected noise in the auditory environment is clutter in the visual environment. Lack of color contrasts, patterned floor and wall coverings, and surfaces loaded with "things" makes attention to visual signals for safety more difficult.

The visual environment is enhanced by bright lighting (two to three times as much for older people), less visual clutter, increased visual contrast, and controlled glare. Generally, light background colors with dark stimuli are best. Halogen bulbs emit a whiter light than incandescent bulbs, last longer, and produce more light per watt. Small, inconspicuous emergency lights that are automatically activated after AC power fails can be placed in bedrooms, hallways, and bathrooms to prevent accidents caused by darkness. These lights provide up to 90 minutes of emergency lighting. A solid-state charger keeps batteries in these devices charged for an expected 15-year life. Motion-sensitive lights in bedrooms and night-lights in bathrooms are inexpensive and helpful in getting safely from bed to bathroom and in finding other light switches.

Signage

Signs are among the most helpful, acceptable, flexible, and inexpensive warning and signaling devices. Signs with large, black letters on white or light backgrounds can be seen with ease. Because of color perception difficulties in some older people, red and yellow colors are preferable to blue-green hues. Simplified, even telegraphic, messages are most effective. For example, a sign with the words "STEP UP" is preferable to one that reads "WATCH YOUR STEP TO PREVENT FALLING" and "NO SMOKING" is more direct than "PLEASE DO NOT SMOKE IN THIS BUILDING."

Signs take many forms and have many uses. Augmented labels on cleaning, personal care, medicinal, and other products may reduce risk of ingestion. Self-adhesive (preprinted or write-on) safety labels are available at home improvement stores. Craft materials (e.g., bubble paint) can be used to make raised letter signs in many colors on wood, fabric, plastic, metal, or paper materials. Many communities have shops specializing in making signs, large and small, for a variety of purposes.

Some household implements are so iconic as to their use that they are themselves a kind of sign. A handrail, for example, suggests taking hold of it. A knob beside a sink is a sign for water. For added safety, however, signs that suggest specific actions are good reminders for the user. For example, a sign such as "HOLD ON" above a grab bar in a bathroom might prevent a fall. Clearly visible, black-on-white signs for "HOT" and "COLD," placed next to faucets, minimizes risk of burns. For single lever faucets, the signs would indicate the direction for each temperature.

Indicators in automobiles are another important type of signage. Big and bold LED (light emitting diode) displays on dashboards are easier to see than meter hands. Buzzers signal unfastened seat belts, but the recent addition of speech warnings is an augmented safety measure. Unfortunately, style and brevity have taken precedence over clarity in some other aspects of automobile signage. Finding the switches can be difficult in some models. Obvious, readable labels on dashboards would clarify the location and use of switches for wipers, defogger, lights, and other devices. (See Chapter 4 for another discussion of technologies for those with low vision.)

Cueing and Way-Finding

Older people who have sensory or cognitive difficulties or both may need environmental cues of additional intensity and duration to reduce confusion that threatens their safety. Whereas familiar surroundings pose few problems, less familiar environments such as those encountered in congregate living facilities or new places may present difficulty.

Visual difficulty and depth perception problems cause many older persons to feel and be unsafe in negotiating stairs, curbs, and other floor level changes. Curb cuts are helpful to the mobility impaired, but not helpful to those who are not able to see where the curb levels change.

Anxiety about falling on curbs causes older people to attend only to where they are stepping, ignoring traffic lights and oncoming vehicles. Iridescent paint on curb and step edges and ramps is simple but very helpful. Hazard adhesive tapes with bold black stripes on yellow backgrounds serve a similar purpose. These tapes or vertical signs mark irregular pavement, wet surfaces, and other hazardous zones.

Additional symbols in the environment may make way-finding and functioning in less familiar environments safer, and therefore, more independent (Calkins, 1988). Simple outline picture symbols of concrete objects have been used successfully in care facilities for persons with dementia. For example, a picture or outline drawing of a toilet, with the word "toilet" beside the picture elicited the best responses. Picture symbols of men and women and the words "restroom" or "bathroom" or "wc" were not as helpful. Short directional arrows have been successful when paired with pictures or words or both to direct older people to a different location. If a person must change directions (e.g., turn right) repetition of the symbols and arrows after the turn is made contributes to maximum effectiveness (Namazi & Johnson, 1991).

Color cueing is successful as a means to facilitate visual recognition and as a mnemonic device with persons who are elderly and confused (Cooper, Letts, & Rigby, 1993). Clear, bright colors are best. Warmer colors (reds, yellows, oranges, browns) are preferable to cooler shades (blues and greens; Alvermann, 1979). Colors can serve as location cues for residents. Colorful canopies placed over doorways may signal entrance to a particular location. A wristband color-coded to a person's room may remind a person of that location. Some patients with progressive dementia eventually lose their ability to discriminate or remember colors or both. Hence, color paired with other symbols may be more effective over a longer time.

Finding one's room (usually the bedroom) is an important task related to feeling safe and secure. Attendance to cues that identify one's room is so strong that when an elderly person is moved to a new room, even within their own home, considerable general disorientation, confusion, and anxiety may ensue. In congregate living situations, a long hallway of doors that look the same creates similar distress. Room numbers have not been very helpful; however, several other symbols have proven to be successful. Some residents respond to a sign with their name in large letters, a photograph, or both beside the room door. A personalized door mat would serve similarly. Painting the door to match a wristband may allow a color-matching strategy. Some older people like to decorate the door or entrance to their room with a personal article they recognize as theirs. Lockable, lighted display cabinets can display personal items or collections safely. These not only provide orientation cues but also add aesthetically to the surroundings (Calkins, 1988).

Although many communication technologies permit elderly persons to continue activity with greater safety, some strategies are employed to restrict access to unsafe situations (Mann, Hurren, Machiko, Bengali, & Steinfeld, 1994). For example, restriction is appropriate when equipment, materials, or areas are too hazardous for safe use by elders. Covers over unused sockets or wall outlets will discourage unsafe behavior. Barriers with signs may be erected. Locks are essential for fuse boxes or storage areas for cleaning supplies or poisonous substances. Such locks can be small and inconspicuous to minimize feelings of loss of control, punishment, or denial.

Location of Safety Messages and Controls

The location of safety communication messages and controls determines, in part, the accessibility and responsiveness to them. It is likely that elders will ignore signs that are difficult to see, do not attract attention, or are hard to understand. Switches in unexpected or inconvenient places will require unsafe maneuvers or extended time to use. Difficulty in opening and closing containers may unnecessarily prevent or delay access.

Generally, the location of signs at the side of door frames is preferable to signs on the front of doors. The latter are difficult to see or not noticed at all when the door is open. In congregate living facilities, signs that protrude from the wall are easy to see. Triangular signs that project at a 45° angle attract attention from several directions. Lighted signs are even more visible, although they would be more institutional in appearance.

Signs accompanying an object or picture are most effective when placed in the line of vision beside or on top of the object or figure. For example, a sign for a handrail placed just above where one is likely to look as the handrail begins is likely to attract attention and promote use of the rail. Likewise, the best placement for signs for hot and cold water is just above the faucet handle.

The evidence is inconclusive concerning the use of floor lines for direction. Signs that direct older persons may be more effective on the floor. The visual orientation of many persons who are older and confused is downward, making the location above or on the wall beside a door difficult to find (Namazi & Johnson, 1991). On the other hand, color changes on floors effectively signal a change in level, for example, the edge of a step or a threshold. Hence, floor color contrasts will misguide elders when level changes are not present. However, the stimulus value for floor level changes may be reduced if colored directional signs are also placed on the floor. The remedy for this situation is to place single word signs and arrows to direct location on the wall, just above the handrail or at eye level. The common gathering room in congregate living facilities is the favored location for general orientation signs, clocks (with lighted faces and large numerals), and schedule boards facilitating independent participation in activities. The common gathering place in a home is often the kitchen or near the dining table. These areas are advantageous in another way. Other residents, family members, and caregivers can provide verbal reinforcement at the same time the sign is read, making the shared message more meaningful and thus stimulating conversation.

Most light switches in residences are 50 to 55 inches from the floor. When possible, lowering the switches to 36 to 40 inches will make them easier to find (approximately where a person's hand is if the arms are at the side). This is especially true if the older person uses a cane or is carrying a purse or tote bag. Pressure switches are easier to manipulate than toggle or turn switches. Light switches are necessary at both the top and bottom of stairways. The location of switches outside the room or area one is about to enter is safer than the usual placement inside a dark room.

The location of stove burner controls at the back of the stove may be safer for children but is more dangerous for adults. They are more difficult to see, and reaching over a heated element is dangerous. A safer location is at the front or at the side of the stove top.

The levers for flushing toilets in home fixtures are usually easily accessible. However, in public restrooms, they may be difficult to reach for an older person, creating a risk of falling, particularly if the floor is wet. Restroom facilities designed for handicapped persons may be safer for some elders. These stalls often have motion sensitive or pressure induced flushing devices as well as grab bars. Because the flushing devices are not as familiar to users as the usual handle, a sign above the pressure button or on the back of the stall door would reduce confusion.

Automobile controls located behind the steering wheel or on a dashboard in places difficult to see or reach create safety hazards. Older persons considering purchase of a new car should examine the controls and indicators to be sure they are accessible, especially at night. Some drivers may find that controls located in a panel between the driver and passenger seats are more convenient to use. It is possible to retrofit automobiles with alternative controls, but that is a more expensive solution.

Packaging is an important consideration in the safe, independent administration of medicines. Unit dosing, in which the pills to be taken in a single dose are packaged as a unit, helps older people avoid taking too little or too much medicine at a time. Some drug packaging is confusing in that each pill is packaged separately, even though the usual single dose is two or more pills. The separate packaging is, in part, an attempt to prevent tampering. That prevention, however, like child-proof pill bottles, has made it difficult for older people to open the packaging. Inability to open the packaging may result in missed doses, which could create a serious risk. Adults without children can request packaging in easy-to-open bottles at the pharmacy. Remembering to take medicine, particularly when several medications are taken on different time schedules, is sometimes difficult. A written schedule helps particularly when someone crosses off times when the medicine is taken. Pill boxes are available in drugstores that are divided into small compartments for each day of a week or month. This device is comparable to a schedule box for other activities.

The technologies discussed previously are those that presume the older person to be the receiver of the message and that activate and guide the responses of the elderly. The following technologies monitor the whereabouts, status, and activities of the elders and direct information to caregivers such as physicians, nurses, family members, and community support networks.

Monitoring Systems

One safety problem that has increased in recent years is that older persons who are cognitively impaired become lost away from home. Signal systems such as WanderCare are now available that permit the monitoring of the location of older people when they are away from home. The older person wears a device on a belt or strap. The device emits a signal revealing the location of the wearer that is received at the "base" or home location. Use of the monitor allows considerable freedom for the older person without the risk of becoming lost.

Computer software is being designed and tested as a prosthetic aid to safety and security. Chute and Bliss (1993) believed that ProsthesisWare offers valuable personal support for safe, independent living. ProsthesisWare is a series of computer software modules, ecologically personalized for the user, that provides support for independent living. SpeechWare is one such module for augmenting oral communication by "text-to-speech" voice output. Other modules address environmental control, activity schedules, sequences of steps in activities of daily living, financial management, and medication schedules and monitoring. Chute and Bliss identified, however, several obstacles to effective use: (a) customization to individual needs and preferences, (b) resistance to high-tech devices by the elderly, and (c) cost.

New technologies are being developed to monitor electronically the health status of individuals in their homes. These incorporate computer-assisted fall detectors and sensors for respiratory failure, sleep disorders, cardiovascular function (heart, blood pressure, pulses), and insulin levels. Stewart and Kaufman (1993) described the computer-based Home Assisted Nursing Care Device (HANC), a system that uses ordinary telephone line transmission of data to a central station. HANC can integrate a variety of home health functions: vital signs monitoring, medication delivery, emergency response, telephone communications, and activity schedules. The HANC is voice activated and uses two-way communications in a "conversational and companion-like manner." At the central station, personnel record and chart all data. Care providers then access data by telephone and modify care plans.

Messaging Systems

Older persons who are away from home need accurate, explicit identification for safety. Basic information cards (name, address, age, person to notify) are effective if kept in a wallet or purse, the usual places for others to look for this information. Lamination of the card will prevent smearing and moisture damage. In addition, Med-Alert bracelets or pendants are important for older people who have special conditions, for example, diabetes, heart conditions, or a tracheostomy. Information about special precautions to be taken, blood type, and the wearer's physician and telephone number is helpful. Medical supply businesses can have these identification devices made.

Drivers cannot easily see pedestrians in dark clothing, especially at night, or anticipate unexpected or slower movements. Older persons who walk for exercise should always wear brightly colored clothing or safety vests. The vests are available in knitted polyester bright orange fabric and are worn over clothing. Fluorescent strips (Scotchlite, Reflexite) on jackets or outer clothing serve the same purpose of notifying the environment.

Telephone Technology

Telephone technology has vastly improved in recent years. Innovative devices and services by telephone afford a number of safety options for elders.

Telephones with larger keys aid those with visual difficulties to dial numbers. The older user can program frequently called numbers to each numbered key so that touching only one key will dial a 7–10 digit number.

Pasting pictures of the person to be called on the keys is a useful strategy for older persons who may not be able to remember or look up numbers. Automatic dialing devices within or attached to telephones permit dialing more numbers with a single stroke. Displays on some devices are small, but can be enlarged or accessed with a lighted magnifying glass. Cordless telephones enable the older person to initiate telephone contact and receive telephone calls from any place within distance of the base transmitter. Carrying cases attached to a belt or shoulder strap permit easy, hands-free portability. Cordless telephones are also useful for socialization of elders.

Cellular telephone technology is a significant development in safety communication. Powered by battery (car or rechargeable battery pack), cellular telephones transmit signals from cell to cell over much longer distances. They provide clear telephone communication while away from home to anyone, including sources of information and aid. In-line personal telephone amplifiers are helpful to elders who are hearing impaired. The portability of cellular phones continues to improve as evidenced by fold-up cellular telephones that fit in pocket or purse.

Voice-activated telephones (Temasek Telephone, Inc.) are another new development that may be particularly useful for the handicapped elderly. These hands-free telephones are answered by voice and permit the user to speak from a distance. Communication partners are heard through a speaker phone. The telephone automatically "hangs up" after a user-determined period of silence. Users can dial out with a single switch scanner, for example, a sip-and-puff switch, selected to meet their needs. Elders who are unable to speak or who are severely speech impaired may find telephone devices for the deaf (TDD) helpful. These systems require a special device that cradles telephone receiver and transmits and receives typed messages.

Another strategy for telephone communication for persons who are hearing or speech impaired is the RELAY system. This system is useful for communication between persons with unmatched capabilities. For example, a person who is severely speech-impaired calls the RELAY station and types the message on a computer. The caller orders a pizza to be delivered. Because the pizza store does not have a way to receive the typed message, the RELAY operator calls the pizza store and relays the message by speaking. (See Chapter 12 for more information on telephone technology.)

Emergency Summoning Strategies

In many communities, expanded 911 service is available through cooperation of the telephone company and the local police department. A person who is elderly subscribes to the service and provides the police department with personal information about the home, special conditions, and neighbors or family members who could respond. When a subscriber calls, the respondent advises the caller or calls appropriate help, for example, ambulance, family member, or doctor. If the caller does not speak when the responder answers, the responder calls a neighbor or family member to go to the caller's home to evaluate the situation.

Lifeline, developed in 1974 by Dr. Andrew S. Dibner, is another personal emergency response system. The older user wears a small, lightweight, waterproof "personal help button" as a pendant or wristband. Depressing the button starts an in-home unit, the Communicator, which then automatically dials the emergency response center. A personal file provides the responder with information on each subscriber. If the response center cannot make voice contact, a relative or neighbor—people who have agreed a priori to be "on call"—is called to check on the elderly person. The units have an advantage over stationary pull-cord call systems used in many congregate living facilities for elders in that the signaling mechanism stays with the person and, therefore, is available for use anywhere that person happens to be within the home.

TRAINING OLDER PERSONS AND THEIR INTERACTORS

Having a sewing machine does not make a person a tailor or seamstress; sewing takes training, learning, and practice. Training is also critical in the strategic use of communication technology for safety. Training older people in their environments and with familiar communicative partners increases safety by maximizing functional performance, thereby reducing the frequency or extent of need for caregiver assistance (Gitlin et al., 1993).

A major reason for the nonuse of communication technology is lack of training. It is difficult to know if the nonuser recognizes the need for training and is unable to get help or if unrealistic expectations for the user or the technology is the primary problem. Experience with augmented communication systems for persons who are severely handicapped suggests that both factors contribute to nonuse. Regardless, to get good safety results from communication technology, the older person must learn how to use the technology effectively to obtain maximum advantage. In addition, training familiar communication partners in the use of the technology leads to better acceptance, use, and satisfaction with the technology.

Training to Increase Safety

The amount of training required for elders and their partners depends on the safety technologies used. Some technologies do not require overt responses from the user. For example, carpeted walls dampen noise, making auditory stimuli easier to hear and more accurately perceived. The older person benefits without having to do anything in response. These are passive technologies and require little or no training.

Technologies, active and interactive, that require overt responses by older users require more training. Without training, some technologies may themselves present safety problems. Improperly used walkers, canes, and wheelchairs actually contribute to many falling accidents. Users benefit from training to notice, recognize, and respond appropriately to the technologies. For example, an older person learns through training to attend to a brightly painted threshold, recognize it as a symbol, understand the hazard message, and alter his or her gait, stepping, and holding behavior. Technologies requiring changes in behavior are active technologies.

Interactive technologies require direct interface of the user with the technology. Interactive technology requires that the user touch, hold, manipulate, or wear the device to benefit from it. When first employed, new interactive technology will be unfamiliar. Some older persons will respond with fascination; others may be phobic or feel clumsy and conspicuous. Increasing familiarity and positive functional outcomes will reduce negative feelings and increase confidence.

Training should focus on appropriate circumstances, techniques, and strategies for using the technology. For example, persons using automatic dosing devices for medication need training (several times, perhaps) to find and press the button. Computer users profit from training in techniques and strategies for using different input and output devices and in software appropriate to their needs. Help files and huge manuals are not always user-friendly. Software training may need to be slower and more repetitive for older people, but older adults can become proficient computer users.

The amount of training required will depend largely on individual factors. Some older people may be acutely aware of environmental cues, divergent in their abilities to solve problems, and clever in their strategic use of aids. Others may not routinely notice cues, and hence, they may not respond. Some are apparently overwhelmed by changes and the need for coping strategies. In some cases, unresponsiveness may be greater because of fear and anxiety about safety. Individual and group training in attending and responding to an environment that promotes safety may reduce fear and focus more thoughtful, less emotional attention. Moreover, training provides collaborative support, which inspires initiative and builds confidence.

Caution! Although training improves attention to the environment, too many environmental cues or augmentations can create auditory or visual clutter that may preclude the ability of older adults to use consistently any or all of the cues. In every situation, the goal is to achieve balance between (a) addressing every need and possibly overloading the person and his or her environment and (b) addressing the most critical needs and developing consistent utilization.

Training of older persons and their caregivers requires the application of behavioral principles. When deciding what to teach, the following suggestions may be helpful. Find the simplest, most consistent element and teach it first. Save exceptions and unusual situations until later. Link new learning with existing knowledge and activities. Remember certain things are easier to do if the new behavior is connected in time or place to an established routine. Give the learner verbal instruction, demonstrate, do it together, and then ask the older person to show you how to do it. Respond with praise and encouragement. Correct if necessary with verbal instruction and demonstration, then ask the learner to demonstrate again, incorporating the corrected behavior (Chafetz & Wilson, 1988). Reinforce often, being careful not to relate to the older person in childish ways.

Communication technology can enhance training, too. Public television, public service programming on commercial television, videotape (all with captioning, of course), and CD-ROM technology may extend training to more older people and their significant others. The success of the media in educating the public about health risks and encouraging behavior change suggests that similar strategies for training may be useful in educating the public about safety risks and reduction.

Along with training the older person in the use of various technologies, both older people and their caregivers need training to recognize changing safety hazards and needs. The safety circumstances of elders are not static; they change as sensory, cognitive, and motor abilities change over time. Being aware of changes and greater dependency may alert caregivers to an "accident waiting to happen." The Carolina Home Injury Prevention for Seniors (CHIPS) Project is a program designed for elders and those who interact with them to identify common environmental and personal risk hazards. In addition to the identification checklist, the program includes a video training program to help educate caregivers about possible interventions to increase safety (South Carolina Educational Television, 1992).

Family, friends, and professional caregivers can assist learning by giving verbal cues that reinforce the strategy for attending to and using available environmental cues. For example, consider an older person who is confused about the location of his or her room and has a colored wristband matching the color of the door. A caregiver's reminder to "Look at your wrist; now find the door that matches" will assist the elder in remembering what to do.

Training for Seeking and Giving Help

Even with every safety precaution employed, accidents will happen. In such instances, communication technology plays an important role in signaling need and summoning help. The efficiency and effectiveness of such communication influence the responsiveness of the environment and may be the difference between life and death.

The use of technology for summoning help requires training for both the older users and the responding environment. Demonstration and practice will facilitate effective and efficient use, increase confidence, and reduce fear. Training procedures may incorporate protocols, written on laminated cards. Training is most meaningful in natural, familiar places where summoning devices are most likely to be used. Some older people may need training to wear personal call buttons all the time and to keep telephones in prominent, easy to reach places.

Training the interpersonal environment to respond appropriately to calls for help is important too. Some communities have well established informal support networks to assist in assuring the safety of elders. Mail carriers routinely check on and communicate with elderly patrons. Organizations of and for elders have regular visiting schedules and response teams for emergencies. Community watch programs, usually organized by local police departments, engage neighbors to help one another. Professionals have an advocacy responsibility to teach elders and their support networks, public and private, about communication technologies and strategies that enhance safety.

There are several training opportunities that help elders themselves to be more responsive to calls for help. Instruction in cardiopulmonary resuscitation (CPR) is available in communities through the American Red Cross, the health department, or a local hospital. Knowing CPR can save lives, where even the best communication technology may not be enough. Older persons participate in many activities together, so they are likely to be the first to know when a peer needs help.

Elders obtain similar value from learning the Heimlich maneuver. Older people often eat and talk together. Swallowing difficulties are common in older persons, and choking or obstruction of the airway with food or other matter is a serious threat to life. In such instances, there may not be time to call someone. As with CPR, training is available through local health departments and the American Red Cross. Training in emergency response techniques can markedly improve the responsive capabilities of elders to the needs of their peers.

SUMMARY

This chapter focused on how a wide variety of simple to complex communication technologies can promote safety for elders in community or institutional environments. Changes in the cognitive, sensory, and motor functioning of elders necessitate vigilance regarding potential dangers and ready access to assistance when needed. Further, changes in the environment or relocation to an unfamiliar environment may pose challenges for elders. Communication technologies that provide elders with clear, unambiguous, and salient information regarding their environment may help them remain active contributing members of their settings. Further, communication technologies that facilitate quick, effective interaction between elders and others, particularly those outside their setting, may prevent problems, summon assistance, and encourage socialization. But the usefulness of communication technologies cannot become real for elders unless either they or significant others in their lives identify the need for such technologies, obtain them, learn to use them, and reinforce their use in daily life. Obtaining technologies that match the needs of the elder with the characteristics of the environment is the first step; using the technologies appropriately and frequently is the essential step. Life is risky, and especially so for elders, but these risks can be minimized or eliminated by the judicious use of communication technologies.

RESOURCES

Summoning/Notification Devices

Care Electronics
5741 Arapahoe Road, Suite 2A
Boulder, CO 80303
303-444-2273
WanderCARE systems notify caregivers when their wanderer leaves home, locating them up to 1 mile away. Free catalog.

Lifeline Systems
640 Memorial Drive
Cambridge, MA 02139
Technology for summoning help.

Temasek Telephone, Inc.
21 Airport Blvd, #G
South San Francisco, CA 94080
1-800-647-8887
Voice-activated telephones.

Technology for Activities of Daily Living

Harris Communications
6541 City West Parkway
Eden Prairie, MN 55344-3248
1-800-825-6758
Closed captioning devices for attachment to older television receivers.

Lab Safety Supply Inc.
P.O. Box 1368
Janesville, WI 53547-1368
1-608-754-2345
Emergency lighting fixtures, traffic vests, fluorescent strips, smoke and carbon monoxide detectors, warning signs, large-letter labels, safety treads, hazard tapes.
LaBuda, D. (1985). *The gadget book.* Glenview, IL: Scott, Foresman and Co.

Special Products for Special People
Flag House, Inc.
150 N. MacQuesten Parkway
Dept. 96453
Mt. Vernon, NY 10550
1-800-793-7900
Mostly products for children, but some for adults.

Training

National Rehabilitation Information Center
8455 Colesville Road
Silver Spring, MD 20910
1-301-588-9284
South Carolina Educational Television (1992). *For safety's sake: A guide to home safety for seniors.* Columbia, SC: South Carolina Educational Television.
1-800-553-7752.

BIBLIOGRAPHY

Abrams, W., & Berkow, R. (Eds.). (1990). *The Merck manual of geriatrics.* Rahway, NJ: Merck & Company.

Alvermann, M. (1979). Towards improving geriatric care with environmental interventions emphasizing a homelike atmosphere: An environmental experience. *Journal of Gerontological Nursing, 5,* 13–17.

Butler, R. N. (1990). Senile dementia of the Alzheimer type (SDAT). In W. Abrams & R. Berkow (Eds.), *The Merck manual of geriatrics* (pp. 933–938). Rahway, NJ: Merck & Company.

Calkins, M. P. (1988). *Design for dementia.* Owing Mills, MD: National Health Publishing.

Chafetz, P. K., & Wilson, N. L. (1988). Communicating effectively with elderly clients. *Seminars in Speech and Language, 9,* 177–182.

Christenson, M. A. (1990). Enhancing independence in the home setting. *Physical and Occupational Therapy in Geriatrics, 8,* 49–65.

Chute, D. L., & Bliss, M. E. (1993). ProsthesisWare: Personal computer support for independent living. In *Life-span design of residential environments for an aging population* (pp. 45–55). [Proceedings of an invitational conference]. Washington, DC: American Association of Retired Persons.

Cooper, B. A., Letts, L., & Rigby, P. (1993). Exploring the use of color cueing on an assistive device in the home: Six case studies. *Physical and Occupational Therapy in Geriatrics, 11,* 47–59.

Czaja, S. J. (1993). Enhancing the home safety of the elderly: Technology and design interventions. In *Life-span design of residential environments for an aging population* (pp. 71–74). [Proceedings of an invitational conference]. Washington, DC: American Association of Retired Persons.

Doty, R. L., & Shuman, P. (1984). Smell identification ability: Changes with age. *Science, 226,* 1441–1442.

Fretwell, M. D. (1990). Comprehensive functional assessment. In W. Abrams & R. Berkow (Eds.), *The Merck manual of geriatrics* (pp. 171–174). Rahway, NJ: Merck & Company.

Gitlin, L. N., Levine, R., & Geiger, C. (1993). Adaptive device use by older adults with mixed disabilities. *Archives of Physical Medicine and Rehabilitation, 74,* 149–152.

Kane, R. L. (1993). The implications of assessment. *The Journals of Gerontology, 48,* 27–31.

Mann, W. C., Hurren, D., Machiko, T., Bengali, M., & Steinfeld, E. (1994). Environmental problems in homes of elders with disabilities. *The Occupational Therapy Journal of Research, 14,* 191–211.

Namazi, K. H., & Johnson, B. D. (1991). Physical environmental cues to reduce the problems of incontinence in Alzheimer's disease units. *American Journal of Alzheimer's Care and Related Disorders and Research, 6,* 22–28.

Rubenstein, L. Z. (1990). Assessment instruments. In W. Abrams & R. Berkow (Eds.), *The Merck manual of geriatrics* (pp. 1189–1200). Rahway, NJ: Merck & Company.

Scheibel, A. B. (1985). Falls, motor dysfunction, and correlative neurohistologic changes in the elderly. *Clinics in Geriatric Medicine, 1*, 671–678.

South Carolina Educational Television. (1992). *For safety's sake: A guide to home safety for seniors.* Columbia, SC: Author.

Stewart, L. M., & Kaufman, S. B. (1993). High-tech home care: Electronic devices with implications for the design of living environments. In *Life-span design of residential environments for an aging population* (pp. 57–65). [Proceedings of an invitational conference]. Washington, DC: American Association of Retired Persons.

Tideiksaar, R. (1986). Preventing falls; Home hazard checklist to help older patients protect themselves. *Geriatrics, 41*, 26–28.

U.S. Consumer Product Safety Commission. (1985). *Home safety checklist.* Washington, DC: Author.

12

An Essential Communication Device: The Telephone

William C. Mann, O.T.R., Ph.D.

INTRODUCTION

Telephones exist almost everywhere: in our homes, stores, airports, bus stations, and on street corners. Almost every household has at least one telephone. We do business on the telephone, keep in touch with our friends and relatives, and use the telephone to alert others when there is an emergency. Within the last 15 years there has been a vast increase in the variety of telephones available and the different features that telephones have to offer. Prices have come down, and choices have increased.

The telephone is especially important for elders with impairments. Almost one-third of all elders live alone (U.S. Senate Special Committee on Aging, 1991, p. 209); for those with limited ability to leave their home, the telephone provides opportunities for socialization. In a study of elders living in rural areas, frequent loneliness was found to be associated with frequent use of the telephone (Kivet, 1979). The telephone also provides a mechanism for calls for help. Finally, many elders use the telephone for shopping, banking, and arranging other personal services.

This chapter first provides an overview of the types of limitations that can be addressed by selecting an appropriate telephone and examples of helpful telephone features. This is followed by a report of a study that examined the use of special telephone features by elders with disabilities.

TELEPHONE FEATURES TO ADDRESS IMPAIRMENTS

Hand Impairment

Hand impairments include painful and swollen joints, stiff or contracted joints, edema, fractures, weakness, and paralysis, all of which can interfere with being able to dial a telephone or hold a receiver. Although a number of conditions can result in impairment of hand function, the most serious in terms of prevalence is arthritis. Arthritis, a serious disabling condition of the joints, affects an estimated 37 million people in the United States, with prevalence greatest among the elderly (Abyad & Boyer, 1992). Estimates from the Longitudinal Study on Aging indicate that approximately 55% of elders have arthritis (Yelin, 1992). Yelin and Katz (1990) determined that, for elders who had arthritis and no other chronic conditions, 66% experienced limitations in physical activities, with 25% reporting limitations in activities of daily living (ADLs) or instrumental activities of daily living (IADLs). For elders who had arthritis and at least one other chronic condition, 82% had limitations in physical activity, and 41% were limited in ADLs. The Consumer Assessments Study at the University at Buffalo (Mann, 1995) determined that 64% of elders with arthritis had at least some difficulty with hand activities and that 12% experienced pain when dialing the telephone.

For elders who have difficulty with movement in their hands and fingers, there are telephone features that can compensate for this limitation. Many telephones now have large buttons, such as the telephone pictured in Figure 12–1, which can make dialing much easier. A redial feature allows the callers to redial a call made to a busy line or to their last conversant using a single button. Many new telephones now have memory features, so that frequently used numbers can be stored for easy retrieval. Some memory telephones have one button memory dialing, such as in Figure 12–1, whereas others require pushing two buttons. A shoulder holder or a gooseneck holder for a telephone can be helpful for a person who has difficulty grasping the telephone (Figure 12–2). For totally hands-free telephone operation, a speaker telephone is often a good alternative.

Memory Impairment

The leading cause of memory impairment in the elderly is Alzheimer's disease, with 1 out of every 10 noninstitutionalized older persons having either Alzheimer's disease or some other organic mental disorder; this increases to almost 1 out of every 2 people over the age of 85 (Mortimer, 1983). For persons with Alzheimer's disease and other con-

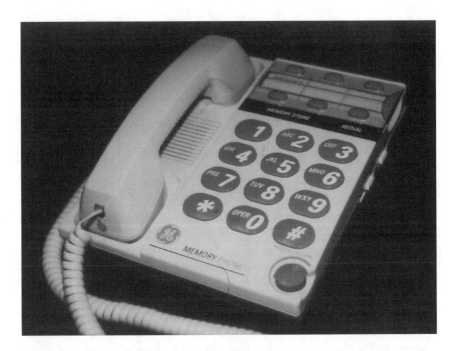

Figure 12-1. This telephone offers redial, memory, speaker output with volume control, and large buttons.

ditions that have an impact on memory, the redial and memory features mentioned before can be very helpful. There are even "picture telephones," so that a picture of the person or place to be called can be placed next to, or right on, the button. Figure 12–3 illustrates a picture telephone developed for children. This telephone could be adapted for elders with memory impairment by using age-appropriate pictures and eliminating the "Playschool" label.

Hearing Impairment

Hearing impairment can make it difficult or impossible to hear the telephone ring, or to hear the other person talking on the telephone. For people who have some hearing, there are two important telephone features: ringer amplification control and voice amplification control. First, it is important to be able to hear the telephone ring, which can be facilitated with a ringer amplification control. Second, a voice amplification control can make it possible for a person to raise the volume on the receiver to an appropriate level. Many telephones have one or both of these features.

Figure 12–2. The shoulder holder attached to this telephone makes it easier for a person with limited grasp to use the receiver.

Figures 12–4 and 12–5 demonstrate two add-on devices that provide amplification for the receiver. The device in Figure 12–4 is added into the line so nothing needs to be attached directly to the telephone. The device in Figure 12–5 is portable—an especially helpful feature for the elder who travels and needs amplification on more than one telephone.

For people with hearing impairment who cannot make use of telephone amplification, special telephones called Telecommunication Devices for the Deaf (TDDs) provide a keypad for sending messages and a digital display for reading the message from the sender (Figure 12–6). TDDs require either that users on both ends of a call have a TDD or that a relay service be used. Relay services are offered in every state. Information on relay services can be found in the front of most telephone books or by calling the local telephone company. Relay services provide a "middle" person who listens to the voice caller and types what the person is saying into a TDD for the person who is deaf. Conversely, the typed messages from the person who is deaf are read by the relay operator to the person who can hear. (For more discussion of hearing loss and devices to facilitate hearing, see Chapters 5, 6, and 11.)

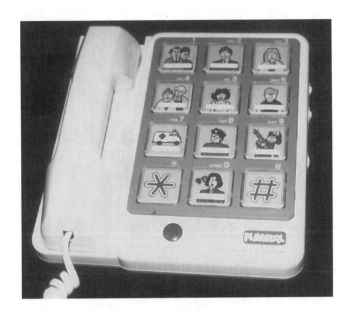

Figure 12–3. This inexpensive picture telephone was developed for children but could be adapted for use by elders with memory impairment.

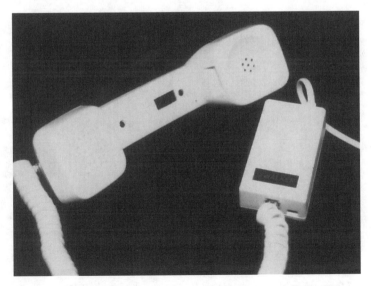

Figure 12–4. This add-on device, called the Phone Amplifier, provides voice amplification for a phone.

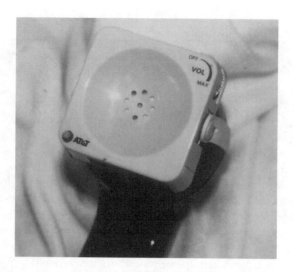

Figure 12–5. This add-on device for providing voice amplification is portable, making it possible to use on a number of telephones.

Figure 12–6. A telecommunication device for the deaf (TDD) makes it possible for persons who are deaf to use a telephone.

Vision Impairment

Vision impairment in older persons has been documented and described by numerous authorities (Kirchner & Scott, 1988; U.S. Senate Special Committee on Aging, 1991). Although it is difficult to determine the exact number of persons who are blind or who have a severe visual impairment, one recent study estimated that 82 out of 1,000 older persons have a serious visual impairment (National Center for Health Statistics, 1990). Visual impairment results in difficulty with reading for 1 out of 5 elderly persons, and 1 out of 20 persons over age 65 cannot see words or letters on a page (U.S. Bureau of the Census, 1986). Most older persons with visual impairments have some functional vision, called low vision. Symptoms of low vision are loss in the peripheral field or in central vision. One term for loss of peripheral vision is tunnel vision. The major causes of vision loss among elders are glaucoma, macular degeneration, cataracts, and diabetic retinopathy (see Chapter 3 for details on vision loss with aging).

There are many telephone features to assist elders with vision impairment. Some telephones have buttons that light up. Telephones with large buttons and good color contrast, such as those in Figures 12–1 and 12–2, make it easier to see the numbers. For persons who use a cordless telephone and forget where they put it down, a paging feature is helpful. When the pager button on the phone is pushed, the base unit of the telephone will buzz, making it easy to locate (Figure 12–7). The memory and redial features discussed previously are also helpful for persons with vision impairment, as they do not need to press as many buttons to make a call. For persons who still use, and do not want to relinquish, their rotary dial telephone, there are templates available that go over the dial, providing large number display.

Mobility Impairment

A number of chronic conditions associated with aging can impact on a person's ability to walk, including arthritis in the joints of the lower extremities, stroke, heart and respiratory conditions, and Parkinson's disease. Symptoms such as shortness of breath, weakness, joint stiffness and pain, and impaired balance can interfere with normal gait. For persons with mobility impairments, there are telephones that can be answered from across the room, such as the remote speaker telephone pictured in Figure 12–8. In this picture, the remote control device used to answer the telephone is shown resting on the telephone speaker. Answering machines provide another option for elders who find it difficult getting

Figure 12-7. This cordless telephone has a pager feature.

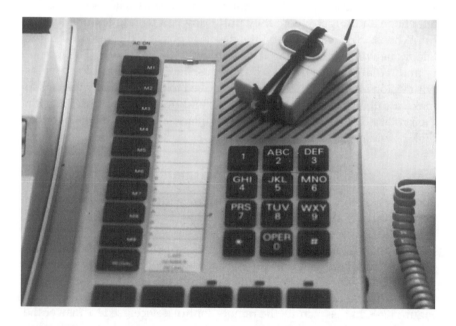

Figure 12-8. This remote speaker telephone can be answered from across the room.

Figure 12–9. An answering machine can be used to monitor calls without leaving one's seat.

up to answer the telephone (Figure 12–9). Calls can be "stored" until the elder is near the telephone, multiple calls can be made at one sitting, and nuisance calls can be ignored. Cordless telephones provide another option. By being able to keep the telephone close by, it is never necessary to get up or move to another location to receive a call. Figure 12–10 illustrates a feature that incorporates some of the latest technology—voice recognition. The user simply says something like "Call Mary" and the telephone automatically dials the number. This telephone would be useful for elders with a number of different types of impairments.

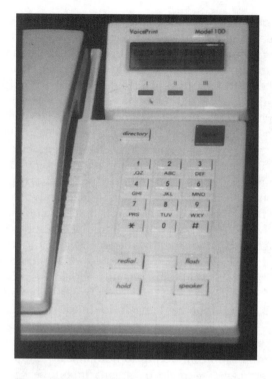

Figure 12–10. This Voice Print Phone incorporates voice recognition technology and can automatically dial a number with a voice command such as "Call Mary."

OTHER CONSIDERATIONS WITH TELEPHONES

In planning for the optimal telephone setup for an elder with impairments, there are several additional considerations that impact on safety and comfort, and installation and placement of the telephone.

Wiring

Many older telephones have not been updated with new modular jacks and wiring. New jacks can be installed by the telephone company, although many people choose to have a relative or friend complete this job. The modular jacks make it easy to add a new telephone. It is important to avoid having long telephone wires cross the floor where people will be walking, as tripping on the wires could result in someone falling and hurting themselves.

Furniture

Often a rearrangement of furniture will make it easier to use the telephone. Placing a table with the telephone on it next to a favorite chair or couch can save steps. This may require some new wiring, which in most cases is not a very difficult task.

Background Noise

Eliminating as much background noise as possible, such as a TV, radio, or conversation, can make it easier to talk on the telephone. Using a remote control to lower the TV volume can make this a simple job, and one that can be accomplished without leaving the chair.

Telephone Maintenance

Problems sometimes arise when a telephone does not work: key buttons may stick, the ringer may not work, and batteries may not charge on a cordless telephone. The first step is to contact the store where the telephone was purchased to inquire about repairs. It is important to consider that it may be less expensive to replace a telephone than to have it repaired. It is always a good idea to ask for an estimate before having any work done on a telephone that is not working properly.

Nuisance Calls

It is not uncommon for elders to be bothered by nuisance calls. They are especially problematic for elders with disabilities. Nuisance calls should be reported to the telephone company. The telephone operator should be able to direct you to the appropriate service representative.

Special Services

Some telephone companies offer special services for older persons and persons with disabilities. Telephone books generally offer such information. In some states, such as California, these services are mandated under state law.

PROBLEMS FACED BY ELDERS IN USING PHONES

Although telephones with helpful features are available, they are not being used by all elders who need them. The study reported here examined telephone use among elders with impairments.

The University at Buffalo Rehabilitation Engineering Center on Aging is conducting a project called the Consumer Assessments Study (CAS). The CAS was designed to determine home-based older persons' needs for assistive devices, as well as to understand the successful use of devices and home modifications. Designed as a longitudinal study, 398 persons age 60 years or older who had disabilities were interviewed in their homes, with follow-up interviews scheduled annually.

In studying the needs of elders for assistive devices, data have been collected along several dimensions: (a) basic demographic information such as education, finances, housing; (b) health status, including number and types of chronic conditions, use of medications, and utilization of hospitals and physicians; (c) functional status, including both activities of daily living and instrumental activities of daily living; (d) psychosocial dimensions, including depression, mental status, self-esteem, and sense of responsibility; (e) social resources; (f) current use of assistive devices; (g) an assessment of the home, yard, and neighborhood; and (h) if there is a family caregiver, a survey of the caregiver's health, psychosocial status, and care burden. Several descriptive studies based on the CAS data have recently been completed (Mann, Hurren, Karuza, & Bentley, 1993; Mann, Hurren, & Tomita, 1993, 1994; Mann, Hurren, Tomita, Bengali, & Steinfeld, 1994; Mann, Hurren, Tomita, & Charvat, 1995; Mann, Karuza, Hurren, & Tomita, 1992, 1993).

One of the findings from the CAS is that a large number of elders with disabilities use telephones with special features. From the sample of 398 elders, 212, or 53%, own at least one telephone with at least one special feature. Table 12–1 provides a summary of these findings. The most common special feature is the cordless telephone, followed by telephones with large numbers and telephones with a memory dial feature. Several elders also use special telephone books, either with enlarged print, or a personal telephone book that is smaller in size and easier to handle.

Table 12–1 also provides a count of the number of problems elders report having with the special feature telephones they own. Table 12–2 provides more detail on the types of problems encountered by elders. The cordless telephone has the largest number of performance problems, such as static or neighbors being able to overhear conversations.

Out of 212 telephones with special features, elders reported 36 problems. This is a problem rate of 17%—rather high for telephones that were primarily purchased to address specific impairments. Most of these problems could be grouped under the following categories: need for repair or maintenance or both, poor device performance, and poor person–device fit. The majority of problems with the cordless telephones relate to poor device performance and the need for repair and/or

Table 12–1. Special features of telephones[a] used by subjects[b] in the Consumer Assessments Study.

Feature	Phones with this Feature		Phones with Problems	
	N	**%**	**N**	**%**
Cordless telephone	100	47	19	19
Telephone with enlarged numbers	72	34	8	11
Memory dial	35	17	2	6
Telephone book with enlarged print and/or smaller size	29	14	0	0
Amplification	14	7	4	29
Speaker phone	9	4	1	11
Telephone answering machine	5	2	0	0
Illuminated key pad	4	2	0	0
Cellular telephone	3	1	0	0
Shoulder holder	3	1	0	0
Devices for dialing rotary telephone	2	1	0	0
Cassette with telephone numbers	2	1	0	0
Telecommunication Devices for the Deaf (TDDs)	1	.05	0	0
TOTAL	**279**		**34**	**12**

[a] Number of telephones = 212; several telephones have more than one special feature
[b] Number of subjects = 398

maintenance. On the other hand, 50% of the problems encountered with the memory dial feature relate to person–device fit.

SOURCES OF INFORMATION

Occupational therapists conduct assessments of the home environment and make helpful recommendations to make it safer and easier to do

TABLE 12–2. Problems experienced with telephone features.

Feature	Number of Problems	Problems
Telephone with enlarged numbers	4	Even with large numbers, cannot see them clearly enough to distinguish among them
	3	Non-vision-related impairment makes telephone difficult to use (e.g., receiver too heavy, not able to dial due to hand impairment)
	1	Number template falls off
Memory dial	3	Cannot use because of severity of cognitive impairment
	1	Maintenance problem—does not work properly
Amplification	2	Cannot distinguish words even with amplification
	1	Telephone whistles
	1	Not able to use because of advanced Alzheimer's disease
	1	Too complicated
Cordless Telephone	9	Does not work properly; interference or static makes it difficult or impossible to hear
	3	Needs more features for other impairments such as larger numerals or backlit keypad
	2	Can overhear conversations from other telephones, or other telephones pick up this telephone's conversations
	2	Maintenance problems such as keys on keypad sticking
	1	Batteries wear out too quickly
	1	Not used optimally; not taken along when moving around in home

daily tasks, including the use of telephones. The American Occupational Therapy Association can be contacted at 301–948–9626 for a listing of occupational therapists who work in a geographic region.

The University at Buffalo Rehabilitation Engineering Research Center on Aging offers a program called Project Link. It is a free service, offering product information on a wide variety of assistive devices. Project Link can be joined by calling 1–800–628–2281. The University at Buffalo Rehabilitation Engineering Research Center also offers a number of other videos, pamphlets, and articles—some directed at health care professions, and others designed for consumers. One consumer-oriented video focuses on telephone features, and provides two examples where elders with disabilities had their telephone systems updated to meet their special needs. To receive a free products catalog, call the 800 number listed previously.

SUMMARY

We all benefit from the convenience features now found in many telephones. For elders, from those with very minor impairments to those with multiple, chronic, disabling conditions, the convenience features become essential tools for successful use of the telephone. We will likely see more developments that prove useful to elders as the technologies behind television, computers, and telephones merge into mainstream communication devices. The challenge will be to assist elders to ensure their successful use of current and future devices.

This chapter detailed the scope of problems elders may have that limit telephone use, from sensory to physical and cognitive disabilities. For each of these disabilities there are numerous telephone adaptations that facilitate access to effective telephone usage. Consumers should be aware of future advances in telephone technologies and make these available to the needs of elders.

There are several places to look for information on telephones. Visiting a department store or an electronics store will provide many choices. There are even special telephone stores in many shopping malls, such as AT&T telephone stores. Many mail order catalogs include telephones in their line of products.

Acknowledgment This research was supported through funding from the National Institute on Disability and Rehabilitation Research, U.S. Department of Education, and the Administration on Aging of the Department of Health and Human Services.

REFERENCES

Abyad, A., & Boyer, J. T. (1992). Arthritis and aging: Current opinion. *Rheumatology, 4*, 153–159.

Kirchner, C., & Scott, R. (1988). *Data on blindness and visual impairment in the U.S.* New York: American Foundation for the Blind.

Kivett, V. R. (1979). Discriminators of loneliness among the rural elderly: Implications for intervention. *The Gerontologist, 19*, 108–115.

Mann, W. (1995). NIDRR rehabilitation engineering research center on assistive technology for older persons. *Generations, 19*, 49–53.

Mann, W., Hurren, D., Karuza, J., & Bentley, D. (1993). Needs of home-based older visually impaired persons for assistive devices. *Journal of Visual Impairment and Blindness, 87*, 106–110.

Mann, W., Hurren, D., & Tomita, M. (1993). Comparison of assistive device use and needs of home-based seniors with different impairments. *American Journal of Occupational Therapy, 47*, 980–987.

Mann, W., Hurren, D., & Tomita, M. (1994). Assistive device needs of home-based elderly persons with hearing impairments. *Technology and Disability, 3*, 47–61.

Mann, W., Hurren, D., Tomita, M., Bengali, M., & Steinfeld, E. (1994). Environmental problems in homes of elders with disabilities. *The Occupational Therapy Journal of Research, 14*, 191–211.

Mann, W., Hurren, D., Tomita, M., & Charvat, B. (1995). Assistive devices for home-based older stroke survivors. *Topics in Geriatric Rehabilitation, 10*, 75–86.

Mann, W., Karuza, J., Hurren, D., & Tomita M. (1992). A study of the needs of home-based elderly persons with cognitive impairments for assistive devices. *Topics in Geriatric Rehabilitation, 8*, 35–52.

Mann, W., Karuza, J., Hurren, D., & Tomita, M. (1993). Needs of home-based older persons for assistive devices: The University at Buffalo Rehabilitation Engineering Center on Aging Consumer Assessments Study. *Technology and Disability, 2*, 1–11.

Mortimer, J. A. (1983). Alzheimer's disease and senile dementia: Prevalence and incidence. In B. Reisberg (Ed.), *Alzheimer's disease: The standard reference* (pp. 141–148). New York: The Free Press.

National Center for Health Statistics (1990). Current estimates from the national health interview survey. *Vital and Health Statistics*, Series 10, No. 176.

U.S. Bureau of the Census. (1986). Disability, functional limitation, and health insurance coverage: 1984/85. *Current Population Reports*, (Series p-70, No 8). Washington DC: Government Printing Office.

U.S. Senate Special Committee on Aging, American Association of Retired Persons, the Federal Council on the Aging, and the U.S. Administration on Aging. (1991). *Aging America: Trends and projections,* Washington, DC: U.S. Department of Health and Human Services.

Yelin, E. (1992). Arthritis: The cumulative impact of a common chronic condition. *Arthritis Rheumatism, 35*, 489–497.

Yelin, E., & Katz, P. P. (1990). Transitions in health status among community-dwelling elderly people with arthritis: A national, longitudinal study. *Arthritis Rheumatism, 33*, 1205–1215.

13

Accessibility to Technology for Older Americans— a Matter of Money

Margo E. Broehle, P.C.

INTRODUCTION

When wealthy sheiks from Saudi Arabia experience heart pains, they fly to the Cleveland Clinic in the United States to receive the very best in modern medical expertise and technology. Although older Americans who are members of the general public do not stay in the special suites reserved for kings and princes, they, too, receive the same medical expertise and have the benefits of the same advanced technology. Indeed, a potentate may have to wait in line behind a retired policeman to receive a heart transplant. What has equalized health care between the very, very wealthy and the average older American?

This chapter explores the issues of access to technology for Americans over the age of 65 and argues that successful implementation of assistive technology is directly related to the availability of third party funding. It focuses on Medicare as the principal insurance program for Americans over age 65. Medicare is not only the major payor in the U.S. health care system, accounting for 28% of all hospital payments, 20% of all physician payments, and 45% of health care spending for elders overall. Medicare coverage policy is also a deciding factor for all medical services for elders, as private insurance companies and Medicaid programs that provide supplemental coverage for amounts not paid by Medicare typically link their coverage to Medicare, paying for only those procedures that are allowable under Medicare.

MEDICARE COVERAGE

Older Americans did not have access to universal health insurance coverage until 1965, when Congress enacted legislation creating the Medicare program (42 U.S.C. 1395, et seq.) to provide federal health insurance for those individuals who were 65 or older, many of whom did not have access to basic medical services. Access to health insurance then, as now, was usually tied to a job, and those people who no longer worked because of age or disability were unable to obtain affordable coverage. The program was subsequently amended to provide coverage for persons with disabilities and those with end-stage renal disease.

In devising the payment system, Congress created two broad categories of covered services and payment mechanisms to provide acute care benefits: Medicare Part A and Medicare Part B. The basic package has changed little since then. Medicare Part A provides for inpatient hospital care, adjunct medical supplies, diagnostic tools, and therapies. Skilled nursing care for rehabilitation (specifically associated with recuperation from hospitalization, and limited to 100 days) is provided. Skilled nursing or rehabilitation benefits provided in the home and prescribed by a physician are covered. Hospice care for the terminally ill is also covered. Part A has a deductible and copayments that must be made by the patient.[1] Everyone over 65 years who qualifies for Social Security or Railroad Retirement benefits is automatically enrolled in Medicare Part A. Although there is a deductible and in some instances a copayment required from the patient, no premium is charged for participation.

Anyone eligible for Part A is also eligible to enroll in Part B. Monthly premiums ($42.50 in 1996) and a deductible payment are required. Medicare Part B pays for 80% of allowable physician and outpatient services. Coverage includes physician services; laboratory and diagnostic tests; X-ray and other radiation therapy; outpatient services at a hospital, rehabilitation facility, or rural health clinic; home dialysis supplies and equipment; limited ambulance services; physical and speech therapy; mammography screening and pap smears; and limited outpatient mental health services. Durable medical equipment and prosthetic devices are covered when provided by a hospital, skilled nursing facili-

---

[1] All statements regarding Medicare coverage are made as of January 1996. Proposed changes to Medicare may alter coverage and the reader is advised to check current statutes.

ty, home health agency, hospice, or as prescribed by a doctor for home health care. Covered items include such items as cardiac pacemakers; corrective lenses needed after cataract surgery; colostomy or ileostomy supplies; breast prostheses following a mastectomy; artificial limbs and eyes; and wheel chairs, hospital beds, and walkers. Part B does not pay for custodial care, long-term nursing care, hearing aids, dental care, routine foot care, routine physical checkups, or outpatient prescription drugs.

TECHNOLOGY AND THE LAWS

Although other laws have been passed that mandate the provision of technology, few provide specific relief for older Americans. The technology provisions included in education legislation, such as the Education of Individuals with Disabilities Act of 1990 (IDEA), which is the reauthorization of the Education for the Handicapped Act of 1975, provides only for students in public schools. The Americans with Disabilities Act of 1990 (ADA), prohibits discrimination against people with disabilities. Its focus, however, is employment, with the provision of technology tied to the work setting where the employer is required to provide those accommodations deemed reasonable for an employee with a disability. ADA requirements mandating building owners to assure equal access to public accommodations have resulted in an increased number of buildings with ramps for people with mobility disabilities, elevators with Braille keypads and voice output for people with visual impairments, and public telephones equipped with amplifiers and TTY connections for people with hearing impairments. ADA provisions do not require that an individual receive technology specific to him or her; indeed, the law specifically states that items for personal use are not required to be provided.

Medicaid (42 U.S.C. 1396 et seq.) was created at the same time as Medicare to provide health care for eligible low-income individuals and is often misunderstood to be similar to, or even part of, the Medicare program. Medicaid is mandated by federal law, but, unlike Medicare, it is administered by each state, with the state having the right to determine the Part B services it will provide. It is financed by state and federal governments, with the federal portion determined by a formula based on the per capita income of the state's residents. Because states share the costs, they are allowed to submit their own plans for providing service that often alter federal coverage rules. There is one Medicare system, but 50 separate and distinct Medicaid systems.

Unlike Medicare, Medicaid eligibility is based on need. Medicaid typically covers health care expenses for all recipients of Aid to Families with Dependent Children (AFDC), and most states also cover the needy elderly, blind, and disabled who receive cash assistance under the Supplemental Security Income (SSI) program. Coverage also is extended to certain infants and low-income pregnant women, and, at the option of the state, other low-income individuals with medical bills that qualify them as categorically or medically needy. Although it is a major source of funding for in-patient nursing home care for indigent older Americans, Medicaid will ordinarily pay for only that technology that qualifies for Medicare payments. Ironically, some states that provide Medicaid services to indigent recipients under the age of 65 may deny payment for the same item to someone over 65. How can this happen? It is because Medicare is deemed to be the primary payor for people over 65, whereas Medicaid occupies the position of secondary payor. If the state's Medicaid plan specifies that the state will pay only for items allowable under Medicare, and Medicare refuses to cover an item, Medicaid will deny coverage as well.

Medical Technology—An Example

Medicare will pay only for those medical procedures, services, or equipment it deems to be medically necessary. What constitutes medical necessity is not a subject of universal agreement or understanding. It is a term that looks to medicine for only a portion of its definition. Other factors influence the determination: politics of cost, politics of voting demographics, politics of big business, politics of medicine. Medical technology adds another dramatic factor to the balance: the effect of rapid change.

The President's Biomedical Research Panel of 1976 stated:

> Fifty years ago the term technology, and for that matter, science, would have seemed incongruous in a discussion of medical practice. In the last 25 years [e]ntirely new disciplines have emerged almost overnight, a research technology has evolved, and the sophistication and power to match. and because of all this, the profession of medicine has begun to experience a transformation unlike anything in the millennia of its existence. (App. A)

The Medicare law was written without the benefit of foresight into the miracles of the future. No specific provision for technology was made. Only those "items or services reasonable or necessary for the diagnosis or treatment of illness or injury or to improve the functioning of a malformed body member" (42 U.S.C. 1395Y(A)(1)) were to be paid for. This language opened the door for technological innovations such as joint replacements, treatments for coronary artery disease, and cataract surgery, all financed by Medicare, and all of which have improved the quality of life and the functioning of millions of elderly people (Davis, 1995). What makes one technology medically necessary and another not? Why is a cochlear implant paid for by Medicare, but the purchase of a hearing aid is not? The answers to these questions are neither easy nor consistent. In order to create a framework for analyzing the issues, let us probe two examples of medical technology, one that has been funded by Medicare and one that has not.

No more dramatic example of the impact of technology exists than that of cataract surgery. A cataract is a clouding of the lens of an eye. Although there may be many causes, most cataracts are the result of bio-chemical changes to the fiber of the lens that occur gradually over time as the lens becomes less uniform, creating variations in its refractivity at different points. This in turn makes the light traveling through the lens scatter, so that the lens is less transparent. These changes are a nearly universal product of aging, with 95% of people over 65 years losing some clarity in one or both lenses (General Accounting Office, 1993).

Until the passage of Medicare assured payment for the treatment of cataracts, cataract treatment was much the same as it had been since the Middle Ages. The only effective treatment is surgical removal of the lens. Pre-1965 surgery was an in-patient procedure, performed with a simple scalpel and a pair of tweezers. After surgery the eyes were cov-ered with gauze soaked in antiseptic, fastened with adhesive, and con-fined by a binocular protective mask. The patient was to lie on his or her back for 24 hours, after which he or she was allowed to change to the unoperated side. In certain cases, the patient's head was held in place by sandbags. Only fluids were consumed for the first few days, as the patient was not to have bowel movements for 4 days. After 3 or 4 days, the unoperated eye was allowed to be left free. After a week the patient was allowed to sit up. Smoked glasses were used until the patient could be fitted with the heavy convex eyeglasses that simulated the natural lens replacement (Perera, 1947).

A dramatic leap forward occurred in 1949 when Harold Ridley observed that fragments of plexiglass from shattered cockpits could be tolerated within the eyes of British airmen. He performed the first inte-rocular lens (IOL) implant, implanting a lens of his own design. Ridley experienced marked success with his patients but, due largely to the still primitive methods of surgery, implants were not always successful. Even even as late as 1970, over 15% of his patients had to have their implants removed (H. R. Rep. No. 506, 99th Congress, 1st Sess. 1985).

The major leap forward was microsurgery using laser techniques. Lasers utilizing semiconductor junctions were discovered in 1962. By

1967, although the major application of laser technology still appeared to be in industrial fields, there was speculation that "[i]f a laser is attached to a microscope, the beam may be directed on small area of tissue and thus permit the possibility of micro surgery," followed with the caution that: "[e]ven at this stage, it is not known exactly what changes are produced in tissue by the impact of a laser beam" (Melia, 1967, p. 25). With the passage of Medicare, assured funding for cataract surgeries for elders seemed likely, and research in lasers for microsurgery began in earnest.

Major improvements in interocular lens technology also took place. Ridley's first lenses were placed in the anterior chamber of the eye, in front of the iris. Posterior chamber lenses were preferred, as these could be placed behind the iris in the same place from which the patient's own natural lens had been removed could reduce postoperative problems. In order to be inserted behind the iris, the lens had to be made of soft and foldable material, a material that had to be developed for the purpose. Again, the assurance of funding for the procedures encouraged the enormous research, development, and testing required to produce such a lens.

By 1987, because of improvements in surgical techniques and lenses, cataract surgery was deemed to be one of the safest and most successful of all major operations (National Institute of Health [NIH], 1987). The improvement of techniques allowed much shorter hospital stays or even outpatient treatment (Jaffe, 1984). Ninety-six percent of Medicare cataract surgery was done on an ambulatory basis in 1987 (Ahern, 1993), down from 2.1 days of inpatient stay in 1984, 4.8 days in 1977, and 7.6 days in 1966 (Reuter & O'Sullivan, 1987).

Surely this must represent a great success story. Millions of Americans who would have been blind regained their full vision. Hospital stays were virtually eliminated. Is this the happy ending to the technology tale?

THE POLITICS OF COST

When Medicare coverage began on July 1, 1966, 19.1 million people aged 65 and over were eligible to enroll, many of whom were without medical insurance coverage and lacked access to acute care services. By 1976, however, the cost of providing medical treatment for older Americans began to be the issue. Enrollment had dramatically expanded, and, partially as a measure of success of the program, life expectancy had grown by over 10 years from 65.6 in 1965 to 76.1 in 1995. Costs had far outstripped the 1965 estimates, and Congress began to consider whether cost savings could be achieved with cataract surgeries in the first of a periodic series of hearings. The first attempt to contain costs was a move to allow optometrists to receive reimbursement for postoperative services. Hearings were held in 1976 on the issue (Health Resources Administration, 1976) and the law was amended in 1980 to allow optometrists to receive reimbursement for follow-up service. In 1976 all cataract surgeries were still inpatient hospital procedures and incorporated almost entirely anterior chamber IOLs, but by 1980, laser surgery was starting and posterior chamber lenses were being used (Safir, 1983). By 1985, with 60% of people over 65 showing signs of cataract and cataracts still the second leading cause of blindness, cataract surgery was the most frequently reimbursed major surgical procedure. Over 1 million surgeries were performed in 1985 and the IOL industry sold over $325 million of lenses. Almost 50% of the lenses implanted were posterior chamber, and laser surgery was common.

Kickbacks from IOL manufacturers were rumored, and hearings were held to investigate (H. R. Rep. No. 506, 1985). The House Report made the unsubstantiated assertion that over 30% of cataract surgeries were unnecessary. Few optometrists were billing Medicare for follow-up services, but it was fairly common for ophthalmologists to refer patients to optometrists for follow-up care, sharing the Medicare fee. This irritated the Inspector General, and Congress held hearings (Medicare Reimbursement for Cataract Surgery, 1985) resulting in further expansion of the optometrist's role in an attempt to reduce costs.

By 1987, when the new reimbursement law was passed, 91% of the lenses were posterior chamber; new microchip technology for removing the natural lens by ultrasonic fragmentation and removal through a very small incision was utilized; and the first foldable silicone lenses were available. This combination of techniques further reduced postoperative complications and recovery time. Inpatient treatment was a thing of the past. Follow-up treatment was minimal and involved only the ophthalmologist. After 11 years of Congressional hearings, the expansion of the optometrist's role provided for in the new reimbursement law in an attempt to contain costs was moot.

The Public Health Service established the Agency for Health Care Policy and Research (AHCPR) in 1989 to improve quality, appropriateness, and effectiveness of health care and to improve access to health care services by conducting and supporting two primary programs: (a) research and analysis of health care costs, quality and access; and (b) medical treatment effectiveness that includes development of clinical practice guidelines (Lavizzo-Mourey, 1993). Senators Heinz and Pryor asked the General Accounting Office (GAO) to investigate cataract surgery costs in 1989. On February 25, 1993, when the AHCPR released its clinical practice guideline *Cataract in Adults: Management of Functional Impairment* in conjunction with the GAO report on cataract surgery, it appeared that the major focus was an attempt to reduce costs (AHCPR, 1993), based on the continued assumption that there were many unnecessary surgeries being performed. (In 1991, 1.35 million cataract surgeries were reimbursed under Medicare at a cost of $3.4 billion, which had raised red flags again.) The GAO report used postsurgery patient surveys to find that somewhere between 2.5% and 24% of all cataract surgeries were unnecessary (GAO, 1993). The agency apologized for not being able to be more precise, noting that the study did not use firm criteria, was conducted in only four states, and excluded certain types of surgery (Chelimsky, 1993).

The AHCPR guideline stated that the mere presence of a cataract does not mean that surgery is needed. Surgery is deemed unnecessary if an individual is able to function normally or if the condition can be corrected with eyeglasses. In October 1995, the Department of Health and Human Services proposed that Medicare adopt coverage standards that reflect the AHCPR clinical guidelines. Under the new policy, reimbursement is available only for individuals who desire the surgery, who are medically fit for the surgery, and whose lifestyle is compromised by functional impairment. Both the cataract and the impairment must be documented in the patient's medical record (60 Fed. Reg. 194, 52,396). The policy does not state how much functional impairment must be present to justify a procedure or even how to measure that impairment. Although HHS hopes to contain costs, it does not appear that the practical impact will be great; physicians will merely document the patient's functional impairment in the medical record to receive Medicare reimbursement (Sandler, 1996).

It is possible to conclude from the cataract example that medical technology that provides great benefits to consumers will, despite fits and starts, political noise-making, and financing challenges, ultimately become almost universally available to those who need it. But before that hasty conclusion is made, let us examine what has happened with a different technology.

A Contrasting Example In Speech-Language Pathology

Two and a half million noninstitutionalized people in the United States have difficulty in making their speech understood to the extent that it is considered a functional limitation (LaPlante, 1991). The actual number of persons with severe communication disability is considerably higher, because people with aphasia, stroke, or other acquired speech impairment, and mental retardation are not included in this figure. Augmentative or alternative communication (AAC) is an area of clinical practice that attempts to compensate (either temporarily or permanently) for the impairment and disability patterns of individuals with severe expressive communication disorders (i.e., persons with severe speech-language and writing impairments) (American Speech-Language and Hearing Association [ASHA], 1989, p. 107). An AAC system is defined as the integration of components, including symbols, aids, strategies, and techniques, that are used by individuals to enhance communication (ASHA, 1991, p. 10).

Potential augmentative and alternative communication users have various disabilities. Many have motor impairments (e.g., cerebral palsy) that affect not only their capacity for speech but also their ability to utilize much mainstream technology such as standard computer keyboards. Others have lost or experienced impairment of speech following a head injury, stroke, or surgery. A third group of users experience diminished oral communication abilities as a consequence of progressive disorders such as Parkinson's disease, multiple sclerosis (MS), or amyotrophic lateral sclerosis (ALS). Still others have serious impairment coincident with cognitive disabilities such as Down syndrome.

Through the 1970s, people who were unable to speak relied on communication boards designed with or without the guidance of a speech-language pathologist. Although these systems served the purpose of communicating basic needs and wants of the person relying on them, communication was often slow, restricted in content, confined to one communication partner, and limited in growth and expansion of language. Rudimentary mechanical systems were cumbersome. Based on a typewriter wheel, the user would select a letter by pressing a switch with a hand or foot, or by using a sip-and-puff method; to make the next selection, the user had to rotate the wheel to reach the correct letter. Saying "Hello" would take 33 "hits." This was exhausting to both the user and the listener.

The use of standard microprocessor technology spurred the development of electronic communication aids, and horizons expanded. Speech output became possible, and prestored vocabulary was available for faster retrieval of language. Early electronic devices allowed the user to utter a limited set of fixed statements, such as "I am cold," "I am hungry," "I have to go to the bathroom," and so forth. For one who has never been able to communicate at all, such phrases are an enormous step forward, and of inestimable value. However, they do not begin to meet an individual's communication needs. The field has continued to develop over the last 15 years, but the pace is much slower than that set in the cataract example. Despite the dedicated efforts of professionals, researchers, and manufacturers in this field, only a fraction of people with severe communication disabilities have been served, and almost none have received benefits under Medicare. Certainly no one argues the importance of speech in our lives. As stated in the *National Strategic Plan* of the National Institute of Deafness and Other Communication Disorders (1995):

- Loss of the voice has profound psychological, social and economic consequences for the individual.
- Spoken language is the most distinct human faculty.
- Language is the uniquely human means of communication through which knowledge, belief, and behavior can be explained and shared. The ability to manipulate language to satisfy needs and desires and to express thoughts, observations, and values is an important human pursuit that directly influences the qualify of life for any individual.
- Language impairments impede social development, employment opportunities and economic self-sufficiency. (National Institute of Deafness and Other Communication Disorders, 1995)

The Examples Compared

The loss of visual acuity because of untreated cataracts and the inability to communicate because of a severe speech disorder represent devastating functional limitations for an individual. Each condition is disabling; each represents an enormous cost to the community. Each has modern technology that can alleviate the effect of the disabling condition.

What demarcates the difference between the availability of an AAC device and cataract surgery? One clear difference is the availability of Medicare funding. Although Medicare will cover communication devices under Part A (only for use while the person is actually in the hospital) to allow people who cannot speak to communicate with hospital and skilled nursing staff (U.S. Congress Office of Technology Assessment [OTA], 1983) it does not cover the devices under Part B because of an administrative decision that the devices are not needed for the functioning of a malformed body member. According to OTA, innovations in the field appear to have been held back by the lack of coverage by Medicare and other insurers (OTA, 1984). States that have elected to provide speech and language services as an optional service under Medicaid must provide AAC devices (*Meyers by Walden v Reagan*, 776

F.2d 241 [8th Cir. 1985])[2] but communication devices remain a specifically excluded item under Medicare and thus unavailable to most older
Americans.

A second difference is that relief for cataracts did exist before 1965,
albeit in the primitive mode of surgery described previously, although
people with severe communication disabilities were typically deemed to
be beyond help. In all of the Congressional investigations and hearings
noted, no one, not even the GAO, proposed returning to the surgery
methods employed in 1964. The government may attempt to restrain
costs by attempting to limit access to the surgery, but it does not suggest
containing costs by returning to pretechnology methods.

STRATEGIES FOR SUCCESS IN FUNDING

Based on the previous examples, one can develop the following assumptions:

1. *Technologies that address a single principal diagnosis have more success in being funded.* People with cataracts may have other medical problems as well, but cataracts are an obvious, specific diagnostic category.
Speech impairment is usually considered as incident to some other diagnosis. There are many different reasons for speech impairment; cataracts
result from one problem: distortion of the lens in the eye.

2. *Technologies that follow the familiar medical service provider system
have more success in being funded.* Cataract surgery is performed by ophthalmologists with additional covered services from allied health professionals such as nurses and optometrists. Medicare requires that all
services be "medically necessary" and in order to receive funding from
insurance, AAC devices must be prescribed by a physician. But physicians do not receive any training or education in the availability of AAC
systems; these systems are not surgical tools; they do not require a
physician to install or train the users. The allied professionals in AAC

[2]Despite the ruling of the Federal Court, funding has been obtained in most states only
after enormous struggle. The far-sighted professionals and policy advocates who have
participated in panels to help write and implement policy and selection criterion for
their state funding departments have donated thousands of hours. The tireless efforts of
one courageous public service lawyer, Lewis Golinker of Ithaca, New York, to obtain
equal access to Medicaid services for people with communication disorders leaves society in his debt. Unfortunately, with the specter of massive changes to Medicaid law, it is
uncertain that these gains so heroically won will not be written out of the coverage policies of the states.

are usually speech-language pathologists who cannot write prescriptions and are typically not affiliated directly with the traditional medical model.

3. *Technology included in professional training curricula has a better success in being funded.* Ophthalmologists study cataract surgery techniques and practice them in medical school and as interns and residents. They enter their practices with current knowledge of the technology and are expected to keep up with it. It would be unacceptable to them not to utilize the technology. Speech-language pathologists can, and many do, receive a graduate degree in speech-language pathology from a highly respectable accredited university without having had one course in AAC. These professionals have no choice but to learn on the job.

4. *Technology has a better chance of being funded when professionals are active lobbyists on behalf of their patients.* Ophthalmologists do not long for the "good old days" when a significant percentage of their older patients would eventually be blind. They expect to employ technology on behalf of their patients and to constantly demand improvements to that technology from manufacturers. Professionals working with people who cannot speak, from pediatricians to geriatricians to speech-language pathologists, are woefully uneducated about the existence and benefits of communication technology.

5. *Technology has a better chance of being funded when professionals are active lobbyists with their legislative representatives.* In 1990, the American Medical Association was 3rd on the list of top 100 political action committee (PAC) sponsors; the American Academy of Ophthalmologists was 42nd and the American Optometry Association was 82nd (Makinson, 1990). Speech language pathologists did not appear on the list.

6. *Technology has a better chance of being funded when consumers are aware of the potential benefits.* Rapid improvement in cataract surgery, technology, and training of the professionals did not occur in a vacuum. Once the advances became available, people with cataracts wanted the benefit of the new techniques. In the AAC example, the consuming public is to a great extent unaware of any technology that could help.

CONCLUSION

Access to acute care medical treatment was the major goal of Congress when it created Medicare. By 1994, over 35 million people received Medicare coverage at a cost of $63 billion, of whom 31 million were persons age 65 or older, and 3 million were disabled. The political pressure has now shifted from access to cost containment. Providing medical technology for elders must be analyzed in the prevailing political context of costs. How do we assess the impact of medical technology on the costs of service? On the quality of care?

The provision of medical services and technology for older Americans is a by-product of Medicare policy. If Medicare does not cover a service, other insurance funders will also deny coverage. The consumer must rely on private payment sources for noncovered items. For elderly consumers, this is often impossible.

Medicare is the bulwark of funding for services for older Americans. Arguing that access to technology should be limited, based on an analysis of the Medicare budget viewed in isolation, is foolish. Successful cataract surgery allows many elderly people to live independently the rest of their lives. These people, if blind, would likely need long-term custodial care, often at taxpayer expense. One finds few success stories about the elderly population in need of a technology not covered by Medicare. A 66-year-old woman who loses her ability to speak and the use of her dominant hand after a stroke becomes despondent over her inability to communicate and commits suicide. A 72-year-old man is no longer able to live independently because he cannot communicate, and spends the rest of his life in a nursing home, a burden to the taxpayers of his state. The costs of technology must be assessed in terms of the improvement of quality of care and the long-term benefit to the community as a whole. Unfortunately, dollars spent from one year to the next on a government program are more readily calculated than dollars saved, or the value of lives improved.

The future of funding for technology is unclear. What is clear is that the availability of Medicare funding is the determining factor in whether technology will be funded for older Americans. The legislation and systems that permit Medicare funding have a significant lag time behind technology development. The definitions contained in the Medicare law are closer to the status of technology and practice of medicine in 1965 than to the level of services available to Americans in the 1990s. Public policy is constrained by budget analysts who view government funding as coming from unrelated, independent pots of money.

Although it is easier to measure money that is already spent from the single pot of Medicare than to consider how to save money for the entire societal pool, what is good for the Medicare budget is not necessarily what will create the greatest good for the community as a whole. Providing technology in the future will require a broader, more creative vision from consumers, professionals, policymakers, and legislators.

RESOURCES

Medicare

Free publications that explain Medicare are available at any local Social Security office, or by writing to

Medicare Publications
Health Care Financing Administration
6324 Security Boulevard
Baltimore, MD 21207

Consumer Information Center
Department 59
Pueblo, CO 81009

REFERENCES

Agency for Health Care Policy and Research. (1993). *Cataract in adults: Management of functional impairment*, (Clinical practice guideline number 4.) U.S. Department of Health and Human Services, Public Health Service (AHCPR Pub. No. 93–054). Washington, DC: Author.

Ahern, K. (1993, April 21). U.S. Department of Health and Human Services, Office of the Inspector General. Personal communication, quoted in Workshop before Special Committee on Aging, United States Senate (103rd Congress, 1st Sess).

American Speech-Language-Hearing Association. (1989). Competencies for speech-language pathologists providing services in augmentative communication. *Asha, 31*, 107–110.

American Speech-Language-Hearing Association. (1991). Report: Augmentative and alternative communication. *Asha, 33* (Suppl. 5), 9–12.

Chelimsky, E. (1993, April 21). *Statement in Workshop before the Special Committee on Aging, United States Senate, 103rd Congress, 1st Sess*. (Serial No. 103–5). Washington, DC: Government Printing Office.

Davis, K. (1995, September 21). Statement in Hearing on Medicare before the Committee on Ways and Means, United States House of Representatives, 105th Congress, 1st Sess.

General Accounting Office. (1993). *Report to Congressional Requesters. Cataract surgery: Patient–reported data on appropriateness and outcomes* (GAO/PEMD–93–14). Washington, DC: Author.

Health Resources Administration. (1976). *Report to the Congress: Reimbursement under part B of Medicare for certain services provided by optometrists*. U.S. Department of Health, Education and Welfare, Public Health Service. Washington, DC: Author.

H.R. Rep. No. 506, 99th Congress, 1st Sess. (1985). Cataract surgery: Fraud, waste, and abuse: A report by the chairman, House Select Committee on Aging, Subcommittee on Health and Long-Term Care.

Jaffe, N. S. (1984). *Cataract surgery and its complications* (4th ed.). St. Louis: C.V. Mosby Co.

LaPlante, M. P. (1991). *Disability in basic life activities across the life span.* National Institute on Disability and Rehabilitation Research. Disability Statistics Report 1.1991. Washington, DC: Author.

Lavizzo-Mourey, R. J. (1993). *Statement in Workshop before the Special Committee on Aging, United States Senate, 103rd Congress, 1st Sess.* Serial No. 103-5. Washington, DC: U.S. Government Printing Office.

Makinson, L. (1990). *Open secrets, the dollar power of PACS in Congress.* Washington, DC: Center for Responsive Politics, Congressional Quarterly, Inc.

Medicare Reimbursement for Cataract Surgery. (1985). Hearing before the House Committee on Ways and Means, Subcommittee on Health, 99th Congress, 1st Sess. (SN99-37). Washington, DC: Government Printing Office.

Melia, T. P. (1967). *An introduction to masers and lasers.* New York: Barnes & Noble.

National Institute of Deafness and Other Communication Disorders. (1995). *National strategic plan.* U.S. Department of Health and Human Services, Public Health Service, National Institutes of Health (NIH Pub. 95-3711). Washington, DC: Author.

National Institutes of Health, U.S. Department of Health and Human Services, Public Health Service. (1987). *Vision research: A national plan, 1983–87—Report of the cataract panel* (NIH Pub. No. 84-2473) Bethesda, MD: Author.

Perera, C. A. (1947). *May's manual of the disease of the eye* (19th ed.). Baltimore: Williams & Wilkins.

Report of the President's Biomedical Research Panel. (1976). Submitted to the President and the Congress of the United States. U.S. Dept. Health, Education and Welfare, Public Health Service (DHEW 76-500). Washington, DC: Government Printing Office.

Reuter, J., & O'Sullivan, J. (1987, June 22). Memo to the Subcommittee on Health, House Ways and Means Committee. Congressional Research Service, Washington, DC: Library of Congress.

Safir, A. (1983). How ophthalmology has changed during my career. Office of Technology Assessment. Washington, DC: U.S. Congress.

Sandler, G. (1996, January 15). Proposed Medicare policy changes could limit payments for cataract surgery. *Ocular Surgery News.* Internet: http://www/slackinc.com/19961b/medicare.htm.

U.S. Bureau of the Census. (1965). *Statistical abstract of the United States: 1965* (86th ed.). Washington, DC: Author.

U.S. Congress Office of Technology Assessment. (1983). *Health Technology Case Study #26: Assistive devices for severe speech impairments* (OTA-HCS-26). Washington, DC: Government Printing Office.

U.S. Congress Office of Technology Assessment. (1984). *Medical technology and costs of the Medicare program* (OTA-H-227). Washington, DC: Government Printing Office.

Index

A

Abbreviated Profile of Hearing Aid Benefit (APHAB), 148–149, 151
AbleNet, Inc., 232
Academy of Neurologic Disorders and Sciences (ANCDS), 231
Accessibility Communication Product Center, 194
Accommodation 46–48
Acoustic immittance, 109–110
Acoustic reflex, 109–110
Acoustical environment, 181–182
Acquired motor speech disorders. *See* Motor speech disorders
Activities of daily living, 76, 79
Adamlab, Inc., 232
Adaptation, 5–7
Adaptive technology. *See* Assistive technology
Advocacy Skills Training Programs, 80
Affordance, 272–274
African Americans, 51, 73
  glaucoma, 51
Age-related macular degeneration (ARMD), *See* Macular degeneration
Agency for Health Care Policy and Research (AHCPR), 345
Aging (*see also* specific sensory changes)
  adaptation to, 5–7, 264–267
  communication, 8–14
  culture, 28–29

definition, 5
expectancy, 2
financial, 7, 30, 341–355
general slowing, 298
network, 80
statistics, 4, 47, 50, 71, 72–73, 79, 103, 130–131, 166–167
wellness, 13–14
Aid to Families with Dependent Children (AFDC), 343–344
Aladden Personal Reader, 87
Alarm clocks, 214
Alerting devices/systems, 175, 246
Alexander Graham Bell Association for the Deaf, 190
Alphabet supplementation, 246, 252, 255
Alzheimer's disease. (*See* Dementia)
Alzheimer's Disease and Related Disorders Association, 231
Amblyopia, 46
American Academy of Audiology (AAA), 190
American Academy of Ophthamology, 64, 99
American Association for Retired Persons (AARP), 190
American Bible Society, 99
American Council for Blind, 99
American Deafness and Rehabilitation Association (ADARA), 190
American Foundation for the Blind, 64, 91, 94, 99
American Indian, 73

Cornea, 43, 57, 59, 75
  dry eye syndrome, 59
  eyelid changes, 58–59
Conversation, 207–208, 225–226
Corrective lenses. *See* Glasses
Cost/benefit ratio, 15
Council on Assistive Devices and
    Listening Systems (COALS,
    Inc.), 192
Council of Citizens with Low
    Vision, 100
Counseling, 151–154
  hearing aids, 151–154
Crestwood Co., 194
Cyber-communities, 26

D

Dehumanization, 334
Delayed Auditory Feedback (DAF),
    251
Dementia
  Alzheimer's disease, 4, 208–209
  characteristics, 11, 208–209, 230
  communication disorders,
      210–211, 230
  communication intervention,
      211–219, 230
  definition, 11, 206–207
  etiologies, 209
  hearing aids, 138
  institutionalized, 11
  multi-infarct, 209
  prevalence, 11, 208
Demographics of aging, 2–5, 10, 11,
    47, 50, 52, 71–74, 103, 130–131,
    140–141, 166–167, 208, 296–297,
    323–324
Depression, 11
  characteristics, 11
  communication, 11
  criteria for, 11
  hearing loss, 104
  vision loss, 63
Diabetes, 47
  diabetic retinopathy, 55–56, 73, 75

macular edema, 56
ophthalmologic monitoring, 56
proliferative retinopathy, 56
Type I, 55–6
Type II, 55
Disability. *See* World Health
    Organization, 132, 166
Disability glare, 268
D.J. Technical Sales, Ltd., 194
Don Johnston, Inc., 232
Drawing, 254
Drusen, 54
Dry eye syndrome, 59–60
Dysarthria. *See* Amyotrophic lateral
    sclerosis; Aphasia; Locked-in
    syndrome; Parkinson's disease

E

Ear (*see also* Hearing loss)
  auditory nerve, 108
  central auditory pathway, 108
  inner, 105–106
  middle, 104–105
  outer, 104–105
  parts of, 104–108
Ectropia, 58–59
Elderspeak, 29, 30–31
Electromagnetic environment,
    182–183
Electronic scrapbook, 217–218
Electrophysiological assessment,
    116–119
Electroretinography, 42
Empowerment, 80
Emergency systems, 313–314
Emergency tactics, 279
Entropia, 58–59
Environment, 12, 17, 179–186,
    263–294 (*see also* Architecture)
  acoustical, 181–182
  as information, 267–271
  as prosthetic device, 272–279
  assistive listening devices,
      179–186
  awareness, 183

ADX 2055